The European Public Servant

A Shared Administrative Identity?

Edited by

Fritz Sager and Patrick Overeem

ecpr PRESS

Cover Image: © iStock #34460612 Filograph

First published by the ECPR Press in 2015

The ECPR Press is the publishing imprint of the European Consortium for Political Research (ECPR), a scholarly association, which supports and encourages the training, research and cross-national cooperation of political scientists in institutions throughout Europe and beyond.

ECPR Press
Harbour House
Hythe Quay
Colchester
CO2 8JF
United Kingdom

Typeset by Lapiz Digital Services

Printed and bound by Lightning Source

British Library Cataloguing in Publication Data

A catalogue record for this book is available from the British Library

Hardback ISBN: 978-1-907-301-74-2
PDF ISBN: 978-1-910-259-52-8
EPUB ISBN: 978-1-910-259-54-2
KINDLE ISBN: 978-1-910-259-5-35

www.ecpr.eu/ecprpress

Series Editors:
Dario Castiglione (University of Exeter)
Peter Kennealy (European University Institute)
Alexandra Segerberg (Stockholm University)

ECPR – *Studies in European Political Science* is a series of high-quality edited volumes on topics at the cutting edge of current political science and political thought. All volumes are research-based offering new perspectives in the study of politics with contributions from leading scholars working in the relevant fields. Most of the volumes originate from ECPR events including the Joint Sessions of Workshops, the Research Sessions, and the General Conferences.
Books in this series:

More on the European Union from ECPR Press

Consultative Committees in the European Union: No Vote – No Influence?
ISBN: 9781910259429
Diana Panke, Christoph Hönnige and Julia Gollub

Parties, Governments and Voters in Finland: Politics under Fundamental Societal Transformation
ISBN: 9781910259337
Lauri Karvonen

Integrating Indifference: A Comparative, Qualitative and Quantitative Approach to the Legitimacy of European Integration
ISBN: 9781907301483
Virginie Van Ingelgom

The Nordic Voter: Myths of Exceptionalism
ISBN: 9781907301506
Åsa Bengtsson, Kasper M Hansen, Ólafur Þ Harðarson, Hanne Marthe Narud and Henrik Oscarsson

Please visit www.ecpr.eu/ecprpress for up-to-date information about new publications.

Table of Contents

List of Figures and Tables

List of Abbreviations

ARAR	Algemeen Rijksambtenarenreglement, by-law to the Dutch CSA
BCE	Before the Common Era
CAP	Common Agricultural Policy
CSA	Civil Service Act
CNCAP	Code of Non-contentious Administrative Procedures
EAS	European Administrative Space
EEC	European Economic Community
ENA	École Nationale d'Administration (National School of Administration)
EP	European Parliament
EU	European Union
FRG	Federal Republic of Germany
GP	Groot Plakkaat Boek: Great Ordinances Books of the United Dutch Provinces (seventeenth and eighteenth centuries)
IEP	Institut d'Études Politiques (Institute of Political Studies)
IFS	Irish Free State
IMF	International Monetary Fund
IPA	Institute of Public Administration
NA	Nationaal Archief: The Netherlands National Archive
NATO	North Atlantic Treaty Organization
NESC	National Economic & Social Council (Republic of Ireland)
NPM	New public management
ODNB	Oxford Dictionary of National Biography
OEEC	Organisation for European Economic Co-operation
OECD	Organisation for Economic Co-operation and Development
OED	Oxford English Dictionary
PA	Public Administration, the science of public administration
PAS	Political–administrative system
PPBS	Planning, Programming and Budgeting System
PSB	Public service bargain
TK	Tweede Kamer: Proceedings of the Dutch Lower House of the States General
WW2	World War II

Contributors

JULIA-CAROLIN BRACHEM is a research assistant at the HIS-Institute for Research on Higher Education, Hannover, Germany.

BERNADETTE CONNAUGHTON is a lecturer at the Department of Politics and Public Administration of the University of Limerick, Ireland.

GERRIT DIJKSTRA is an assistant professor at the Institute of Public Administration of Leiden University, The Netherlands.

NIELS HEGEWISCH is a research assistant at the Institute for Political Science of the Ernst-Moritz-Arndt-University, Greifswald, Germany.

PASCAL HURNI is a PhD candidate at the Center of Competence for Public Management of the University of Bern, Switzerland.

LARS JOHANNSEN is an associate professor at the Department of Political Science and Government of Aarhus University, Denmark.

CÉLINE MAVROT is a research assistant at the Center of Competence for Public Management at the University of Bern, Switzerland.

PATRICK OVEREEM is an assistant professor at the Institute of Public Administration of Leiden University, The Netherlands.

JOANNE PAUL is a lecturer at the New College of the Humanities, London, United Kingdom.

KARIN HILMER PEDERSEN is an associate professor in Comparative Politics at the Department of Political Science and Government of the University of Aarhus, Denmark.

JOS RAADSCHELDERS is a professor of Public Administration at the John Glenn School of Ohio State University, United States.

CHRISTIAN ROSSER is a fellow at the Center of Excellence "Cultural Foundations of Social Integration" of the University of Konstanz, Germany, and a research associate of the University of Zurich, Switzerland.

MARK R. RUTGERS is a professor of Philosophy of Public Administration in the Department of Political Sciences of the University of Amsterdam, The Netherlands.

FRITZ SAGER is a professor of Political Science at the Center of Competence for Public Management of the University of Bern, Switzerland.

KOEN STAPELBROEK is an associate professor at the Department of Public Administration of the Erasmus University Rotterdam, The Netherlands.

GAYIL TALSHIR is a senior lecturer in the Department of Political Science of the Hebrew University, Jerusalem, Israel.

MARKUS TEPE is a professor of Political Science at the Institute of Social Sciences of the University of Oldenburg, Germany.

CASPAR VAN DEN BERG is an assistant professor at the Institute of Public Administration of Leiden University, The Netherlands and visiting fellow at the Princeton Institute for International and Regional Studies, Princeton University, United States.

FRITS VAN DER MEER is a professor in Comparative Public Sector and Civil Service Reform of Leiden University, The Netherlands.

Acknowledgements

We want to thank Mark Bevir, Jörn Ege, Stephan Grohs, Tamir Libel, and Richard J. Stillman, II, for their helpful contributions to the ECPR Joint Sessions panel '*The European Public Servant: A Shared Administrative Identity?*' held at the 2012 ECPR Joint Sessions meeting in Antwerp on which this volume is based.

Fritz Sager and Patrick Overeem
March 2015

Part One

Searching for a European Public Servant

Chapter One

Introduction: The European Public Servant's Shared Identity

Fritz Sager and Patrick Overeem

Towards a European administrative space

As the economic, political and cultural integration of Europe advances, the organisation of European administration becomes more complex. Consequently, the need for a shared administrative identity among the member states of the EU becomes more salient. Europeanisation can thereby take two directions. Héritier *et al.* (2001: 3) define Europeanisation as 'the process of influence deriving from European decisions and impacting member states' policies and political and administrative structures'. In this perspective, Europeanisation is triggered from above, but it also grows from below. Risse, Cowles and Caporaso (2001: 3) take on the inverse perspective and define Europeanisation as '*the emergence and development at the European level of distinct structures of governance*, that is, of political, legal and social institutions associated with political problem solving that formalizes interactions among the actors, and of policy networks specializing in the creation of authoritative European rules' (emphasis in original). Europeanisation in this perspective takes place at the supranational rather than at the member state level. These notions of Europeanisation share the institutionalist claim that a common institutional framework such as the EU results in common political practices, and eventually, a shared culture or even identity. Following Olsen (2010: 158), '[i]nstitutionalization as a process implies that an organizational identity is developed and legitimacy in a culture is built'. The growing literature on the European public sphere takes on this perspective when maintaining 'that national public spheres become Europeanised if the discourses within these spaces evade the boundaries of certain national debates and assume transnational, European points of view' (Nitoiu 2013: 33; *see* Koopmans and Statham 2010: 43). Given that EU compliance research finds the implementation of EU policy and hence the process of Europeanisation as described here to be conditional upon well-functioning administrative structures, it is striking that the question of a European administrative identity has not been given the same attention as the European public sphere so far. The case is even more surprising as some fifteen years ago, the Organisation for Economic Co-operation and Development (OECD), in its paper 'European principles for public administration', highlighted the need for the construction of a collective European administrative identity as follows:

> No *acquis communautaire* exists for setting standards of horizontal systems of governance or national public administrations. Targets and orientations for public administration reform in the perspective of EU accession are therefore less distinct. However, over time a general consensus on key components of good governance has emerged among democratic states. These components include the rule of law principles of reliability, predictability, accountability and transparency, but also technical and managerial competence, organisational capacity and citizens' participation. Despite the lack of an *acquis communautaire,* this consensus has established principles for public administration shared by EU Member States with different legal traditions and different systems of governance. [...]
>
> Shared principles of public administration among EU Member States constitute the conditions of a 'European Administrative Space' (EAS). The EAS includes a set of common standards for action within public administration that are defined by law and enforced in practice through procedures and accountability mechanisms. Countries applying for EU membership should take these standards into account when developing their public administrations. Although the EAS does not constitute an agreed part of the *acquis communautaire,* it should nevertheless serve to guide public administration reforms in candidate countries. In EU Member States these standards, together with principles established by the constitution, are usually embedded in or transmitted by a set of administrative laws, such as administrative procedures acts, administrative process acts, freedom of information acts and civil service laws. (OECD 1999: 5)

While meant as an introduction to the enumeration of 'administrative law principles as a set of criteria to be applied by candidate countries in their efforts to attain the administrative capacity required for EU Membership' (OECD 1999: 6) for practitioners of public and administrative law, this long quote reads like a research agenda for social scientists.

What is striking about the European Administrative Space, however, is that it is abstract rather than concrete, conceived as a set of principles rather than a community of people. In much of the thought and talk about an integrated European public administration, the public administrator is still conspicuously absent. Yet this social figure, the 'public servant', as most Europeans know him or her, is crucial. After several centuries of increasingly strong statehood and bureaucratisation, the type of the public servant has taken a central place in the European mind. This is even the case in a time when, as many hope or fear, the nation state with its bureaucracies seems to recede again: the Europeanised public servants or 'Eurocrats', both in Brussels (Leidenfrost 2011) and in the member state capitals (Geuijen *et al.* 2008), are regarded as key players in the process of continental integration. So it seems that no shared European administrative space can exist without a clear idea of the role and characteristics of the public servant. In this book, we aim to enrich the literature about administrative Europeanisation with much-needed historical and theoretical background. Sociological institutionalism distinguishes three ways in which harmonisation processes such as Europeanisation can take place: first, coercive isomorphism describes the development of structural similarities, where organisations are forced to change by external forces such as formal supranational power (supranationalism); second, normative isomorphism, driven by horizontal interorganisational interaction as can be found in soft law (intergovernmentalism); and third, as an actual counter-concept to Europeanisation, where uncertainty encourages imitation (DiMaggio and Powell 1983). Historical institutionalism, in addition, emphasises the crucial role of a shared ground for any sort of harmonisation to take place at all. There is a normative edge in this view in the sense that a certain amount of commonality is a necessary condition for integration.

Following up on this historical institutionalist assumption, the main question this volume addresses is whether European thought (in different periods of time and across different places) offers such a shared idea of the public servant and of public service more generally as can serve as a cornerstone for the project of building a common European administrative identity in the increasingly integrating continent.

Despite its centrality to the European project, surprisingly little analysis of the idea of the public servant in Europe exists. So far, very little research has been done on the question of a European administrative identity: neither whether such thing exists nor how it may develop. Indeed, compared to the history of political ideas more generally, the subfield of the history of administrative ideas is still rather underdeveloped. Our book aims to contribute to this scholarly and practically relevant endeavour by analysing – from the perspectives of political and administrative theory and conceptual history – the similarities and dissimilarities of historical and contemporary ideas on the public servant as a relevant political actor in Europe. As collective identity relies not only upon the mutual recognition of shared values, but also on the confrontation with 'foreign' values (Albert and Whetten 2004: 89; Hobsbawm 2004: 109), it is crucial to address the development of both inter- and extra-European administrative thought in a comparative manner. Whether we identify such thing as a European public servant depends not only on similarities among European public servants but also distinctions that can be noted from non-European public servants.

In this comparative perspective, it seems inevitable to pay special attention to the contrasts and commonalities of the European notion of the public servant with that of its counterpart in the United States. Although not original – European and American administrative thought in general have been compared more often (Stillman 1997; Rutgers 2001) – there is no getting around the fact that the (Anglo-) American tradition has clearly been *the* most important reference point for and influence on the development of modern European administrative theory and practice. A number of influences from other parts of the world may be graciously acknowledged (the Chinese merit system is a case in point), but no tradition of administrative thinking has exerted an influence on the European understanding of public service and the public servant even closely comparable to that of the American tradition. This influence does not deny instances of independent conceptual development in Europe, let alone of the reversed pattern of early and ongoing 'Europeanisation' on the other side of the Atlantic: both these developments will be made amply clear in this volume. However, the American influence is a historical given, which every study of our topic must recognise.

In current debates, both academic and practical, there are several competing approaches to public administration. Whereas economic and managerial approaches emphasise administrative values such as efficiency, effectiveness and economy (e.g. Schedler and Proeller 2003; Hood 1991), neo-progressive approaches stress the importance of public servants' responsibility and reliability (Lowery 1999; Goodsell 1994). Other scholars suggest that it is time to rediscover Weberian bureaucracy (Olsen 2006). According to Max Weber (1978: 223; *see* Pierson 2004: 16), 'the development of modern forms of organization in all fields is nothing less than identical with the development and continual spread of bureaucratic organization'. This suggests that the modern public servant, in Europe and elsewhere, should be the classical bureaucrat, but of course other (and older) ideas and ideals are available as well (Sager and Rosser 2009; Sager *et al.* 2012).

Our book contributes to the examination of the intellectual roots of such different administrative approaches in order to find out to what extent their respective values may serve as an ideational foundation for a potential European administrative identity.

This volume

In this book, we chart so far unexplored territory by pushing the study of public administration more towards that of the history of (political) concepts, and at the same time establish a direct link with the political study of Europeanisation. The attempt brings together hitherto mostly unconnected strands of political scientific, administrative and historical research. The volume is built around the following four sub-questions:

a. How has the public servant been conceived (in different periods of time and at different places) throughout the history of European thought?
b. How do the European conceptions of the public servant compare with and/ or reflect the influences of other conceptions, in particular American ones?
c. To what extent do different conceptions of the public servant converge in times of European integration?
d. Is it possible to identify a shared conception of the public servant that can serve as a building block for a common European administrative identity?

These sub-questions will be answered in the order in which they are listed, but in an accumulative rather than a serial manner: Each one presupposes the other(s) and when all sub-questions have been addressed, an answer to the volume's main question will be formulated. The book has a logical and chronological order and is divided into six parts: The first part aims at developing a common understanding of our topic and a concept to capture it, and the second part looks into older notions of public service preceding the formative nineteenth century, which is treated in Part Three. Part Four addresses specifically the American influence on European administrative science in the twentieth century, after which Part Five investigates the Europeanised public servant in the EU in more detail. We conclude in Part Six by summing up the findings with regard to our initial question: *Is there a shared administrative identity in Europe?*

In the following chapter, Jos Raadschelders offers some of the main conceptual and methodological assumptions that can be used for analysing the changing role and identity of the public servant in Europe. Raadschelders presents cornerstones for a general assessment of European ideas of the public servant throughout the volume.

Part Two and Three deal most explicitly with the historical development of the concept of public servant (sub-question a). Part Two, entitled 'Older notions of public service', goes back to the early modern period and is opened up by Joanne Paul's analysis of the sixteenth-century figure of the king's counsellor as the European public servant's ancestor (Chapter Three). She concentrates on the important relationship between public service and advice to rulers through a close scrutiny of sixteenth-century discourse, exploring the purpose of counsel, the figure of the counsellor and the emergence of a republican view of liberty captured in the idea of *parrhesia* – speaking truth to power. From such an investigation we are able to identify a clearly articulated figure who serves the interests of the people by giving truthful, fearless advice to the monarch. This has implications for contemporary discourse regarding the revival of an 'ideal' of public service. By turning to the sixteenth-century development of the political counsellor, we begin to understand the growth of an essential, yet often marginalised figure in the public service tradition – the political counsellor.

Mark Rutgers in his contribution (Chapter Four) discusses the oath of office as a characteristic of public office, especially for public servants. In most European countries the oath of office is still in place as a symbolic *rite de passage* when entering public office. Being symbolic may suggest that it is not a very important or substantial matter, but this obscures the fact that it is clearly important for many, and probably more important than signing a contract. It is particularly clear in the case of legal professionals and when public officials have to give evidence in a legal context. Thus, the oath of office as the symbolic act of accepting public responsibility and of receiving public authority is central to the professional status of public servants. The oath of office legitimates a certain degree of the discretionary power of bureaucrats *vis-à-vis* elected politicians. Finally, there is a much more instrumental approach: the oath of office as a tool to try and commit people to behave in a desired mode.

Part Three continues the exploration of conceptual history, concentrating in three chapters on the pivotal nineteenth century. In Chapter Five, Niels Hegewisch addresses the question of the extent to which public servants should be granted political influence. He points out that the separation-of-powers doctrine offers two conflicting normative assessments: politically influential public servants can be perceived as protecting as well as endangering the citizens' freedom. Hegewisch depicts both sides of this coin from a history-of-ideas perspective by analysing early nineteenth-century German thought about the public servant and his relation to politics. The chapter develops two opposing perceptions of the public servant: either as a necessary evil that needs to be constricted as far as possible or as a welcomed complement to the legitimised political actors. The historical analysis is connected to contemporary debates. Hegewisch argues that the role of a shared European administrative identity is to mediate between these two extremes.

Koen Stapelbroek's chapter (Chapter Six) then enquires into the possibility that the rise of new administrative practices around 1900 might be conceptually related to the emergence of a European space. Neither the prospect of a united Europe nor the idea of extensive public services as a requirement of modern politics existed until this period. The thesis advanced here, by drawing upon the intellectual tradition of the political theory of pluralism, is that the idea of the 'administrative state' developed along with the notion that the state might not need to be as sovereign as traditional thinking presupposed. If a large part of modern government did not involve political decision-making but instead administrative processes that optimised socio-economic processes, this created a previously unthinkable scope for transferring public administrative structures to the European level.

Gerrit Dijkstra, Frits van der Meer, and Casper van den Berg treat the protected status as characteristic of the European public servant (Chapter Seven). They examine in depth the transformation process leading to the increasing protection of public servants in France, the United Kingdom, German territories and The Netherlands in the nineteenth and early twentieth centuries, looking at similarities and differences in their national 'paths'. A comparative historical analysis using a public service bargain (PSB) perspective provides the necessary critical look at often too strongly defined national identities in shaping public service systems, particularly at the higher hierarchical levels. The relation between defining public servants' rights and duties on the one hand, and maintaining the rule of law on the other, coincided with the transformation of public servants from their role as personal servants to a ruler or a ruling class into an instrument to assist in the development of the public interest and thus to enforce public decisions within the context of the rule of law. On the formal side of things, the need for able, skilled and professional officials enhanced the development of the *Rechtsstaat*, the expansion of government tasks, and the growth of government intervention more particularly in the latter decades of the nineteenth century. On the informal side, however, this relatively clear and linear development is much less present. The history of informal rights and obligations, protection and employer–employee relations turns out to be much more complicated.

Part Four, 'The Americanised public servant in Europe' (dealing with sub-question b), consists of three chapters, each of which addresses a transatlantic transfer of administrative ideas between Continental Europe and the United States. In Chapter Eight, Christian Rosser starts by examining the extent to which the administrative thinking of early American Progressives was informed by Hegelian political philosophy. Comparing Hegel's reflections on the state and public administration with those of Woodrow Wilson and Frank J. Goodnow, he illustrates how the Hegelian line of thought contributed to the identity formation of American Public Administration. Rosser outlines Hegelian political philosophy in Germany, and then chronicles its transmission across the Atlantic and its subsequent translation and dissemination into American administrative thought. The chapter concludes with a discussion of Hegelian philosophy as a source of inspiration for dealing with current problems regarding the role of public administration both in Europe and the United States.

In the following chapter Céline Mavrot sets out to identify the American 'genes' in French administrative science by focusing on the post-war shifts in the composition of the public service as well as in the study of administration. Until WW2, the study of public administration in France was quasi-monopolised by administrative law. After the war, however, many initiatives flourished in order to create an administrative science. The initial sketches of this new academic discipline came mainly from public law professors and Councillors of State, and were presented as a necessary complement to administrative law. Administrative science was intended to provide a more flexible theoretical framework than traditional administrative law, which was accused of being unable to accompany the development of the State any more. Mavrot analyses particularly the work of one of the main post-war initiators of this newly born administrative science: Georges Langrod. It is shown how he relied on Herbert Simon and the importation of the case method in order to establish a body of French administrative science.

Pascal Hurni (Chapter Ten) follows with a similar endeavour for Germany, looking at the impact of cybernetics on German public administration and its contribution to the *Neo-Verwaltungswissenschaft*. In the aftermath of cameral science's schism at the end of the nineteenth century, German administrative science rapidly became dominated by jurisprudence. From the 1960s, however, a public administration based on social science's epistemology could establish itself in German academe. Hurni argues that the concept of cybernetics contributed to the forming of the *Neo-Verwaltungswissenschaft* by broadening the scholarly discourse after WW2: cybernetics suggested conceiving of public administration as an integral part of the political–administrative system. Consequently, public administration was no longer regarded as a mere implementer of the executive branch's will, but became an interesting topic for political science and sociology. Thus, cybernetics not only added public administration as a research topic to social science, but also helped to establish a paradigm shift in theory and methodological approach.

Part Five turns to the Europeanisation of public servants in the EU (sub-question c) with chapters spanning the far west and the far east of the continent. Bernadette Connaughton starts with an analysis of Irish officials' interaction with the EU policy-making process (Chapter Eleven). This chapter explores whether Irish officials in central government departments have developed an official European identity and whether participation in EU fora shapes their role perceptions and practices. In the first section of the chapter the concept of Europeanisation is considered as a means of understanding how engagement with the EU has the potential to shape national official identity. The second section unpacks the characteristics of public service that have influenced the identity of Irish officials from independence in 1922 to EU membership in 1973. This is further considered in the third section, which presents a discussion of how Irish officials approach their EU policy work. The overview offers insights into official attitudes, career trajectories and identity, which remains influenced by the ethos and norms of the national public service.

In Chapter Twelve Karin Hilmer Pedersen and Lars Johannsen look into the changes in public administration and in the identity of public servants after the breakdown of the Soviet regime. Fundamental reconstructions of the political, economic and administrative systems of the Central and East European countries were necessary in order to 'return to Europe'. The reconstructions in the Baltic States (Estonia, Latvia and Lithuania) have been remarkable successes. They have become members of EU and NATO and, with determination, have fought off several deep economic recessions without endangering democracy. Public administrations have undergone complete changes in their legal environment and deep structural reorganisation, combined with a high degree of turnover among staff. This has turned previous Soviet administrations into capable modern administrations. The question highlighted in this chapter is whether the public servants have also returned to Europe in the sense of sharing common European values and administrative identity. Pedersen and Johannsen find that the core principles of integrity and neutrality have been internalised and many, though not all, public servants see responsiveness to citizens' participation as positive in administrative development.

Part Six, finally, is dedicated to the question of whether there is at present a shared administrative identity in Europe and what it looks like (sub-question d). Julia-Carolin Brachem and Markus Tepe (Chapter Thirteen) start with the comparative exploration of public servants' value orientations in France, Germany, Sweden and the United States, representing distinct administrative traditions. The empirical findings obtained from a multivariate analysis of the World Values Survey 2005/6 can be summarised as follows: the cross national comparison of government employees' *Basic Human Values* shows that in contrast to government employees from the US, government employees from Great Britain, France, Germany and Sweden all share the higher values of *Self-Transcendence*. This observation is corroborated in the within-country analysis, which reveals that government employees have higher values of *Self-Transcendence* and lower values of *Self-Enhancement* than their private sector counterparts, even after controlling for a full range of socio-demographic and occupational factors. This distinct motivational value pattern might provide a promising basis for (further research on) the development of a European administrative identity.

In the penultimate chapter (Fourteen), Gayil Talshir adopts a more theoretical and normative approach, concentrating on the implications of public servants' training programmes. Bureaucracy, in the Weberian model, was the quintessential mark of the modern state, and with it perhaps the symbol of disenchanted, albeit professional, politics. Yet, in the praxis of professionalising the public service, its training became a key feature of the different political cultures of European nations. On the theoretical level, this chapter challenges Weber's notion of disenchantment, using the image of national bureaucracies as a case in point and arguing that while the professional bureaucrat was to portray an image of disinterested profession, the image of the public servant became essential in reflecting the political culture of the different nation-states. It thus symbolised political re-enchantment. The comparative analysis of public service training (ideal and praxis) in France, Great Britain and Germany demonstrates the diverse models of public service and hence of state–citizen relationship, but also the grave effect of neoliberalism on the transformation of the image and training of the public service. Paradoxically, it is the current, converging model of the 'effective bureaucrat' that better resembles Weber's notion of disenchantment as well as facilitating a European model of public administration.

In the concluding chapter (Chapter Fifteen), we wrap up the findings of the preceding chapters in order to find a tentative answer to our main questions: is there such thing as a European administrative identity, where does it stem from, and what is it like? Our answers combine insights provided in this volume and point to research gaps. They also take into account the current crisis of the European idea and address the question whether a conception of the European public servant may serve to underlie the project of European administrative integration or whether its fundament is too fragile to serve such a grand purpose.

It is clear that the empirical answers that the chapters in this volume provide to the ambitious question of *whether there is a shared administrative identity in Europe* cannot be definite. Our attempt is to address a so far open research field, and emphasise a historical perspective that has been lacking to date. As will become clear in the final chapter, this attempt is considered a starting point for future research rather than the conclusive truth.

References

Albert, S. and Whetten, D. A. (2004) 'Organizational identity', in Hatch, M. J. and Schultz, M. (eds) *Organizational Identity: A reader*, Oxford: Oxford University Press, pp. 89–118.

DiMaggio, P. J. and Powell, W. W. (1983) 'The iron cage revisited: institutional isomorphism and collective rationality in organizational fields', *American Sociological Review*, 48(2): 147–60.

Goodsell, C. T. (1994) *The Case for Bureaucracy: A public administration polemic*, Chatham NJ: Chatham House Publishers.

Geuijen, K., Hart, P. 't., Princen, S. and Yesilkagit, K. (2008) *The New Eurocrats: National civil servants in EU Policymaking*, Amsterdam: Amsterdam University Press.

Héritier, A., Kerwer, D., Knill, C., Lehmkuhl, D., Teutsch, M. and Douillet, A. -C. (2001) *Differential Europe: The European Union impact on national policymaking*, Lanham, MD: Rowman & Littlefield.

Hobsbawm, E. J. (2004) *Nationen und Nationalismus: Mythos und Realität seit 1780*, Frankfurt/Main: Campus.

Hood, C. (1991) 'A public management for all seasons', *Public Administration*, 69(1): 3–19.

Koopmans, R. and Statham, P. (eds) (2010) *The Making of a European Public Sphere: Media discourse and political contention*, Cambridge: Cambridge University Press.

Leidenfrost, M. (2011). *Intimate Brussels: Living amongst Eurocrats*, Berlin: Lexxion.

Lowery, D. (1999) 'Answering the public choice challenge: a neoprogressive research agenda', *Governance: An International Journal of Policy and Administration*, 12(1): 29–55.

Nitoiu, C. (2013) 'The European public sphere: myth, reality, or aspiration?' *Political Studies Review*, 11(1): 26–38.

OECD (1999) 'European principles for public administration', SIGMA Papers, No. 27. OECD Publishing, pp. 1–28.

Olsen, J. P. (2006) 'Maybe it is time to rediscover bureaucracy', *Journal of Public Administration Research and Theory*, 16: 1–24.

—— (2010) *Governing Through Institution Building: Institutional theory and recent European experiments in democratic organization*, Oxford/ New York: Oxford University Press.

Pierson, C. (2004). *The Modern State* (2nd edn), London/New York: Routledge.

Risse, T., Cowles, M. G. and Caporaso, J. (2001) 'Europeanization and domestic change: Introduction', in Cowles, M. G., Caporaso, J. and Risse, T. (eds), *Transforming Europe: Europeanization and Domestic Change*, Ithaca, NY: Cornell University Press.

Rutgers, M. R. (2001) 'Traditional flavors? The different sentiments in European and American administrative thought', *Administration and Society*, 33(2): 220–44.

Sager, F. and Rosser, C. (2009) 'Weber, Wilson, and Hegel: Theories of modern bureaucracy', *Public Administration Review*, 69(5): 1136–47.

Sager, F., Rosser, C., Hurni, P. Y. and Mavrot, C. (2012) 'How traditional are the American, French and German traditions of public administration? A research agenda, *Public Administration*, 90(1): 129–43.

Schedler, K. and Proeller, I. (2003) *New Public Management*, Bern: Haupt.

Stillman, R. J., II. (1997) 'American vs. European public administration: does public administration make the modern state, or does the state make public administration?' *Public Administration Review*, 57(4): 332–8.

Weber, M. (1978). *Economy and Society: An outline of interpretive sociology*, Roth, G. and Wittich, C. (eds), Berkeley/Los Angeles, CA/London: University of California Press.

Chapter Two

Changing European Ideas about the Public Servant: A Theoretical and Methodological Framework

Jos C. N. Raadschelders

Introduction

We can expect that the concept of 'public servant' to be time and context bound, but we cannot really ever determine the extent to which it is time and context bound. Hard measures that cross borders and time are inconceivable. However, and specifically in Europe, we can trace whether the definition and expectations of the public servant changes contingent upon changes in the institutional (i.e. political-administrative) and societal context. Given the title of this edited volume (*The European Public Servant: A Shared Administrative Identity?*), and its intention of discerning how public servants in Europe have been perceived historically this chapter is limited to perceptions rather than including practices as well. One limitation is that only appointed career public servants are considered, that is, those who are subordinate to elected officeholders. Technically, the designation 'public servant' would also include the latter, but in this volume they are excluded. Also, the concept of civil service is really one that has been used only in the past two centuries. The term 'administrative staff' (*see* Weber's *Verwaltungsstab*) encompasses all those working for those in political power at all times. Thus, the main title to this piece could be 'From administrative staff to civil service in Europe', but for reasons of consistency with the volume title and other contributions in this volume I will use the term 'public servant'.

Another reason to see whether perceptions of and about public servants have changed is because the organisational and societal context in which they work has allegedly changed. A brief detour into these changes in the past twenty years or so is necessary, because how public servants are perceived is to some degree dependent upon that organisational and societal context. Indeed, we shall see later how much that has also been the case in the past. Many scholars suggest that public sector reforms have intensified in terms of scope and content since the mid-1970s/ early 1980s (e.g. Peters and Pierre 2001: 1), that turbulence and transformation since the early 1980s ended the incremental change hitherto (e.g. Nolan 2001), and that these rapid, systematic changes can be expected to continue for decades (e.g. Baker 2002: 10). The most visible reforms are those associated with new public management (NPM), a term that covers a great variety of operational level reforms. However, the extent to which NPM reforms can be implemented (so not its longer-term impacts) seems to depend upon whether it occurs in a majoritarian electoral system or in a more proportional system (Pollitt and Bouckaert 2011; Pollitt and Dan 2011: 39, 45, 47). Indeed, in the continental European consensual and multi-party systems, NPM reforms have been much more limited. Have they had effects upon the structure and functioning of the public service? Not really. In most countries, public service traditions (*see* this section below) have not been fundamentally uprooted. For instance, in The Netherlands, NPM was recently concluded to have little influence upon the administrative elite. NPM has not given rise to a new generation of public managers (Van der Meer and Raadschelders, forthcoming).

Meanwhile, these NPM reforms surfaced in a context where attention shifted from *government* to *governance*, suggesting that government is no longer the primary player in (re)solving collective problems and that, instead, government is one among many players who together influence the steering of society. Central to one set of theories about governance is that it concerns managing of and through networks (Chhotray and Stoker 2009: 26). Whether the shift from government to governance is truly an empirical change remains to be seen. After all, most of the governance literature focuses on the system-level rather than on specific governance arrangements within organisations (*ibid.*: 11). Is it empirically the case that government has moved away from hierarchy to networks? Did government bureaucracies network significantly less prior to the 1980s? Knowing that in several West European countries (e.g. Austria, Germany, The Netherlands, Scandinavian countries) corporatism is an important feature of the state since at least WW2, we should conclude that networking is not something that has developed in the past twenty years. These questions about the novelty of networks will not be answered since they are not central to the subject matter of this chapter and volume, but it is important to point out that when it comes to governance and networking, there is a big gap between perception and empirical reality. Also, let us not forget that government is still the only actor that can make binding decisions for an entire population. No other societal actor has that kind of encompassing authority. In that sense the state is certainly not 'hollowed out', and its public servants are still pivotal to policy making. However, with the Thomas theorem in mind, if such a shift to governance is perceived, it may have consequences for the role and position of public servants.

In this chapter I will first outline some ideas about theoretical frameworks and methodological approaches for studying why and how ideas about the public servant change over time. Next, I shall sketch the development of the public service by briefly looking at the millennia preceding the middle of the eighteenth century. This is followed by a section on the four decades between 1780 and 1820, since they represent a watershed in the development of European government. It is also the period when the concept of public service emerged (in contrast to political office), so I will discuss early modern and modern conceptions of public service. The question whether European conceptions of public service are converging is then addressed. In the concluding section the question is discussed whether national administrative traditions still play an important role in how public service is defined and perceived. Is there a European conception that is Hegelian and Weberian in nature and that describes a desired situation? Are public servants the new guardians of the state (Hegel) and are they neutral suppliers of policy advice and supporters of whoever is elected into political office (Weber)? Whatever the answers, I think that those whoever fills the ranks of the middle and higher public service nowadays must have rather uncommon capabilities in order to meet the changing social-economic and political-administrative environment.

Brief reflections on theories and methods

The theme of this volume, i.e. whether a common European administrative identity could be based on a shared idea of the public servant, requires that we consider the different angles from which this topic can be approached. As stated above, I will focus on the public servant. More specifically, I will look at some ways in which the role and position of administrative staff and of public servants in the political-administrative institutional arrangement have been conceptualised.

From a synchronic perspective several examples come to mind, such as principal-agent theory, Aberbach, Putman and Rockman's model of political-administrative interaction, and Peters' model of political-administrative interaction. In principal-agent theory, and in correspondence with the primacy-of-politics principle, the principal is the political officeholder and the agent the public servant who enjoys information advantage, expertise and longevity in office. A drawback of principal-agent theory is that it adheres to methodological individualism, which regards social structures and causes as dependent on and inherent to individuals. In this view, institutional structures do not exist in and of themselves. Historical institutionalism, in contrast, considers institutions as important independent or trans-individual contexts for human action, but in this approach human agency is constrained by path dependency. Thus, stability is emphasised rather than change. A middle ground might be possible in methodological localism, which departs from the notion that large social structures and phenomena influence social outcomes, but sees these structures as embodied in the actions and states of socially constructed and situated individuals (Little 2009: 163). This middle ground appears to be visible in the attempt by Peters et al. (2005) to capture both continuity and change when analysing political and policy change and, I would add, shifts in political-administrative relations.

Both Aberbach et al.'s (1981) and Peters' (1985) models conflate juridical and sociological perspectives upon the relation between politicians and public servants (see for example Raadschelders and Van der Meer 1998: 32; Lee and Raadschelders 2008: 428). In the juridical perspective politicians and public servants are clearly separated (image I in Aberbach et al. 1981; the formal-legal model in Peters), the former being elected, the latter appointed. It is also a normative perspective on this relationship, since according to the primacy-of-politics doctrine politicians ought to be the principals. However, as has been increasingly recognised in the twentieth century, career public servants are indispensable to policy making. Politicians depend upon public servants to a larger extent than we realise and this has been empirically confirmed (e.g. Page and Jenkins 2005; Page 2012). This then represents a sociological perspective that emphasises realities on the ground. Whereas Aberbach *et al.* and Peters provide models that categorise different types of political-administrative relations, much more descriptive literature is available both in Europe and in the US (*see* for an overview: Raadschelders and Van der Meer 1998).

Some of that comparative literature is diachronic in nature, describing the development of the public service over time. Max Weber described administration as developing from a traditional, via a patrimonial, to a bureaucratic stage. Under traditional administration authority emanates from the ruler(s), and their administrative staff (*Verwaltungsstab*) consists of personal rather than public or bureaucratic servants (1980: 130). Patrimonial administration is distinct in the sense that a ruler's legitimacy is supported by bureaucratic officials and accepted by a society's elite (e.g. eunuchs; the Pope as patrimonial ruler of the Catholic Church), or where the ruler has a bureaucratic staff but shares authority with, for example, a body of aristocrats (as in European feudalism) (Weber 1980: 134–40, especially 140; 148).

Drawing upon Weber's stage model, but focusing on administrative staff and public servants only, Raadschelders and Rutgers (1996: 71–89) distinguished five phases in the development of the public service in the Western world. In the first phase (the early and high Middle Ages), the administrative staff operated very much as a personal servant to the ruler, with no distinction being made between public and private spheres. As states consolidated their authority at the expense of regional lords (especially in England and France), state servants emerged (fifteenth to eighteenth centuries). These state servants worked as an administrative staff for the state. Some of them were recruited on the basis of some degree of merit (e.g. a law degree). These state servants are distinguishable from a personal staff that tends to the ruler's needs. In the third stage, the administrative staff truly becomes a public service, serving the people rather than the ruler (from the late eighteenth/early nineteenth century). The public service has become a bureaucratic organisation that operates within clear legal boundaries, is professional and meritorious, is as transparent as possible and treats everyone as equal under the law (i.e. impersonal). Both the second and the third stage become formalised during the 1780–1820 period (*see* below). Raadschelders and Rutgers also suggested a fourth (protected service, including a full-time job with salary and pension in money, since the early nineteenth century) and a fifth phase (a professional service: the Civil Service Acts since the late nineteenth century), with Raadschelders later suggesting that these latter two are elaborations of the third stage (2003: 327). These two examples of stage models clearly suggest convergence towards a bureaucratically embedded public service, but has that been the case?

From a sociological perspective, it is easier to see differences in the role and position of public servants in various states. For instance, Painter and Peters have linked public service status to different national administrative traditions (*see* Table 2.1).

Table 2.1: Four Western administrative traditions

	Anglo-American	Napoleonic	Germanic	Scandinavian
State and society	Pluralist	Interventionist	Organicist	Organicist/ welfarist/open government
Organisation of government	'Limited government'; UK: unitary, with weak 'local self-government'; US: 'compound republic'	The indivisible 'Jacobin Republic'; hierarchical and centralised (Spain: semi-federalised)	Integrated; cooperative federalism and interlocking coordination	Decentralised through administrative and/or political decentralisation
Civil service	UK: quite high status, unified, neutral, generalist, permanent; US: low status, upper ranks temporary, politicised	France: very high status, permanent, specialised elite training, segmented 'corps' (S. Europe, lower status, politicised)	Very high status, permanent, legal training; upper ranks permanent, but can be openly partisan	High status, professional, non-politicised (Sweden: segmented and decentralised)

Source: Adapted from Painter and Peters 2010: 20.

This overview does not clearly show, however, that in some countries a broad definition of public service is used that includes anyone working in the public sector in an appointed career position (e.g. Scandinavian countries, The Netherlands, where a juridical perspective dominates), while in other countries a more restricted concept of public service exists that includes only those who perform core tasks of public administration: they would include professionals in public management and administration and professionals exercising state power (such as police, customs, and so on) (OECD 1999: 21).

Table 2.1 does not show either that when one shifts from a legal to a more sociological perspective, a distinction then becomes visible in some countries between higher-level and lower-level public servants. Thus in England, the public service refers to those working for ministers accountable to Parliament, roughly 10 per cent of the total public workforce (Fry 2001: 20–1). In France and Germany a distinction is made between middle- and higher- (*fonctionnaire, Beamte*) and lower-level (*employé, Angestellte*) personnel.

How can we determine whether ideas about what public servants are have changed? For that we should look at primary, contemporary sources such as legal documents, newspapers, periodicals, regulations in the work environment ('codes of the shop floor'), and etiquette and political philosophical literature ('moral authorities'). These types of sources were used profitably in a project that attempted to trace changing attitudes towards political corruption in The Netherlands between 1650 and 1950 (Hoenderboom 2013; Kerkhoff 2013; Kroeze 2012). Looking at contemporary sources will enable the researcher to reconstruct ideas about a given concept or practice in the context of models, theories, or frameworks of reference relevant to a particular period. In other words, through interpretative understanding (i.e. *Verstehen*) anachronism can be avoided. Specifically with regard to conceptions of the public servant, I will consider some modern conceptions (those emerging in the eighteenth and nineteenth centuries) below. Another way to reconstruct role and position of the public servant in the larger political-administrative structure is to study administrative histories and to this I now turn.

From heritage and skills to merit

From antiquity until the late eighteenth century the professionalism of an administrative staff was understood tacitly in terms of specific skills that subordinates were supposed to have in order to aid those who governed. Several examples come to mind. First, the training schools for scribes in Ancient Egypt and Mesopotamia. Second, the 'instruction literature' such as in Ancient Egypt (e.g. the *Instruction of Ptah-Hotep*, the *Admonition of Ipu-Wer*; see Pritchard 1955: 412–14 and 441–4) and in the medieval Mirrors of Princes (*Fürstenspiegel*, such as Machiavelli's *The Prince*) with advice to rulers, and/or offspring and/or subordinates on how to govern. Third, the medieval *cartularia* (books with collections of deeds, contracts, charters and documents relating to a person, family or institution) providing clerks with examples of various types of official documents and correspondence. Fourth, the earliest handbooks of public administration with detailed instructions on how to keep records and conduct correspondence. However, the first of these handbooks also contained chapters on statistics, government and constitution, organisation of departments, appointments of functionaries, and extensive descriptions of public sector jobs (Seckendorff 1656). The second handbook had chapters on various policy areas such as health and water management, the distribution of food and transport and the management of buildings (De La Mare 1705–38). In the course of the eighteenth century a number of scholars and social commentators would describe the functions of government as including public health, care for the poor, care for children, education, i.e. that we now call welfare tasks (*see* Christiaan von Wolff in the middle of the eighteenth century: *see* Rutgers 2001) and social justice in general (*see* Condorcet 1795) (*see* below). From this I conclude that the initial focus on stylistic (composition) and physical writing skills for clerical jobs was augmented from the seventeenth century, with the need for ideas and knowledge about the role and position of government in society.

In the early modern age, those who governed (what we now would call 'political elites') and those who helped govern (today referred to as 'civil servants') relied on the type of education privy to the elites, which was a broad-based orientation in literature, history and philosophy, capped by travels in foreign lands such as the Grand Tour for young gentlemen in Europe from the late Middle Ages up to the early twentieth century. Young Americans, especially in the eighteenth century, were encouraged to travel to Europe. We know that George Washington wanted his stepson, John Parke Custis (1754–81), to travel to Europe after completing studies in Greek, French, mathematics and the law and customs of other countries (Cook 2012: 53). That this did not happen is because Custis was not much interested in studying.

Heritage and nepotism were long considered sufficient for entry into middle- and higher-level public office, but these were slowly but surely eclipsed by competency and merit. Several European authors have been urging for competent administrators since the early eighteenth century. With regard to the United States, as early as 1936 Mosher and Kingsley wrote that 'The credit for setting the standard of competency as the primary criterion for qualifying for an appointive position goes to President Washington' (1936: 17). Van Riper even suggested that Washington had inaugurated a merit-based system of employment that was largely maintained by presidents after him (1983: 479). However, President Washington emphasised neither technical competence nor specific administrative skills. What he looked for was 'fitness of character', as judged by personal integrity, standing in the community and place of residence (White 1948: 259). 'Character' was still important but is today more commonly understood in the context of 'meritorious service' (i.e. competence *and* public service character) (Ingraham 1995; 2006: 487). Professionalisation took off in Europe with the establishment of professorial chairs in *Kameralistik* (Germany) and in *science de la police* (France) from the early eighteenth century. In the United States this happened in the decades following the Pendleton Act of 1883. That this started in Europe as early as it did had everything to do with some major and unprecedented changes in the institutional superstructure and the organisational structure of the public sector in the decades between 1780 and 1820.

1780–1820: Watershed in the history of government and the concept of public servant

In reference to the upheavals in America and Europe, the American historian Robert R. Palmer dubbed the second part of the eighteenth century as the period of the Atlantic Revolutions when a call for equality, liberty and brotherhood successfully challenged the dominance of monarchs, aristocrats, clergy and merchants in the trade and craft guilds (1959, 1964).[1] It actually resulted in the creation of a type of government not before seen in the history of humankind, and this is best analysed by characterising what changes took place at the constitutional, organisational and individual levels (Kiser and Ostrom 1982). It is important to pay attention to this briefly, since to greater or lesser extent what happened back then gave rise to our modern (Western) conception of a public servant and that conception has spread across the globe.

---

1. Koselleck (1972) refers to the 1750–1850 period as *Sattelzeit*, the time bridging ('saddling') the *Ancien Régime* and the modern age. Administrative history's *Sattelzeit* is perhaps shorter (1780–1820) when considering the decades that actual reforms were not just advocated but actually implemented (*see* below why 1780–1820 were important years). At the same time, professionalisation of the civil service had started in France and Germany earlier, that is, in the early eighteenth century.

At the constitutional level, i.e. of the institutional superstructure that is both the foundation for and context within which government operates, there have been at least four major changes: separating the public and private sectors, separating church and state, the creation of constitutions, and the separation of politics from administration. I shall briefly address each of these in turn.

Separating public and private spheres

Until the late eighteenth century positions in the upper reaches and strata in all societies were held by people who belonged to one single social, economic and political elite. Thus it was that local, regional and national government administrators (what we nowadays would call political officeholders) also held positions in, say, the British East India Company or major office in one of the guilds. Also, high-ranking clerics could hold major office in government (e.g. Cardinal Richelieu in France). Furthermore, positions in what we would define today as career public servants or policy bureaucrats were also held by members of the same elite, as preparation for higher (political) office. In other words, there was no distinction between public and private sectors, as understood today. The Roman distinction between *res publica* (public thing) and *res privata* (private property) is quite different. It only became possible to separate the public from the private sphere by the idea that government existed not as an instrument of the elites but as a mechanism to protect all people against violence from foreign aggressors and against injustice and oppression from within, to provide people with public works and education so as to advance the interests of all (*see also* next section) and to protect people from the power of government. The contemporary understanding of public (government) and private (predominantly the economy, but also other societal organisations) spheres dates back to John Locke, and came to full flower in the works of Adam Smith (Kennedy 2010: 164–7).

Separating church and state

In the slipstream of this development, church and state, *de facto* separate since the twelfth century, became *de iure* separated in the national constitutions that were rapidly adopted everywhere (the American in 1787; the French in 1791; the Dutch in 1798) (Raadschelders 2002: 6). This is a monumental development, because hitherto the state had been intertwined with other societal organisations such as organised religion. From this moment, the state would dominate the public realm, and organised religion was relegated to the private realm.

Establishing a constitutional foundation to the state and its public sphere

Indeed, capturing the foundation of society in a legal document, a constitution, is another major innovation in the history of government. This did not come out of the blue, for its origins can be traced back to Aristotle's ideas about the good constitution as a mix of oligarchy and polis, to Roman natural law (connecting law to natural principles of equity and justice), and Germanic law and feudalism (i.e. ruler and lords bound by mutual obligations and reciprocities). These three fed into the contemporary understanding of constitutionalism which includes (1) limiting state power *vis-à-vis* society and (2) separating powers within the state (Lane 1996: 20–5). These powers were initially identified as those of legislative, executive and federative (i.e. foreign affairs; Locke) but the most common is that between legislative, executive and judiciary (Montesquieu). At no time was administrative staff considered a (political power) in and of itself. With that, constitutionalism provided not only a new context for the relation between rulers and people, but also for the interaction between rulers and administrative staff.

Separation of politics from administration

These first three changes at the constitutional level concern the institutional context in which the 'new' public servant was going to work, namely as subordinate to one (in the case of the executive) or several (in the case of a collegial body) political officeholder(s). From research done in the 1980s in four Dutch municipalities (Raadschelders 1994), I recall reading some correspondence between the mayor and municipal secretary (*see* the city manager in the United States) stored in the archives of the town of Purmerend (in the province of North Holland) in the early nineteenth century. They were brothers, they belonged to the local elite, and they had occupied public office for decades. They conveyed to each other that they found it very difficult to adapt to their respective positions of 'superiority' and 'subordination'. Should those born to rule (*noblesse oblige*) not be treated as equals, as partners in the administration of their town? Difficult it may have been for a few decades, but the idea stuck hold that those in higher 'public' offices should be elected as representatives of the people, i.e. politicians, while those at subordinate levels should be selected on the basis of specifically defined administrative skills, training and experiences.

This last development especially had direct consequences at the organisational and individual levels. At the organisational level there are two major developments: departmentalisation and separation of office from officeholder.

Departmentalisation

Departmentalisation became widespread. While there had been government departments before the late eighteenth and early nineteenth centuries (Raadschelders 2002: 12), the idea structuring the bulk of the public sector in clearly identifiable units that were organised as a bureaucracy (i.e. with unity of command, a clear line structure, and so on) that was subjected to the primacy of politics is yet another product of the eighteenth century. Collegial organisation where one office was held by a group of people – and this was the normal situation at middle and higher managerial levels (e.g. the regents of the orphanage, church masters) – was from here on limited to elective office (e.g. legislative bodies) and sometimes also to judicial office (e.g. the High Court).

Separation of office and officeholder

The second development at the organisational level was to separate office from officeholder. Throughout history it had been quite common to acquire a position on the basis of kinship or friendship. Offices could be inherited and even sold, and it was possible to hold multiple offices at the same time. First urged by Popes Celestine I and Leo I (fifth century) (Miller 1983: 84), and later reiterated by Martin Luther (Hattenhauer 1978: 15), the separation of office and officeholder was not common practice until the late eighteenth/ early nineteenth century. This started in 1780 with the creation of a number of committees by George III, king of England, that were charged to look into the sale of public office and so-called sinecure offices (Cohen 1941: 20). This resulted in a series of public service reforms, such as Act 23 GEO III, c.82 (1783), which abolished sinecure offices in the Exchequer upon the demise of the officeholder, who was then – if necessary – replaced by a salaried official. Other departments followed quickly (Chester 1981: 138).

Developments at constitutional and organisational levels naturally had consequences at the level of individual officeholders. The separation of politics and administration happened with an eye on two important issues: to make administrators less dependent upon their 'political bosses', yet still subordinate to the latter and not beholden to other external influences, and to increase their substantive qualifications for holding a career public service position.

Adequate salary and pension in money

Government jobs below the top ranks often required one to two days a week at most. Except for the elites, anyone working in a government job had to augment that income with employment elsewhere. Since salary was paid in money *and* in kind, and since there was no formal pension system, those working in a government job were highly dependent upon patronage. The fact that they worked other jobs as well opened the door for corruption. It is in the early nineteenth century in Europe that administrative positions in government become full-time jobs, compensated with a salary in money that was sufficient to sustain a family. Equally important, government employees were no longer required to work until very old age, because of the establishment of a retirement age and pension system. Starting in the seventeenth century with military pensions, by the 1820s several German states had established retirement (with a maximum age between 65 and 70) and pensions (Wunder 2000: 28; Chester 1981: 129). To have a sufficient salary and pension in money was one of the features of Max Weber's ideal-typical bureaucracy: at one stroke career public servants were made somewhat autonomous from political officeholders as well as no longer beholden to other employers. In return, career public servants were expected to serve the elected administration to the best of their ability, which included appropriate educational background and experience. It is to this that I now turn.

Modern conceptions of public service: Early roots and nineteenth-century ideals

Against the background of the above, it is no surprise that professionalism became a cornerstone for normative ideas about what a career public servant should be in this modernised government. In the late medieval conception of an administrative or public service state, as advocated by the legal and political theorist Filips van Leiden (c. 1325–82), administrative staff were portrayed as servants of the state (which in Van Leiden's view was equal to the ruler[2]) (Romein and Romein-Verschoor 1973: 27) and thus as personal servants (*see* above).

From the middle of the seventeenth century, this was no longer considered acceptable, at least not among some political philosophers and theorists. In the eyes of political philosopher Johann Althusius (1557–1638) designated public ministers should work on behalf of the population, and he viewed this as a universal symbiotic association.[3] They are mandated as trustees or stewards of the people (Overeem 2014). The German scholar Christiaan von Wolff (1679–1754) firmly believed that administrators needed to be trained and examined in administration, and should work to improve the common good (for what he called the 'Eudamonic state', somewhat comparable to the welfare state). Sale of office, accumulation of office (this was quite common at the upper levels of early modern elite administration), and inadequate pay ought to be avoided (Rutgers 2001). Some years later, in his *Der Herr und der Diener, geschildert mit Patriotischer Freyheit* (1759), the German political philosopher Friedrich Carl von Moser (1723–98) was convinced that the educated, paternal prince needed a skilled, well-functioning, loyal and patriotic administration. He was very critical of the fact that administrative office could be bought, of inappropriate behaviour of officials, of the fact that some were unfit for public office and of remuneration practices at court (as mentioned in Richter 2014; *see also* Schumann 1954: 5). Two years later he published another book titled *Beherzigungen* (1761), in which he stressed firmly the importance of civil rights grounded in a contract between ruled and ruler (Schumann 1954: 11). In the Dutch Republic several authors (who often also served in high administrative positions) wrote pamphlets condemning nepotism, patronage and the abuse of power by administrative elites, advocating that public servants (in this case I do refer to both political and administrative officeholders) should first and foremost serve the general, not personal interest. They also favoured rotation of office because 'government officials who are never forced to return to the status of citizen are likely to believe they are masters' (as quoted in Kerkhoff 2014).

---

2. This notion 'lived' well into the seventeenth century: *see* James I (King of England and Ireland, 1603–25; he was James VI as King of Scotland, 1567–1603), 'I am the husband and the whole Isle is my lawful wife; I am the head and it is my body' (quoted in Cohen 1994: 30), and Louis XIII (King of France, 1601–43), 'l'État c'est moi' (translation: 'the state is me') (Dyson 1980: 137).

3. Reminiscent of Althusius' discussion of politics as the art of association, but not mentioning him, is Alexis de Tocqueville (2000: 492) noting that in a democracy the science of association is the mother science. De Tocqueville's views on this were reiterated by V. Ostrom (1974: 93–4).

In the spirit of Althusius before him, the German philosopher Hegel (1770–1831) labelled public servants as the new guardians (*see* Plato's guardians, i.e. the philosopher-kings) of democracy, because they combined practical wisdom with practical experience and skills (Jackson 1986; Shaw 1992). The same sentiment could be found in *Lehre vom Modernen Staat. Vol. 1, Allgemeine Statslehre* (1875) by the German legal scholar Johann Caspar Bluntschli (1808–81): public servants are guardians of the general will and are appointed on the basis of a thorough education and competency (Rosser 2014).

Hegel influenced Max Weber's (1864–1920) formulation of the bureaucratic ideal type (Gale and Hummel 2003; Spicer 2004) and especially with those dimensions that concern bureaucracy as a personnel system (the other dimensions are about bureaucracy as organisation), including: office held by individual functionaries, who are subordinate (to political officeholders), who are appointed, who are knowledgeable, who have expertise, who are assigned by contractual agreement in a tenured (secure) position, and who fulfil their office as their main or only job, who work in a career system, who are rewarded with a regular salary and pension in money, who are rewarded according to rank, who are promoted according to seniority, and who work under formal protection of their office. These elements also show some similarity with what Bluntschli advocated, but in contrast to him, Weber favoured an apolitical administrative apparatus.

To be sure, Weber's bureaucratic ideal type has become so dominant a concept in public administration scholarship that we are inclined to think that it is of West European or even Prussian origin, and forget that there was at least one historical precedent. Indeed, central to the Confucian idea of government is that career public servants are recruited on the basis, among other things, of their knowledge, policy contribution and experience (Liu 1959: 212, 216).

In Europe the career public service was depoliticised from the early nineteenth century, while in the US this did not happen until the late nineteenth century (for an explanation of this *see* Nelson 1982). By the end of the nineteenth century a professional public service had come into being in the Western world with increasing emphasis on technical and specialist expertise and bureaucratisation.

Is a European conception of public servant emergent?

The various studies in this volume seek to provide a historical background and narrative about conceptions of public servants in the past three to four centuries and, possibly, provide direction to the search for a European public servant. In this section we can look at two elements: the context within which the public servant works, and society's view of the public servant.

NPM reforms and the shifting perspective towards governance and networks have allegedly changed the context within which public servants work. The Thomas theorem comes to mind: when people perceive situations as real, then they are real in their consequences. So, while there is little empirical research, and thus a lack of evidence, that we actually shifted from 'traditional' administration to emphasising management and from 'traditional' bureaucratic hierarchy to networking and collaborative governance, it might well be that the public servant looks upon her/ himself more than ever as a public manager. But that too has so far escaped any serious empirical enquiry.

It has been suggested that one of the possible consequences of this embrace of governance and of networks is that public servants spend less time on policy advice and more on management. Again, tiresomely, there is no empirical evidence to back this up. The only quantitative study of how public servants spend their time that I know of (demonstrating, perhaps, grave limitations in my knowledge of the literature) is that by Brehm *et al.* on time spent on internal, administrative supervision (2003). There are, though, qualitative studies that suggest that middle- and higher-level public servants spend significant amounts of time on policy making (which would include advising) (Page and Jenkins 2005; Page 2012). And this is not something that has emerged in the past twenty years or so, as Bevir suggests that there is now widespread recognition that public servants, street-level bureaucrats, and so on, do not just implement legislation but also interpret, make and redefine public policy (2010: 160). At the time that Frank Goodnow urged that judicial, quasi-judicial, statistical, semi-scientific and organisational administrative functions ought to be removed from political influence (1900: 78–9), no doubt inspired by the widespread corruption fresh in anyone's memory, public servants were already extensively involved in developing policy content before decision making through networks (*see* Carpenter 2001, especially the title of his book). Four decades after Goodnow, Leys noted how public servants had become significantly more independent, with legislators responsible for laying down general policy and public servants providing the substantive details and plans of action (1943: 10). Today, more than a century after Goodnow, public servants are even more involved through secondary legislation (*see* Furlong 2003; Gordon 1999; Page 2001) and through policy making (Page and Jenkins 2005; Page 2012).

As well as the lack of empirical evidence, it seems that the NPM, network and collaborative governance literatures do not pay much attention to the normative implications of infusing the public sector with principles drawn from the business sector. If the new public servant is a public manager and/or entrepreneur, to whom is she/he accountable? Can policy making be separated from the execution of policy? This policy/operations dichotomy 'is a perfect vehicle for allowing ministers to absolve themselves of their responsibilities to Parliament by defining any problems as "operational matters" and hence deferring responsibility to chief executives' (Du Gay 2000: 132). If this arms-length style of administration is preferred, does it mean that these public managers, i.e. middle- and higher-level public servants, can be held directly accountable before a legislature?

The problem with this question, and in general with the notion of a shift to governance and networks, is that 'shift' seems to be understood as synonymous with 'replace'. That, I am sure, is not the case. Middle- and certainly higher-level administrators still do both policy advising and management. And so they should. In a legal sense, little has changed in their position in the political-administrative system: they are still subordinate to political officeholders (cabinet ministers, mayors, governors), and are expected to give the best possible advice on policy proposals. The extent to which their input is valued varies from country to country but is generally higher in northwest Europe than in southern Europe or the United States. Are there elements in the contemporary notion of the public servant in Europe that suggest some degree of convergence towards a shared conception? Are they, indeed, not (perceived) as just state servants (as was the case in the fifteenth to eighteenth centuries) but also – and more importantly – as public servants whose first charge it is to advance the common good? Above we have seen that ideas about such a public servant had already emerged as early as the early seventeenth century, and were enacted in law from the early nineteenth century.

One issue with regard to the question whether a shared perception of a European public servant is emerging concerns existing administrative traditions. No matter how strong the drumbeat for NPM measures, for networking, for collaborative governance, and so forth, may be, these administrative traditions or cultures cannot be legislated away or reformed out of the picture. The varied successes with NPM reforms in different countries should be sufficient to point out that these national cultures do not change by way of active agency but over time. And they will change, just as the initial conception of an administrative staffer as personal servant changed to that of being a state servant, and that to our contemporary notion of public servant. Each of these changes took time. The change towards a public service was discussed by very few political theorists and philosophers (e.g. Althusius, Von Wolff, Von Moser), but then only on the margins (Overeem 2012: 22), before it became practice, and it became practice before it was formalised in regulation (pensions, retirement age) and legislation (Civil Service Acts). Perhaps we are entering a new age of networked governance with public managers, an age that requires a new type of public servant. But, by all means, before we jump into suggesting all sorts of changes, let us first consider what facts exist to support the idea that we have moved away from bureaucratic hierarchy and government. I reiterate, government is still the only actor that can make binding decisions on behalf of an entire population. And that makes public servants still important and necessary contributors to public policy. Reducing them to public managers would harm rather than support the European administrator of the future.

Concluding remarks

The historical perspective in this volume provides depth in the sense that it removes us from the hustle and bustle of the time in which we live. For example, the public administration literature has been buzzing in the past twenty years with concepts such as governance, networks, collaboration and so forth. And these concepts are *discussed* as if they are novel, but there is ample evidence that *practices* of governance, networking and collaboration go back much farther. If that is the case, then the question is whether the role and position of public servants has changed in the past twenty years or not. Also, is there a European concept of public servant, and upon what sources and evidence can we determine this? Does a legal perspective dominate contemporary (European?) conceptualisations in which the public servant is one who loyally, but not uncritically, serves the cabinet in power? That public servant has the uncommon capability of serving successive political officeholders even when they are of different political ilk, while keeping an eye out for trends and movements in society. Or does a more sociological perspective dominate, where public servants are the eyes and ears of the political officeholder, weighing what is politically, socially and financially feasible. That public servant is a highly trained professional with an advanced degree who has the skills both to help develop and to execute policy. Perhaps one can even say that both perspectives, or conceptualisations, are relevant to understanding the role and position of the public servant today. In both perspectives the public servant is also committed to treating everybody as much as possible as equal before the law. It is that type of public servant that has become the norm used by international forum organisations such as the International Monetary Fund (IMF) and the World Bank when advising on administrative reforms in developing countries. It is, however, a public servant rooted in a specific political-administrative culture. At best, Europe is a confederacy of states, and while many of its policies have assumed supranational proportions, the implementation of these policies is still done in the various countries by public servants at the national, regional and local levels of government, i.e. in countries with different political-administrative traditions.

References

Aberbach, J. D., Putnam, R. D. and Rockman, B. A. (1981) *Bureaucrats and Politicians in Western Democracies*, Cambridge, MA: Harvard University Press.

Baker, R. (ed.) (2002) *Transitions from Authoritarianism: The role of bureaucracy*, Westport, CT/London: Praeger.

Bevir, M. (2010) *Democratic Governance*, Princeton, NJ: Princeton University Press.

Brehm, J., Gates, S. and Gomez, B. (2003) 'Donut Shops, speed traps, and paperwork: Supervision and the allocation of time to bureaucratic tasks', in Krause, G. and Meier, K. J. (eds), *Politics, Policy and Organisations: Frontiers in the scientific study of bureaucracy*, Ann Arbor, MI: University of Michigan Press, pp. 133–59.

Carpenter, D. P. (2001) *The Forging of Bureaucratic Autonomy: Reputations, networks, and policy innovation in executive agencies*, Princeton/Oxford: Princeton University Press.

Chhotray, V. and Stoker, G. (2009) *Governance Theory and Practice: A cross-disciplinary approach*, Houndmills: Palgrave Macmillan.

Chester, N. (1981) *The English Administrative System 1780–1870*, Oxford: Clarendon Press.

Cohen, E. W. (1941) *The Growth of the British Civil Service System 1780–1939*, London: George Allen & Unwin.

Cohen, I. B. (1994) *Interactions: Some contacts between the natural sciences and the social sciences*, Cambridge, MA/London: MIT Press.

Condorcet, M. de (1795) *Outlines of an Historical View of the Human Mind*, London: J. Johnson.

Cook, S. A. (2012) 'George Washington: Progenitor of American public administration theory', unpublished PhD dissertation, Florida State University.

De La Mare, N. (1705–10) *Traité de la Police*, Paris: J. and P. Cot.

De Tocqueville, A. (2000) *Democracy in America* (trans. and ed. with introduction by Mansfield, H. C. and Winthrop, D.), Chicago/London: University of Chicago Press.

Du Gay, P. (2000) *In Praise of Bureaucracy: Weber, organization, ethics*, London: Sage.

Dyson, K. H. F. (1980) *The State Tradition in Western Europe: A study of an idea and institution*, New York: Oxford University Press.

Fry, G. K. (2001) 'The British civil service system', in Bekke, A. J. G. M. and van der Meer, F. M. (eds) *Civil Service Systems in Western Europe*, Cheltenham: Edward Elgar, pp. 12–35.

Furlong, S. R. (2003) 'Bureaucratic agencies, evolution of delegation of authority/power', in Rabin, J. (ed.) *Encyclopedia of Public Administration and Public Policy*, New York: Marcel Dekker, pp. 130–4.

Gale, S. A. and Hummel, R. P. (2003) 'A debt unpaid – reinterpreting Max Weber on bureaucracy', *Administrative Theory & Praxis*, 25(4): 409–18.

Goodnow, F. (1900) *Politics and Administration: A study in government*, New York: Macmillan.

Gordon, S. (1999) *Controlling the State: Constitutionalism from ancient Athens to today*, Cambridge, MA/London: Harvard University Press.

Hattenhauer, H. (1978) *Geschichte des Beamtentums* (vol. 1, *Handbuch des öffentlichen Dienstes*), edited by Wiese, W. (ed.) Cologne: Heymann Verlag, C. pp. 4–315.

Hoenderboom, M. (2013) *Scandal, Politics and Patronage: Corruption and public values in The Netherlands (1650–1747)*, Ridderkerk: Ridderprint.

Ingraham, P. W. (1995) *The Foundation of Merit: Public service in American democracy*, Baltimore/London: Johns Hopkins University Press.

— (2006) 'Building bridges over troubled waters: Merit as a guide', *Public Administration Review*, 66(4): 486–95.

Jackson, M. W. (1986) 'Bureaucracy in Hegel's political theory', *Administration & Society*, 18(2): 139–57.

Kennedy, G. (2010) *Adam Smith: A moral philosopher and his political economy*, Houndmills: Palgrave Macmillan.

Kerkhoff, A. D. N. (2013) *Hidden Morals, Explicit Scandals: Public values and political corruption in The Netherlands (1748–1813)*, Amsterdam: Ponsen & Looijen.

— (2014) 'Early modern development in Dutch public administration: Patriot and Batavian authors on public morality (1770s–1813)', *Administrative Theory & Praxis*.

Kiser, L. L. and Ostrom, E. (1982) 'The three worlds of action: a metatheoretical synthesis of institutional approaches', in Ostrom, E. (ed.) *Strategies of Political Inquiry*, Beverly Hills: Sage, pp. 179–222.

Koselleck, R. (1972) 'Über die Theoriebedürftichkeit der Geschichtswissenschaft', in Conze, W. (ed.) *Theorie der Geschichtswissenschaft under Praxis des Geschichtsunterrichts*, Stuttgart Klett-Cotta:, pp. 10–28.

Kroeze, D. B. R. (2012) *Een Kwestie van Politieke Moraliteit: Politieke corruptieschandalen en goed bestuur in Nederland, 1840–1940*, Hilversum: Verloren.

Lane, J. -E. (1996) *Constitutions and Political Theory*, Manchester/New York: Manchester University Press.

Lee, K. -H. and Raadschelders, J. C. N. (2008) 'Political–administrative relations: impact of and puzzles in Aberbach, Putnam, and Rockman, 1981', *Governance*, 21(3): 419–38.

Leys, W. A. R. (1943) 'Ethics and administrative discretion', *Public Administration Review*, 3(1): 10–23.

Liu, J. T. C. (1959) 'Eleventh-century Chinese bureaucrats: some historical classifications and behavioral types', *Administrative Science Quarterly*, 4(2): 207–26.

Little, D. (2009) 'The heterogeneous social: New thinking about the foundations of the social sciences', in Mantzavinos, C. (ed.) *Philosophy of the Social Sciences: Philosophical theory and scientific practice*, Cambridge: Cambridge University Press, pp. 154–78.

Miller, M. (1983) 'From ancient to modern organization: the Church as conduit and creator', *Administration & Society*, 15(3): 275–93.

Mosher, W. E. and Kingsley, J. D. (1936) *Public Personnel Administration*, New York: Harper & Brothers Publishers.

Nelson, M. (1982) 'A short ironic history of American national bureaucracy', *Journal of Politics*, 44(3): 747–78.

Nolan, B. C. (ed.) (2001) 'Introduction', in Nolan, B. C. (ed.) *Public Sector Reform: An International Perspective*, Houndmills: Palgrave, pp. xix–xxxiv.

OECD (1999) *European Principles for Public Administration*, Sigma Paper no.27, Paris: OECD.

Ostrom, V. (1974) *The Intellectual Crisis in American Public Administration*, Tuscaloosa, AZ: University of Alabama Press.

Overeem, P. (2012) *The Politics-Administration Dichotomy: Toward a Constitutional Perspective*, Boca Raton: CRC Press.

— (2014) 'Johannes Althusius on public administration', *Administrative Theory & Praxis* 36(1): 31–50.

Page, E. C. (2001) *Government by Numbers: Delegated legislations and everyday policy-making*, Oxford/Portland: Hart Publishing.

— (2012) *Policy without Politicians: Bureaucratic influence in comparative perspective*, Oxford: Oxford University Press.

Page, E. C. and Jenkins, B. (2005) *Policy Bureaucracy: Government with a cast of thousands*, Oxford: Oxford University Press.

Painter, M. and Peters, B. G. (eds) (2010) 'Administrative traditions in comparative perspective: Families, groups and hybrids', *Tradition and Public Administration*, New York: Palgrave Macmillan, pp. 19–30.

Palmer, R. R.(1959) *The Age of Democratic Revolution: A political history of Europe and America 1760–1800* (vol. 1), Princeton, NJ: Princeton University Press.

— (1964) *The Age of Democratic Revolution: The struggle* (vol. 2), Princeton, NJ: Princeton University Press.

Peters, B. G. (1985) 'Politicians and bureaucrats in the politics of policy making', in Lane, J.-E. (ed.) *Bureaucracy and Public Choice*, London: Sage, pp. 256–82.

Peters, B. G. and Pierre, J. (eds) (2001) 'Civil servants and politicians: The changing balance', *Politicians, Bureaucrats and Administrative Reform*, London/New York: Routledge, pp. 1–10.

Peters, B. G., Pierre, J. and King, D. (2005) 'The politics of path-dependency: political conflict in historical institutionalism', *Journal of Politics*, 67(4): 1275–300.

Pollitt, C. and Bouckaert, G. (2011) *Public Management Reform: A comparative analysis – New Public Management, governance and the neo-Weberian state* (3rd edn), Oxford: Oxford University Press.

Pollitt, C. and Dan, S. (2011) *The Impacts of the New Public Management in Europe: A meta-analysis, European Commission: Work Package 1 of Cocops* (Coordinating for Cohesion in the Public Sector of the Future), Brussels: European Commission.

Pritchard, J. (1955) *Ancient Near Eastern Texts relating to the Old Testament*, Princeton, NJ: Princeton University Press.

Raadschelders, J. C. N. (1994) 'Understanding the development of local government: theory and evidence from the Dutch case', *Administration & Society*, 25(4): 410–42.

—— (2002) 'An administrative history perspective on church-state relations: On the varied impacts of Judeo-Christian heritage and organized religion', in Raadschelders, J. C. N. (ed.) *Church and State in European Administrative History*, Vol. 14 of the Yearbook of European Administrative History, Baden-Baden: Nomos Verlagsgesellschaft, pp. 1–20.

—— (2003) *Government: A public administration perspective*, Armonk, NY: M. E. Sharpe.

Raadschelders, J. C. N. and Rutgers, M. R. (1996) 'The history of civil service systems', in Bekke, A. J. G. M., Perry, J. L. and Toonen, T. A. J. (eds) *Civil Service Systems in Comparative Perspective*, Bloomington, IN Indiana University Press, pp. 67–100.

Raadschelders, J. C. N. and van der Meer, F. M. (eds) (1998) *L'entourage administratif du pouvoir executive/Administering the Summit*, Cahier d'Histoire de l'Administration no.5. Brussels: Ets. Bruylant.

Richter, S. (2014) 'German "minor" thinkers? The perception of Moser's and Justi's works in an enlightened European context', *Administrative Theory & Praxis*, 36(1): 52–73.

Romein, J. and Romein-Verschoor, A. (eds) (1973) 'Filips van Leiden, circa 1325–82: De eerste regent', *Erflaters van onze Beschaving*, Amsterdam: Querido, pp. 13–32.

Rosser, C. (2014) 'Johann Caspar Bluntschli's organic theory of state and public administration', *Administrative Theory & Praxis*, 36(1): 32–51.

Rutgers, M. R. (2001) 'The prince, his welfare state, and its administration: Christiaan von Wolff's administrative philosophy', *Public Voices*, 4(3): 29–45.

Schumann, D. W. (1954) 'Goethe and Friedrich Carl von Moser: a contribution to the study of Götz von Berlichingen', *Journal of English and German Philology*, 53(1): 1–22.

Seckendorff, V. L. von (1976 [1656]) *Teutscher Fürstenstat*, Glashütten im Taunus: Detlev Auvermann.

Shaw, C. K. Y. (1992) 'Hegel's theory of modern bureaucracy', *American Political Science Review*, 86(3): 381–9.

Spicer, M. W. (2004) 'Note on origins: Hegel, Weber, and Frederician Prussia', *Administrative Theory & Praxis*, 26(2): 97–102.

van der Meer, F. M. and Raadschelders, J. C. N. (2014) 'Administrative elites in The Netherlands from 1980 to 2011: making the invisible visible', *International Review of Administrative Sciences*, 80(4): 726–45.

van Riper, P. P. (1983) 'The American administrative state: Wilson and the Founders – An unorthodox view', *Public Administration Review*, 43(6): 477–90.

Weber, M. (1980) *Wirtschaft und Gesellschaft: Grundriss der verstehenden Soziologie*, Tübingen: J. C. B. Mohr.

White, L. D. (1948) *The Federalists: A study in administrative history 1789–1801*, New York: Free Press.

Wunder, B. (ed.) (2000) 'Die Entwicklung der Alters- und Hinterbliebenenversorgung im öffentlichen Dienst in Deutschland (18.-19. Jahrhundert)', *Pension Systems for Public Servants in Western Europe (19th/20th c.)*, Baden-Baden: Nomos Verlagsgesellschaft, pp. 1–53.

Part Two

Older Notions of Public Service

Chapter Three

Serving the Public by Advising the Ruler

Joanne Paul

Introduction

Much like this volume itself, early modern English discussions of public service emerged out of a meeting of intellectuals in Antwerp. Almost precisely five centuries ago, in 1515, the humanist Thomas More travelled to Bruges in the diplomatic service of Henry VIII.[1] During a break in negotiations, he visited Antwerp to meet with Peter Giles, a city magistrate and fellow humanist. There, they had the discussion that would form the inspiration for a second – fictional – meeting of minds in Antwerp: book one of More's *Utopia*, published a year later in 1516. In this text, the characters of More and Giles meet with a third – fictional – interlocutor, Raphael Hythloday, and debate the merits and disadvantages of a life of public service. When Peter Giles suggests that Hythloday 'enter some king's service', Hythloday objects that he does not wish to 'enslave himself to any king', prompting Giles to clarify that he 'meant not that you should be in servitude [*servire*] to any king, only in his service [*inservire*]' (More 2002 [1516]: 13),[2] upon which the character of More connects this idea of service to the public benefit.[3] Underlying these discussions is the recognition that such public service is best performed by providing counsel to a king in the context of the royal court.

This may seem an odd and out-of-the-way place to begin a historical appraisal of the European public servant; after all, European public service in its present context takes place in democracies, not monarchies, and scholarship regarding its function and purpose has seldom had much to say about advisers. When it does, a stark distinction is often drawn between public servants, who offer impartial and legitimate 'policy advice', and those 'outsiders' who offer illegitimate and partial 'political advice' (*see* Table 3.1).

Special advisers, it has been suggested, 'complicat[e] the relationship between the "key actors"' in governance – politicians and their public servants (Walter 1986: 2) – by introducing a 'possible third group' (Dror 1987: 202; *see* Baum 1982).

---

1. All biographical details pertaining to More from Baker House, 'More, Sir Thomas (1478–1535)', ODNB Online (accessed 4 September 2013).

2. Original dates of publication are in square brackets. Language and editorial conventions differ significantly between editions.

3. I have employed modern editions where possible and employed my own modernisations to spelling and grammar where no modern edition exists; original text is given in footnotes.

Table 3.1: The distinction between policy advice and political advice

'Policy advice'	'Political advice'
Technical and professional alternatives	Likely electoral or media consequences
Outcome of objective/rational analysis	Subjective
Substantive	Self-interested
From non-partisan career public servants	From partisan, committed sources
Permanent and 'official'	Temporary and 'unofficial'
'Inside'	'Outside'
Seen as 'pure' or legitimate	Seen as 'shabby' or illegitimate

Source: Weller 1987: 149.

This divide between advisers and public servants has been recognised as pervasive but 'essentially artificial' (Weller 1987: 149), not only because neither group is in practice limited to these 'types' of advice (*see* Baum 1982: 546–52; Chabal 1993: 54; Topf 1993: 182–3) but also because, at least in the British context,[4] 'special advisers' who offer 'political advice' are in fact deemed also to be civil servants.[5] Although distinct from '*permanent*' civil servants, in that they do not have to be appointed by merit nor offer impartial advice, they are still '*temporary*' civil servants, and thus fall under the Civil Service Order (1995), as well as having their own *Code of Conduct for Special Advisers* (2009; *see* James 2007: 64–6).

Thus it is that in recent decades (and in the UK especially following the 1997 Blair administration; *see* Blick 2004: 2; Fawcett and Gay 2010: 25), attention has turned to these 'people who live in the dark' (Blick 2004) in an attempt to illuminate their roles, relationships and, in a few cases, their history (*see* Peters and Barker 1993; Laugharne 1994; James 2007; Connaughton 2010; Gay 2010; Gains and Stoker 2011; Fleischer 2012). Attempts, however, to recover a pre-twentieth century history of advisers in the context of public service have been largely shallow and under-researched, lacking an appreciation for methodological developments and changes in the field of history from which they draw.[6] For instance, Laugharne's 1994 study traces the use of specialist advisory committees to the early Middle Ages, through to developments in sixteenth-century political administration (Laugharne 1994: 21–2). Although interesting, this suggestion is

---

4. For a survey of these relationships across other European countries *see* James 2007. For instance, Denmark and Sweden have a system much like that of the UK, whereas in Spain there is a top tier of permanent civil servants who are also politicised, and in France and Italy there is a mixed group of advisers and civil servants.

5. There are also arguments that, rather than posing a threat to the 'traditional' relationship between public servant and minister, such advisers in fact support and benefit it; *see* Eichbaum and Shaw 2008.

6. For instance, Dror 1987 declared that 'key features of relations between rulers and advisers have not changed very much' since their evolution 5,000 years ago, an assumption that also lies behind Goldhamer 1978, an ambitious volume but one that generally lacks historical rigour.

given without reference or analysis, and fails to incorporate the move in recent historiography towards combining analysis of institutions with an awareness of the history of political ideas (*see* Guy 1997: 3–8). When histories of public service advice do mention Renaissance and early modern political thinkers – such as Machiavelli (Chabal 1993: 51) and Bacon (Walter 1986: 3, 8) – they do so without contextual consideration or engagement with the text as a whole.[7] In other words, recent attempts to shine a light on the hidden history of the adviser have failed to take a truly integrated historical perspective that brings institutional and intellectual histories to bear on a subject sitting at the nexus of these concerns.

Of course, a complete and thorough history of such a subject cannot be attempted here. In what follows, I will be providing a piece of this project, by following the trail left by More and highlighting some of the main developments and debates in the early sixteenth-century English discourse of counsel.[8] In particular, it is worth being attentive to the role that the figure of the counsellor had in the English humanist attempt to integrate elements of neo-classical republican thought into a (increasingly restrictive and dangerous) monarchical context. The counsellor was an agent of republican freedom through public service; a lesson that is clearest in the early sixteenth-century humanist focus on the concept of *parrhesia* – freedom of speech in the context of unequal power relations. For these thinkers, the position of counsellor to a king could indeed constitute servitude, even outright slavery, but through *parrhesiastic* speech, this role could be turned into one of public service and thus constitute an important element of freedom.

The Henrician political counsellor[9]

The English sixteenth-century figure of the political counsellor was thoroughly indebted to the revival of a neo-Roman, specifically Ciceronian, view of public service (*see* Pocock 1993: 395; Guy 1995; Colclough 1999). This is not to say that there were not previous traditions of political counsel; medieval texts repeatedly emphasised the importance of a counsellor who would provide prudent advice to a king, paralleling the rule of reason over the emotions in the attainment of virtue (Ferster 1996). This figure was derived from the Aristotelian recognition that Plato's ideal 'philosopher king' was unattainable, especially in the context of hereditary monarchy, and so the king must rule guided – even governed – by the advice of a philosopher

---

7.   This is in contrast to the move towards the contextualism associated with the methodology of the 'Cambridge School'; *see* Skinner 2000.

8.   The choice of England is based upon my own research; any European country would also have a fascinating history with its own nuances to explore. Because of the interrelated nature of what has been termed the humanist 'republic of letters' at the time, I also consider the influences of prominent continental theorists, such as Erasmus and Castiglione, as their works were read widely in England.

9.   Much of what follows is taken from my unpublished PhD thesis, 'Counsel and command in Anglophone political thought, 1485–1651' (Queen Mary, University of London 2013).

(Chroust 1968: 17; Barker 2006: 16–7). This message is best captured in one of the most widely read and circulated texts of the Middle Ages, the pseudo-Aristotelian *Secretum Secretorum* (Williams 2003: 1), in which the character of Aristotle himself offers advice to the young King Alexander, emphasising the importance of such prudent counsel for a prince who is 'but one man' (*Secretum Secretorum*, sig. F, iv^r). Importantly, the character of Aristotle resists giving his advice and does so only at the persistent solicitations of Alexander. Although he acquiesces to giving his counsel via letters to the young king, he refuses to actually join his court. This role of an absent, even semi-divine or otherworldly, philosopher-counsellor is repeated throughout the medieval literature, for instance in Christine de Pisan's *L'Épistre de Othéa a Hector* (1399–1400), in which the role is filled by the Goddess of Prudence or, in an English context, in John Gower's *Confessio Amantis*, in which the wise Genius guides and rules the young passionate Amans.[10]

In none of these cases are the advisers in question understood to be members of the princely court. The absence of courtly advice is noted by the fifteenth-century *Mum and the Sothsegger* (Anonymous 2000), a dialogue between two courtly figures – Sothsegger (or truth-teller) and Mum (who is resistant to giving truthful advice). When Sothsegger attempts to find guidance on giving courtly counsel to princes, he must admit that the topic is 'new', for no such text exists (Ferguson 1955: 74). Sothsegger himself is visited by an otherworldly advice-giver, who suggests that he write a series of truthful advice-books to his prince, to fill the hole in the literature and fulfil his duty. Importantly, however, Sothsegger's service is not due to the public as a whole, but to his prince as his feudal liege-lord; if Sothsegger should serve his prince with his body and soul, he ought to also serve him with his advice.[11] This same duty is expressed by the *Regement of Princes*, written contemporaneously to *Mum*, by Thomas Hoccleve, a poet and Clerk of the Privy Seal. Like Sothsegger, Hoccleve's character receives advice from a wise old man, who also suggests that he deliver counsel to his prince, but once again he does so only out of a sense of reciprocal duty; Hoccleve hopes that upon giving his advice, his prince's 'free grace' will fall upon him (ln. 1904), solving his significant financial woes.

It is only with the Renaissance revival of Ciceronian humanism that this duty to offer advice becomes understood as more than just an extension of a reciprocal feudal relationship. The philosopher and the courtier become combined in the figure of the political counsellor, a conscious rearticulation of the Roman *vir civilis*, who has a moral duty as a citizen to lead an active life of public service, in this case offering his advice to his monarch.

---

10. 'Genius' is here used in the sense of a 'tutelary god or attendant spirit allotted to every person at his birth, to govern his fortunes and determine his character, and finally to conduct him out of the world'; OED Online (accessed 5 September 2013).

11. 'And as my body and my beste/ oute to be my liegis,| So rithffully be reson/ my rede should also' (ln. 74).

This is laid out in the work of one of the leading humanists of the Northern Renaissance, Desiderius Erasmus, whose advice to the future Emperor Charles V is immortalised in his *Institutio principis Christiani* (*The Education of a Christian Prince*), written in 1509 and published in 1516. Here he repeats the lesson that counsel is designed as a pragmatic addition to the Platonic ideal of the philosopher king in the context of hereditary monarchy; although it is true that a commonwealth can only be happy when 'philosophers are put at the helm, or those to whose lot the rule happens to have fallen embrace philosophy'[12] (Erasmus 1997[1516]: 2), this is unlikely to happen through succession; thus 'When there is no power to select the prince, the man who is to educate the future prince must be selected with comparable care' (*ibid*. 6). Importantly, this is conceived of as a *public* service, for 'a country owes everything to a good prince; but it owes the prince himself to the one whose right counsel [*recta ratio*] has made him what he is' (*ibid*. 6). The prince is just the vessel through which the virtue (or indeed vice) of such a figure flows. In placing the philosopher in the context of the court, Erasmus makes clear that he is rejecting the Greek view of contemplative philosophy in favour of an active Roman conception (*see* Nelson 2004: 13–15, 22). Countering the objections of 'some idiot courtier, who is both more stupid and more misguided than any woman ever was', who might protest that Erasmus is 'making a philosopher for us, not a prince', Erasmus clarifies that 'philosopher' does not mean someone who is clever at dialectics or science but someone who rejects illusory appearance and undauntedly seeks out and follows what is good' (1997[1516]: 15). In other words, a philosopher is not someone divorced from reality, but heavily embedded within it, a wise, active citizen who makes up for the defects of a hereditary system by guiding and shaping a young prince.

A similar figure is conceived of by Baldassare Castiglione in his *Libro del Cortegiano* (1513–28), but instead of changing the definition of 'philosopher' to place him in the context of the court, as Erasmus does, Castiglione reassigns the role to the courtier himself. He, like Erasmus' 'idiot courtier', thinks that a philosopher is ill suited to deliver advice to a prince, for if such a one should endeavour to show a prince:

> plainly and without any circumstance the horrible face of true virtue and teach them good manners and what the life of a good Prince ought to be, I am assured that they would abhor him at first sight, as a most venomous snake, or else they would make him a laughing stock, as a most vile matter. (Castiglione 1994[1561]: 298–9)[13]

---

12. This is a reference to a line in both Plato's *Republic* (5.473d) and *The Seventh Letter* (which may or may not be a work of Plato, 326b), commonly repeated throughout the humanist literature on counsel.

13. 'plainlie and without enie circumstance the horrible face of true vertue and teache them good manners and what the life of a good Prince ought to be, I ame assured that they wolde abhorr him at first sight, as a most venemous serpent, or elles they would make him a laughinge stocke, as a most vile matter'.

Rather than a philosopher becoming more like a courtier, as in Erasmus, for Castiglione the courtier ought to become more like a philosopher, who will 'lead [his Prince] through the rough way of virtue' (*ibid.* 299).[14] As Hoby summarises in his 1561 English translation of the text:

> The final end of a courtier, whereto all his good conditions and honest qualities tend, is to become an Instructor and Teacher of his Prince or Lord, inclining him to virtuous practices; And to be frank and free with him, after he is once in favour in matters touching his honour and estimation, always putting him in mind to follow virtue and flee vice. (*ibid.* 371)[15]

There is reason, however, in both cases to question whether the figure in question is indeed a *counsellor*, and to suggest that he may instead be a *tutor*, for as Erasmus – and probably Castiglione – well knew, there was an important distinction between these two roles in classical thought, set out by the philosopher Seneca in Epistle XCIV ('On the value of advice') in his *Epistolae morales ad Lucilium*.[16] Castiglione, as Hoby makes clear, defines his ideal courtier as an 'Instructor and Teacher', and Erasmus' subject is 'the man who is to educate the future prince' (1997[1516]: 6), not the counsellor. For Erasmus, it is 'fruitless to give advice on the principles of government' – as a counsellor would – 'without previously setting a prince's mind free' (*ibid.* 11) through philosophic instruction in 'established principles and ideas [...] from theory and not from practice' (*ibid.* 20).[17] Erasmus' emphasis is on the tutor who teaches his prince about philosophical principles, not the counsellor who guides his prince on daily political matters.

For the full realisation of this latter figure – the political counsellor as public servant – we return to *Utopia*. As we have already seen, in Book One the characters engage in a debate over the merits of entering a king's court and serving the public through giving advice. This is once again couched in a debate between

---

14. 'leade him throughe the roughe way of vertue'.

15. 'The final end of a courtier, whereto al his good condicions and honest qualities tende, is to beecome An Instructer and Teacher of his Prince or Lorde, inclininge him to vertuous practises: And to be francke and free with him, after he is once in fauour in matters touching his honour and estimation, alwayes puttinge him in minde to folow vertue and to flee vice'.

16. Here Seneca distinguishes between 'that department of philosophy which supplies precepts appropriate to the individual case' (94.1) and the 'dogmas [decreta] of philosophy and the definition of the Supreme Good', which are universally applicable. The former, for Seneca, are the domain of action and advice, the latter contemplation and instruction: 'Training teaches contemplation, and admonition teaches conduct [contemplationem instituo tradit, actionem admonitio]' (94.45). Because virtue can only be complete through its performance ('right conduct both practises and reveals virtue'), and counsel aids in virtuous action, then counsel must be necessary to virtue ('if right conduct is necessary to virtue, and if, moreover, admonition makes clear right conduct, then admonition also is an indispensable thing'). Finally, this advice is even necessary when instruction has failed, for all by nature carry the 'seed of everything that is honourable', but this is only 'stirred to growth by advice, as a spark that is fanned by a gentle breeze develops its natural fire' (94.29). One does not need instruction to get value from precepts and advice.

17. Note that this is precisely the opposite view taken by Seneca, who makes this distinction, but still thinks advice is important even when there is no previous instruction.

Greek contemplative philosophy and a Ciceronian emphasis on the active life of politics (*see* Skinner 1987). Following Giles' suggestions regarding Hythloday's aptitude for advice-giving, the character of More also takes up this view, telling Hythloday that aside from any benefit it may or may not have to his own interests, his 'advice to a prince' would 'be of the greatest advantage to the public welfare' (More 2002 [1516]: 27). Hythloday, however, has not read his Seneca, and misunderstands, retorting that 'If I proposed wise laws [*decreta*] to some king, and tried to root out of his soul the seeds of evil and corruption, don't you suppose I would be either kicked out forthwith, or made into a laughing stock?' (*ibid.* 28). More tries to correct his mistake, making the distinction between Hythloday's 'school philosophy', which has no place 'in the councils of kings' for it 'supposes every topic suitable for every occasion' – in other words it is the sort of universal dogma associated with instruction – and 'another philosophy, better suited for the role of the citizen', which is more adaptive (*ibid.* 34–5). By offering his advice in *this* way, Hythloday could fulfil his role as active citizen and benefit the commonwealth as a whole, even if it did not bring benefit to him as an individual.

Thomas Elyot and *parrhesia*

It has often been contended that More's exploration of the costs and benefits of public service in *Utopia* derived from his own struggle to decide between the contemplative and active life, a question arguably at the forefront of his mind in 1515 (*see* Suzuki 1988). As history teaches us, More did indeed decide to pursue an active political life, advising Henry VIII and rising to one of the highest positions in his government, before resigning in protest to the English Reformation and dying on the block for his refusal to acknowledge the king's religious superiority. It would seem from *Utopia* that More knew well the dangers of the life he chose to pursue before he embarked upon it, but did so regardless, as was his civil duty to do so.

More's younger contemporary, Thomas Elyot, also saw such a duty in giving truthful counsel, and wrote at length about it, as we shall see. Elyot entered public service a short while after More, in 1523, as clerk of the king's council, and was knighted as reward for his work in 1530.[18] The next year he composed his first text on the figure of the counsellor, *The Book Named the Governor*, which, like previous works on the subject, emphasised the role of a wise philosopher-courtier who guided the prince to virtuous action through his advice. Like More, Elyot saw such advice as forming a middle way between philosophical contemplation and political action – it is 'the last part of moral Sapience, and the beginning of sapience politic' (1962[1531]: 241). Importantly, all the lessons of the *Governor* are towards one purpose only, which is public service. As Elyot explains in his closing paragraphs: 'these things that I have rehearsed concerning consultation ought to be of all men in authority substantially pondered, and most vigilantly observed, if they intend to be to their public weal profitable, for the which purpose only they be called to governors' (*ibid.* 241).

---

18. All biographical details concerning Elyot from Lehmberg 2008.

In the same year that the *Governor* was published, Elyot was appointed to the prestigious position of ambassador to the imperial court. This posting, however, did not last long. Henry had hoped Elyot would use his position to advance the cause of his separation from the emperor's aunt, Catherine of Aragon, but Elyot's sympathies lay with Catherine, and he was unwilling to bend to the king's will. He was recalled after only three months and returned in 1532 in disgrace and in debt, with little hope of returning to royal favour. It has been suggested that upon his return, which also followed closely on the heels of More's resignation from the chancery, Elyot may even have counselled Henry himself against his decision to break with Rome and marry Anne Boleyn, endangering not only his career but even his life (Walzer 2012a: 26–7). By the opening of 1533, Elyot's cause was truly lost – Henry had married Anne and broken with the Pope – as was his political career. It is thus no surprise that this year saw a productive contemplation from Elyot on the prospect of offering truthful political counsel. He published no less than three works on the subject in quick succession: *Pasquil the Plain, Of the Knowledge Which Makes a Wise Man* and *The Doctrinal of Princes*.

In order to understand how such works, especially the first two,[19] explore the project of introducing a space for republicanism in a monarchical – even tyrannical – context, we must revisit the tenets of republican freedom.[20] Renaissance republicans, drawing on their Roman predecessors, considered it to be essential for liberty that government be conducted by the will of the community as a whole, hence the emphasis on active citizenship. To be dependent on the arbitrary will of another was synonymous with slavery, whether or not this will is ever exercised over you, for even if only unconsciously, such subjection limits and alters your speech and action (Skinner 1998, 84), as Elyot himself wrote in his *Banket [Banquet]of Sapience* (1564[1539]), quoting from Terence, playwright of the Roman Republic: 'They be out of liberty, that do not labour in their own business, they sleep at another man's slumber, and set their feet where another man steps' (1564[1539]: 34ʳ).[21] This leads to a concern for those who are the 'truest' citizens in the state, 'that is, on those who devote themselves to public service by acting as advisers and counsellors to the rulers and governments of modern Europe', as it is these figures who are 'speaking and acting as conscience dictates in the name of the common good' (Skinner 1998: 87). These figures thus become the most important bulwark against a state's complete loss of liberty, and thus its enslavement.

But there is a slight paradox here, for although the counsellors to kings are the republican champions of a commonwealth's liberty, they themselves exist in 'slavish conditions', as they are consistently dependent upon the arbitrary will of the ruler that they serve, in ways that – most importantly – serve to limit their

---

19. The final text of 1533, which I will not be treating in what follows, is a translation of Isocrates' Ad Nicoclem, a piece of advisory literature that emphasises many of the same themes of the danger of virtuous counsel present in the other two texts; *see* Walzer 2012a: 36–7.

20. Which are summarised in Skinner 1998, to which I am indebted in what follows.

21. 'They be out of libertie, that do not labour in their owne businesse, they slepe at an other mannes winke, and set their feete where an other man steppeth.'

ability to speak truths that will benefit the commonwealth (Skinner 1998: 89). In other words, at first glance, Hythloday is quite correct to suggest – at least according to a neo-Roman perspective – that to enter the court of a king is to enter a relationship of *servitude*, not *service*. Thus the question becomes, how does one turn the position of king's slave into public servant?

This is precisely the issue that Elyot sought to address in 1533, and he did so in the same way as his republican predecessors, by turning to the concept of *parrhesia*. Although embraced by Roman and neo-Roman writers, *parrhesia* was a Greek concept, central to the good functioning of a democracy (Colclough 1999: 183–4). In general, it can be seen to have four essential elements (adapted from Foucault 2001):

- *(primarily)* A truthful speech act;
- *(which contains)* A critique of either speaker or audience (usually the latter);
- *(given in the context of)* A power differential – speaker must be less powerful than the audience;
- *(resulting in)* A sense of risk or danger in speaking this truth.

Thus *parrhesia* requires precisely the context in which a courtly counsellor finds himself – which is why, even in Greek philosophy, it often appears in this context (*see* Foucault 2001: 22, 86–106) – and it provides a way out of the quandary that More, Elyot and their contemporaries found themselves – albeit a dangerous one. Although *parrhesia* requires a situation of unfreedom – the *parrhesiastes* must be dependent upon the arbitrary will of his listener – it is also the key to escaping it. By no longer allowing this dependence to limit a willingness to speak the truth that will benefit the commonwealth – offering counsel to the monarch that he/she does not wish to hear – the *parrhesiastes* becomes free, opening the potential of the liberation of the commonwealth as he/she does so. *Parrhesia* presupposes enslavement but through its very action constitutes freedom (*see* Foucault 2001: 19; Colclough 2005: 252).

For Elyot, such *parrhesia* was essential to the project of public service he had outlined in his *Governor*. As he writes in this text: 'O what damage have ensued to princes and their realms where liberty of speech hath been restrained?' (1962[1531]: 108).[22] In 1533, he saw before him precisely such a situation of limited liberty of speech. More had resigned his post, unable to offer his truthful counsel to Henry VIII, and Elyot had been removed from his for similar reasons. His first attempt to grapple with *parrhesia* in such a context comes with his *Pasquil the Plain*, a dialogue between three characters epitomising three courses of action in giving counsel to a prince: Pasquil, the frank speaker, Gnatho, who argues that flattery is the best way to counsel a king, and Harpocrates, who favours silent acquiescence. From the outset, Pasquil is presented as the quintessential *parrhesiastes* (Walzer 2012b); Gnatho notes that he has an 'old custom in railing',[23] despite the 'damage and hindrance' (Elyot 1533a: 4[r–v]) he has sustained because of it. He advises Pasquil

---

22. The original reads 'domage', which is more akin to 'loss' than damage.
23. 'olde custome in raylying'.

to leave aside his 'indiscrete liberty in speech'[24] for it is unprofitable (*ibid.* 4^v), as it does not lead to change in what he criticises, but only his own detriment and loss of place. For Pasquil occupies the same extra-institutional position as Elyot in 1533; whereas the flattering Gnatho and silent Harpocrates have their master's ear, Pasquil has been exiled from the council chamber for his frank speech.

But does that mean that he should not speak as he does? It has been suggested that Elyot is not wholly behind his title character's *parrhesiastic* speech (Walzer 2012b), and as it is a dialogue, some middle way between the characters might be expected. However, to say that Elyot viewed Pasquil's method of counsel on a par with that of his interlocutors misses some important points, especially regarding republican freedom and *parrhesia*. First, Gnatho and Harpocrates' places within the council chamber are no great advantage beyond their own self-interest, as Pasquil himself makes clear. In the case of Gnatho, because he believes that the 'opportunity and [right] time'[25] to give counsel 'always do depend on the affection and appetite of he that hears them',[26] his 'counsel is but a vain word',[27] allowing his hearer to 'do as he desires' (Elyot 1533a: 6^r).[28] Harpocrates, Pasquil suggests, is like someone who stays silent when he sees a sword raised against his king and thus his 'counsel is not worth three halfpence' (*ibid.* 29^r).[29] Counsellors such as these 'serve for nothing' (*ibid.* 29^r).[30] Neither stands in the way of their master's affections and appetites, and thus they exert no influence through their counsel. Furthermore, as their speech is limited – indeed becomes negligible – by their desire to please the master upon whom they are dependent, they are truly slaves.

Pasquil, on the other hand, proves quite conclusively that he is subject to no one. An 'old Roman' (*ibid.* 2^r), he speaks his mind without concern for reward or punishment. Regardless of what others might judge of what he has said, his 'thought shall be free' (*ibid.* 32^r). Furthermore, unlike the official councillors Gnatho and Harpocrates, 'dumb counsellors'[31] who 'cause many things to be brought to an unlucky conclusion' (*ibid.* 29^v),[32] Pasquil actually does his duty as a counsellor, for through his open 'railing' men might perceive and repent of their vices. Thus it is that, as Elyot makes clear in his address to the reader, 'venomous tongues and oppositional wits [...] do more mischief, than Pasquil's babbling' (*ibid.* 2^v).[33]

---

24. 'vndiscrete libertie in speche'.
25. 'oportunitie & tyme'; for more on the meaning of opportunity and time in Pasquil *see* Walzer 2012a and 2012b; Paul 2014.
26. 'alwaye do depende on the affection and appetite of hym that hereth them'.
27. 'counsaylle were but a vayne worde'.
28. 'do as hym lyste'.
29. 'counsayle is not worth thre halfpens'.
30. 'serue for nothynge'.
31. 'dumme counsailours'.
32. 'cause many thynges to be brought to an vnlucky conclusion'.
33. 'venomous tunges and ouerthwart wittes [...] doeth more myschieffe, than Pasquillus babillinge'.

Finally, although this topic is not fully taken up in *Pasquil*, the frank speaker is also truer to himself, and in this way also more free (*see* Foucault 2001). Flatterers like Gnatho dress themselves up in gaudy and meaningless apparel and opinions, just to please the appetites of those they serve. A *parrhesiastes* like Pasquil, on the other hand, dresses as plainly as he speaks, the truth of his speech and himself presented without need for excessive ornamentation. This issue of knowing and being true to oneself forms the backbone of much of the debate in Elyot's second work of 1533: *Of the Knowledge Which Makes a Wise Man*. Even more than *Pasquil*, *Of the Knowledge* is a clear and conscious reflection on the issue of *parrhesiastic* counsel in the court of kings, as it takes as its inspiration one of the classical examples of such an exchange: Plato and the tyrant Dionysius.

Citing Cicero, Elyot opens the piece by expressing his desire through his work to benefit his country, before turning to the issue at hand – the definition of wisdom. He sets it up as a tension between the three classical ways of life – contemplation, political activity and self-interest – citing the speech of Plato as the answer, for although 'at first sight it seemed to me to be very dissolute and lacking the modesty that belonged to a philosopher, when I better examined it, therein appeared that which is best worthy to be called wisdom' (1533b: vi^v).[34]

The dialogue itself is between Plato, returning from exile after counselling the tyrant, and Aristippus, a wily counsellor in Dionysius' court (Walzer 2012a: 27). In answer to Aristippus' questions regarding his slave's garb, Plato notes that he has lately 'been so often in peril of being lost',[35] for 'commonly men do call him lost, who despairs of his life, or of a free man is made a slave' (Elyot 1533a: 2^r),[36] though they will discuss in due course whether or not this is an accurate use of the term. Plato goes on to tell Aristippus how he was called to Dionysius' court, only to find it declining into tyranny. When Dionysius asked him to discourse on the excellent qualities of a king, Plato took it as a 'good opportunity to warn him of his blindness and folly' (*ibid.* 3^r),[37] for which he was condemned and sold as a slave. In conclusion of his tale, Plato notes to Aristippus that all the trials he endured do not change his commitment to virtue and truth, just as the 'twice selling of me, nor this vile habit of a slave or bondman may change my estate or condition' (*ibid.* 5^{r-v}).[38] In other words, even being made a slave and dressing as one does not change Plato's standing as a free man, a status connected with his commitment to telling the truth despite all peril.

---

34. 'at the first syghte it semed to me to be very dissolute and lackyng the modestie that belo[n]ged to a philosopher: but whan I had better examined it, therein appered that whiche is best worthy to be called wysedome'.

35. 'bene so often in perile to be loste'.

36. 'commenly men do calle hym lost, which despayreth of his lyfe/ or of a free man is made a slaue'.

37. 'good oportunitie to warne hym of his blyndenes and foly'.

38. 'the twise sellynge of me, nor this vile habite of a slaue or bondman may chau[n]ge mine astate or condicion'.

In response to the accusation that Plato spoke 'inadvisedly', knowing that Dionysius would not suffer criticism, Plato responds by arguing that to do otherwise would have gone against his reputation as a wise man, committed to virtue, and they both conclude that Plato was right to tell Dionysius the truth 'according to his profession', for to do otherwise would be 'dissemblance'. Having agreed on this, they turn to the question of what wisdom it was that Dionysius sought in Plato, what knowledge Plato ought to have expressed in order to fulfil Dionysius' expectation of wisdom. After a lengthy dialogue, they come to the conclusion that the 'knowledge which makes a wise man' is not any specific form of knowledge, but rather the performance of that knowledge proper to each individual. In other words, if Plato was wise as Dionysius expected 'it ought to be declared by operation', for 'although wisdom be knowledge, yet by knowledge only none may be called a wise man' (*ibid.* 90^v).[39] Because Plato's philosophical training involved a commitment to truth and virtue, to declare anything other than this before Dionysius would not have been wisdom.

In doing so, further, Plato exposed Dionysius' own lack of a king's wisdom, demonstrating to all that he must be a tyrant. Dionysius' enslavement of Plato was proof of his frustration with Plato's lack of dependence upon his will, for Plato declares that he remains unthreatened by any of the bodily punishments that might be inflicted upon him: 'by taking liberty from me, and making me a slave, he more declared my words to be true, and thereby had the larger example, whereby he might the better have known himself' (*ibid.* 109^v).[40] By the end of the text it is clear that it is Dionysius who is truly unfree, enslaved to his passions and lost to himself and Plato who is wise and free. This reversal of position, importantly, is only possible through Plato's use of *parrhesia*.

Conclusions

So let us return from this brief foray into the past to consider once again the contemporary position of the public servant as the adviser of political leaders. What can this tradition of republican freedom expressed through the sixteenth-century political counsellor teach us about the function and purpose of modern-day European public service advisers? First, it is worth remarking on some of the striking parallels that continue to exist between the historical figure we have been investigating and the contemporary figure with which we began.[41] Scholars of modern-day public service note that there continues to be a 'court culture' in which public servants and advisers must operate (*see* Walter 1986: 7–12; Dror 1987: 189; *see* Rhodes 2005 for the 'court politics' of the Blair years). This is most

---

39. 'all though wisedome be knowlege, yet by knowledge onely none may be called a wise man, but operation'.

40. 'by takyng libertie from me, and makyng me a slaue, he more declared mi wordis to be true, and therby had the larger example, wherby he mought the better haue knowen hym selfe'.

41. This is of course not to say that there is continuity or a lack of change, but rather that these parallels may indicate some hidden assumptions inherited from the past.

important in the relationship of 'advisers and rulers' that pervades that culture (Plowden 1987: 170). Essential to this is the continuing expectation that 'an adviser is failing in his principal duty if he does not offer advice' (Plowden 1987: 172), as well as the power differential that places the adviser at the arbitrary mercy of his minister. This can render 'the work of an adviser [...] either useless' like that of Gnatho and Harpocrates, 'or dangerous' like that of More, Elyot, Pasquil and Plato (Baum 1982: 548). As the seminal study by Peters and Barker (1993) makes clear: 'An adviser who thinks that some absolute truth or faith must be maintained by his minister may well come to grief when it becomes clear that such "truth" has only the value which the government's leaders are willing to accord to it' (55; *see also* Blick 2004: 2). In other words, there is no question that 'as adviser, the public servant is [still] responsible for 'speaking truth to power' (*see* Wildavsky 1987).

Second, and perhaps more importantly, advice continues to be seen as a way of promoting democratic principles in a context that may not be seen as being sufficiently transparent. Receiving advice 'helps governments appear more open and democratic', reducing the appearance that they are ruling *over* the people, rather than ruling *for* them (Peters and Barker 1993: 1). This positive democratic view of the function of advice stands in stark contrast to the reputation that such special advisers themselves have come to acquire. As Tony Wright, Labour MP and chairman of the Commons Select Committee on Public Administration, mused in 2002, special advisers are 'ranked somewhere alongside paedophiles in the lexicon of media opprobrium' (quoted in Blick 2004: 9). This has, unsurprisingly, done little for the 'ideal of public service' among such a group (*see* O'Toole 2005). As Bromell notes, there is a continuing question of '[what] "success" looks like in the policy advice role' (2010: 58).

The revival of an understanding of the historical development of the public service adviser might go some way towards remedying some of these pervasive and pernicious issues. If this role is understood within a tradition of the *parrhesiastes* and conceptions of republican values, an 'ideal' and concept of 'success' might be recaptured. Through the re-adoption of such principles, public service advisers can start to see themselves, and reciprocally to gain a reputation, as servants to the public as a whole, rather than as slaves to those who appointed them.

References

Anonymous (2000) *Richard the Redeless and Mum the Sothsegger* (ed.) Dean, J. M., Kalamazoo, MI: Medieval Institute Publications.

Baker House, S. (2008) 'More, Sir Thomas (1478–1535)', *Oxford Dictionary of National Biography*, Oxford University Press. Available at http://www.oxforddnb.com/view/article/19191 (accessed 4 September 2013).

Barker, A. (2006) 'On the receiving end: the hidden protagonist of Plato's Laches', in Spencer, D. and Theodorakopoulos, E. (eds) *Advice and its Rhetoric in Greek and Rome*, Bari: Levant Editore, pp. 31–46.

Baum, H. S. (1982) 'The advisor as invited intruder', *Public Administration Review*, 42(6): 546–52.

Blick, A. (2004) *People Who Live in the Dark: The history of the special adviser in British politics*, London: Politico's.

Bromell, D. (2010) 'The public servant as analyst, adviser, and advocate', in Boston, J., Branstock, A. and Eng, D. (eds) *Public Policy: Why Ethics Matters*, Canberra: Australian National University Press, pp. 55–78.

Castiglione, B. (1994[1561]) *The Book of the Courtier*, translated by Hoby, T., Cox, V. (ed.) London: Everyman.

Chabal, P. (1993) 'Advice-giving, time constraints and ministerial efficiency', in Peters, B. G. and Barker, A. (eds) *Advising West European Governments*, Edinburgh: Edinburgh University Press, pp. 51–8.

Chroust, A. -H. (1968) 'Aristotle's criticism of Plato's "philosopher king"', *Rheiniches Museum für Philologie* 111(1): 16–22.

Colclough, D. (1999) '"Parrhesia": the rhetoric of free speech in early modern England', *Rhetorica: A Journal of the History of Rhetoric*, 17(2): 177–212.

— (2005) *Freedom of Speech in Early Stuart England*, Cambridge: Cambridge University Press.

Connaughton, B. (2010) '"Glorified gofers, policy experts or good generalists": a classification of the roles of the Irish ministerial adviser', *Irish Political Studies*, 25(3): 347–69.

Dror, Y. (1987) 'Conclusions', in Plowden, W. (ed.) *Advising the Rulers*, Oxford: Blackwell, pp. 185–206.

Eichbaum, C. and Shaw, R. (2008) 'Revisiting politicization: political advisers and public servants in Westminster systems', *Governance*, 21(3): 337–63.

Elyot, T. (1533a) *Pasquil the Playne*, London.

— (1533b) *Of the Knowledeg* [sic] *Whiche Maketh a Wise Man*, London.

— (1564[1539]) *The Banket [Banquet] of Sapience*, London.

— (1962[1531]) *The Book Named the Governor*, in Lehmberg, S. E. (ed.) New York: E. P. Dutton.

Erasmus, D. (1997[1516]) *The Education of a Christian Prince*, Jardine, L. (ed.) Cambridge: Cambridge University Press.

Fawcett, P. and Gay, O. (2010) 'United Kingdom', in Eichbaum, C. and Shaw, R. (eds) *Partisan Appointees and Public Servants: An international analysis of the role of the political adviser*, Cheltenham: Edward Elgar, pp. 24–63.

Ferguson, A. B. (1955) 'The problem of counsel in Mum and the Sothsegger', *Studies in the Renaissance*, 2: 67–83.

Ferster, J. (1996) *Fictions of Advice: The literature and politics of counsel in late medieval England*, Philadelphia: University of Pennsylvania Press.

Fleischer, J. (2012) 'Policy advice and institutional politics: a comparative analysis of German and Britain', unpublished PhD thesis, University of Potsdam.

Foucault, M. (2001) *Fearless Speech*, Pearson, J. (ed.) Los Angeles: Semiotext(e).

Gains, F. and Stoker, G. (2011) 'Special advisers and the transmission of ideas from the policy primeval soup', *Policy Press*, 39(4): 485–98.

Gay, O. (2010) 'Special advisers' (SN/PC/03813), London: House of Commons Library. Retrieved from: http://www.parliament.uk/documents/commons/lib/research/briefings/snpc-03813.pdf

Goldhamer, H. (1978) *The Adviser*, New York: Elsevier.

Guy, J. (1995) 'The rhetoric of counsel in early modern England', in Hoak, D. (ed.) *Tudor Political Culture*, Cambridge: Cambridge University Press, pp. 292–310.

—— (1997) 'Introduction', in *The Tudor Monarchy*, London: Arnold, pp. 1–12.

Hoccleve, T. (1999) *The Regiment of Princes*, Blyth, C. M. (ed.) Kalamazoo, MI: Medieval Institute Publications.

James, S. (2007) 'Political advisors and civil servants in European countries', *Sigma*, 38: 1–70.

Laugharne, P. J. (1994) *Parliament and Specialist Advice*, Liverpool: Manutius Press.

Lehmberg, S. (2008) 'Elyot, Sir Thomas (c. 1490–1546)', *Oxford Dictionary of National Biography*, Oxford: Oxford University Press, Available at http://www.oxforddnb.com/view/article/8782 (accessed 4 September 2013).

More, T. (2002 [1516]) *Utopia*, Logan, G. M. and Adams, R. M. (eds), Cambridge: Cambridge University Press.

Nelson, E. (2004) *The Greek Tradition in Republican Thought*, Cambridge: Cambridge University Press.

OED Online, *Oxford English Dictionary*, Oxford University Press, available at http://www.oed.com/view/Entry/77607?redirectedFrom=genius (accessed 5 September 2013).

O'Toole, B. J. (2005) *The Ideal of Public Service: Reflections of the high civil service in britain*, London: Routledge.

Paul, J. (2014) 'The use of *Kairos* in Renaissance political philosophy', *Renaissance Quarterly*, 67(1): 43–78.

Peters, B. G. and Barker, A. (eds) (1993) 'Introduction', in *Advising West European Governments*, Edinburgh: Edinburgh University Press, pp. 1–14.

Plato (1966) *The Republic* in *Plato in Twelve Volumes*, vol. 7, trans Bury, R. G., Cambridge, MA: Harvard University Press

—— (1969) *The Seventh Letter* in *Plato in Twelve Volumes*, vols 5 and 6, trans Shorey, P., Cambridge, MA: Harvard University Press.

Plowden, W. (1987) 'Relationships between advisers and departmental civil servants', in Plowden, W. (ed.) *Advising the Rulers*, Oxford: Blackwell, pp. 171–4.

Pocock, J. G. A. (1993) 'A discourse of sovereignty: observations on the work in progress', in Phillipson, N. and Skinner, Q. (eds) *Political Discourse in Early Modern Britain*, Cambridge: Cambridge University Press, pp. 377–428.

pseudo-Aristotle (1511) *Gouernaunce of Kynges and Prynces*, trans Lydgate, J., London.

Rhodes, R. A. W. (2005) 'The court politics of the Blair presidency', *Senate Occasional Lecture*, Parliament House.

Seneca (1971) *Ad Lucilium Epistulae Morales: Epistles 93–124*, trans Gunmere, R. M., Cambridge, MA: Harvard University Press.

Skinner, Q. (1987) 'Sir Thomas More's *Utopia* and the language of Renaissance humanism', in *The Languages of Political Theory in Early-Modern Europe*, Pagden, A. (ed.) Cambridge: Cambridge University Press, pp. 123–57.

— (1998) *Liberty Before Liberalism*, Cambridge: Cambridge University Press.

— (2000) *Visions of Politics: Volume I: Regarding Method*, Cambridge: Cambridge University Press.

Suzuki, Y. (1988) 'Thomas More on politics as a profession', *Moreana*, 25(97): 29–40.

Topf, R. (1993) 'Advice to governments – some theoretical and practical issues', in Peters, B. G. and Barker, A. (eds) *Advising West European Governments*, Edinburgh: Edinburgh University Press, pp. 182–90.

Walter, J. (1986) *The Ministers' Minders*, Melbourne: Oxford University Press.

Walzer, A. (2012a) 'The rhetoric of counsel and Thomas Elyot's *Of the Knowledge Which Maketh a Wise Man*', *Philosophy and Rhetoric*, 45(1): 24–45.

— (2012b) 'The rhetoric of counsel in Thomas Elyot's *Pasquil the Playne*', *Rhetorica: A Journal of the History of Rhetoric*, 30(1): 1–21.

Weller, P. (1987) 'Types of advice', in Plowden, W. (ed.) *Advising the Rulers*, Oxford: Blackwell: 149–57.

Wildavsky, A. (1987) *Speaking the Truth to Power: The art and craft of policy analysis*, New Brunswick, NJ: Transaction.

Williams, S. J. (2003) *The Secret of Secrets: The scholarly career of a pseudo-Aristotelian text in the Latin Middle Ages*, Ann Arbor, MI: University of Michigan Press.

Chapter Four

A History of the Oath of Office in The Netherlands

Mark R. Rutgers

Introduction

The oath of office has been, and possibly still is, a feature that is specific to public office. In most countries, the oath remains a *rite de passage* for those entering public office.[1] A swearing-in constitutes the acceptance of public responsibility and the reception of public authority. According to John Rohr, in his classic *Ethics for Bureaucrats* (1989), the oath is central to the professional status of public servants.

This chapter's focus will be on the history and development of the oath of office in The Netherlands.[2] Back in the sixteenth century, the Dutch could well have been the earliest to allow a solemn promise to replace the oath. In 2006, the Dutch also became the most recent to make the oath of office a legal obligation.

This chapter starts with an overview of the origins of the oath, followed by a definition and a description of the oath of office as object of study. The subsequent sections outline the historical development of the oath of office in The Netherlands in six stages. The chapter closes with observations on the contemporary status of the oath of office.

Old origins

The origins of oaths are rooted in prehistory.[3] The oldest evidence comprises treaties, histories and myths recounting sworn, broken and avenged oaths. To swear an oath is regarded as the ultimate guarantee that one's statement or promise is to

---

1. Denmark is the main exception.
2. References to archive material in this chapter are given in the notes. For the sake of brevity, references to seventeenth- and eighteenth-century decisions by the States General of the United Provinces in the Great Ordinances Books (Groot Plakkaat Boek) will be referred to as 'GP', volumes I through IX. References to the proceedings of the Dutch Lower House of the States General (Tweede Kamer) will be referred to as 'TK' and the proceeding of the States General as HSG. The Dutch National Archive (Nationaal Archief) will be abbreviated as 'NA'. Unless relevant, titles of other archive sources will not be translated.
3. Main sources consulted were Bauer (1884); Ernste (1895); Friesenhahn (1928/1979); Hirzel (1902); Kolmer (1989); Plescia (1970); Prodi (1993); Tyler (1834); Van den Doel (1989); Van Leeuwen (1881).

be trusted, that it is sincere and true. In simple terms, an oath is a calling upon the gods as a witness, a self-invoked liability for breaking one's word. Oaths were thus linked to religion and the occult (*see* MacLachlan 2008: 91). An oath is no more or less than a special act of promising. And the oath taker is meant to prepare to be doomed (whatever this means), if a statement proves untrue or a promise is broken.

Oaths, in particular those pledging loyalty to the king, were highly important for keeping social and political order intact (Bachvarova 2008: 183; Gregoire 1991: 351). Historically, their power was so immense that an oath was seen as equivalent to the truth. A sworn statement could not be disputed, for doing so would amount to blasphemy. Most civilisations ascribe extreme importance to the precise wording, accompanying gestures and location of oath taking. Any deviations can invalidate an oath, as exemplified in 2009 when Barack Obama had to redo his presidential oath of office due to an imprecise reading and recitation of the wording at his inauguration ceremony.

The ancient Greeks are considered among the most promise-conscious and widespread users of oaths (Karavites 1992: 2; MacLachlan 2008: 91). Oaths have even been considered the very foundation of democracy (Plescia 1970: v). All kinds of public functions required an oath: 'the oath of investiture, which was always necessary' (Plescia 1970: 14). The Greek word for oath is *horkos*, derived from the Greek word for 'fence'. The suggestion thus is that an oath is a fence against deceit and disorder in an effort to create what Kitts (2005: 64) calls a common reality.

The consequence of the oath was certainly not constant over time. For instance, until the end of the sixth century BCE, divine wrath seemed to suffice as the envisaged repercussion of breaking an oath (Plescia 1970: 87). But eventually the patient wait for godly intervention would be buttressed by immediate earthly punishments. Increasingly, oaths came to be replaced by legal contract in most social and economic interactions (Carawan 2008: 75).

Greek oath tradition influenced the Romans (Connolly 2008: 204). Yet it was the Romans who imbued oaths with legal status, resulting in implications not just for the person of the emperor, but also his function and his legal successors. Over time, the Romans also introduced the obligation to swear by one's own gods, as this seemed the most effective technique to secure commitment from a religious person.

A high regard for the power of an oath is illustrated by the acceptance of oaths as binding even if taken under force. Despite objections by Cicero, for one, this became the dominant view in Western tradition. In the Roman Catholic tradition a forced oath can only be made valid or relieved by a bishop or the Pope. In the fifth century, refusal of a state-ordered oath was declared heresy. In the early Middle Ages, the oath became a Christian sacrament, integrating old Greek and Roman as well as Germanic law customs in Judeo-Christian traditions (Prodi 1993: ix), and most likely also encompassed the adoption of the Germanic gestures.[4]

---

4.   In particular the raising of the hand and/or two fingers (the latter being the Dutch gesture). Christian interpretations of the gestures were sometimes added later on. The ancient Greek and Roman gesture of a raised arm survives as the traditional Olympic oath gesture (be it less raised nowadays, so as to avoid association with the infamous Nazi gesture, which was also copied from the Romans).

During the Middle Ages, oaths were obligatory under many circumstances. They ranged from the pledging of loyalty between a king and his people to promises made among inhabitants of a city concerning public function, as well as in application to the work of millers, brewers, butchers, gatekeepers, apothecaries and even brothel keepers (Kolmer 1989: 118). A refusal to swear implied an inability to carry out one's profession. In socio-economic dealings, the replacement of oaths by contracts grew with the development of the legal system. In the political and public setting, however, oaths remained of great importance. Over time, special oaths of office developed concerning the duties of a member of a public body or collegium (Friesenhahn 1928/1979: 64).

Although their gravity can hardly be underestimated, oaths were just as often not taken seriously. Stories about cheating and perjury abound, not least in Greek mythology. Plato and, later, Cicero would even complain that belief in the gods was withering and that oaths were thus no longer reliable.

The oath of office

Cicero famously called the oath an *affirmatio religiosa*, a religious affirmation. This description captures the more common understanding of an oath. Equally renowned is Thomas Hobbes' definition: '*Swearing, or Oath, is a Forme of Speech, added to a Promise; by which he that promiseth, signifieth, that unlesse he performe, he renouncesth the mercy of his God, or calleth to him for vengeance on himselve*' (Hobbes 1651/1979; 73, emphasis in original). Bentham (1817/2005: 1) has added that an oath is 'a ceremony composed of words and gestures'.

Reducing the oath to a religious act is unsatisfactory from a social scientific perspective, as religion itself is a social phenomenon. Historically, an oath can also refer to anything that is of special relevance to the oath taker (*see* Hirzel 1902: 15). Legally and morally, the non-religious, secular solemn affirmation, or civil oath, has become commonplace (*see* Friesenhahn 1928/1979: ix); 'in terms of a secular ethics we believe that oaths bind in conscience' (Rohr 1986: 189). To conclude, an oath – a swearing – can be religious or civil depending on the warranty provided.

The oath of office is made at the time of investiture in a public function. At such a ceremony, magistrates, generals, public servants, inter alia, swear to act in accordance with the laws and customs, to judge fairly, and so on. In this context, a public official is granted access to the most influential sphere in society, state power. The bestowed public authority can be used for the general interest, but also abused for personal interests. Officeholders are therefore required to provide the highest warranty and commitment they can give as a person. To this purpose, the oath of office creates a double link: first, between oath taker and fellow citizens; second, between an individual's conscience and the common good, i.e. between the most personal and the most public moral spheres (*see* Rutgers 2009: 8).

An oath of office generally consists of three parts: an opening formula ('I swear' or 'I solemnly promise'); followed by the promise(s) sworn by; and last, a closing formula with reference to the nature of the warranty provided ('So help me God' or 'This I promise'). A valid oath involves specific gestures and sometimes attributes a specific time and/or place or style of dress; in other words, certain rituals are an integral part of an oath (*see* Gaudemet 1991: xiii). The ritual and its symbolic aspects are important for the social-psychological effect of an oath (*see* Rutgers and Steen 2010). Ever since the Middle Ages, official oaths have in principle always been recorded (Cialdini 2001: 71; *see* Kolmer 1989: 351). Over time, the oath of office, or oath of investiture, evolved to encompass three different oaths in terms of the promises sworn by. To start with, there is the oath of purification, whereby someone declares that the office was obtained in a proper manner. Next, there is an oath of loyalty – the political oath – to the nation, the constitution and the people. Finally, there is an oath of performance – the professional oath – concerning the correct execution of the office (with prudence, dedication, and so on).

To conclude, we can define a (full) oath of office as *a social-linguistic act providing the highest warranty a person can give according to his or her moral convictions and beliefs for promises concerning fair attainment of office, loyalty towards a political regime, just use of public authority and proper execution of tasks, which is accepted as such by the social community and is accompanied by rituals, including specific gestures.*

The oath in Dutch history

To unravel the history of the oath of office in the Dutch Republic and, later, what would become the Kingdom of The Netherlands, it is useful to distinguish six historical phases. They are not strictly chronological, but rather concern specific aspects of the development.

From the Middle Ages to the Dutch Revolt (793–1581)

The Low Countries share in a broader European legacy. During the age of Charles the Great (c. 742–814), the official closing formula of the oath was: '*Sic me adjuvet Deus*'[5] or 'So help me God'. The oldest evidence of the Dutch version dates from 1551 (Van Es 1911: 109). Although the Roman Catholic Church declared refusal of an oath heresy, in 793 Charlemagne allowed for a non-religious oath 'in verbo tantum et veritate promittere' (Van Es 1911: 41, 108) albeit not for public functionaries.

The oldest surviving oath for administrators in the Low Countries dates from 1413: the oath for the accounting office at Rijsel.[6] It demanded loyalty to the Duke of Burgundy, pledging to guard his interest in his territory and to fulfil duties promptly and loyally as registrar and accountant, as well as to be friendly, loyal and trustworthy towards others. Other surviving late medieval oaths of office also demanded political loyalty and proper execution of office. Absent, though,

---

5. Capitularia of 802.
6. Eed van de Rekenmeesters Rijselse Rekenkamer, Archive Département du Nord, B 31.f. 1r. (Thanks to Mario Damen for calling this oath to my attention.) Rijsel, once the capital of Flanders, is in present-day Lille, France.

were oaths of purification – unsurprising perhaps in an age of highly personal relations. An oath dated 12 April 1477 is the oldest known document to contain an expression that the oath must be delivered 'in the hands of' the oath receiver,[7] as is still customary. It hearkens back to the tradition of a vassal placing his hands in those of his ruler when swearing fealty.

A true Dutch history of the oath starts mid-sixteenth century, being a by-product of independence. The Dutch Revolt was catalysed by various adversities (e.g. high taxes, religious intolerance) that led to the denouncement of Philip II of Spain as monarch. Leading this revolt was William of Orange, Philip II's sworn representative, or stadtholder (*stadhouder*).[8] In keeping with the medieval notion of an oath as mutually binding the sovereign and his people, William argued in his *Apology* (Oranje 1568) that the king had broken the oaths necessary to maintain his privileges to the Low Countries (86; *see* Black 1993: 44). The formal declaration of independence[9] on 26 July 1581 also portrayed Phillip II as a perjurer. The States General took an oath of renunciation;[10] an oath on 29 July 1581 required public functionaries to denounce Philip II and swear loyalty to the States General.[11]

Religious issues (1552–1816)

In 1552, Menno Simons declared that the Bible – specifically, Matthew Chapter Five – rejects oaths. Simons' followers, the Mennonites,[12] along with others, such as the Amish, the Baptists, the Quakers and the Hernhutters, objected to the oath on religious grounds. However, the two most dominant Protestant leaders, Luther and Calvin supported oath taking. The influential Heidelberger Catechism of 1563 explicitly rejected the Baptists' position and to the contrary stipulated that an oath by God's name can be sworn if required by an earthly authority, and false swearing was regarded one of the most serious sins deserving the death penalty (Schaab 1993: 24).

Opposition to the oath was as such not an invention of the Reformation. Prominent early church fathers, in particular Augustine and Aquinas, were opposed to the oath. In the Middle Ages, swearing without a religious formula was also often allowed if the oath taker instead swore 'by the truth of men and women' (*bij mannen- en vrouwenwaarheid* (Van Es 1911: 6)), a custom that survived in the courts into the early nineteenth century.

In modernity, the first mandate to relieve the obligatory oath came from William of Orange in person. Baptists petitioned him to instruct the town of Middelburg to permit them to live and work without having to take a citizen's oath (*de poortereed*). In 1566, William ordered the town council accordingly, but to no

---

7. Damen, M. (2000), pp. 46–9.
8. Original terms in Dutch are given in parentheses in this chapter.
9. 'Het Plakkaat van Verlatinge' (*see* Mout 2006).
10. This is disputed by some historians (*see* de Kort and Rutgers forthcoming).
11. NA no. A. 1.01.01.01, no. 245, no. 28.
12. After Simons' first name, Menno.

avail. In 1577, he had to intervene again, this time with fierce arguments in favour of freedom of conscience (Van Es 1911: 113). In 1578, another request by Baptists indicates that some towns did indeed allow for a solemn promise to be sworn, i.e. an oath without invoking God. There remained strong objection to allowing such a civil, rather than religious oath. However, on 28 March 1588, all Mennonites in the Dutch Republic were permitted freedom of conscience by the States General[13] and to swear just by the truth of men and women. However, this did not apply to people in public office. Still, the main Protestant denomination (*de Gereformeerde synodes*) kept attempting to abolish this unholy swearing until at least 1624. The City of Amsterdam, for example, only regulated the civil oath in 1699. According to Van Es (1911: 64), over time only the province of Holland (and not the six others that then existed) ever fully acknowledged freedom of conscience in all its towns and courts. Public office required a religious oath, the only known exception to this rule applying to the guardians of orphanages in four towns.[14]

The issue of accepting religions other than Christianity for an oath remained equally disputed. Here Amsterdam proved a forerunner; in 1616, the city required people of Jewish origin to take the oath according to their own customs.

Naissance of the oath of office (1656–1795)

In the period 1581–1795, at least 150 references to oaths can be found in formal resolutions by the States General.[15] The majority concerns oaths for military and marines, primarily demanding political loyalty. Other oaths concern a wide range of public functionaries, such as members of high councils, the grand pensionary (*Raadpensionaris*) and the board of the Dutch East India Company. Besides loyalty, they often specify instructions for a particular function. A substantial number of oaths were for professions, such as millers, beer brewers and wine merchants. Stopping tax evasion was their core concern. For example, a resolution of 2 May 1642[16] demanded wine merchants to take the oath or else have their businesses closed down. Often, there was opposition to requisite oaths, sometimes even resulting in rioting – an indication that the oath was not regarded merely as a formality. Finally, there were oaths specifically for public servants. This was a longstanding custom in the cities, though would eventually become a matter of state. The States General had very few public servants, yet they swore to their function-specific instructions that demanded, for instance, proper bookkeeping or adequate office hours, as well as ardent work, duty and loyalty. In some cases, a fine was imposed in instances of oath violation.

The resolution of 24 February 1656[17] may be seen as the earliest oath of office for public servants in the republic. It demanded that all those accepting a

---

13. Ordonnantie 28 March 1588, GP V, p. 96.

14. Enkhuizen, Den Briel, Wormer and Vlaardingen.

15. In the collected ordinances published over two centuries in GP. *See also* note 2.

16. GP I, pp. 2256–7.

17. GP III, p. 102.

function – be it political, military, religious or civil – take an oath of purification. The formula read:

> That I swear, that I, in order to acquire [the function] did not promise or give, nor will promise or give, any gift, good or donation to any person, be it outside or within the administration, directly or indirectly in any way.

The promise had to be sworn with the oath taker placing his hands in the hands of the oath receiver, i.e. the chair of the relevant collegium. Clearly, the oath was directed at fighting against corruption and nepotism. A resolution in 1675[18] stated specifically that buying an office is ruinous for the state and therefore demanded an oath of purification for political functions, such as burgomasters and town councillors. That oath was explicitly required to be taken in public. Laxity soon crept in, though. A resolution in 1690 thus reminded people that earlier ordinances should be obeyed.[19] Again, a resolution on 10 December 1715[20] specifically targeted corruption and introduced the requirement that all oaths be recorded. Another resolution on the same day[21] made a further point by sharply formulating the case against corruption: no devout regents (*regenten*) or public servants (*beampten*) should accept gifts and let themselves be corrupted. No distinctions should be made between higher and lower functions,[22] and cases of perjury and corruption could be brought to court up to ten years after the fact. The forbidden acts listed in the earlier resolution grew, as did the catalogue of unacceptable gifts. Finally, the resolution also elaborated the list of functionaries to which it applied.

Just ten days later,[23] another resolution addressed the need to eradicate tendencies towards private gain. It introduced the huge reward of 1,000 guilders, amnesty in case of complicity to find offenders and full anonymity of witnesses who came forward. Also, fraudulent functionaries would immediately be fired, and half of the fine would be given to witnesses and the officer who made the charges.

Again, on 23 January 1748,[24] an elaborate resolution was accepted by the States General. It outlined the oaths to be taken in the towns and provided four different formulas for different functions. Burgomasters had to take an oath in the hands of the sheriff (*schout*), councillors in the hands of burgomasters, and so on. All oath takers had to be registered and reported to the States General within eight days.

---

18. GP III, pp. 102–3.

19. GP IV, pp. 379.

20. GP V, pp. 684–6.

21. GP V, pp. 684–6.

22. It was considered inappropriate to treat social non-equals as equals (*see* Kerkhoff 2013).

23. GP V, p. 689.

24. GP VII, pp. 108–11.

Disputes and a new formula (1795–1828)

In 1795, the Dutch Republic was overthrown and, with the aid of the French, the Batavian Republic was established. The old regime was replaced by a people's republic, later a kingdom (with Napoleon's brother Lodewijk Napoleon Bonaparte as monarch) and, finally, it became a French province. Following Waterloo, in 1814, the Kingdom of The Netherlands was established. Besides bringing fundamental changes to the future The Netherlands' state organisation, the events also culminated in major oath turmoil.

The very declaration proclaiming the Batavian Republic on 30 January 1795 referred to 'forced and illegal oaths' of the old regime and relieved everyone from them.[25] The next day, the formula of the oath was changed into the simple: 'This I swear' ('Dat zweer ik'). The idea was to have only a civil oath, like the French 'Je le jure'. However, it was quickly deemed unsatisfactory, for what was one swearing by? The Court of Holland (*Hof van Holland*) suggested an oath for all representatives of the people and all functionaries (Van den Doel 1989: 220). The problem, however, was that the oath was very much disputed by authors of the Enlightenment. Famously, the era's champion, Kant, argued that a promise is a promise, regardless of any swearing. This was not a religious consideration, but followed from the attempt to ground morality in reason (*see* Feith 1892: 3; De Waal Malefijt 1907: 69; Kolmer 1989: 57).

And yet, in February 1795, a warning was issued that the oath, as specified in the old constitution, was not annulled, but rather that the authority had changed.[26] On 10 February 1795, public servants were urged to swear by a new oath.[27] On 9 March 1795, a new oath formula was sent to all local administrators, demanding they swear loyalty to the new Batavian Republic, recognise that sovereignty resides with the people, be loyal to its representatives and act as good and loyal administrators would. However, objections were raised, for should all citizens not swear such loyalty?

A new decision was made on 11 December 1795. Reinstated was the old closing formula: the right hand with two fingers raised and utterance of the line 'So help me God almighty'. Equally, the option to take a civil oath was reinstated for religious objectors.

Nevertheless, continued upheaval compelled the National Assembly to appoint a committee to advise on the oath in March 1796. In its ensuing report, the committee pointed to the many objections to the oath and the respect once granted to conscientious objectors. The report thus suggested as a formula: 'I regard myself subjected to the full force of punishment, if ever I am so honourless to perjure my legally accepted bond, or, whenever I have been found so honourless as to have declared this against the truth' (Hahn 1796). According to the new decision, a religious formula should never be ordered and a civil formula should be valid in all circumstances.

---

25. Strictly speaking, only the old regime could do this.
26. Nieuwe Nederlandse Jaarboeken p. 195, CLI, deel I, 5 Feburary 1795.
27. Nieuwe Nederlandse Jaarboeken p. 224, CLXIX, deel I, 10 Feburary 1795.

Discussed in the National Assembly, the report ushered in support for the idea that the state should not mingle with theological arguments and that freedom of conscience should take priority. The oath of office would also only be a civil oath (De Waal Malefijt 1910: 20).[28] In the constitution (*Staatsregeling*) of 1798 it was stated that recognition of an 'Almighty Divinity' was essential for social bonds; nevertheless, it stuck to a civil oath (Van Es 1911: 137). After a coup in 1798, the new regime again demanded an oath of loyalty from all public functionaries. In the same year, it was also decided that the oath should not be allowed because it relied on superstition and had nothing to do with true religion. Confusion prevailed, as the following year an official committee called attention to the continued practice of oath taking and, moreover, the distinction made between oaths by Baptists and oaths by others. The new constitution of 1801 included a simple swearing: 'I promise loyalty to the constitution and subjection to the law' (Van Es 1911: 161). But in the next version of 1805, the religious oath returned. This was in line with Napoleon's restoration of the religious oath in France (De Waal Malefijt 1907: 70). Of notable interest is that in 1808 the Jewish population in The Netherlands found official recognition for their own specific oath ritual.

Finally, at the end of all this turbulence – when the Batavian Republic was annexed as a French province – two formulas came to be used: the old 'So help me God almighty' and 'This I promise'. When Napoleon was defeated, the present-day Kingdom of The Netherlands was established. The son of the last republic's stadtholder, William V, was installed as sovereign King William I. The constitution of the Kingdom of The Netherlands of 1814 states in article 62 that all members of the States General, i.e. the parliament, would have to take the religious oath in accordance with the customs of their respective religious denominations. This would have a big impact later on.

When the French formally left The Netherlands in 1816, King William I publicly declared that everyone was relieved of the oath of loyalty and obedience to the previous regime. Royal Decree number 88 of 14 March 1815 had determined that public servants were officially appointed only once they had performed their oath – evidence that the oath of office was still used. Years later, Royal Degree number 40 of 2 April 1828 gave rise to some turmoil, as it regulated that salary would be paid only after the oath of office was performed. This was inconsistent with existing practices.

A lot of correspondence followed between the monarch, the general accounting office and ministers. The result was a new Royal Decree stating that a new oath formula would be drafted and implemented by the year-end. The Minister of Home Affairs subsequently drafted this proposal,[29] ordering that the oath be taken by all those with tenure and a fixed yearly salary and in general employment of the state or provinces. The highest in charge of a governmental organisation should receive the oath. Furthermore, the oath should be personal, so as to avoid giving an individual any chance to deny having taken the oath. And finally, it contained three

---

28. Most authors discussing these events, however, use a religious definition of the oath, and consequently argue that the oath was (by definition) abolished.

29. NA 2.02.01, inv. no. 3083, no. 103.

parts: a civil oath, a professional oath (*een ambtseed*) and an oath of purification. These oaths should be performed in accordance with the customs prescribed by the oath taker's religious denomination. The result was a Royal Decree on 31 October 1828,[30] which contained three different versions: formula A for secretaries-general and chief administrators of the state departments with all three oath parts; formula B for lower-ranking officials comprising an oath of loyalty to the king, accurate execution of all instructions, incorruptibility and confidentiality; formula C for clerks and writers who were paid by the hour or according to quantity for their copy work and who only swore to obedience and confidentiality. By the end of 1828, it seemed that all public servants had performed the oath of office as required.

The oath query (1846–1916)

Generally speaking, the oath was not a big issue in the early nineteenth century. In the period 1842–3, the oath of office made a brief appearance, as Parliament decided on punishing any public servant executing his job without having taken the oath.[31] Yet, soon after there was an entirely new development: atheism. In 1846, the High Court (*Hoge Raad*) decided that exemption from a religious oath was allowed only on religious grounds. The verdict relied on a reading of the French version of the 1814 constitution,[32] which referred to someone's *culte*, or denomination, as grounds for exemption. But objections failed, and a relaxed acceptance of refusing the religious oath meant few problems for the next seventy years.

A possible reason for this was the new constitution of 1848, a watershed innovation with regard to parliamentary powers and freedom of religion. It would, however, take decades before the consequences would become effective in political and legal practice – among these unappreciated consequences was the untenability of the requisite religious oath for public office.

Politicians and academics started to voice the idea that freedom of religion implied that nobody should be forced to take the religious oath. But, in practice, people refusing this could be fined or even imprisoned. An illuminating case, from 1869, is of a father who was allowed to refuse a religious oath because he was Baptist. However, his son, who also refused although he was not yet a baptised member of the congregation, was sent to prison for three days (Van Es 1911: 195).

Oath refusal recurred regularly in parliament and in the courts. What is more, in new legislation oath and promise (*eed en belofte*) were sometimes allowed and sometimes not.

An incident in 1881 triggered a parliamentary debate that became known as the oath query (*eedskwestie*). It involved a new town council member of no religious denomination who took the religious oath in public, adding 'that he doesn't care' about having to invoke God (Ernste 1895: 3, note 1). The incident resulted in

---

30. NA 2.04.26.02 inv. no. 549, no. 293.

31. 1842/1843 B. TK 26, TK articles 18 and 19.

32. The constitution was also available in French as the kingdom originally encompassed the southern Low Countries, which split off in 1830 to become Belgium.

a request by MP Heydenrijck, a Catholic liberal, to bring up discussion of the oath with the government. In the debate, which took place from 6 to 8 October, Heydenrijck stated that it is abject to force someone to perform a religious oath. A fierce debate followed. Minister of Justice Modderman argued that atheists lack morality. On hearing about a civil oath being allowed, MP Mackay asserted: 'It was as if I felt the state shook on its very foundations. This touches upon one of the most sturdy pillars the State rests upon' (in *Eedsquestie* 1881: 99). Some MPs suggested atheists start their own church where they could refuse the oath. Liberals and socialists, mainly, invoked the constitutional freedom of religion. However, Heydenrijck's proposal for free choice did not get the vote.

Still, in 1881, socialist MP Van Houten took up the issue again, after the mayor of Assen refused to inaugurate an elected socialist town council member because he refused the religious oath. Van Houten published an article on the issue and requested a debate in parliament (Van Houten 1882). The only result of the debate was a vote stating that requiring a forced oath by law should be reduced to a minimum and called upon the government to revise the law accordingly.

A year later nothing had changed, and MP Schaepman, who was also a Catholic priest, revisited the issue. He was appalled that non-believers were still forced to swear by God's holy name. There were atheists and this should be recognised, Schaepman maintained. Nothing happened. Neither did anything come of the highly appraised 1883 treatise on the constitution by J. F. Buys, who stressed that freedom of choice with regard to the oath was in line with the spirit of the constitution (1883: I, Article 83).

New cases arose and in 1884 the High Court again[33] judged that refusal of the religious oath was only allowed for those of a religious denomination. And in parliament, during budget debates, the government was again requested to change the laws.[34] It was actually suggested that the matter could be resolved by grouping atheists with children and the mentally ill, who were exempted from the oath. Others opposed such changes, arguing that atheists could perhaps leave the country (Schuurbeque Boeije 1884: 19). Yet the notion of atheists swearing by God was an issue; so, it was argued, they should be declared unable to perform the oath of office and be thus excluded from all public functions. But change was in the air.

On 14 and 15 October 1885,[35] two seemingly minor changes were introduced: the phrase 'according to one's denomination' was removed from the constitution and freedom of choice was granted to the king, his ministers and MPs. The next year, members of the provincial parliaments and town councils were also included. But in all other circumstances, free choice was rejected by the government.[36] Even then, the obligatory religious oath was still included in many laws, including the municipal law. As a consequence, in 1894 a town council member was still forced either to swear the religious oath, or to give up his seat (Ernste 1895: 1). A subsequent

---

33. Weekblad van het Regt no. 4996, 17 March 1884.
34. HSG II 1883–4, pp. 442–80. *See also* Weekblad van het Regt no. 4973, 10 January 1884.
35. HSG II 1884–5, B. 111, p. 106.
36. HSG II 1888/1889 B. A, Chapter 1, p. 7.

proposal by MP Gerritsen[37] to change municipal and provincial laws was accepted on 28 May 1896. Freedom of choice was now assured for all elected politicians.

Debates surrounding other obligatory oaths continued. In 1901, the oath for the public functionaries of the national health board (*gezondheidsraad*) was abolished, for the first time permitting a particular group of public servants – health inspectors – to perform a civil oath. The next year, the same happened for labour inspectors.[38] In neither case was there fierce debate! When the general oath of office for public servants was discussed in a cabinet meeting in 1908, it came to light that different formulae were used and practices varied between departments. The cabinet concluded that formula B, as established in the Royal Decree of 1828, would suffice and swearing would only be required upon first appointment.[39]

The next year a Royal Decree[40] made the choice of oath contingent on religious conviction (*godsdienstige overtuiging*). As a result, the High Court finally revised its interpretation of the provision to read: 'there is no legal obligation to performing the [religious] oath' (Van Es 1911: 212). This seems to restate that refusal was still only allowed on religious grounds. However, the High Court concluded in a case before it that there remained no legal ground to demand of atheists any oath, for the oath law applied only to people of a religious denomination.[41]

The government was quicker than ever to provide an emergency law: the Law on Performance of the Oath (*Wet vorm van de eed*). It became effective on 25 July 1911.[42] Its Article 1 states that if an oath is required according to a law, it must be performed by raising the two first fingers of the right hand and stating: 'So help me God almighty' (unless someone's religion prescribes differently and demands the oath be done otherwise). Article 2 states that in cases with a witness in a civil or penal court case, the oath provided in Article 1 is replaced by a promise if the person called upon to perform the oath: (1) belongs to a church or congregation that forbids taking the oath or (2) does not belong to a church or congregation and provides reasonable grounds for why he objects to taking the oath.

Article 2's shortcoming was that it did not really regulate the civil oath, but only provided a brief formula. Moreover, the core issue – who was obliged to take a religious oath – remained unresolved, as the High Court pointed out in 1913.[43] In April 1916, a new Oath Law (*Eedswet*) became effective. Article 1 reads: 'In every instance where a law prescribes an oath has to be taken or legal consequences are in place, the person in question can choose instead of the [religious] oath to perform a promise, or in relevant cases, an affirmation [i.e. a civil oath]'. [44]

---

37. Gerritsen was a personal friend of Charles Bradlaugh, who famously succeeded in getting the British Parliamentarian Oaths Act changed in 1888.
38. KB 26 January 1903; Staatsblad 1903, no. 38L.
39. NA 2.04.26.02 inv. no. 549.
40. KB 289 20 August 1909.
41. Weekblad van het Regt no. 8955, 18 February 1910.
42. TK 1910–1 B. 138; Staatsblad 1911 no. 215.
43. Weekblad van het Regt no. 9574.
44. Staatsblad 1916 no. 174.

What remained was the requirement to provide adequate reasons for refusing a religious oath so as to test a person's sincerity and prevent him from cheating his way out of an oath. Regardless, from hereon in, religious and civil oaths were legally equivalent for all citizens.

Oath of office and integrity (1920–2006)

As oaths were required for almost all public functions – be it for the member of the board of architects, the art councillor or the tax collector – it took many years before all laws and regulations were adapted to ensure the equality of an oath and a promise.[45] The oath of office figured specifically in a Royal Decree of 1920.[46] This decree introduced an obligatory oath for all state public servants (*rijksambtenaren*); although, as we have seen, this obligation had already been established over a century earlier. However, Minister of Agriculture and Trade Van IJsselstein was extremely annoyed with the practices he encountered concerning oath of office. This amounted to the government drawing up a new decree, which referred to the Royal Decree of 1828[47] and, as before, indicated that formula B be used. It stated that the oath could be performed orally but also – a novel introduction – in writing. Alongside the decree, a letter dated 6 September 1920[48] provided additional provisos: that the oath be performed only upon a public servant's first appointment, not in instances of promotion, and that an official report be made of the performance of the oath.

In 1929, the first Dutch Civil Service Act (*Ambtenarenwet*) was introduced. It included the order that public servants act properly, though the oath of office was not required. The existing arrangement by Royal Decree was apparently adequate.

There were a few other oath-related issues, such as in the 1920s concerning the acceptability of an oath by socialists, Catholics and, in the 1930s, the national socialists (the fascist party).

After WW2, the oath became an even less prominent issue. It surfaced, for instance, in 1951 when a debate arose on whether the oath was allowed to be performed in the Frisian language.[49] In 1969, the oath of parliamentarians resurfaced as a topic.[50] A plea was made to do away with the difference between religious and civil oaths and to allow just one formula to which everyone would answer 'yes' (as in a civil marriage). The result was a proposal to renew the Oath Law of 1916. The renewed law (*Eedswet* 1971)[51] did away with the requisite

---

45. For instance, functionaries in the accounting office got a free choice (1926–7 TK bijlage 225.5, p. 39). A year later in the regulation for specific courts of justice (Raden van Beroep) (1928–9 TK, appendix 59.7, p. 4).

46. KB 23 August 1920, no. 293; NA 2.02.01 inv. no. 6579, no. 293.

47. The 1828 documents were rediscovered during the course of this project in the 1920s files.

48. NA 2.04.26.02 inv. no. 549.

49. The Frisian language was accepted as an official language in education in 1955 and in administration as late as 1995.

50. 21 January 1969. TK handelingen 1258, 1259, 1274.

51. HSG II 1968–9, 10260; HSG 1970–1, 10 260.

so-called proof of sincerity for a civil oath. Finally, religious and civil oaths were legally equivalent, but the formula and gestures were not harmonised: in fact, the civil oath was left entirely without any specific gestures.[52]

A major overhaul of the constitution in 1983 kept the obligation of the oath intact, but all oath formulas were removed. The argument was that in order to make changes easier, the wording of the oath should be a matter of ordinary laws and regulations.

In 1994, when the oath of office resurfaced in a parliamentary debate on police personnel, curiously, the law distinguished explicitly between an oath of purification and a separate professional oath; this was long since the case only for these public servants.[53] The general formula for state public servants was reaffirmed in 1998,[54] and prescribed in the General Rules and Regulations for Civil Servants (*Algemeen Rijksambtenarenreglement*).[55] The ministries were required to make their own internal regulations for the performance – and most seem to have done so.[56] The oath of office was discussed primarily in the context of increasing awareness of integrity issues. This also was the prime perspective when the oath of office again became a topic of parliamentary discussion in 2003–4 on the renewal of the Civil Servants Act (1929). The government proposed including the oath of office in this formal law, whereas before it was regulated by Royal Decree, i.e. without the full force of parliament. However, the government explicitly took codes of conduct as the main tool; the oath of office figured just as one of several options in a 'set of integrity measurements'.[57] The oath was seen as an instrument in creating awareness among public servants about their use of discretionary power and possible risks to their integrity. Also new was the fact that no oath formula would be prescribed, but that government organisations were expected instead to develop their own, so as to 'adjust as much as possible to the specific culture in a government organisation'.[58]

In parliamentary debate, reservations were voiced regarding the open nature of the proposals. Some argued that the oath lacked adequate force or that signing the obligatory code of conduct would do the job well enough. Others applauded the oath, seeing it as a means 'to call upon the highest possible authority'.[59] In its response,[60] the government stressed again that the oath was 'an instrument' in

---

52. This suggests it is not really an oath, a view that is in line with the dominant limited religious interpretation of an oath.

53. Staatsblad 1994, no. 214; Staatsblad 2006, no.129.

54. Staatscourant 1998, no. 184, p. 9.

55. Recent version: Staatsblad 2003, no. 394.

56. For instance, the regulation on oath and promise, Ministry of Internal Affairs of 13 August 1998 and Ministry of Justice of 10 May 1999.

57. Huberts and Nelen (2004–5), pp. 55–6.

58. Memorie van toelichting van de regering bij de wijziging van de Ambtenarenwet. TK 2003–4, 29 436, no. 3, p.18.

59. TK 2003–4, 29 436, no. 6.

60. TK 2003–4, 29 436, no. 7.

the context of maintaining integrity among the public service, and only the newly employed would have to swear, as all others would already know what is relevant.

The renewed Civil Service Act was approved of and formally published on 22 December 2005.[61] It implied that the new requirement of the oath of office would take effect on 1 March 2006. There is some information available on the effect of this law. In 2008, research showed a rise in performance of the oath of office: 100 per cent in the central government and 80 per cent at the lowest in municipal government (independent agencies were not included in the study).[62]

A final occurrence in parliamentary debate to be mentioned here took place in 2008. The issue concerned police departments allowing their recruits to take the oath according to Muslim tradition.[63] This subject got a lot of publicity in the national press. The answer of the minister was that it was already taken care of as it was simply not allowed.

Finally, a strange twist of history saw the formal introduction of an obligatory banker's oath in January 2013 (*see* De Bruin and Dolfsma 2013). For the first time in centuries, a political oath became obligatory by law for functionaries not working in the public sector. The idea was to infuse people working in banking with awareness of their public role, as well as to create more trust in their sector. It remains to be seen whether the oath will succeed in doing so.

Concluding observations

The history of the Dutch oath of office reveals a sustained, even if at times disjointed, relevance: it has served as a symbolic and moral statement. It developed from feudal oaths, evolving to include instructions for functionaries and, since the mid-seventeenth century, oaths of purification in an effort to curb corruption. The formulas and rituals, still in use today, can be traced back to at least the Middle Ages. One interesting exception is that the gestures linked with the civil oaths, such as swearing by 'the truth of men and women', have disappeared altogether. Generally speaking, the history of the oath shows a lot of continuity. This includes the debates on its meaning, as well as the tendency for its obligations and regulations to be forgotten after a while. It seems plausible that the 2006 oath of office will share in this fate.

The oath of office has always been an obligatory one. An important historical development concerns the kind of oath that was demanded, rather than the obligation per se, although, as we have seen in the period of 1795–1814, this was explicitly discussed as well. The freedom to choose between a religious and a civil oath proved the main struggle over the centuries. It was only truly resolved in 1971, although the oath law still reflects the distinction between a religious oath and a 'solemn promise'. The latter has never gained the full ritualistic aspects of a religious oath; its solemnity remains underdeveloped and everyday parlance

---

61. Staatsblad 2005, p. 695.

62. 21 April 2008, dossier 28844, no. 13, pp. 13–14.

63. TK 2008–9, aanhangsel, p. 2315.

clearly reveals a sense of lower esteem for it as something less binding – probably because it does not involve (the belief in) an avenging god.

An outstanding issue is whether an oath of office is needed as a foundation for the legal system. That is, the oath is symbolic in a very meaningful sense (just as signing contracts is symbolic): it has legal power. Perhaps the most lasting stronghold for the oath of office as more than a tool to guarantee integrity is its relevance in a legal context. Proof of this came in 2009 in The Netherlands, when a number of suspects of violent robbery and rape had to be released after it turned out that one of the judges involved in warranting their arrest had not yet taken the oath of office, implying it was not an official judge who had issued the warrant (luckily, this annihilation of the warrant could be reversed later).

History shows how the oath of office has been a feature specific to public office. It would probably be seen as strange if a private firm required an oath of loyalty – and an oath of purification clearly is not in place either. In practice, some people will be proud to perform an oath of office, others will not care and some will object. At the same time, an oath still has a special ring to it, as evidenced by its frequent inclusion in the narratives of books and movies. The question, though, remains: is there a future for the oath of office? Perhaps, though let it be noted that the declining status of the oath as a means to secure promises began as early as the seventh century BCE. It is therefore all the more surprising that, as stated at the beginning of this chapter, the past years have witnessed calls to introduce, or reintroduce, a public oath of office for functions in the private sector to ensure the public interest. Yet a state-ordered banker's oath could just as well quicken the demise of the oath of office; it may be dismissed as a mere marketing tool for bankers, rather than a moral commitment to the public interest, and this may reflect back on the general status of the oath of office (*see* Rutgers 2013).

Despite much scepticism about their effects – doubt has been cast ever since Plato – oaths still seem to have some magical power in contemporary society. As Bachvarova (2008: 182) states: '[T]he oath derives its power from the social framework in which it is embedded'. Overestimating the meaning of the oath in contemporary society could be just as problematic as underestimating how formidable its meaning may in fact still be.

References

Bachvarova, M. R. (2008) 'Oath and allusion in Alcaeus fr.129', in Sommerstein, A. H. and Fletcher, J. (eds) *Horkos: The oath in Greek society*, Bristol: Phoenix Press, pp. 179–88.

Bauer, B. (1884) *Der Eid: Eine Studie* [The Oath: a study], Heidelberg: Carl Winter's Universitätsbuchhandlung.

Bentham, J. (1817/2005) *'Swear not at all' containing an exposure of the mischievousness as well as antichristianity of the ceremony of an oath*, London: Elibron Classics.

Black, A. (1993) 'Der verborgene Ursprung der Theorie des Gesellschaftsvertrages' [The hidden origins of the theory of social contract], in Prodi, P. (ed.) *Glaube und Eid: Treueformeln, Glaubensbekenntnisse und Sozialdisziplinierung zwischen Mittelalter und Neuzeit*, Munich: Oldenbough, pp. 31–48.

Buys, J. T. (1883) *De Grondwet: Toelichting en kritiek* [The constitution: clarification and critique], vol. 1, Arnhem: Gouda Quint.

Carawan, E. M. (2008) 'Oath and contract', in Sommerstein, A. H. and Fletcher, J. (eds) *Horkos: The Oath in Greek Society*, Bristol: Phoenix Press, pp. 73–80.

Cialdini, R. B. (2001) *Influence, Science and Practice*, 4th edn, Boston, MA: Allyn & Bacon.

Connolly, S. (2008) '"Ομνύω ύτòν τòν Σεβαστόν" ["I swear by Augustus himself"]: the Greek oath in the Roman world', in Sommerstein, A. H. and Fletcher, J. (eds) *Horkos: The oath in Greek society*, Bristol: Phoenix Press.

Damen, M. (2000) *De staat van dienst: De gewestelijke ambtenaren van Holland en Zeeland in de Bourgondische periode (1425–1482)*, Hilversum: Verloren.

De Bruin, B. and Dolfsma, W. (2013) 'Oaths and codes in economics and business – introducing the special issue', *Review of Social Economy*, 71(2): 135–9.

De Kort, P. and Rutgers, M. R. (forthcoming) *Eden en Afzweringen rondom het Plakkaat van Verlaetinge van 1581* [Oaths and oaths of denunciation around the Plakkaat van Verlaetinge of 1581].

De Waal Malefijt, J. J. (1907) *De Eed ter beslissing van het geding* [The oath in deciding in lawsuit], unpublished doctoral dissertation VU Amsterdam, Utrecht: Wentzel.

—— (1910) *De Eed* [The Oath], Utrecht: Ruys.

Eedsquaestie in de Tweede Kamer: Interpellatie van den Heer Heydenrijck, De [The oath query in the Second Chamber (Parliament): Interpellation of mister Heydenrijck] (1881), The Hague: Susan.

Ernste, G. W. (1895) *Eed of Verklaring* [Oath or declaration], Amsterdam: H. Eisendrath.

Feith, R. (1892) *De Decisoire Eed* [The decisory oath], Leiden: Van Doesburgh.

Friesenhahn, E. (1928/1979) *Der politische Eid* [The political oath], Darmstadt: Wissenschaftliche Buchgesellschaft.

Gaudemet, J. (1991) 'Ouverture' [Opening], in Verdier, R. (ed.) *Le Serment. I. Signes et fonctions*, Paris: Éditions du Centre National de la Recherche Scientifique, pp. xiii–xiv.

Gregoire, J. -P. (1991) 'Le serment en Mésopotamie au IIIe Millaire avant notre Ère' ['The oath in Mesopotania in the 3rd millennium before our time'], in Verdier, R. (ed.) *Le Serment. I. Signes et fonctions*, Paris: Éditions du Centre National de la Recherche Scientifique, pp. 345–65.

Hahn, J. G. H. (1796) Rapport door Hahn uitgebragt, J. G. H. van wege Commissarissen op den 11 Maart 1796 benoemd; houdende derzelver consisteratien en advys op het stuk van den Eed (1796) [Report by Hahn, J. G. H. of the Committe on the Oath] in *Dagverhaal der handelingen van de Nationale Vergadering representeernde het Volk van Nederland (1796–1798)*, The Hague: Van Schelle en comp, pp. 612–16.

Hirzel, R. (1902) *Der Eid: Ein Beitrag zu seiner Geschichte* [The Oath: a contribution to its history], Leipzig: Hirzel.

Hobbes, T. (1651/1979) *Leviathan*, London: Dent.

Huberts, L. W. J. C. and Nelen, J. M. (2004–5) *Corruptie in het Nederlands Openbaar Bestuur*, TK 2004–5, dossier 17050, pp. 55–6.

Karavites, P. (1992) *Promise-Giving and Treaty-Making: Homer and the Near East*, Leiden: Brill.

Kerkhoff, T. (2013) *Hidden Morals, Explicit Scandals: Public values and political corruption in The Netherlands (1748–1803)*, doctoral thesis, Leiden University.

Kitts, M. (2005) *Sanctified Violence in Homeric Society: Oath-making rituals and narratives in the Iliad*, Cambridge: Cambridge University Press.

Kolmer, L. (1989) 'Der promissorische Eid im Mittelalter' [The promissory oath in the Middle Ages], *Regensburger Historische Forschungen*, vol. 12, Regensburg: Kallmünz.

MacLachlan, B. (2008) 'Epinician swearing', in Sommerstein, A. H. and Fletcher, J. (eds) *Horkos: The oath in Greek society*, Bristol: Phoenix Press, pp. 91–101.

Mout, M. E. H. N. (2006) *Plakkaat van Verlatinge 1581* [Declaration of removal], Facsimile from original edition, The Hague: Staatsdrukkerij.

Oranje, Willem I Prins van (1568/1933) *Verantwoordinge, verklaringhe ende waerschowinghe mitsgaders eene hertgrondighe begheerte des edelen, lancmoedighen ende hooghgeboren Princen van Oraengien* [Apology], Amsterdam: Schenk.

Plescia, J. (1970) *The Oath and Perjury in Ancient Greece*, Tallahassee: Florida State University Press.

Prodi, P. (1993) 'Der Eid in der Europäischen Verfassungsgeschichte: Zur Einführung' [The Oath in European constitutional history: introduction], in Prodi, P. (ed.) *Glaube und Eid: Treueformeln, Glaubensbekenntnisse und Sozialdisziplinierung zwischen Mittelalter und Neuzeit*, Munich: Oldenbough, pp. vii–xxix.

Rohr, J. A. (1986) *To Run a Constitution: The legitimacy of the administrative state*, Lawrence, KS: University Press of Kansas.

— (1989) *Ethics for Bureaucrats: An essay on law and values*, 2nd edn, New York/Basel: Marcel Dekker.

Rutgers, M. R. (2009) 'The oath of office as public value guardian', *American Review of Public Administration*, 40(4): 428–44.

— (2013) 'Will the phoenix fly again?' *Review of Social Economy*, LXXI(2): 1–28.

Rutgers, M. R. and Steen, T. (2010) 'Confounding public values and public service motivations: towards a concept of public value commitment', paper presented at the Copenhagen Public Value Consortium Biennial Workshop 2010: Heterogeneity and Convergence in Public Values Research, Research workshop, Leiden, The Netherlands, June 2010.

Schuurbeque Boeije, M. J. (1884) *De Eedsquaestie* [The oath question], Zierikzee: Ochtman & Zoon.

Schaab, M. (1993) 'Eide und andere Treuegelöbnisse in Territorien und Gemeinden Südwestdeutschlands zwischen Spätmittelalter und Dreissigjährigem Krieg' ['Oaths and other loyalty declarations in regions and municipalities in south-east Germany in between the late Middle Ages and the Thirty Years' War'], in Prodi, P. (ed.) *Glaube und Eid: Treueformeln, Glaubensbekenntnisse und Sozialdisziplinierung zwischen Mittelalter und Neuzeit*, Munich: Oldenbough, pp. 11–30.

Tyler, J. E. (1834) *Oaths: Their origins, nature, and history*, London: Parker. J.W.

van den Doel, H. W. (1989) 'Geschiedenis van de ambtseed' [History of the oath of office], Bestuur, 8(7): 220–7.

van Es, W. J. L. (1911) *Het Eedsvraagstuk* [The oath question], Leiden: Eduard IJdo.

van Houten, S. (1882) 'De Asser eedskwestie' [The oath issue in Assen], *Vragen des Tijds*, 8: 37–46.

van Leeuwen, E. H. (1881) *De Eed en de Moderne Staat: Eene studie* [The oath and the modern state: a study], Utrecht: Breijer. C. H. E.

Part Three

The Formative Nineteenth Century

Chapter Five

Two Sides of the Same Coin: The Public Servant as a Political Actor in Nineteenth-Century German Thought

Niels Hegewisch

Introduction

In the course of developing a shared European administrative identity the question arises: to what extent should public servants be granted political influence? This is a pressing question since the empirical observation largely undisputed for decades is that public servants are relevant political actors, and their influence continues to rise. But it is far from clear what normative conclusions are to be drawn from that observation. The separation-of-powers doctrine is pivotal to this question, being not only a cornerstone of Western statehood but also an important component of the ideational foundation of a shared European administrative identity. Unfortunately, two conflicting normative assessments of politically influential public servants are inherent to the doctrine, like two sides of the same coin: given the preservation of the citizens' freedom as the doctrine's normative core, politically influential public servants can be perceived as protecting as well as endangering it.

In my contribution I show both sides of this coin from a history-of-ideas perspective. I show that German thought during the first half of the nineteenth century not only observed the rising political influence of public servants but also developed two opposing perceptions of this phenomenon: either as a necessary evil that needs to be constricted as far as possible or as a welcomed complement to the legitimised political actors. Arguments for both enabling and restraining public servants' political influence by protecting them from politics and vice versa were developed against this background. I elaborate from a historical perspective on which side the two-sided coin should land if flipped in order to resolve the problematic juxtaposition between the desirability and undesirability of politically influential public servants. Additionally I contribute to the first of the four sub-questions underlying this volume – how has the public servant been conceived in the history of European thought? – by presenting two opposed perceptions of politically influential public servants, exposing the historical continuity of the present problem, and evaluating arguments for two antithetical solutions.

The analysis proceeds in three steps. First, I explain what is meant nowadays by public servants exercising political influence and show why this is problematic and why this is conceived as problematic. Second, I argue that in the German case this problem has a long history, dating back to the beginning of the nineteenth century when two crucial developments coincided: the formation of modern public administration and early forms of the constitutional state with its pivotal feature of the separation of powers. Third, I contrast the endorsement with the problem of politically influential public servants by constructing bundled patterns of arguments elaborated from a rather broad corpus of selected sources.

The present perspective

What does it mean precisely to speak of public servants as relevant political actors? First of all, this refers to the common scholarly understanding that on the institutional level public administrators are generally involved in the different stages of formulating and implementing policies. This is a longstanding finding dating back to the early days of the study of public administration. Subsequently this finding has been confirmed and refined over decades by numerous mostly empirical studies (*see* Raadschelders, Chapter Two in this volume).

For my question, it is crucial to stress that public servants are involved in all phases of the policy cycle. They play a part in setting the political agenda and formulating policies by gathering relevant information necessary for adequate legislation, ruling out unrealisable alternatives, and formulating legal texts involving highly complex matters. Moreover, public servants are in charge of substantiating enacted policies in various social contexts. They are entrusted with evaluating whether certain policies have fulfilled their goals or not. In short, public servants are involved in the vast majority of decisions made in modern political systems (exemplary for many other studies: Jann 1998; Jann and Wegrich 2003; Page 2012; Scharpf 1973).

This poses a problem for the theory of a separation of powers which, being a cornerstone of modern statehood, 'has shaped Western thought on the state and its administration' (Overeem and Rutgers 2003: 174). In contrast to the closely observed political influence of public servants in constitutional reality, the theory of a separation of powers confines itself to a rather simple distinction between two government functions – the making and the executing of law – which are assigned exclusively to three government bodies – legislative parliament, executive government and adjudicative courts (*see* Vile 1998: Chapter One; Schmidt 2010: 311; Senn 2012: 335). According to a very common view public administration is considered as a part of the executive branch, hereby strictly limited to the application of law, and subordinated to government (Kropp and Lauth 2007: 24; Riklin 2006: 357, 419). Any political influence exceeding these narrow limits is to be refused (Overeem and Rutgers 2003: 177). Or, as Raadschelders phrases it in his chapter, 'at no time was administrative staff considered a (political power) in and of itself' (Chapter Two).

Given the fact that in practice public servants successfully push the doctrine's narrow boundaries, a wide gap opens between the separation-of-powers theory and administrative reality. One could say that public administration on the institutional level as well as public servants on the individual level are located in a blind spot of the separation-of-powers doctrine, whereas government and parliament, with the courts, form its visible surface (Hegewisch 2011).[1] This state of affairs is theoretically unsatisfying and keeps the separation-of-powers doctrine from becoming a resilient component of the ideational foundation of a shared European administrative identity (Carolan 2009: 253).

The underlying problem becomes clearer when we pay attention to the ambiguity towards the exercise of state power as such that is inherent to the idea of a separation of powers. It is necessary to highlight that 'the doctrine does not have a univocal interpretation in Western thought' (Overeem and Rutgers 2003: 175; *see* Rutgers 2000). The protection of the citizens' freedom as the doctrine's normative core is undisputed (Vile 1998: 14). But the doctrine does not state whether the freedom of the citizens it ought to preserve refers to a negative freedom from the state or rather a positive freedom through the state (Möllers 2008: 43–5). Instead two conflicting promises go with the idea of a separation of powers, one being to moderate state power in order to protect the citizens' negative freedom, the other to enable the exercise of state power in order to protect the citizens' positive freedom (Di Fabio 2004: 619; *see* Overeem 2012: 32). Naturally, this ambiguity affects the perception of public servants as relevant political actors, if only because there is no exercise of state power without them.

The hitherto sketched ambiguity of the separation-of-powers theory should show that if one does not want to abandon the very idea of preserving the citizens' freedom through a differentiation of government functions and bodies in the context of a shared European administrative identity, constitutional theory and administrative practice have to be more consistent. Therefore, it is worthwhile to discuss how to approach public servants' overall involvement in the policy process from the initial position of the doctrine's normative core (*see* Overeem 2012: Chapters Two–Three).

I argue that there is a fundamental conceptual vagueness inherent in the separation-of-powers doctrine regarding the question whether politically influential public servants should be perceived as a threat or rather as a contribution to the preservation of the citizens' freedom and how they could be enabled or restrained to be so. Given the pivotal significance of the doctrine for modern Western statehood the ideational foundations of a shared European administrative identity are affected by this ambiguity as well. Possible solutions are to be found in a continuum that is unfolded between the two poles of a *protection of public servants* from politics or a *protection of politics* from public servants.

Historical roots of the present problem

At this point, a turn towards the history of ideas is illuminating as similar questions about the legitimacy and the range of political influence exercised by public servants emerged in Germany as early as the first half of the nineteenth century – the 'century of administration' (Stolleis 1992: 229) – when three circumstances that still characterise the outlines of the present problem were given

---

1. Riklin criticises the mainstream theory of a separation of powers for its unrealistic and marginalising (*stiefmütterlich*) treatment of public administration (2006: 419). The conventional theory is appropriate, in his eyes if at all, only to the political systems of the seventeenth and eighteenth centuries (*ibid.*: 357).

at the same time: (1) a state that demanded to intervene in society (Langewiesche 1989), (2) by making use of a professional public administration (*see* Wunder 1986: Chapter One; Ellwein 1993; Raadschelders and Rutgers 1996), and (3) the regulation of the relationship between the state and its citizens by means of law including (usually constitutionally guaranteed) basic rights (Grimm 1988: Chapters Two–Four; Boldt 1993: Chapter Eight; Daum 2012: Chapter Eleven).

When modern forms of public administration ultimately became prevalent, their effect was an increase of state power paralleled by administrative professionalisation and bureaucratisation. The exercise of political power by public servants not only became widespread in practice but also increasingly apprehended in political thought. Simultaneously the ruling dynasties strived to reinforce an enlightened absolutism as the dominant system of government after the distortions of the French Revolution and its aftermath in the Napoleonic Wars had weakened the corporative state (Korioth 1998). But at the same time monarchs saw themselves confronted with growing demands for liberalisation, democratisation and a bourgeois state with the rule of law (Wehler 1987: 297–322). The separation-of-powers doctrine was vital for these demands; consequently, it became an influential concept in political discourse at the same time as the political influence of public servants started to grow significantly.

This historical situation led to a border-crossing discussion in the German *Gelehrtenrepublik* primarily among legal scholars and administrative practitioners about the question whether political influence exercised by public servants was desirable or objectionable – a discussion that has not yet been analysed in depth. Thus we lack detailed knowledge of what it meant for the German case when it was realised in political thought that public administration 'did not fit the separation of powers' (Overeem and Rutgers 2003: 176). Admittedly, at that time there was no coherent discourse that could justifiably be labelled 'the rise of public administration as a problem for the separation-of-powers doctrine'. But in spite of that, I argue that the manifold remarks on public administration and public servants that were undoubtedly present in political thought at that time (Damkowski 1969; Koselleck *et al.* 1992: 69–96) resorted frequently but sometimes unintentionally to the idea of a separation of powers – especially in the form of protecting the citizens' freedom as its normative core. This assumption rests on an approach that exceeds the habitual constriction on paramount thinkers like Hegel[2] (*see* Sager and Rosser 2009) and has been

---

2. Hegel wanted to give public administration 'a separate, special place beside the established constitutional powers, or even an elevated place above them, outside the separation-of-powers framework' (Overeem 2012: 31). Overeem argues that in spite of this, 'Hegel was not unconcerned about the danger of administrative dominance, but he was confident that it could be countered without much difficulty' (*ibid.*; *see* Hegel 1970: §295, §297). However, it is particularly remarkable that despite the prevailing opinion that 'the shadow of Hegel's *Elements of the Philosophy of Right*, with its heralding of the Prussian bureaucracy falls over much of German political and administrative thought' in the nineteenth century, Hegel was scarcely mentioned in the period between 1821 and 1848 (Overeem 2012: 40). It is all the more remarkable because an organic conception of the state, commonly associated with Hegel, was widespread (Stolleis 1992: 123–6, 133–8).

labelled 'democratic' by the historian Hans Rosenberg because it includes a vast corpus of source material and does not take into account success or neglect in terms of historical or present reception (1972: 10–11). This approach allows me to highlight in the following, the fruitfulness of a usually overlooked or underrated department of the archive of German political thought by applying a cross-section through sources that are commonly hidden in the shadows of the alleged great thinkers and singling out two opposing perceptions of public servants as relevant political actors.[3]

The starting point when analysing sources in the aforementioned respect is the widely shared observation that, on the institutional level, public administration played an increasingly powerful role in the political process. Despite monarchical attempts to restore pre-revolutionary absolutism, awareness spread among publicists, academics and administrative practitioners all over Germany that state and society had reached a level of complexity that rendered any kind of monarchical self-government impossible. Like in other European countries, many German thinkers came to realise that 'with the expansion of public administration [...] more than ever, the preservation and realisation of liberty and other constitutional values would depend on the role and position of public administration within the state' (Overeem 2012: 47). Among them was Carl A. von Malchus, a former high-ranking public servant who held several leading positions in different states in the Rhineland. Malchus put the aforementioned observation in a nutshell when stating that 'no state can be thought of without an administration' (1823: 2).[4] A more elaborate and representative description was put forward by the Hanoverian public servant and eventual professor of *Staatswissenschaft* Gustav Zimmermann, a conservative, who observed that:

> there is probably no country where the personal power of the rulers has unimpairedly stayed the same when its internal condition evolved into a state which the whole world knows as 'cultivated'. (1845: 176)

And further:

> But as soon as this period [the 'cultivated' state] begins in the life of states the public power is committed by the condition of the people to develop considerable activities. But on the other hand forms of administrative business will grow and start to entangle themselves with the nature of political actions. Then the rulers and their viceroys will start to lose their influence and personal care within the regular business of government. (*ibid.* 179)

---

3. For the selection of sources I have relied on earlier studies that have combed through the sources of that period thoroughly but with a different focus (mainly: Damkowski 1969; Koselleck *et al.* 1992: 69–96; Stolleis 1992; Pahlow 2000; Racky 2005). In addition I have used a rich contemporary bibliography (Walther 1854).

4. All sources are translated by the author. I thank Douglas Voigt (London) and Knut Langewand (Warwick) for their assistance.

The diagnosis of an over-challenged monarchical autocrat was shared by numerous authors, for example by another Hanoverian, the political publicist and public servant August W. Rehberg, who exposed the 'mock of absolute self-government' (1807: 125). In 1807, Rehberg presented a sharp critique of Prussian administration that was, in his eyes, based on the outdated idea of monarchical self-government. Since no monarch had all the necessary skills available for absolute self-government, Rehberg warned that any attempt to do so would exceed human capacities, and was therefore doomed to fail, leading necessarily to the 'greatest disadvantages' (*ibid.* 125–6). Notions like this were commonly shared during the entire period. They occurred in all parts of Germany and were not bound to a particular ideology (*see* Grävell 1808: 10–11; Haller 1816–25, vol. 3: 50; Cucumus 1825: 415; Brewern 1835: 288; Bülau 1836: 128–9; Schmitthenner 1843: 498).

This observation about the increasing influence of public administration at the institutional level of the political process laid the groundwork for arguments either for protecting public servants from politics, or for protecting the political process from public servants. As Zimmermann pointed out, the monarchs had no choice other than establishing 'administrative institutions for regular state affairs specially designed to technically fulfil its political tasks'. Out of this resulted 'a ring fence [enclosure] for the ruler which takes away from him an important part of executive powers both indirectly and *de facto*'. Hence there was an 'excessive power of administration, partly in its relationship to the rulers, partly in its relationship to the ruled' (1845: 183).

In the words of Sylvester Jordan, a seminal liberal professor of constitutional law at the University of Marburg, 'one does not go too far by saying that the weal and woe of the subjects and the flourishing of the state depends on the quality of public servants, and the success or failure of new institutions is largely due to their influence' (1828: 376). From the observation that 'almost all rights of the executive were exercised by public servants either directly or indirectly' (*ibid.*) a normative assessment of the observed political influence of public servants was a logical conclusion. It stood to reason that 'freedom [...] or the lack of freedom in a people nowadays rather depends on the style of administration than the style of government' (Schlosser 1816: 10).[5]

The conclusions drawn from this observation – which were, admittedly, quite often uttered unintended, scattered, or casual – can be bundled into two consistent but opposing perceptions of public servants that resort to aspects of the doctrine of a separation of powers and interrelate as two sides of the same coin. The first argues for politically influential public servants both as a necessary complement to the primary political actors and as a safeguard of the citizens' freedom. The other sees politically influential public servants as a potential problem, not only for the primary political actors but also as an infringement of the citizens' freedom.

---

5. The quote is also attributed to the German historian Barthold Niebuhr (Wilson 1887: 211).

Two opposing perceptions

Protecting public servants from politics

In this section, I elaborate from the sources a favourable perception of public servants exercising significant political influence through participation in implementing as well as formulating policies. This perception was granted to public administration at the institutional level but was based on qualities that were attributed to public servants at the individual level. Arguments for protecting public servants from politics were formulated bearing in mind public servants' alleged specialised abilities, corpuses of knowledge and guidance by a service ethic. These arguments aimed at allowing public servants leeway when implementing and when participating in formulating policies.

Many authors linked public administration to attributions that legitimised the exercise of political influence. Roughly speaking, these attributions can be divided into two classes – professionalism and independence – and are based on individual qualities of public servants. Public servants were thought of as being guided by a 'moral compass' (Burkhardt 1821: 548–9), an 'indissoluble love of the truth', 'duty' (*ibid.* 198–9), 'strength', 'honour', and 'zeal' (Wehnert 1836: 8–10). They also were considered to have command over 'specialised education and knowledge' (Jordan 1828: 258) comparable to those of physicians or mechanics (Brewern 1835: 158–61). Because of the unique individual qualities of its members, public administration was seen as the designated 'direct care-taker of the purposes of the state' (Wehnert 1836: 31).

As one important condition for public administration becoming the anticipated professional and independent actor in the political process it was considered necessary for public servants to be granted leeway when implementing policies (Rehberg 1807: 48; *see* 42–9). This required a solid measure of independence from both formal legislation and political instruction by government and parliament. Neither had public servants to be bound too rigorously to the 'dead letter of the law', nor did they require permission for every aspect of policy implementation (Emmermann 1819: 35). On the contrary, only by acting autonomously would they be able 'to realise what is most appropriate to the particular circumstances', which ultimately allows the state to protect freedoms (Rotteck 1840: 213). In this sense common statements should be understood that neither a law-making parliament nor an instructing government could rightfully claim to possess the 'godlike omniscience' that would be necessary to deny the justifiable leeway of public administration (Schoen 1831: 338). Karl von Rotteck, a profiled liberal thinker and advocate of the rule of law, argued that legal guidelines for administrative action were not supposed to exceed the necessary minimum (1840: 330–1). This line of argumentation was unproblematic for conservative thinkers who tended to oppose a constitutionally guaranteed rule of law in any case. For instance, the Prussian public servant Gottlieb J. M. Wehnert criticised any very detailed control of public administration as a 'harmful separation and juxtaposition of the state powers' (1836: 33). He warned of overly 'limiting the power that could do good in order to prevent its misuse' (*ibid.* 31). In addition, it was feared that without sufficient autonomy, public servants would degenerate intellectually as well as morally and thus eventually turn against the common good (*see* Brewern 1835: 211–18). This fear was memorably expressed in the metaphorical juxtaposition of public administration as an 'inanimate automaton' in which public servants were not more than 'dead wheel[s] of a machine' (Schoen 1831: 338) on the one hand, and on the other hand as an organism in which public servants resembled body parts that functioned 'lively and reasonably' (Emmermann 1819: 35) in their designated area for the benefit of the whole. The latter would pave the way for public administration's 'free and busy spirit', which maintained the state (Wehnert 1833: 95; cf Pölitz 1833: 315–20). In the words of Pölitz: 'Clockworks, mill wheels, windmills, and steam engines are machines; but the state is a living whole which like all life on earth has its organic limits that are often incommensurable with the laws of pure mechanics' (1833: 314).

Accordingly, it was demanded that public administration would be granted significant influence in the formulation of policies – if only because the law-making or, in most cases, law-approving parliament was suspected of pursuing only the particular interests of the educated and wealthy elites it represented. Besides, parliament was deemed incompetent due to the lack of administrative expertise of most of its representatives. None of this applied to public administration, in the eyes of its advocates; it was considered independent from particular interests. Because of their specialised training, merit-based recruitment, and practical experience, public servants were regarded as particularly able to care for the common good, the interest of the state and the technical details relevant for just and practical legislation. Thus public servants were naturally depicted as the most competent lawmakers (Zachariä 1839–43, vol. 4: 89–90). Consequently, it was quite often demanded that especially high-ranking public servants were given the possibility of both initiating legislation and participating in its deliberation. Indeed, neglecting the experience, knowledge and ethical guidance of public servants would only demonstrate a wanton disregard for basic efficiency. Incorporating public administration in the making of law could mean either forming committees staffed (among others) with experienced public servants who initiated or evaluated proposals for legislation (Behr 1810, vol. 2: 80–4; Emmermann 1819: 31; Jordan 1828: 357–8; Rotteck 1840: 332), to make sure that a significant share of parliamentary law-makers also were experienced public servants (Burkhardt 1821: 399; Zöpfl 1846: 262), or it could mean administration or government participating in deliberations about legislation (Eiselen 1828: 107–10). At the most extreme, it was even argued that public administration passed as a proper replacement for any kind of parliamentary representation not least because, in contrast with parliamentarians, its members were the true representatives of the people as they stemmed from a wider range of social strata than most members of parliament (Bülau 1836: 137–8; Rotteck 1840: 336–7; Zachariä 1839–43, vol. 6: 121). Closely linked to this aspect was the perception of public administration as a perfect moderator of the conflicted relationship between the monarch and his government on the one hand and the aspiring civil society on the other hand (Brewern 1835: 37–9). Public servants were expected to criticise required actions openly when they considered them unlawful or harmful. Beyond that they were even expected to disobey their superiors if their criticism remained unheard. Therefore, because of the competence and virtue of its members, public administration resembled a firewall that could be erected between a malicious monarch or government on the one side and the citizens on the other (Heffter 1829: 141–2; Mohl 1837: 54–5). Politically influential public servants were thus desirable when they functioned as the 'guardians of physical welfare and the true liberty of the people [...], its natural friend' (Rohmer 1848: 44), or a 'guarantee of the constitution' (Buddeus 1833: 55–6). Thus, monarch and government could rule more effectively when conflicts were moderated and the citizens were confident that their rights would not be harmed by the state.

Neither professionalism nor independence in the realm of public administration emerged by itself. The professionalism of public servants implied that they needed to acquire two different qualities: specialised skills and knowledge, and general intellectual capacities. Given the increased complexity of state and society, public servants were expected to be 'scholars' in the field in which they were appointed, in contrast to noble or upper-class dilettantes who administered because they inherited a position or desired a challenging recreational pursuit (Haller 1820–1, vol. 2: 156; cf. Rehberg 1807: 158). Public servants were widely required to have received an academic education within their area of competence. In other words, public administration had to be protected from unqualified public servants regardless of their social status. This, for example, was the position of Friedrich Bülau, a rather conservative censor and professor for constitutional law at the University of Leipzig, who stated that 'official duties are nowadays more than an occasionally practiced secondary occupation. They require years of costly preparation. They require the entire man', (1836: 101; cf. Dresch 1810: 268–9; Malchus 1823: 17; Jordan 1828: 258; Blome 1832: 8). In most cases, especially for the higher ranks, this meant the study of law or cameralism (cf. Lindenfeld 1997: 89–141). The French example was frequently referred to when clarifying public servants' need for academic education. The former public servant Johann K. I. Buddeus argued that in post-Napoleonic France public servants were 'skittish adventurers' appointed to office 'after they had failed in other undertakings' (1833: 48). By this definition, 'scientific spirit' was removed from public administration (*ibid.*).

Beyond specialised skills and knowledge, public servants were expected to possess a more general intellectual ability in terms of a 'presence of mind', 'quick wit' (Gönner 1808: 161), 'power of judgement' (Emmermann 1819: 34), and 'knowledge of human nature' (Zachariä 1839–43, vol. 4: 88). This was partially thought to be inherent but also acquirable through studies in fields that were, unlike law or cameralism, seen as free from utilitarian considerations (Rehberg 1807: 90). The influential scholar of legal history Karl H. L. Pölitz assessed a 'spiritual consecration by ideas' more significant for the qualification of public servants than technical or legal textbook knowledge (1833, vol. 3: 310). He demanded that public servants 'represent the ideas of their era' in order to 'relate their office to the purpose of the state' in every respect (*ibid.*). 'Only men of ideas (*Ideenmänner*) are suitable for the higher ranks, the men of mere notions (*Begriffsmänner*) are solely suited for simple tasks' (*ibid.*; *see* Wehnert 1833: 104–6).

Public administration's independence, in addition, was considered to derive from public servants' genuine service ethic as the anticipated product of a 'moral education' (Brewern 1835: 232), including such things as 'community spirit', 'love of justice' (Anonymous 1844: 104–5), 'honor' and 'decency' (Rehberg 1807: 81), 'strength of character' (Zachariä 1840, vol. 4: 88), 'duty' (Burkhardt 1821: 198), and so on. Only an impeccable character was therefore suited for office. In order to be independent and focused on the common good, however, more aspects were required, in particular material security, which would dissipate fear for personal and familial well-being. Material security referred mainly to a lifelong and sufficient regular income ensuring at least the subsistence of the public servant and his relatives (*see* Gönner 1808: 107–10; Malchus 1823: 17; Brewern 1835: 163–5 Bülau 1836: 85). For example, the high-ranking public servant Friedrich W. Emmermann from Nassau demanded that 'every office nourishes a man decently' (1819: 36). Beyond that, material security of public servants extended to pensions as well as funds for widows and orphans (*see* Dresch 1810: 269–70; Cucumus 1825: 419–25; Jordan 1831: 95–6; Schoen 1831: 340). Furthermore, it was of vital importance that this secured position remained unaffected when an officeholder would be removed from office (unless a court found him guilty of violations of criminal law). Georg von Brewern, a legal scholar at the University of Dorpat (Tartu),[7] characterised this aspect as 'the vital question regarding the independence of public servants' (1835: 270–1; *see* Emmermann 1819: 36–7; Burkhardt 1821: 198–9; Buddeus 1833: 51–6; Welcker 1990: 317–21; *see also* Chapter Seven in this volume). Only when materially secure could public servants feel truly liberated from 'chicanery and arbitrariness' by their superiors (Malchus 1823: xxiv).

These pronouncements of public servants' genuine qualities were contrasted with the contemporary administrative reality, which was perceived to be deficient. On the one hand, the struggle for the independence of public servants through material security was nowhere fully implemented. Rehberg stated that officeholders without a personal fortune 'live nearer to shortage than luxury', for they were kept in an 'unnatural and indecent spareness' (1807: 156–7). The state was seen as 'sinning against its servants' (Grävell 1808: 6; *see* Brewern 1835: 170–2). On the other hand, the professionalism of public servants was seen as subverted by nepotism, patronage and the sale of offices reserved for the members of the nobility and the financial aristocracy. This occurred despite the fervent arguments that neither talent nor virtue could be purchased or inherited (*see* Dahlmann 1835: 249; Zachariä 1839 ;43, vol. 6: 153; Schmitthenner 1843: 506). The sale and heritability of public offices were consequently deemed a sign of 'political barbarism' for they degraded public administration to a pension institution for certain fractions

---

7. Brewern's widely neglected dissertation 'Das Verhältnis der Staatsverwaltungsbeamten im Staate' (1835) alludes to many of the subjects in question here and is not only a rich source for administrative thought in the early nineteenth century but also a good example of the fruitfulness of commonly neglected sources from that period.

of society (Schoen 1831: 335; *see* Anonymous 1844: 155–6; Krug 1827: 111–12). Therefore both had to be replaced by an open and merit-based competition of those most suited for public office (*see* Gönner 1808: 159–69; Behr 1810, vol. 2: 138–40; Wangenheim 1815: 264; Harl 1822: 637–8; Welcker 1990: 316).[8]

Protecting politics from public servants

Now I shall briefly elaborate the alternative perception that public servants should be denied political influence and limited to the implementation of policies under the watchful guidance of government and attentive supervision of parliament and citizens. This perception, like its counterpart elucidated above, was based primarily on qualities which were attributed to public servants as individuals. Public servants were seen not only as guardians of the common good and the citizens' freedom but also as power-hungry and over-ambitious individuals who tended to misuse entrusted power to the detriment of the citizens' freedom. Accordingly, authors argued in favour of limiting the political influence of public administration and establishing tight control over its members.

It is notable that some of the same authors I use to elaborate the argument for protecting a politically influential public administration from politics also point out its potential for impairing citizens' freedom. Among them were conservative public servants like Rehberg as well as liberal legal scholars like Zachariä. A negative perception of public administration was based primarily on a pessimistic anthropology and therefore related to the individual level of public servants. The basic assumption was that by nature all human beings tended to misuse entrusted power for their own benefit. A simple equation applied: the greater the entrusted power, the more compelling is its misuse to gain prestige and power for one's own benefit to the detriment of the common good or the rule of law (Anonymous 1834: 21). This basic assumption of a pessimistic anthropology was implied when Rehberg stated that 'imperiousness [...] is inevitably connected with great power' (1807: 106; *see* Zachariä 1839–43, vol. 6: 262) as well as in Grävell's citation of the proverb 'opportunity makes a thief' (1808: 317).

Ironically, some of the same parameters that were welcomed to enable the exercise of political influence by public servants and presented in the preceding section were also apprehended as a potential threat to citizens' freedom. In the first place, this applied to public servants' leeway when implementing policies. Facing substantially indeterminate law (or governmental instructions) it was suspected that public servants were given 'free rein for arbitrariness' (Bülau 1836: 120). This was considered all the more threatening given the continuously increasing complexity of state and society and the subsequently growing need for complex and general legislation. With respect to this tendency it seemed inevitable that public servants would be granted increasingly extensive discretion regarding the

---

8. The postulated competition focuses on academic exit exams, theoretical entrance exams, traineeships and interviews conducted by committees consisting of experienced public servants (*see* Gönner 1808: 164–7; Behr 1810, vol. 2: 139–45; Eiselen 1828: 313–16).

implementation of policies. Authors with a pessimistic anthropology feared that this discretion would offer public servants a permanently growing and all the more compelling incentive to indulge in unjust malpractice, unbridled passion and a selfish thirst for power. The threat was perceived as real especially regarding high-ranking public servants, who were alleged to establish their 'own realms of despotism in the state' by making the citizens their vulnerable and helpless subjects (Burkhardt 1821: 314–15). In a nutshell, the members of an insufficiently programmed and controlled public administration were feared to become 'the whip of the nation' (Bülow-Cummerow 1842: 101). From this angle it was necessary to provide protection for the citizens from the 'fallacy or lack of goodwill' and ultimately the despotism of public servants (Behr 1810, vol. 2: 123). This was not least because a substantially indeterminate legislation was seen to 'enable the villain to act upon its own sweet will but baffle the righteous about what is right and how it is asserted' (Burkhardt 1821: 50–1). In this grim scenario there was left no doubt that public servants 'can cause harm for the citizens without formally leaving the path of law by a hair' (Bülau 1836: 120). As a result, it was even feared that the arbitrariness of public servants usurped the position of the law (*ibid.*: 78).

The perception of a politically influential public administration as a threat involved not only the implementation of policies, but also their formulation. And again this perception was based on negative qualities attributed to public servants. The warning of an anonymous critic that public servants had become the real 'masters of legislation' (Anonymous 1834: 74) by commonly abusing the dependency of the monarch, government and parliament on their administrative skills and knowledge, is, in my view, paradigmatic. Other critics seconded describing how high-ranking public servants intentionally promoted particularly vague legislation opening the doors to their arbitrary interpretations until there were virtually no legal boundaries for administrative leeway (Heinzen 1845: 123). Furthermore, public servants were suspected of utilising their position as intermediaries between citizens and the monarch or the government. Since the only way for the citizens to reach the monarch's ear was through public administrators, complaints and petitions could easily be twisted to serve the latter's selfish needs. Rule over the official communication channels was seen as a powerful instrument in the hands of the members of public administration to exercise an almost unnoticeable but effective indirect control of monarch and government. The aforementioned anonymous critic saw this potential for power clearly:

> The path to the ear of the monarch, even to the one with a truly good and just will, only leads through many serpentine windings around the thousands of little pillars which support the vaulted dome of his throne; and through them innocent and righteous laments can be heard: about being aggrieved by public servants, about the unjust interpretation and execution of initially wise laws, about the curtailment of rights, about the violation and restraint of vital functions of the people. The monarch, upon hearing the cries for rebellion and the wails of the terrifying crowd, shuns the light of truth before the throne and hardens his heart, arms his hand and strikes a blow unto the head of the innocent people and not unto the parting of the wicked. (Anonymous 1834: 64)

As if that were not enough, it became risky to raise a complaint about a public servant under those circumstances, since any complaint – appropriate or not – resembled an insolence requiring retaliation from the public servant's perspective (*ibid.*).

Another thread of arguments warned that a powerful public administration would develop a life of its own. This meant that public servants, if not programmed and controlled by external political actors, were less oriented to the common good, the rule of law and 'the most precious interests of the citizens', but all the more by a self-referential interest in the undisturbed efficiency of public administration's 'machine-like operation' (Brewern 1835: 228–9). It was feared that public administration would become, for its members, an end in itself resembling 'an independent reign in the state' that produced specific interests different from that of the state (Bülau 1836: 226). The young Karl Marx sharpened this criticism in his comments on Hegel's philosophy of law by labelling public administration 'bureaucracy'[9], meaning a closed caste of public servants inspired by 'Jesuitical, theological spirit' (1962: 316). The bureaucrats preserved their mysteries according to Marx through a 'hierarchy of knowledge', and in so doing they continuously took possession of the state until, ultimately, the purpose of the state was entirely subordinated to the purposes of bureaucracy (*ibid.*).

This pessimistic and fearful view of public administration was carried to extremes by Karl Heinzen, a former public servant, later revolutionist in southwest Germany during the Revolution of 1848–9, and publicist on gender equality and the justification of revolutionary violence after his emigration to the United States. In the aftermath of the involuntary end of his administrative career in the lower Prussian tax administration and due to degrading personal experiences, Heinzen transformed from a loyal public servant into the public administration's castigator in the heated atmosphere in the wake of the revolution. Allegedly based on his own experiences, he described how an administrative discretion unleashed by overly generalised and therefore indeterminate legislation, lawfully paved the way for public servants' 'narrow-mindedness, pedantry, conceit, inhumanity, and arrogance', leaving the citizens to their mercy (1845: 144–5). In Heinzen's eyes, public servants tended to prize their own interests and desires eagerly over those of the state and its citizens.

> Instead of being their offices' servants they use it to solely appear as masters. Louis XIV said: 'I am the state!'[10] Plenty of writing desk kings and *Büreauludwige* strive to emulate the king by saying: my office – *c'est moi!* (*ibid.* 144)[11]

Heinzen particularly criticised Prussia, where in his view since the days of Frederick William III high-ranking public servants had virtually disempowered the legitimate leaders. Like the Praetorian Guard in the Roman Empire, the army

---

9. For the use of the term at that time: Mohl (1862).

10. German in the original.

11. French in the original.

of public servants in Prussia was initially a mere instrument of absolutist power that managed to usurp the king's sovereignty (*ibid.* 17).

The challenge that arose from this dystopian perception of politically influential public servants and their alleged aspiration for a 'regiment of administrators' that would subject the state to its needs was met by arguing in favour of various means of legitimate political actors tightly controlling public servants (Mohl 1862: 121; *see* Rohmer 1848: 37–8, 42–4). And again, these means, which aimed primarily at the individual level of public servants, illustrate insightfully the perception that public servants threatened the citizens' freedom. First of all, the constitutional order of the *konstitutionelle Monarchie* was designed to subordinate public administration under monarchical prerogative and to subject it to governmental instruction. From this angle only the monarch and his government (not the public servants) counted as the truly selfless and righteous actors (Pölitz 1827: 477; *see* Weber 1827: 184; Jordan 1831: 68). It was therefore considered the task of monarch and government to constrain the public servants' thirst for power, for instance by authoritatively specifying generalised legislation for its practical use by public servants (Dahlmann 1835: 90). It was argued that ministers should continuously supervise every aspect of administrative practice in order to sanction misconduct by public servants immediately. Accordingly, the ministers' role in the political process was characterised by Wehnert as that of deputies to the monarch and 'leaders as well as guards of a right and accurate administration' (1833: 42). It was deemed important that public administration was not driven by petty selfish interests that were attributed to public servants and denigrated as the 'spirit of administration' (Mohl 1862: 125). On the contrary, guidance of public servants by 'statesmen' (*ibid.* 121), and animated by 'political spirit' (*ibid.* 125), was demanded. In practice, this subordination of public servants under governmental instruction was thought to be achieved mainly by three powers comprised in the monarchical prerogative and delegated to the government: the power of organisation, the power of discipline and the power of positions. All in all, it was assumed that these would prevent public servants from counting their offices as personal property and developing an 'aristocracy of administrators' (Brewern 1835: 116; *see* Haller 1820–1, vol. 2: 141–3, 148–51). In this view, only tight control by monarch and government would guarantee public servants' primary orientation towards the common good and the rule of law. Accordingly, it was argued that citizens should be granted the right to disobey public servants if the latter exceeded their powers (Schmitthenner 1843: 496).

The perception of politically influential public servants as a threat to citizens' freedom can be illustrated further by sources that argue about parliamentary and public control of public administration. Karl J. A. Mittermaier, a professor of law at the universities of Heidelberg and Bonn, suspected public servants of exercising their power arbitrarily, but was at the same time equally confident that this attempt was deemed to break like a wave against the 'permanent alertness of the representatives of the people', if they were given the proper means to control public administration

(1821: 310; *see* Roßbach 1844: 105).[12] Otherwise it was feared that the seemingly inevitable 'bureaucratic aristocracy' of public servants would 'paralyse the noble virtue of the people [and] sacrifice their highest and holiest interests to public servant's greed and obsession with power' (Anonymous 1834: 143; *see* Behr 1810, vol. 1: 202–5). Finally, a perception of public servants as a threat to citizens' freedom was the starting point of arguments for a tight supervision of public administration by the public. It was pointed out that both the ruled and the rulers had a mutual interest in effectively supervising how public servants made use of their entrusted power. Public servants, both high ranking and low ranking, were suspected of ignoring the common good if they were not being watched by the 'thousand eyes' (Zachariä 1839–43, vol. 6: 269) that formed together the 'judgement seat of public opinion' (Dahlmann 1835: 99–100). The remarks of an anonymous author can serve as a typical example in this respect: he recommended that monarch and government 'allow unconditional freedom of speech and refrain from obstructing that public opinion expressed itself loud and clear', because then they would 'not need to make other arrangements for guaranteeing the responsibility of head administrators' (A. W. 1818: 242; *see* Mohl 1862: 120). Obviously, distrust towards public servants' orientation to the common good was present in those and other demands for a constitutional guarantee of freedom of speech as well as freedom of the press. It was argued that only by these means would citizens be able to bypass the official communication channels that were under the control of public servants and inform the monarch and government directly about grievances in the realm of public administration (Welcker 1990: 304–5, 312–13, 319; *see* Behr 1810, vol. 1: 207–25; Zöpfl 1846: 299). Therefore Mohl considered it a civic duty to push the envelope of the right to protest against grievances in the realm of public administration. In Mohl's eyes, citizens who refrained from that 'deserve to be treated as worthless' by public servants (1862: 126; *see* Mohl 1837: 221).

Conclusion

German thinking between 1800 and 1850 offers rich material for reflection on the question whether a shared European administrative identity should be built on the endorsement by or rather on the rejection of politically influential public servants. My broadly based cross-section of the vast German literature about state, constitution and administration has revealed two opposing viewpoints on politically influential public servants with a view to the protection of the citizens' freedom: the protection of public servants from politics and vice versa. It was possible to hereby elaborate that the roots of this problem are inherent to the separation-of-powers doctrine which is an important component of the ideational foundation of a shared European administrative identity.

---

12. These means were the obligation of ministers and high-ranking public servants to justify themselves to the parliament if asked to (Mohl 1837: 10–11). Correspondingly parliament had to be conferred the right to obtain information about any possible bureaucratic procedure (Rotteck 1840: 256). Finally, the contemporary practice of an extensive official secrecy was in this context criticised as incommensurable with parliamentary supervision of public administration (Kronburg 1821: 287–8).

The arguments analysed here can serve to develop pointedly two opposing solutions for resolving this juxtaposition. In so far as a shared European administrative identity has been shaped by sources that argued for protecting public servants from politics, a perception of public servants would apply that sees them as contributing to the protection of citizens' freedom. The separation-of-powers doctrine had to adapt to administrative practice by explicitly including public servants and public administration as relevant political actors. In other words, what is already taking place in practice but remains overlooked in theory had to become an explicit feature of the separation-of-powers doctrine. Conversely, insofar as a shared European administrative identity has been shaped by sources that argue for protecting politics from politically influential public servants the separation-of-powers doctrine remained largely unchanged and administrative practice only had to adapt. Public servants as individuals and public administration as an institution had, in practice, to be strictly reduced to purely executive activities guided by parliamentary law or governmental instruction. Public servants had to be denied the exercise of political influence of any kind.

But there is more to learn from German thinking in the period in question than an elaboration of these rather extreme alternatives. Strikingly, many authors who argued in favour of granting leeway to public servants as well as including them in the formulation of policies did also warn against completely unleashing power-hungry public servants. Following those authors a dichotomous confrontation of protecting politics from public servants seems too harsh. Instead, the best protection *from* politically influential public servants seems to be a protection *of* them. Protecting citizens' freedom might be best achieved by both protecting what makes politically influential public servants contribute to the citizens' freedom and enclosing what endangers it. Past discourses might not provide us with complete institutional designs for a tension-free relationship between the separation-of-powers theory and administrative practice but suggest a tendency of how to achieve it. The task of a shared European administrative identity therefore would lie in mediating between the two extremes. Ideally, the two-sided coin, flipped to decide for either a protection of public servants or protecting from them would not tip to one side or the other but land on its edge.

References

A. W. (1818) 'Ist eine oberste controllirende Behörde für den Staat nothwendig? und welches kann der Zweck einer solchen Behörde seyn?', *Journal für Deutschland*, 12: 230–80.

Anonymous (1834) *Von den Aristokratien, den Geschlechts-, Geld-, Geistes- und Beamtenaristokratien und der Ministerialverantwortlichkeit in reinen Monarchien*, Leipzig: Hinrichs.

— (1844) 'Vom Civil-Staatsdienste: Betrachtungen über einige Verhältnisse desselben nach dem gegenwärtigen Standpunkte der Gesetzgebung und der Doctrin', *Deutsche Vierteljahresschrift*, 1: 87–156.

Behr, W. J. (1810) *System der Angewandten Allgemeinen Staatslehre oder der Staatskunst (Politik)*, 3 vols, Frankfurt am Main: Andreä.

Blome, O. von (1832) *Ueber den Organismus der Staatsverwaltung, insbesondere ueber die Trennung der richterlichen und administrativen Gewalt*, Hamburg: Perthes & Besser.

Boldt, H. (1993) *Deutsche Verfassungsgeschichte*, (vol. 2: Von 1806 bis zur Gegenwart), Munich: Deutscher Taschenbuch Verlag.

Brewern, G. von (1835) *Das Verhältnis der Staatsverwaltungsbeamten im Staate*, Leipzig: Frantz.

Burkhardt, J. M. V. (1821) *Staats-Wissenschafts-Lehre mit Rücksicht auf die gegenwärtige Zeit*, Leipzig: Rein.

Buddeus, J. K. I. (1833) *Die Ministerverantwortlichkeit in Konstitutionellen Monarchien: Monographie eines alten Geschäftsmannes*, Leipzig: Köhler.

Bülau, F. (1836) *Die Behörden in Staat und Gemeinden: Beiträge zur Verwaltungspolitik*, Leipzig: Göschen.

Bülow-Cummerow, E. von (1842) *Preußen, seine Verfassung, seine Verwaltung, sein Verhältnis zu Deutschland*, vol. 1, Berlin: Veit und Comp.

Carolan, E. (2009) *The New Separation of Powers: A theory for the modern state*, Oxford: Oxford University Press.

Cucumus, C. (1825) *Lehrbuch des Staatsrechts der konstitutionellen Monarchie Baierns*, Würzburg: Stahelsche Buchhandlung.

Dahlmann, F. C. (1835) *Die Politik, auf den Grund und das Maaß der gegebenen Zustände zurückgeführt*, vol. 1, Göttingen: Dieterich.

Damkowski, W. (1969) *Die Entstehung des Verwaltungsbegriffes*, Cologne: Carl Heymans Verlag.

Daum, W. (ed.) (2012) *Handbuch der europäischen Verfassungsgeschichte im 19. Jahrhundert: Institutionen und Rechtspraxis im gesellschaftlichen Wandel*, vol. 2, Bonn: Dietz.

Di Fabio, U. (2004) 'Gewaltenteilung', in Isensee, J. and Kirchhof, P. (eds) *Handbuch des Staatsrechts der Bundesrepublik Deutschland*, (vol. 2: Der Verfassungsstaat), Heidelberg: C. F. Müller.

Dresch, L. von (1810) *Systematische Entwicklung der Grundbegriffe und Grundprinzipien des gesammten Privatrechts, der Staatslehre und des Völkerrechts*, Heidelberg: Mohr und Zimmer.

Eiselen, J. F. G. (1828) *Handbuch des Systems der Staatswissenschaften*, Breslau: Max.

Ellwein, T. (1993) *Der Staat als Zufall und Notwendigkeit*, (vol. 2: Die öffentliche Verwaltung in der Monarchie 1815–1918), Opladen: Westdeutscher Verlag.

Emmermann, F. W. (1819) *Die Staats-Polizei in Beziehung auf dem Zweck des Staats und seine Behörden*, Wiesbaden: Schellenberg.

Gönner, N. T. (1808) *Der Staatsdienst aus dem Gesichtspunkt des Rechts und der Nationalökonomie betrachtet*, Landshut: Krüll.

Grävell, M. C. F. W. (1808) *Anti-Platonischer Staat: Oder welches ist die beste Staatsverwaltung?* Berlin: Maurer.

Grimm, D. (1988) *Deutsche Verfassungsgeschichte: 1776–1866, Vom Beginn des modernen Verfassungsstaats bis zur Auflösung des Deutschen Bundes*, Frankfurt am Main: Suhrkamp.

Haller, C. L. von (1816–25) *Restauration der Staats-Wissenschaft oder Theorie des natürlich-geselligen Zustandes der Chimäre des künstlich-bürgerlichen entgegengesetzt*, 6 vols, Winterthur: Steinersche Buchhandlung.

— (1820–1) *Restauration der Staats-Wissenschaft oder Theorie des natürlich-geselligen Zustandes der Chimäre des künstlich-bürgerlichen entgegengesetzt*, 3 vols, 2nd edn, Winterthur: Steinersche Buchhandlung.

Harl, J. P. (1822) *Entwurf eines Polizei-Gesetzbuchs*, Erlangen: Palm.

Heffter, A. W. (1829) *Beiträge zum deutschen Staats- und Fürstenrecht*, Berlin: Reimer.

Hegel, G. W. F. (1970) *Grundlinien der Philosophie des Rechts oder Naturrecht und Staatswissenschaft im Grundrisse* (Original published 1821), Frankfurt am Main: Suhrkamp.

Hegewisch, N. (2011) 'Im "toten Winkel"? Verwaltung und Gewaltenteilung in Deutschland und in der Schweiz in der ersten Hälfte des 19. Jahrhunderts', paper presented at the conference on administrative reform in Switzerland during the nineteenth and twentieth century at the Swiss Federal Archive, Bern, September 2011.

Heinzen, K. (1845) *Die Preußische Büreaukratie*, Darmstadt: Leske.

Jann, W. (1998) 'Politik und Verwaltung im funktionalen Staat', in Böhret, C. *et al.* (eds) *Politik und Verwaltung auf dem Weg in die transindustrielle Gesellschaft*, Baden-Baden: Nomos, pp. 253–82.

Jann, W. and Wegrich, K. (2003) 'Phasenmodelle und Politikprozesse: Der policy-cycle', in Schubert, K. and Bandelow, N. C. (eds) *Lehrbuch der Politikfeldanalyse*, München and Wien: Oldenbourg, pp. 71–104.

Jordan, S. (1828) *Versuche über allgemeines Staatsrecht, in systematischer Ordnung und mit Bezugnahme auf Politik vorgetragen*, Marburg: Garthe.

— (1831) *Lehrbuch des allgemeinen und deutschen Staatsrechts*, Cassel: Krieger.

Korioth, S. (1998) '"Monarchisches Prinzip" und Gewaltenteilung – unvereinbar? Zur Wirkungsgeschichte der Gewaltenteilungslehre Montesquieus im deutschen Frühkonstitutionalismus', *Der Staat*, 37(1): 27–57.

Koselleck, R., Schindling A. and Wunder, B. (1992) 'Verwaltung', in Brunner, O., Conze, W. and Koselleck, R. (eds) *Geschichtliche Grundbegriffe: Historisches Lexikon zur politisch-sozialen Sprache in Deutschland*, vol. 7, Stuttgart: Klett-Cotta, pp. 1–96.

Kronburg, A. von (1821) *Encyclopädie und Methodologie der practischen Staatslehre nach den neuesten Ansichten der berühmtesten Schriftsteller dargestellt und ergänzt*, Dresden: Arnold.

Kropp, S. and Lauth, H.-J. (2007) 'Einleitung: Zur Aktualität der Gewaltenteilung', in Kropp, S. and Lauth, H.-J. (eds) Gewaltenteilung und Demokratie: Konzepte und Probleme der 'horizontal accountability' im interregionalen Vergleich, Baden-Baden: Nomos, pp. 7–27.

Krug, W. T. (1827) 'Amt', in Krug, W. T. (ed.) *Allgemeines Handwörterbuch der philosophischen Wissenschaften nebst ihrer Literatur und Geschichte*, vol. 1, Leipzig: Brockhaus, pp. 110–112.

Langewiesche, D. (1989) '"Staat" und "Kommune": Zum Wandel der Staatsaufgaben im Deutschland des 19. Jahrhunderts', *Historische Zeitschrift*, 248: 621–35.

Lindenfeld, D. F. (1997) *The Practical Imagination: The German sciences of state in the nineteenth century*, Chicago: University of Chicago Press.

Malchus, C. A. von (1823) *Politik der inneren Staatsverwaltung oder Darstellung des Organismus der Behörden für dieselbe: Mit Andeutungen von Formen für die Behandlung und für die Einkleidung der Geschäfte, vorzüglich jener in dem Gebiete der inneren Staatsverwaltung*, Heidelberg: Mohr.

Marx, K. (1962) 'Kritik des Hegelschen Staatsrechts [1843]', in Lieber, H.-J. and Furth, P. (eds) *Frühe Schriften*, vol. 1, Stuttgart: Cotta, pp. 258–426.

Mittermaier, K. J. A. (1821) 'Beiträge zur Lehre von den Gegenständen des bürgerlichen Processes', *Archiv für die civilistische Praxis*, 4: 305–70.

Mohl, R. von (1837) *Die Verantwortlichkeit der Minister in Einherrschaften mit Volksvertretung*, Tübingen: Laupp.

—— (1862) 'Ueber Bureaukratie [1846]', in *Staatsrecht, Völkerrecht und Politik*, Tübingen: Laupp, pp. 99–130.

Möllers, C. (2008) *Die drei Gewalten: Legitimation der Gewaltengliederung in Verfassungsstaat, europäischer Integration und Internationalisierung*, Weilerswist: Velbrück Wissenschaft.

Overeem, P. (2012) *The Politics-Administration Dichotomy: Toward a Constitutional Perspective*, 2nd edn, Boca Raton, FL: CRC Press.

Overeem, P. and Rutgers, M. (2003) 'Three roads to politics and administration: ideational foundations of the politics/administration dichotomy', in Rutgers, M. R. (ed.) *Retracing Public Administration*, Amsterdam: Elsevier, pp. 161–84.

Page, E. C. (2012) *Policy without Politicians: Bureaucratic influence in comparative perspective*, Oxford: Oxford University Press.

Pahlow, L. (2000) *Justiz und Verwaltung: Zur Theorie der Gewaltenteilung im 18. und 19. Jahrhundert*, Goldbach: Keip.

Pölitz, K. H. L. (1827) *Die Staatswissenschaften im Lichte unsrer Zeit*, vol. 1, 2nd edn, Leipzig: Hinrichs.

— (1833) *Staatswissenschaftliche Vorlesungen für die gebildeten Stände in constitutionellen Staaten*, vol. 3, Leipzig: Hinrichs.

Raadschelders, J. C. N. and Rutgers, M. R. (1996) 'The history of civil service systems', in Bekke, A. J. G. M., Perry, J. L. and Toonen, T. (eds) *Civil Service Systems in Comparative Perspective,* Bloomington, IN: Indiana University Press, pp. 67–100.

Racky, M. (2005) *Die Diskussion über Gewaltenteilung und Gewaltentrennung im Vormärz*, Frankfurt am Main: Lang.

Rehberg, A. W. (1807) *Ueber die Staatsverwaltung deutscher Länder und die Dienerschaft des Regenten*, Hannover: Hahn.

Riklin, A. (2006) *Machtteilung: Geschichte der Mischverfassung*, Darmstadt: Wissenschaftliche Buchgesellschaft.

Rohmer, F. (1848) *Deutschlands alte und neue Bureaukratie: Mit einem offenen Worte über das gegenwärtige bayerische Ministerium*, Munich: Kaiser.

Roßbach, J. J. (1844) *Die Lebens-Elemente der Staaten*, Würzburg: Thein.

Rosenberg, H. (1972) *Politische Denkströmungen im Vormärz*, Göttingen: Vandenhoeck & Ruprecht.

Rotteck, C. von (1840) *Lehrbuch des Vernunftrechts und Staatswissenschaften*, vol. 2, 2nd edn, Stuttgart: Hallberger.

Rutgers, M. (2000) 'Public administration and the separation of powers in a cross-Atlantic perspective', *Administrative Theory & Praxis*, 22(2): 287–308.

Sager, F. and Rosser, C. (2009) 'Weber, Wilson, and Hegel: Theories of modern bureaucracy', *Public Administration Review*, 69(6): 1136–47.

Scharpf, F. W. (1973) 'Verwaltungswissenschaft als Teil der Politikwissenschaft', in idem (ed.) *Planung als politischer Prozess*, Frankfurt am Main: Suhrkamp, pp. 9–32.

Schlosser, C. F. (1816) *Ueber Staatsverfassung und Staatsverwaltung: Aus dem Französischen von Fievée übersetzt und mit Anmerkungen begleitet*, Frankfurt am Main: Hermann.

Schmidt, M. G. (2010) *Wörterbuch zur Politik*, 3rd edn, Stuttgart: Kröner.

Schmitthenner, F. (1843) *Zwölf Bücher vom Staate, oder systematische Encyklopädie der Staatswissenschaften*, vol. 3, Giessen: Heyer.

Schoen, J. (1831) *Die Staatswissenschaft geschichts-philosophisch begründet*, Breslau: Korn.

Senn, M. (2012) 'Gewaltenteilung', in Cordes, A. and Stammler, W. (eds) *Handwörterbuch zur deutschen Rechtsgeschichte*, vol. 2, Berlin: Schmidt, pp. 335–41.

Stolleis, M. (1992) *Staatsrechtslehre und Verwaltungswissenschaft: 1800–1914*, Munich: Beck.

Vile, M. J. C. (1998) *Constitutionalism and the Separation of Powers*, 2nd edn, Indianapolis, IN: Liberty Fund.

Walther, O. R. (1854) *Handbuch der juristischen Literatur des 19. Jahrhunderts*, Weimar.

Wangenheim, K. A. von (1815) *Die Idee der Staatsverfassung in ihrer Anwendung auf Wirtembergs alte Landesverfassung und den Entwurf zu deren Erneuerung*, Frankfurt am Main: Körner.

Weber, H. B. von (1827) *Grundzüge der Politik oder philosophisch-geschichtliche Entwickelung der Hauptgrundsätze der innern und äußern Staatskunst*, Tübingen: Laupp.

Wehler, H.-U. (1987) *Deutsche Gesellschaftsgeschichte*, (vol. 2: Von der Reformära bis zur industriellen und politischen 'Deutschen Doppelrevolution', 1815–1845/49), Munich: Beck.

Wehnert, G. J. M. (1833) *Über den Geist der Preußischen Staatsorganisation und Staatsdienerschaft*, Potsdam: Riegel.

—— (1836) *Die Politik des Civilstaatsdienstes*, Potsdam: Riegel.

Welcker, C. T. (1990) 'Staatsdienst', in Rotteck, C. V. and Welcker, C. T. (eds) *Staats-Lexikon: Encyklopädie der sämmtlichen Staatswissenschaften für alle Stände [1845–1848]*, 2nd edn, 12 vols, Frankfurt am Main: Keip, pp. 297–322.

Wilson, W. (1887) 'The study of administration', *Political Science Quarterly*, 2(2): 197–222.

Wunder, B. (1986) *Geschichte der Bürokratie in Deutschland*, Frankfurt am Main: Suhrkamp.

Zachariä, K. S. (1839–43) *Vierzig Bücher vom Staate*, 7 vols, 2nd edn, Heidelberg: Winter.

Zimmermann, G. (1845) *Die Deutsche Polizei im neunzehnten Jahrhundert*, vol. 1, Hannover: Schlüter.

Zöpfl, H. (1846) 'Grundsaetze des allgemeinen und des constitutionell-monarchischen Staatsrechts', 3rd edn, Heidelberg: Winter.

Chapter Six

A Not-So-Statist State: The European Public Servant and the Political Theory of Pluralism

Koen Stapelbroek

Introduction: The possibility of a European public service

Discussing the 'European public servant' as the ideal-typical incarnation of a 'shared administrative identity' can take many different forms. The aim of this chapter is to explore how the space within which the figure of the 'European public servant' moves *may* have been created in the early decades of the twentieth century. This chapter provides – in a rather schematic way – an outline of the conceptual development, such as took place within the political discourse of pluralism, which would have been required to shape the notion of a shared administrative understanding. The main argument is, first, that such a conceptual development would have had to take place in the light of previous history in which an internationally shared, or united, administration was pretty much unthinkable; second, that its key elements, the modern idea of Europe as simultaneously a social and a political entity and the modern idea of administration, arose roughly at the same time; and third, that the nature of their interrelation can be grasped through the political theory of pluralism.

One thing that is easily overlooked is that the possibility for creating a European public service depends on there being sufficient scope for such an institution and that before 1900 such scope did not exist. Until the early twentieth century the existence of international organisations (state and non-state) was not a common feature in the global political landscape. What is more, there was a fairly simple and straightforward reason for this. International organisations that could be said to hold any sway were generally understood to affect the sovereignty of the state. The idea of a united Europe had been around until at least the early eighteenth century, but was known as a pariah concept, a groundless utopia, rather than a viable vision of a future political and economic configuration that could integrate nations. At the same time, the idea of public service or administration did not until this time entail a concern for objectives that lay outside the traditional state-directed spheres of political control and management. How come that, rather suddenly, these things changed? What were the (social, economic, political, administrative, legal or intellectual) contexts in which public services did assume new functions within the state? And how could these functions translate into mission statements or legitimations for the creation of an *international* democratic society that arguably endure until this day?

In this chapter the approach will be mainly conceptual and, indeed, hypothetical. International organisations today play a major role within the global political realm and the future of the European public service is likely to have an increasing impact on how we will look at the successes and failures of modern democratic governance. Still, while there are both sufficient urgency and ample empirical data available to engage with the recent development of European administrative services, the question why a transfer of decision-making processes from the state to the interstate level could take place, along with new ideas about administration, merits attention and is relatively uncharted territory. The question here, then, is not how international organisations, and European ones in general, actually function. It has often been argued by realists in the field of international relations that international organisations in the twentieth century function as platforms from which states try to further their interests. Instead, the question is how it became thinkable in the first place that they might not function in this way.

A great many international organisations, both of an intergovernmental and of a non-governmental character, emerged during the early decades of the early twentieth century. This has been acknowledged and confirmed by various introductory texts and research writings on the subject (MacKenzie 2010; Reinalda 2009; Herren 2009; Barnett and Finnemore 2004; Iriye 2002; Archer 2001; and earlier Mangone 1954). Most of these works have been written from retrospective and strongly disciplinary viewpoints that differ in method (these include constructivist and functionalist viewpoints and are often dictated by strands within international relations theory). As such, they do display not so much a historical interest in why these institutions arose, but rather enquire how they did or did not change international power dynamics. A basic temporal structure that is common to these histories, which in itself seems adequate enough, identifies the creation of the League of Nations as a turning point in the history of international organisations. In general these histories distinguish various famous interstate political organisations (think of the Central Commission for the Navigation of the Rhine or the 1899 and 1907 Peace Conferences in the Hague) as manifestations of the wider dynamics of global politics and international law of the period. The question remains, what made the establishment of these institutions possible?

International organisation, civilisation, commerce and administration

The wider intellectual question as to what vision inspired the establishment of international organisations around 1900, thus, seems of a different category from the ones that have inspired recent texts on the subject. The idea that there was indeed a vision that was not simply political in the most obvious sense is easy to recognise. The way in which the Union of International Associations, which was founded in 1907 and driven by a cosmopolitan civilising ideal, saw itself, is but one example. In a book published in 1957 on the history of international organisations published by this same organisation, the author stated some of its main aspects in the opening lines of the work:

> As the British historian Arnold Toynbee has well said: 'this is the first age since the dawn of history in which mankind has dared to believe it practicable to make the benefits of civilisation [...] available to the human race'. We owe it to the development of a spirit, and a mechanism, of international co-operation. (Speeckaert 1957: iii)

In other words, Speeckaert claimed, albeit rather profusely, that there was something decisively new that international organisations from the early twentieth century were trying to achieve that was aimed at the entirety of humankind and that had previously been impossible to realise. The 'mechanism' of international cooperation was not primarily political, or state-bound, but was inspired by a 'development of spirit' and could spread the 'benefits to civilisation' beyond the privileged nations, or within those nations, that, so far, had access to them.

While it remains hard to judge clearly such rhetorical testimonies to the novelty of international organisations and their purported modernising powers, some of the contours can be gleaned. Interestingly, with regard to international administration the same author described the development of pioneering institutions like the International Telegraphic Union, which was established in 1865 as a specific instantiation of the civilising power of international cooperation. Administrative functions within societies formed a branch of decision-making that could be easily depoliticised. Once this process was set in motion:

> descending from the sphere of purely political conventions, where it was concerned, in its own exclusive right, so to speak, with war, peacemaking and, incidentally, commerce, the law of nations started to tackle "international administration", regulating according to its own ideas the varied activities involved in the common affairs of the peoples of the world. (Descamps 1894: 2, quoted by Speeckaert 1957: xvi)

The idea was that the 'common affairs' of 'the peoples of the world' could be organised more efficiently, that this could be done on a universal scale, and that doing so was a matter of acting upon 'the law of nations' beyond the realm of 'political conventions'. This was more than a claim that administrative tasks need not be political, and would be more efficiently organised and executed once this was recognised. The real claim came from identifying the 'law of nations' as an objective source, independent of the political will of states, for the regulation of 'common affairs' that took place in all societies.[1] In much the same way, the author saw 'commerce', the exchange of goods among peoples, as a natural object of

---

1. The nexus between peaceful civilisation and international administration was also a main theme during the 1950s in publications from the Carnegie Foundation, one of the major private funding agencies that echoed the spirit of the times and its social and political missions.

the law of nations that ought not to be dominated by political considerations. As Speeckaert argued, discussing the original impact of commerce upon peace:

> Undoubtedly it was commerce more than anything else which developed peaceful relations between peoples. With the improving means of transport and communication an imperious urge arose to supplement home grown food by commodities only to be found in far off regions. For their manufacturing industries men searched far and wide for raw materials and available locally. Thus international commerce entered upon the scene. (Speeckaert 1957: v)

The problem that intersected with the relation between commerce and peace had been that 'the sixteenth and seventeenth centuries saw the acceptance of the conception of an international society composed of sovereign and equal states'. The reality of early modern Europe was 'a long way off the idea of international co-operation [...] for the betterment of humanity' (Speeckaert 1957: vi). The reality of interstate competition that had been developed in those centuries had distorted the original civilising powers of 'commerce', which had now to be and – through international cooperation – could be restored.

A major change had come in 1815, when at the Congress of Vienna 'an international concern for economic and monetary affairs [...] led to the proclamation of freedom of navigation of international rivers and the abolition of the slave trade'. Preceding the early twentieth century as the turning point in human history when international cooperation was linked with universal global civilisation, Speeckaert asserted that a century earlier 'such concern [for economic and monetary affairs by separate states] gave birth to the world's first truly international organisations, with which the present chronology opens' (Speeckaert 1957: vi–vii).[2]

The association of the sovereignty of states with restrictions on the potential for humanity to generalise civilisation, remained unaccounted for in this short text. Speeckaert did, however, indicate that previous standard ideas of international relations as revolving around power at the level of government had recently given way to a new approach that would help to dissolve the previous impediment. New outlooks on the history of humankind shed a different light on the determinants of human progress and this had had a salutary impact on ideas about international relations. As Speeckaert noted:

> new tendencies in historical research, which lay emphasis on the study of the material and spiritual life of human societies, have suggested quite a different orientation in the field of international relations. In this perspective relations between governments are no longer the centre of interest; what is important is the history of relations between people. (Speeckaert 1957: iv)

---

2. This issue is the topic of a forthcoming paper 'The ordering of trade at the Congress of Vienna: a Dutch, European and global perspective', as part of a project on 'The Vienna Congress and the transformation of international law'.

If these quotations provide mere snippets of the basic vision that inspired the establishment of international organisations from around 1900 and how their establishment was understood to mean something rather important, the answer provided in this chapter is that a possible explanation may be provided through the political theory of pluralism, which is known primarily as a theory of the state. This theory gained some measure of popularity around the time that international organisations emerged onto the scene and when the tasks of public services, first of all in growing industrialised cities, widened to include a range of social and economic spheres that subsequently became integrated into European welfare states. When the central principles of pluralism – notably its critique of sovereignty – and its reception by some scholars of international law are applied to the international realm the main characteristics emerge of an understanding of states that fits with a different logic of interstate relations; one that ultimately could be aligned with the two notions of Europe and modern public service that are central in this volume. The purpose of the following is to provide an outline of the dimensions of the intellectual challenge involved in bringing these two elements within the same frame from a historical point of view.

A problematic legacy: The idea of Europe

The idea of the European public servant hinges crucially on two concepts that now seem relatively unproblematic but whose present-day understanding can be argued to stem from the early decades of the twentieth century. These two concepts are the one of Europe as somehow a state-like entity with shared legal rules, social norms and institutional orderings; and that of the public service where the term stands for a category of impartial professionals who are hired in permanent works contracts by the state, whose tasks extend beyond the exercise of power and control into the realm of managing public provisions that promote the socio-economic development of the population.

Both the notions of Europe and of the public or civil service (or public administration – these terms will be used interchangeably) existed of course long before the turn of the twentieth century. Public services, where specialists served the common good rather than the private interest of rulers, had actually become the norm and were systematically institutionalised at the state level in the late eighteenth and nineteenth centuries, before they gradually became professionalised and protected by labour agreements.[3] But according to some this development was not in itself sufficient to make for a 'modern' public administration, as will be discussed in the next section.

Concerning the idea of Europe, whenever, for instance, dynastic succession crises in early modern Europe had to be settled, reference would be made to the idea of Europe (or to Christianity, which served as a synonym) as a system of sovereign territories ruled over by monarchs or oligarchies, whose different cultures shared the same historical source, which lay in the history of the Roman

---

3. *See* the framework presented by Jos Raadschelders in the Chapter Two of this volume where the history of administration is traced back to antiquity.

Empire and its successive downfall.[4] This latter idea of a divided Europe lay at the basis of a great many eighteenth-century outlooks on international peace and trade. Somehow its shared Roman history could be the basis for a future European reintegration, whatever form this might take. This was how Voltaire described the condition of Europe during the time of Louis XIV:

> For a long time past the Christian part of Europe – Russia excepted – might be considered as a great republic divided into several states, some of which were monarchical, others mixed, some aristocratic, and others popular; but all corresponding with one another; all having the same basis of religion, though divided into several sects, and acknowledging the same principles of public and political equity, which were unknown to the other parts of the world. It is from these principles that the European nations do not make slaves of their prisoners; that they respect the persons of their enemies' ambassadors; that they agree together concerning the pre-eminence, and some other rights belonging to certain princes; such as the emperor, kings, and other lesser potentates: and particularly in the prudent policy of preserving, as far as they are able, an equal balance of power among themselves; by continually carrying on negotiations, even in the midst of war, and keeping ambassadors, or less honorable spies, at one another's courts, to give notice to the rest of the designs of any single one, to sound the alarm at once over all Europe, and to prevent the weaker side from being invaded by the stronger, which is always ready to attempt it. (Voltaire 1752: 11)

Despite these kinds of statements, the eighteenth century was not a favourable time for the idea of Europe. Following a failed attempt, prior to the conclusion of the Peace of Utrecht, to provide a legal-political structure for containing the foreign trade of Europe's dominant states and their global aspirations, Europe became a pariah concept. The most famous illustration of this is the reputation of the Abbé de Saint-Pierre's *Project for Perpetual Peace*, which, published in its full version in 1713 and informed by the negotiations that took place before and at Utrecht, concluded that a lasting peace required the establishment of a federal European government. During the eighteenth century, while interstate 'Jealousy of Trade' continuously sparked global commercial warfare, Saint-Pierre's *Project* would be commonly referred to as 'the dream of an honest man'.[5] While the restoration of commerce – however the normative principles of commerce were understood – was considered necessary, the range of political solutions seemed generally illusive. Europe, as the idea that states might be willing to sacrifice part of their sovereignty to a higher political agency, was generally deemed a groundless utopia. In the light

---

4.   With regard to Europe and the longer history of the concept, *see* Pagden (2002); Wintle (2009).

5.   This qualification was a European commonplace, said to have come from the Cardinal de Fleury. For 'Jealousy of Trade' as the main problem of eighteenth-century politics (Hont 2005). The notion of 'Perpetual Peace' also became the title of one of Immanuel Kant's most famous works from 1795 and, in a dehistoricised form, continued to attract attention in international relations theory (Easley 2004).

of this background, which continued until the early twentieth century, the question is in order how the idea of Europe as a political unity in some form ever assumed a different association? What changes in the political and conceptual landscape could have allowed for such a connotative shift?

Another problematic legacy: Public service and the common good

The birth of modern public administration theory is commonly associated with texts written by Woodrow Wilson (1887) and Max Weber (1994 [1919]) (*see* Sager and Rosser 2009; Rosser 2010; Walker 1989; Rabin and Bowman 1984; Stillman 1973), who both argued from a historical perspective of the state. While this commonplace might also be questioned, here the two texts are used to suggest that both arguments about the place of public administration within states derived from a general theory of modern politics.

To start with Weber, it is not always recognised that his theory of administration, which was included in his lecture *Politics as a vocation* [*Politik als Beruf*], derived in reality from a historical theory of the state. From the first sentences onwards and through the notion of 'expropriation', Weber explained the transformation of politics in Europe since the fall of the Roman Empire as a process moving in the direction of an archetypal idea of the state. The main characteristic of the European state that came down from history was that it was an institution for the centralisation of power, territorial ownership and exercise of the means of coercion. Within this conception of the state, the element of administration played a key balancing role. The emergence of the figure of the administrative official emancipated its status compared with earlier periods when there had been private ownership of political power, and when professional administrators were servants to the ruler. While the professional politician in the modern state still faced ethical dilemmas and had to make hard choices that transcended the level of given legal arrangements, civil servants, by way of forming a politically independent intermediary force, regulated the relation between politics and the citizenry.

Outside the standard readings of the text and its historical meaning amidst the turmoil of the German Revolution in 1919, its implications for the possible existence and scope of public administration (and in the final instance of international organisations) need to be underlined. Weber's outlook on the European development of forms of government had a flipside. The same compounded process of 'expropriation' that produced representative democracies with administrative officials tended to a form of political relations within the state that was characterised by a struggle among various components. From the first sentences of his text onwards Weber defined the state through concepts of power, coercion and control. That function remained intact over time and was carried over into the modern era of government where it lost nothing of its legitimacy. It was within the boundaries of this historically grown and explicable conception of the state as a structure of authority and territorial dominion that administrative officials engaged with the regulation of social relations, not in the least with economic dynamics determined by what Weber called the 'spirit of capitalism'. In contrast with Marx, Weber's capitalism was thus located within the realm of the state (for pointers in this direction based on Weber's *Economy and Society* [*Wirtschaft und Gesellschaft*], *see* Tribe 2013). Precisely because of this, the objectives of social policy and administrative actions were situated within a different spectrum from the objectives of the politics of the state, indeed of the tasks of the professional politician. The general ideas of the common good, if Weber can be imagined accepting such a concept, of politics and the public service, respectively, thus diverged and can easily be understood as mutually contradictory under certain circumstances. While politics stuck to the traditional idea of the interest of the national state, the public service operated for the good of a 'social economy' that functioned according to principles of action that changed over time and corresponded to changing norms of rationality.

Wilson's famous 1887 article, likewise, was based on an invited lecture. In his speech, which gained fame only much later as a founding text of academic public administration, he gave some preliminary ideas about how to solve the problem he had identified in his own doctoral thesis entitled *Congressional Government: A Study in American Politics* (1885). As is well known, Wilson identified administrative questions, in contradistinction with constitutional and political questions, as almost technical issues that required a professional capacity to solve them rather than political choice. The modern state as it had emerged since the eighteenth century, with the advent of financial speculation and public debts, required a different outlook on government. Modern politics could no longer be dominated by discussions about constitutional law and forms of rule, but was constrained to redevelop itself along lines that had already been explored overseas by German and French political theorists (Wilson 1887; *see also* Wilson 1892).

The study of administration, not by coincidence the title of Wilson's article, helped to identify the workings of a separate sphere within modern political decision making from which socio-economic renewal independent from political choice or constitutional identity could be developed. It was this insight that arguably lay at the basis of Wilson's later academic works and directly fed into the agenda that set him off onto a career as a professional politician.

While Wilson did not speak the language of power, authority and control, unlike Weber, in arguing for a separation of political from administrative questions, he did firmly locate the realm of the public service within the classical paradigms of the idea of the state. The study of administration was, as Wilson made very clear, a new addition to the science of politics, a new 'branch'. Administrative questions represented the latest generation of innovations within the science of the state and were built on the foundations of constitutional and political questions. By virtue of this new addition it would become possible, he claimed, to reconcile the apparently mutually exclusive concepts of socialism and democracy. The major challenge for modern political science, focused on the new role of the public service thus was 'a question of policy primarily but also a question of organization, that is to say of *administration*' (Wilson 1968: 562).

The pluralist theory of the state and its contexts

While Wilson and Weber positioned the public service within the state not only as a relatively new addition, but also as a somehow politically 'independent' part of the state that functioned according to different principles, other theorists went a step or two further. The very idea that political and administrative questions – the respective realms of power and of socio-economic stability and development – could oppose each other within the state was taken to be a sign of a fundamental misconstruction and a reason for a general rethinking of the state. Much as Speeckaert, as we saw, located a change in political sensibilities around 1900 that inspired new forms of international organisation, a number of political writers in the same period likewise questioned the fundamental principles of the classical theory of the sovereign state and set out to replace them with a new set of principles of an altogether different character.

Political thinkers commonly denoted by the term pluralists associated the rise of new administrative practices and the extension of public services with a process of historical change. Around 1900, following the so-called 'second industrial revolution', European and American cities faced the predicament of rapid urban growth coupled with steepening social inequality and a range of health, sanitation, housing and education problems. Thus, a scenario played out that had been anticipated since the mid-eighteenth century, where the internal architecture and historically entrenched moral principles within commercial societies produced their own limits to further development (Topalov 1994; Hont 2005). On the one hand this crisis was of a socio-economic nature and required municipal governments to expand their activities to deal with the backlash of modern economic growth, thus giving rise to new public goods and services, public–private partnerships and international networks of local officials (Couperus 2011; Gaspari 2002; Saunier 2001). On the other hand this led to more theoretical questions about the relation between authority and responsibility. As Harold Laski argued, legitimate state interference depended on whatever form socio-economic structures took at a certain point in time:

> Men cease to regard slavery as 'natural' as it becomes difficult, by its means, adequately to exploit those forces. The rights of women are transformed from a philosopher's eccentricity into claims socially recognised by the law when the relations of the productive process require that recognition. Education becomes a state-matter instead of one of purely private concern as soon as industry acquires a corps of workers who can read and write. The degree of state-interference in industry depends on the degree to which the defenders held to promote for the productivity of the material forces upon which the society depends. Our attitude to the House of Lords is governed by the view we take of its relationship to the legislation we think desirable; this, in its turn, is involved in a conception of social good, which is born, in predominant part, of our place in the scheme of social relationships. (Laski 1935: 97)

This line of reasoning (which was also endorsed by Speeckaert, we saw, when he associated the rise of international organisations around 1900 with 'new tendencies in historical research') made the legitimacy of state action flexible.[6] It detached the determinants of the progress of humankind from a historical perspective based on the evolution of forms of government and attached it to a sociological or socio-economic outlook on the development of human societies. What the state should do, according to the latter approach, depended not upon its sovereignty and its free will and power to act, but on what the nature of social relations and economic modes of production expected from the state. This was argued by Léon Duguit (on Duguit's intellectual contexts, *see* Laborde 2002), a French public lawyer from Bordeaux who was a pupil of Émile Durkheim:

> What, then, is the state in fact performing? Its function is to provide for certain public needs, which each day are growing more varied, more imperative and more numerous. The whole theory of the state, indeed, is contained in the idea of public need. It is the performance by the mass of officials of their social function – the determination that some public need shall be served by government in a certain fashion. Administrative acts are simply the fulfilment of the statute – the creation of a special situation corresponding to the social need therein satisfied. These are not political in character – that is rather their corruption. They are simply technical operations that, like any other social act, are submitted, for the general validity, to the rule of law, whence their necessity is ultimately derived. (Duguit 1919: *xx–xxi*)

Duguit's inversion of the sovereign political 'will' and historical 'social facts' made the legitimacy of the state dependent upon its activities. Whereas the sovereign in the previous 'theory of the state' had a right to act by virtue of the legal constitutional construction of authority, in the new 'theory of the state' the right of the state was constituted by its activities: the degree to which public services responded to 'public need' confirmed the legal right of authority as a necessary condition for the continuity of the state. In Duguit's view, this was no *political* structure of accountability (such an idea about administrative acts 'corrupted' the proper role of the state), but much more straightforwardly a 'social' one in which the state, like any other (think of private) provider of goods, could be held accountable for the effects of its actions on individual well-being:

> State activity emanates from individual wills, but it is essentially collective in its end; which is the organisation and management of public services. It follows that if the organisation or management of such a server should particularly prejudice a group or individual, the funds of that service should repair the damage so long as the relation of cause and effect between act and damage is traceable. If the service is centralised it falls upon the general funds of the state. (Duguit 1919: 206)

---

6.   This historical view resembles the intellectual framework underlying G. D. H. Cole's 'Guild socialism', which was left unexplored in the most recent study of relations between American progressives and British 'socialist pluralists' (Stears 2002).

These were insights with profound repercussions in practice for the role of the state in modern societies that seemed to fit with a tide of new ideas emerging within various academic disciplines:

> We seem on the threshold of a new political synthesis. The movement towards what is vaguely called the socialization of law is, in fact, symptomatic of something far deeper and wider in its bearings. Distinguished thinkers over the world have not hesitated to examine with scant respect the traditional theory of representative government. Psychologists like Mr Graham Wallas, sociologists like M. Emile Durkheim, political theorists like Mr Ernest Barker, publicists like Mr Herbert Croly and Sir Sidney Low, are all of them insistent that the classic defence of representative government – in the main, a product of the Benthamites – has broken down. The great society has outgrown the mould to which the nineteenth century would have fashioned it. The life of the community cannot longer be contained in or satisfied with its merely political achievement. (Duguit 1919: x)

Thus, Duguit saw his new idea of the state as a reorientation of the science of politics and society. It was no longer possible to merely focus on the 'political achievement' of 'representative government'. The nineteenth-century liberal theory of the state was up for revision because the societies it was supposed to manage had created new dynamics that called for a different role for the state: a role that was both more active and involved in 'public need', but that was also derived from a much less privileged position of the state.

The combination of these two elements fit with the practical challenges and initiatives of the time. Both on the urban level and on the level of international relations it became necessary to contemplate new modes of authoritative action – be it the provision of goods or the maintenance of peaceful global commercial relationships. Here Duguit's ongoing attacks in his written œuvre on the theory of the sovereign state could feed into movements of regionalism and internationalism that reduced the role of the state as the privileged agency for democratic society. At the same time the question (and it was a theoretical as well as a practical problem) was how to conceptualise and arrange authoritative action as subservient to general universal objective norms, or otherwise define external normative criteria that specify what public actors should be doing and how their performance might be evaluated.

The pluralist theory of interstate relations: Theoretical principles

Duguit's transformation of the idea of the state, as it was stripped off the notion of sovereignty, held a certain scope for transpiring into an argument about transnational politics. Whereas the problem in contemplating an international society since the early eighteenth century had been the problem of interstate sovereignty, the so-called modern theory of the state, which was inherently anti-sovereign, could conceptualise the nature of international society according to its own normative register of responsibility, solidarity, accountability and legitimate public action. It did not need to transfer sovereignty somehow from the national to the international level. Rather it had to imagine another 'superior' universal normative basis for legitimate action – interference in existing socio-economic structures.

Indeed, pluralist writers themselves understood that the consequences of their 'sociological' understanding of the relation between society and public provisions was not limited to the realm of the state, but might be translated into a different take on international relations from the one that had become dominant in international diplomacy (Kolb 2012). As such it was welcomed and adopted by certain public lawyers who understood the insights of pluralism as a key to redefining justice, responsibility and solidarity not only as objects of civil and administrative law, but equally as providing higher order norms according to which state interference might be judged across national borders, and based on which interstate relations might be reformed.

One of the key figures in forging this new theory could have become Léon Duguit himself. Yet Duguit passed away just before he made public his views on 'intersocial law' – as he entitled his own vision of international law, presumably to emphasise its different orientation from more conventional approaches to international law. In an article from 1930 in the *Revue Générale de Droit International Public* Marc Réglade restated some of the main elements of how Duguit had approached the renewal of 'international public law' (Réglade 1930).[7]

Réglade first argued that just as the liberal theory of the state of the nineteenth century was no longer satisfactory, so in international relations, the reality of global trade and politics no longer fit with the legal structure of political diplomacy:

> The old individualist subjective conception of right, which no longer suffices in the field of civil law, proves its insufficiency even more in the field of international law. As Mr Politis shows very rightly, the old frames are breaking down in each part. The old conception of the sovereignty of states, understood as moral persons in their fundamental rights, does not permit taking into account numerous limitations that are caused by that same sovereignty and that, by consequence of establishing new rules of international law, multiply themselves. (Translated from Réglade 1930: 382)

It was necessary to redirect the organisation of international authority through bypassing the existing sovereignty of states. One way of doing so, Réglade supposed, might not be to change anything immediately in legal institutional terms, but only to agree generally to suddenly understand state sovereignty in a completely different light as subservient to socio-economic relationships and to some objective set of rights that reflected these relationships. Acting upon this agreement would fit naturally with anticipating the establishment of an international sovereignty that dissolved state sovereignty and would itself be

---

7.   The articles published in a commemorative special issue of the *Archives de philosophie du droit et de sociologie juridique* devoted to the works of Duguit in 1932 provides similar and additional ideas.

equally subservient to the same norms and rights that were dictated by the forms of the modern societies it presided over:

One needs to look for a foundation outside of states that is superior to their sovereignty and that is imposed onto one. That is to say that, if one maintains the idea of sovereignty, one changes the concept. One does not consider it any longer a power that is superior to right itself, but simply one that is superior in relation to subordinate authorities in civil law, only admitting (in the actual state of practical means of realising international law) human institutions that are superior to sovereignty and that can address orders to states. That does not preclude one from being subordinate to international law from now on, anticipating that state sovereignty shall disappear one day and that it subjects itself to another sovereignty, the sovereignty of the international community which, itself, will be only a supremacy, subjected to right, if one arrives at realising a superior authority to that of states in order to apply international law. (Translated from Réglade 1930: 382)

While this approach to realising 'international law' – which at that time was still a much more speculative concept than it is nowadays (Koskenniemi 2001) – seemed thinkable, it would not really be workable:

But, as the doyen Duguit and Mr Politis have said, it will be preferable to exclude the idea of sovereignty because this term has been liable for a long time in the language of public law to bring about considerable delay to the progress of international law and the establishment of international authority within which true peace can be secured for the world. (Translated from Réglade 1930: 382)

The alternative to what otherwise would be a long-term voluntary reform process that, in the light of history, would come with large risks of failure, involved creating an objective principle and conception of international law that would ultimately make it possible to treat policy questions that were formerly part of state politics as technical decision-making problems about the progress of humankind:

It is this doctrinal effort that consists in substituting for the sovereign will and the subjective fundamental rights of states as the foundation of international law, an objective principle that is superior and prior to these that one could call the objective conception of international law. It is this doctrinal effort that Duguit and his school have realised with regard to civil law, and that remains to be accomplished in the field of international law. (Translated from Réglade 1930: 382)

While this argument as a whole perhaps seems not very specific it captures the spirit of the time when these arguments chimed well with powerful critiques of interbellum political diplomacy and were easily connected to the uncertain establishment of the League of Nations, attempts to further develop international law in theory and practice, and the various types of movements that coupled reformist ideas to international associationalism as a way to settle fundamentally the perceived crises of the time (Sick 2002, 2003). The point here, however, is not the sociological analysis of the matches between the international side of the pluralist thought of Duguit and his circle and its contexts, but the simple idea that in this complex of ideas the link between administrative acts and international integration was pretty seamless: within a new regime of international law that followed the dissolution of state sovereignty, decision-making would be depoliticised and would become the object of technical administrative processes.

Peace and administration: A Dutch perspective

Duguit's theory of the state became internationally known, influential and was also often criticised in the years following its appearance. The Dutch law scholar Hugo Krabbe adopted an interesting position among those who were inspired by Duguit's views. In his main work, *The Modern Idea of the State*, Krabbe, as the translators in the preface explained, tried to mitigate the radical aspects of Duguit's theory of the state. Rather than accepting or criticising Duguit's definition of the state as the collectivity of its actions, which was often considered as too radical a departure from the traditional idea of the state, Krabbe sought to preserve Duguit's critique of sovereignty while providing an 'explanation of the modern state in terms of the sovereignty of law' (Krabbe 1922: *lxxxi*). Like Duguit, Krabbe believed strongly that the traditional concept of the state, which combines the notions of sovereign will, centralisation of power and legal personality, had reached its limits and had become obsolete. The good news was that any modern theory of the state had merely to provide a formal description of the practice that had already grown (Krabbe 1922: 3–11):

> Thus juristic dialectic continues to be cultivated, while political practice is already revealing to us the effective truth of an entirely different idea. We must now turn our attention, therefore, to this modern idea of the state, which is absolutely opposed to the of sovereignty, with its postulate of an authority standing outside the law. Thus we shall see clearly that more and more political idea communities are ruled not by external powers, but by inner spiritual forces dwelling in men and working out from them. Everywhere, in every field of social life, appears the new rule, law, with the full certainty that sometime there will fall to his lot over the entire globe that unlimited and undivided rulership which the best of our race at all times longingly desired. (Krabbe 1922: 10–11)

Krabbe explained in his book that in everyday reality the privileged position of the state in society had been transformed. Whereas in previous times the administrative roles of the state could easily be captured under the category of public law, in recent decades a great number of new tasks had become part of what the state did. These new tasks ranged from the provision of clean water, sanitation, education, public transport and telecommunication services and connected the spectrums that had previously been part of state policy and of private market initiative. In legal terms, the realms of public and private law were ever more difficult to separate. Besides this distinction had become less important. Within the new reality, or practice, of the state, any service provided privately or publicly had to be accounted for according to the same norms. Thus, the idea that the state was responsible for the effects of its actions and the idea that the state's actions had to be responses to a public need had in practice already been realised to a large degree (Krabbe 1922: 122–3).[8]

Krabbe's hostility to the traditional theory of the state went back a long time, at least to his inaugural lecture in Groningen of 1894. In his early works Krabbe signalled a division between two models of the state that each came with an outlook on administrative law. First there was the 'police state' (*Politiestaat*), the traditional sovereign state that exercised control through its actions. Then there was the 'State of Law' (*Rechtsstaat*): the state's sovereignty was conceived as derived from public law. Interestingly, the contradistinction between these two models as expressed in the first sentences of his 1894 lecture echoed some famous statements of Woodrow Wilson's published lecture from 1887:

> To the latest tasks of the human sciences belongs the science that deals with the study of the structure of social life, that exposes the organizations that comprise more or less necessarily the lives of men. Only in this century did this science come into being, and only could come into being because only this latest timeframe can identify these many widely branched spiritual organisations, which more than all eventful political occasions at this moment determine the shape of social reality.
>
> Yet there has always been one spiritual organization that has been the object of scientific consideration. This is the society in dependence of which man has always lived, through the existence of which his servitude to an authority that did not derive from him revealed itself most clearly, and which, despite the major sins that have been committed in a name, has always remained recognised and honoured as completely necessary. We know the society under the arbitrary name of: state, and it is from the reality of her personal life that the history of all times is a testimony. (Krabbe 1894: 5–6)

Perhaps Wilson's article on administration and Duguit's theory of the state had a formative impact on Krabbe's later work.

If Krabbe in his main text was concerned mainly with the legal, political theoretical and administrative issues of Duguit's theory of the state, he also touched upon the international dimension in the last chapter of the book (Krabbe 1922: 233–74). It was here that he criticised the existence of an international culture of diplomacy in which power bargaining through alliances and treaties remained

---

8. Many of these developments where governmental and private authorities combined and the range of public services was extended took place at an urban level. It might be said that the welfare state of post-WW2 was preceded by the welfare city of the early twentieth century. It was also in 1928 that a student of Krabbe, named Van Poelje became the first public administration professor in The Netherlands at what is now the University of Rotterdam.

as much in place as it had been in previous centuries and that he cited with great approval the contemporary Dutch law scholar Cornelis van Vollenhoven whose plan to let the Dutch state play a moral leading role (be a 'guiding state', was the expression) involved emphatic support for the establishment of independent international institutions of legal arbitration and political coordination that for the time being should form an external source of power and control over state behaviour (Krabbe 1922: 272–4).

There was something in this last notion that seemed contradictory about Krabbe's argument and it was picked up by John Dewey when he reviewed Krabbe's 'The modern idea of the state'. As Dewey pointed out, the style of Krabbe's work was quite speculative and the book was full of German metaphysical disquisitions about spirit and right that were hard to make sense of (Dewey 1923: 406–7). But also, it was peculiar that an author like Krabbe, whose main principle seemed to be his rejection of the sovereignty of the state, argued for the establishment of international institutions that took over the very sovereign roles that states had fulfilled earlier. The immediate answer, as Dewey pointed out himself, lay in Krabbe's idea that 'the phase of sovereignty is one which the international community must pass through, as did the national community', which Dewey called a form of 'evolutionary fatalism' (Dewey 1923: 407–8).

Dewey's critique of Krabbe resembled W. W. Willoughby's critique of Duguit's works (Willoughby 1920). The problem from an 'American' point of view (*see* Gunnell 2004) was that writers like Duguit, Krabbe and Laski seemed to trade in illogical arguments and had little to offer:

> To these pluralists it seems advantageous either to deny the personality of the state, as is done by Duguit, or, by taking the other extreme, to exalt its personality into the realm of reality but at the same time to assert, that, in this respect, other corporate institutions, whether churches, trade-unions, or functional organizations, have a real personality that should be respected. (Willoughby 1920: 505)

While these operations seemed 'worthless' in the eyes of Willoughby, who deemed Duguit and these other writers 'incapable of distinguishing between the ideas of personality and sovereignty as legal concepts, and [...] questions of actual power, moral right, or political expediency' (Willoughby 1920: 504), F. W. Coker, in a review of a work by Duguit, held that 'Duguit's doctrines have been singularly misconceived in this country', and merited a more contextually and intellectually sensitive reconstruction in the light of other continental European theories of public law not to be mistakenly 'regarded as loose, and as anarchistic in logical tendency' (Coker 1918: 539).

Coker's judgement combines well with Dewey's interpretation that Krabbe engaged with the crisis of 'representative government', which had 'broken down [...] because of lack of technique' and needed 'some method [...] by which organized social interests shall become the law-making bodies' (Dewey 1923: 407).

Conclusion

The argument in this chapter does not prove that pluralist theories of the state and of international relations were actually influential (for instance through analysis of actual impact on their context) in bringing about the shift in ideas that was necessary to allow for imagining a shared European space within which administrative action played a major role. Nor was the aim here to develop a full-blown political theory of international organisation of administrative agencies. What the argument does show, however, is that around 1900 a certain current of political thought that sought to renew the match between representative democracy and society did so by combining reformist views on international coordination (possibly integration) and the provision of public services through administrative agencies. Within the reform vision of these political writers the depoliticisation of a large part of government activities, by turning them into administrative tasks, and the decentralisation and internationalisation of government structures were intrinsically related. Once these wider reform objectives are recognised, the project that Duguit and others were engaged in at the time becomes more interesting and relevant for our day, as not merely an 'anti-statist' theory of politics that called for *more* government. If with regard to ideas on the state Duguit's ideas had a notable impact on the theory of democracy devised by Robert Dahl (Snyder 2007: 118), it might be pertinent to investigate further specific ideas about administration and the public service that were invented around 1900 as a basis for general political theories that have developed since then and others that could have been a response to the challenges of that and our time.

References

Archer, C. (2001) *International Organizations*, 3rd edn, London: Routledge.

Barnett, M. and Finnemore, M. (2004) *Rules for the World: International Organizations in Global Politics*, Ithaca, NY: Cornell University Press.

Coker, F. W. (1918) 'The law and the state by Leon Duguit', *American Political Science Review* 12(3): 536–8.

Couperus, S. (2011) 'In between "vague theory" and "sound practical lines": transnational municipalism in interwar Europe', in Laqua, D. (ed.) *Internationalism Reconfigured: Transnational ideas and movements between the World Wars*, London: Tauris, pp. 67–89.

Descamps, E. E. F. (1894) *Les Offices Internationaux et leur Avenir*, Brussels: Hayez.

Dewey, J. (1923) 'The modern idea of the state', *Columbia Law Review*, 23(4): 406–8.

Duguit, L. (1919) *Law in the Modern State*, translated by Laski, H., New York: Huebsch.

Easley, E. (2004) *The War Over Perpetual Peace: An exploration into the history of a foundational international relations text*, London: Palgrave.

Gaspari, O. (2002) 'Cities against states? Hopes, dreams and shortcomings of the European Municipal Movement, 1900–1960', *Contemporary European History*, 11(4): 597–621.

Gunnell, J. G. (2004) *Imagining the American Polity: Political science and the discourse of democracy*, University Park PA: Pennsylvania State University Press.

Herren, M. (2009) *Internationale Organisationen seit 1865: Eine Globalgeschichte der internationalen Ordnung*, Darmstadt: Wissenschaftliche Buchgesellschaft.

Hont, I. (2005) *Jealousy of Trade: International competition and the nation-state in historical perspective*, Cambridge, MA: Harvard University Press.

Iriye, A. (2002) *Global Community: The role of international organizations in the making of the contemporary world*, Berkeley, CA: University of California Press.

Kolb, R. (2012) 'Politics and sociological jurisprudence of inter-war international law', *European Journal of International Law*, 23(1): 233–41.

Koskenniemi, M. (2001) *The Gentle Civilizer of Nations: The rise and fall of international law 1870–1960*, Cambridge: Cambridge University Press.

Krabbe, H. (1894) *De Werkkring van den Staat*, Groningen: Wolters.

—— (1922) *The Modern Idea of the State*, New York: Appleton.

Laborde, C. (2002) *Pluralist Thought and the State in Britain and France, 1900–1925*, Basingstoke: Macmillan.

Laski, H. (1935) *The State in Theory and Practice*, New York: Viking Press.

MacKenzie, D. (2010) *A World Beyond Borders: An introduction to the history of international organizations*, Toronto: University of Toronto Press.

Mangone, G. J. (1954) *A Short History of International Organization*, New York: McGraw-Hill.

Pagden, A. (ed.) (2002) *The Idea of Europe from Antiquity to the European Union*, Cambridge: Cambridge University Press.

Rabin, J. and Bowman, J. S. (eds) (1984) *Politics and Administration: Woodrow Wilson and American public administration*, New York: Marcel Dekker.

Réglade, M. (1930) 'Perspectives qu'ouvrent les doctrines objectivistes du Doyen Duguit pour un renouvellement de l'étude du Droit International Public', *Revue Générale de Droit International Public*, 37(4): 381–419.

Reinalda, B. (2009) *Routledge History of International Organizations: From 1815 to the present day*, New York: Routledge.

Rosser, C. (2010) 'Woodrow Wilson's administrative thought and German political theory', *Public Administration Review*, 70(4): 547–57.

Sager, F. and Rosser, C. (2009) 'Weber, Wilson, and Hegel: theories of modern bureaucracy', *Public Administration Review*, 69(5): 1136–47.

Saunier, P. -Y. (2001) 'Sketches from the Urban Internationale, 1910–50: voluntary associations, international institutions and US philanthropic foundations', *International Journal of Urban and Regional Research*, 25(2): 480–3.

Sick, K. -P. (2002) 'A Europe of pluralist internationalism: the development of the French theory of interdependence from Emile Durkheim to the circle around Notre Temps (1890–1930)', *Journal of European Integration History*, 8(2): 45–68.

— (2003) 'A new idea of Europe: the liberal internationalism of the Nouvelle Revue Française (1919–25)', *European Political Economy Review*, 1(1): 105–17.

Snyder, R. (2007) 'Robert A. Dahl: Normative theory, empirical research, and democracy', in Munck, G. L. and Snyder, R. (eds) *Passion, Craft, and Method in Comparative Politics*, Baltimore, MD: Johns Hopkins University Press, pp. 113–49.

Speeckaert, G. P. (1957) *The 1978 International Organisations Founded since the Congress of Vienna*, Brussels: Union of International Associations.

Stears, M. (2002) *Progressives, Pluralists, and the Problems of the State: Ideologies of reform in the United States and Britain, 1909–1926*, Oxford: Oxford University Press.

Stillman, R. (1973) 'Woodrow Wilson and the study of administration: a new look at an old essay', *American Political Science Review*, 67(2): 582–8.

Topalov, C. (1994) *Naissance du Chomeur 1880–1910*, Paris: Albin Michel.

Tribe, K. (2014) 'What is social economics?' *History of European Ideas*, 40(5): 714–33.

Voltaire (1752) *The Age of Lewis XIV*, Dublin: Faulkner.

Walker, L. (1989) 'Woodrow Wilson, progressive reform, and public administration', *Political Science Quarterly*, 104(3): 509–25.

Weber, M. (1994) 'The profession and vocation of politics', in Lassman, P. and Speirs, R. (eds) *Weber: Political writings*, Cambridge: Cambridge University Press, pp. 309–69.

Willoughby, W. W. (1920) 'Law in the modern state by Léon Duguit', *American Political Science Review* 14(3): 504–6.

Wilson, T. W. (1885) *Congressional Government: A study in American politics*, Boston, MA: Houghton.

— (1887) 'The study of administration', *Political Science Quarterly,* 2(2): 197–222.

— (1892) *The State: Elements of Historical and Practical Politics: A sketch of institutional history and administration*, Boston, MA: Heath & Co.

— (1968) 'Socialism and democracy', in Link, A. S. (ed.) *The Papers of Woodrow Wilson*, vol. 5, Princeton, NJ: Princeton University Press, pp. 559–62.

Wintle, M. (2009) *The Image of Europe*, Cambridge: Cambridge University Press.

Chapter Seven

Traditions, Bargains and the Emergence of the Protected Public Servant in Western Europe

Caspar F. van den Berg, Frits M. van der Meer and Gerrit S. A. Dijkstra

Introduction

In Chapter Two of this volume, Raadschelders alludes to the transformation of 'administrative staff', serving a ruler, into a 'civil service', serving the people. The central part of this transformation, which took place from the late eighteenth or early nineteenth century onwards, is the institutionalisation of public servant protection, that is, protection against arbitrary dismissal and the security of a salary and pension in money (Weber 1980; Raadschelders and Rutgers 1996). Without the institutionalisation of this protection, the public servant would not have been able to divert his primary allegiance – whether consciously or not – from the ruler to the people. Why and how did the European public servant become protected and how did this alter the definition and expectations of public officials? This is what the present chapter aims to describe and clarify.

As government tasks expanded and state intervention grew from the beginning of the nineteenth century, the need for able, skilled and professional officials who could make and enforce public decisions increased. Personalist appointments based on nepotism and political criteria were seen increasingly as a political and administrative evil in this period, but that did not mean they soon disappeared: in many parts of Western Europe it took a long time to ban this old custom by formal-legal means. Moreover, the *practice* of non-merit selection and promotion on the ground proved to be even stickier: informal rights and obligations, protection and employer-employee relations gave way only very sluggishly to a merit-based and protected bureaucracy.

In this chapter we will examine in depth the transformation process leading to this increasing protection of public servants in The Netherlands, France, the German territories[1] and Great Britain in the nineteenth and early twentieth centuries. We thereby synchronically cover parts of Europe that customarily fall within the Anglo-American, Napoleonic and Germanic administrative traditions (Painter and Peters 2010), and diachronically examine the period that Raadschelders distinguishes as the 'watershed in the development of government' (1780–1820) and the period of further constitutionalisation and parliamentarisation in Western

---

1. By 'the German territories' we mean the twenty-six kingdoms, grand duchies, principalities, free Hanseatic cities and imperial territories that would unite in 1871 to form the German Empire.

Europe (1820–1950). Countertrends of the last three or four decades are not included here as they have been analysed elsewhere (*see* Van der Meer *et al.* 2012).

For the purposes of this chapter, we will look at similarities and differences in the national 'paths' of development. While the Painter and Peters model (2010) offers an apparently neat typology of traditions, it tends to emphasise similarities *within* clusters of countries that 'belong' to a certain tradition and to downplay the similarities *across* countries that have been influenced by specific traditions (Van den Berg 2011). In this chapter, we therefore add a public service bargain (PSB) perspective, which is premised on generic insights from social exchange theories rather than on historically informed ideal-typical constructions. The combination of a historical-institutional and a PSB approach allows for the necessary critical look at these national bureaucracy-shaping paths.

The remainder of this chapter is organised as follows. In the next section we will discuss the PSB perspective in more depth. Next, the cases of The Netherlands, France, the German territories and Great Britain will be examined respectively. In the final section we will draw some comparative conclusions and reflect on the similarities and differences in development lines.

Public sector bargains

Although differing with respect to the exact timing, most European countries have developed an extensive legal framework for their administrative apparatus over the past century-and-a-half. It can be considered a vital component of what has been called a bureaucratic and *Rechtsstaat* revolution in the nineteenth and early twentieth centuries (Van der Meer 2009). This law-making endeavour cast public sector labour relations into a variety of acts, statutes, codifications and legal frameworks. As a result, these relationships became more durable and transparent and the room for arbitrary interpretation of norms and undue actions was limited.

Applying present-day vocabulary to this historical process of law making, we could say it concerned the establishment in laws of existing and emerging PSBs. Hood and Lodge (2006) have expressed and analysed the relationship between politicians and public servants in terms of such PSBs. In their view, this relationship at a given time in a given political system is the outcome of a political exchange between the two actor groups. Such a bargain includes implicit or explicit arrangements in which (1) politicians gain some degree of loyalty, expertise and competency from public servants, and (2) those public servants obtain a place in the government structure, protection, responsibility and rewards.

The bargained outcome of this exchange offers both types of actors benefits that are accepted formally or informally and that guide the behaviour of the actors involved. In this sense, the PSB perspective does not conflate the juridical and the sociological perspectives on political-administrative relations (as the models by Aberbach *et al.* 1981 and Peters 1985 do, *see* Raadschelders in this volume), but leaves room for arrangements that are enshrined in law as well as those that are tacitly understood.

The two broad types of bargains are systemic and pragmatic bargains, where systemic bargains refer to systems where the public servant is part of a broad constitutional or social bargain, and pragmatic bargains refer to systems where the public servant's position is a more or less convenient agency arrangement between politicians and bureaucrats.

The systemic bargain is again divided into two subtypes: the consociational and the Hegelian bargain. In a *consociational* bargain, members of different ethnic, national, caste, racial or religious groups in the public service provide 'glue' to bond the society together. What they get in exchange is a share of administrative power in the form of overt or *de facto* quotas for different social groups. In a *Hegelian* bargain, public servants are not seen as mere agents of politicians, but as quasi-autonomous actors, more like judges, functioning as guardians of the welfare of the society or the constitutional order as a whole. Public servants operate as trustees in exchange for high status and relatively high rewards.

The pragmatic bargain consists of three types: the Schafferian, hybrid and managerial bargains. In the *Schafferian* bargain, public servants provide loyalty and competent service to the government of the day in exchange for trust, anonymity, merit selection and permanent tenure. The *managerial* bargain sits at the other end of the scale, in which bureaucrats accept public blame for errors in exchange for a measure of autonomy within their defined managerial space and perquisites. They represent a blame/credit trade-off for politicians and a blame/autonomy trade-off for public servants. The *hybrid* bargain is between the Schafferian and the managerial PSBs in which politicians share the blame with public servants rather than transferring it to them, and public servants have no defined sphere of autonomy, similar to Aberbach and Rockman's 'Image IV' (Aberbach and Rockman 1988; Hood 2001; Van der Meer *et al.* 2013; Hondeghem and Van Dorpe 2013).

The word 'bargain' suggests (two) directly involved (contractual) actor groups. We argue that this is overly simplistic, given that the bargains do not seem to be confined to just politicians and public servants. Moreover, rather than looking at 'politicians' and 'bureaucrats' as unitary players, the varying rationales and interests within each group should be taken into account. This means first that within the group of politicians, ministers should be distinguished from members of parliament and party officials. Second, there is a relevant distinction between top public servants and the rest. Third, a disaggregation should be made between functionally politicised and functionally bureaucratised senior public servants. In addition, where relevant, we should not exclude trade unions, professional associations, academics (in this case labour and constitutional lawyers and political science and public administration experts). This refinement of the PSB approach is discussed more extensively elsewhere (Van der Meer *et al.* 2013).

The Netherlands

In The Netherlands, an important change with respect to the legal provisions pertaining to public officials took place during the Batavian Republic (1795–1801), when the country was under strong political and intellectual influence of post-revolutionary France. With the establishment of the unitary state and the creation of central government departments at its centre, a new and more bureaucratic public service came into existence.

As a consequence, all public servants received a so-called 'decision of appointment' and a personal salary. The decision of appointment also specified other aspects of the employment, thereby formalising the previously informal notion of permanence of appointment. The introduction of pre-entry exams for the lower ranks is an indication of the increasing importance given to a specified level of competence and, as a result, to merit as a recruitment criterion (*see* Raadschelders in this volume). Still, for many positions at the various levels of the bureaucracy, family ties remained important until well into the latter part of the nineteenth century (Quack 1913).

Only extraordinary circumstances, such as misconduct, extreme negligence of duties, or other strong violations, could lead to dismissal (apart from general cutbacks for financial reasons). In the first half of the nineteenth century, if a minister wished to dismiss an individual public servant, he had to file a motivated request to the king to do so. In that sense public servants were protected primarily by the king and only secondarily by the law. This 'pact' between the king and the public servant, in opposition to the executive politician, resembles the situation in the German lands, which accounts for the initially suspicious attitudes by public servants in those territories against formal public service legislation, which would put an end to the practice that the king could serve as a guarantor of public servants' interests against their direct employer, the executive politician (*see* discussion on German territories, below). At the municipal level, the appointment and dismissal of officials was reserved to the sheriff (*schout*), the mayors (*burgemeesters*), and/ or the municipal council (*raad*), but only after the provincial council had given its approval.

In the first half of the nineteenth century, the relationship between employer (the state at whatever level or in whatever form) and the employee (the public official) still had strong patriarchal, personal and arbitrary features (Van IJsselmuiden 1988). In the higher echelons of the national bureaucracy, however, officials did consider themselves to be servants of the state (Randeraad 1994). Although permission for dismissal was necessary from a higher level, appointment, evaluation, salary and pension depended on the personal ties between the superior and the subordinate and many issues were not legally enforceable. In the early nineteenth century the bargain that was broadly in place was one of paternal care on the part of the superior on the one hand and one of loyalty, obedience, accuracy, secrecy and integrity on the part of the subordinate on the other.

From the middle of the century, the situation changed under the new parliamentary system that developed from 1848 onwards. At the central level the potential patriarchal benevolence of the monarch lost its significance and ministers exercised their powers more fully. The patriarchal element gradually moved to the background, but it was not before 1931 (following the adoption of the Civil Servant Act in 1929; *Ambtenarenwet*, CSA) that a formal law on the dismissal of public servants would take effect (*see* below). Although the need for a professionalised apparatus with duties and rights enshrined in law was recognised, the process of creating the current legal basic framework took a considerable time.

The drafter of the modern Dutch constitution, Johan Rudolf Thorbecke, did emphasise in 1848 the importance of a legal anchoring (Thorbecke 1848) as did most legal experts (for instance Ferf 1864) and public servants (such as Bachiene 1848), but this approach was not adopted in law until much later (Van IJsselmuiden 1988; Stekelenburg 1999). The expectation that legal provisions regulating the position of public servants would lead to higher financial costs was an important reason for parliamentarians not to support this proposal.

The process of obtaining this law and formalising the position of public servants took another fifty years of pressure by public sector labour organisations and constitutional lawyers (Krabbe 1883; Krabbe and Fokker 1897). Even though there were examples in Germany, notably the *Reichsbeamtengesetz* of 1873, of how to establish the arrangements, it actually required the founding of a specific association to attain a public law status for public servants. Interestingly, the resistance did not come primarily from the ministries of the interior or of justice but rather from the wider political classes and parliament for fear of rising costs and increasing centralism.

From 1866 onwards the concern for the rise of political radicalism among the democratically disenfranchised parts of the population helped to get the discussion on defining the rights and obligations of public servants going again. As part of the so-called social question (the struggle for better social and economic conditions and political representation for the underprivileged classes), the government led by Prime Minister Kuyper introduced a strike ban in the Penal Code for public servants and railway employees (1903). While this was part of the same process of recognising the distinctiveness of public service within the total labour force, it would be misguided to see this as the primary and direct motive for a special (public law) status for public servants, as sometimes is argued (*see* for instance Van der Heijden 2008). As has been shown above, the discussion about this special status predated the measure of Kuyper's government by at least half a century. Also, if the ban on strikes was the direct motive for the proposing of the 1929 Civil Service Act, it is surprising that it took twenty-six years before it was actually adopted. Therefore, the ban on strikes might have been helpful but was by no means decisive to the introduction of public service legislation in The Netherlands.

Whatever the direct causes may have been in 1929, the Civil Service Act was adopted. The accompanying by-law (ARAR) for central government was issued in 1931. Likewise a service act was enacted for the military in 1931. Both CSA and ARAR regulate and define the constitutional and legal position of public servants and thus establish what has been called a public law status (Van der Meer 2011; Dijkstra and Van der Meer 2011: Bekke and Van der Meer 2000). In case of labour disputes, from 1931 onwards public servants could turn to administrative law courts instead of using standard civil law procedures (Van IJsselmuiden 1988; Stekelenburg 1999).

Casting these developments in the concepts central to the PSB framework, we observe that the early nineteenth century bargain was mostly agency-oriented and Schafferian, as politicians gave up their right to hire and fire public servants at will and offered protected permanent bureaucratic offices, and the public servants offered competence, loyalty and obedience in return. When ministerial responsibility replaced the royal prerogative in 1848, the position of the competent public servant became more formally institutionalised and the bargain moved towards a more systemic one, with the public servant being part of a fundamental constitutional settlement. This systemic type of bargain was further entrenched as a consociational bargain with the introduction of the CSA in 1929.

France

The case of France is particularly interesting, as it has witnessed many regime changes during the course of its modern institutional history. Although the French administrative system has been described in more recent years as suffering from political–administrative sclerosis (Bréchon *et al.* 2000; Cole *et al.* 2005; Suleiman 2008; Bezes and Jeannot 2011), especially around the turn of the eighteenth and nineteenth centuries it was really one of the hothouses for administrative change, although the remnants of an older, more personalist culture did survive long afterwards.

In the period of the Third Republic, personal relations and social criteria were still of importance, especially for the higher positions, which were in the hands of the political officials. Bezes and Jeannot (2011: 191) state that '[during] the Third Republic many parliamentarians increased their use of the Chamber of Deputies to gain control over and to colonise specific ministries (Interior, *Ponts et Chaussées*, Education) with state field administration'. Some would argue that the personalist character of the France administrative system still exists (Suleiman 2008; Van den Berg 2011). Thus the French system has always been a concoction of a modern, rationalised administrative system with patrimonial features.

What we now see as quintessential features of the French (often but less correctly called the Napoleonic) system were already in existence before the French Revolution. Meininger (2000) points to the creation of a service to perform technical tasks like public works and roads. In addition she points to the creation of a specific corps of civil engineers (1716) and of *École des Ponts et Chaussées*, the first *grande école* (Meininger 2000, Bezes and Jeannot 2011). Although Napoleon did not create these institutions, as some erroneously think, he did follow their example and established many more state training schools for the various corps. His policy aimed at creating a government monopoly on the regular education system from *lycées* to universities and the specialised government training schools (*grandes écoles*) and thus providing government with a meritocratic basis. In addition, emphasis was put on bureaucratic roles, career development in terms of career predictability, and the formation of integrated labour markets operated by the ministries and reinforced by a system of corps, some of which are nested within one ministerial department, and others extending across multiple ministries and agencies. These elements were designed during the Napoleonic period, although most of the measures were implemented in later years (Silberman 1993; Bezes and Jeannot 2011). The advantage of the French corps system is that professional expertise is rewarded and specialists are valued. A disadvantage is the large degree of fragmentation and corps particularism, especially with respect to the power of the so-called *Grands Corps*. Each of these corps had its own labour conditions, management and promotion systems, and of course culture.

From the early days of the nineteenth century, administrative law has been applied to the public officials working for the central state regarding recruitment, career, dismissal, financial position and other rights and duties related to their position in administration. The Conseil d'État served as a disciplinary organ for state public agents, in the sense of a type of professional association upholding the professional norms and standards. As Meininger (2000) argues, public servants, with the exception of clerks, were protected from then onwards from being prosecuted or sued for facts related to their public activities.

During the whole period till the present, the French public service remained highly fragmented due to its proliferated corps system. The existence of cross-ministerial groupings of officials with the same conditions of service and their own particular methods of internal management and promotion led – in the words of Bezes and Jeannot (2011: 183) – to a 'highly Balkanised administration', resulting in diminished effectiveness and efficiency in the public service. Even though the fragmentation and diversity across the corps have been a topic of concern for many years, only in the 2000s were efforts made to curb the powers of the corps and diminish their number.

The necessity of moving towards a general statute for the public service had been discussed as early as the 1930s and led to the enactment of a general public service law by the Vichy regime in 1941 (Baruch 1997; 2000). This law was corporatist in nature and intended to ensure the cooperation of the public servants in terms of political loyalty while having disciplinary authority to control the service. After the war this Vichy law was replaced by a so-called republican law (prepared already by the provisional government established in 1944 and its communist vice-premier Thorez), in which, contrary to the Vichy law, public servants had the right to strike. This legislation however, only concerned central government administration; local government and the health care services had their own statutes dating from 1952 and 1955, respectively.

An important change was made by the socialist President François Mitterrand in 1983 and the communist minister for the public service Anicet Le Pors, who defined three parts of the public service: the central state, territorial government and the health service. The important part of this law was the extension of public servant status to local government and the health care sector and the creation of more rights for public servants. For each of these three branches specific legislation was formulated. Meininger (2000) explains these reforms in part by pointing at the ideological agenda of the Communist Party, which was part of the ruling coalition at that time and delivered the minister for public service affairs.

From the PSB perspective, we see that despite the various regime changes and institutional engineering that have taken place in France since the early nineteenth century, the bargain between politicians and bureaucrats in terms of the protection of the latter has remained remarkably constant: the dominance of administrative law in combination with a relatively high degree of corporal self-regulation places the French bargain from the nineteenth century right through to the late twentieth century in the category of systemic Hegelian bargains, in which the public servant functions as a trustee with quasi-judicial autonomy to protect the constitution and advance general public welfare. While this applies to all of the French career bureaucracy, the bargain for the members of the ministerial cabinets is more hybrid: the cabinet public servant provides competent service with party or personal loyalty to the government or the minister.

Germany and the German territories

Germany is often seen as the country that exemplifies the larger group of administrative systems with a specific public servant status. The crucial element in the German system is the so-called *Beamtentum* or career public service. Besides these *Beamter*, Germany has always known personnel whose employment is arranged according to private law (*Angestellten*, white-collar workers; and formerly *Arbeiter*, or blue collar workers) and the *politische Beamter* who can be dismissed from their (elevated) positions on political grounds and then return to the career bureaucracy either in a regular position or on half-pay (*Ruhestand*) (Fisch 2007). The basic elements of the German career service have been (Goetz 2011):

- Attribution of administrative tasks that involve the use of 'sovereign authority' (*hoheitliche Aufgaben*) to officials rather than contract employees;
- The need for formal educational qualifications, professionalism, seniority and political neutrality;
- Recruitment of officials to one of four public service categories (basic, intermediate, executive and higher services);
- Lifelong tenure;
- Full-time service (meaning officialdom as a principle task);
- The absence of the right to strike.
- A special commitment of public servants to the state, which finds its complement in the special responsibility of the state *vis-à-vis* its officials and their dependents (*gegenseitige Treuepflicht*).

Historically, the establishment of rights and duties in public law was deemed a necessary condition for *Beamter* to perform their job in realising the 'high' (*Obrigkeit*) functions of the state and the exercise of public power with its possibilities of enforcement. Discussing the legal situation of public servants before the creation of the German Wilhelmine Empire in 1871 implies taking into account of the variation in applicable legislation in the separate states. The first example of the conversion of public servants from servants of the king to servants of the state and the definition of the legal position is to be found in the *Allgemeinen Preußischen Landrecht* (1794). In that code's Chapter Ten (second volume), titled: 'Von den Rechten und Pflichten der Diener des Staates', provisions regarding public servants can be found. The first distinctive public service law act (defining recruitment based on merit, employment for life and administrative protection through the courts) was enacted in Bavaria in 1805 (*Hauptlandespragmatik* 1805) by Montgelas. The secularisation of abbeys (*Reichbistumer*) and the incorporation of smaller independent states into Bavaria (1799–1805) made integrating the different public service regulations a primary task for the new Bavarian government; hence the perceived necessity of the *Hauptlandespragmatik*.

This new law was viewed with the highest degree of suspicion by higher public servants who feared to lose their autonomy with the introduction of a bureaucratic public service order (Gotschmann 2007). Only with the rise of an ambitious bourgeoisie did these public servants seek an alliance with the executive (at that time the king).

The legislation in Bavaria was the model for legislation enacted under imperial rule after 1871. An imperial public service law was enacted in 1873. Thus the model of the German *Beamtentum* described above was completed (Grindle 2012). This model was not fundamentally changed after the demise of the Empire and the rise of the Weimar Republic; thus securing a certain level of administrative stability. After Adolf Hitler came to power in 1933 a new law (*Wiederherstellung des Berufsbeamtentums* [Law for the Restoration of the Professional Civil Service], April 1933) was issued. While it nominally emphasised the importance of the *Beamtentum* principle, in reality clauses were included to get rid of so-called 'undesirable' public servants. Thus the public service was purged of real or imagined political opponents and officials with a Jewish background (Goetz 2011). Moreover, in the German Civil Service Law of 1937 a 'civil servant' was defined as 'the executor of the will of the state based on the National Socialist German Workers' Party' (Goetz 2011: 47).

After WW2 the career public service was quickly restored in the Western occupied zones (contrary to the Soviet occupied zone) and to a certain degree purged from overtly national socialist adherents. Many officials could keep their position because the new leadership wanted to retain key public servants, as long as they had not been too directly involved with the Nazi regime. The Allies, too, wanted to leave the basic legal and organisational framework of public administration intact as much as possible (Goetz 2011). The legal position of public servants was reinstituted under public law in 1950 and enshrined in the Basic Law of 1949, with 'its explicit safeguards for the "traditional principles" of the civil service' (Goetz 2011: 47; *see also* Barner 1997).

The German PSB with respect to the protection of the public servant has to be viewed in the light of the distinction between *Beamter* and *Angestellten*. *Beamter* have historically fitted within the category of Hegelian systemic trustees, like their French colleagues, and have to a large degree remained so (despite the radical aberration between 1933 and 1945) up until the late twentieth century. The protection of *Angestellten* historically conforms more to the pragmatic Schafferian bargain, in which private rather than public law applies, the public servant provides loyalty and competent service to the government of the day and politicians give the public servant permanent protected tenure, but in recent decades it has also taken on some characteristics of the pragmatic hybrid bargain.

Great Britain

In line with Raadschelders and Rutgers' (1996) argument, the origins of the British public service can be traced to the royal household (*see also* Page 1992; Van den Berg 2011). The eighteenth- and nineteenth-century process of modernisation in Great Britain was accompanied not only by unprecedented industrialisation but also by the acquisition of a vast overseas empire, which necessitated a substantial expansion of many offices of state and training of officials. British officials visiting China in the first years of the nineteenth century were impressed by the Chinese imperial examination system for bureaucrats and they recommended the establishment of a national training college for administrators of the British East India Company. The modern examination system of the late Qing dynasty was created in 1806 (Elman 2002). For the general British system of governance the situation looked very different.

At the beginning of the nineteenth century, the British state in general and its administration in particular did not resemble the modern bureaucratic state it would be near the end of that century. Offices could be sold from one official to the other, public and private accounts were not necessarily separated, and posts were poorly remunerated, which led to relatively unattractive employment for capable citizens. The lack of ambitious and capable entrants to the public service as well as military debacles laid bare the inefficiencies of the apparatus. In addition, the political benefits of patronage and cronyism diminished and the disadvantages of an 'unprofessional' public service increased.

Together, these conditions and the rising influence of Benthamite utilitarian ideas (Fry 1979) led to the famous Northcote and Trevelyan report (1854), which shaped what came to be known as the Whitehall model and institutionalised elements such as political impartiality, permanence, the internal labour market, elitism and secrecy for the (top) public service (Greer and Jarman 2011).

The work of the conservative politician Stafford Northcote and the public servant Charles Trevelyan has to been seen within the framework of the Victorian modernisation movement where in all fields of life and parts of the public domain initiatives were started to modernise crumbling institutions and rationalise existing services and provide new ones. Interestingly enough, the last recommendation made in the Northcote-Trevelyan report was to develop a civil servile law. It has often been mentioned that the recommendations made in the Northcote-Trevelyan report were implemented only slowly and in a piecemeal way; this particular recommendation took more than 150 years to be put into law (*see* below).

In direct response to the Northcote-Trevelyan report, a Civil Service Commission was set up in 1855. Its main task was to oversee the introduction of a permanent, unified and politically neutral public service. A clear division between mechanical work and policy formulation and implementation was established, which created the mechanical and administrative classes. Since Northcote-Trevelyan, the main course of action has been to ensure a trustworthy and reliable public service. This has been maintained through a combination of the following ideas: (1) civil nature, meaning that public servants are separate both from the military service and from the political institutions of Parliament and Cabinet; (2) permanence, meaning that public servants retain their jobs when there is a change of government; (3) unity, meaning that the public service as an institution is centrally organised and that service-wide rules apply; (4) non-political appointments, meaning that selection and promotion are based on merit rather than party-political patronage or seniority; and (5) anonymity, meaning that public servants have no public profile, but that their ministers are answerable to Parliament and the public (Parris 1969; Dargie and Locke 1999; Fry 2000). The civil service system in Great Britain, based on these principles and shaped by most of the Northcote-Trevelyan Committee's recommendations, proved to be sufficient for nearly a century. During this period, the British public service emerged as a 'unified service with a sense of cohesion and set of common values'.

Given our periodisation we finish at this point in time but some remarks concerning the aftermath of the Northcote-Trevelyan report still have to be made. Recently, we have witnessed a formalisation of the position of these public servants with the adoption of the Constitutional Reform and Governance Act 2010. Most of the substance of this act found its origins in the 2007 White Paper called 'The Governance of Great Britain' (UK Government 2007). With the adoption of this act Great Britain got a public service law for the first time, as Northcote and Trevelyan had proposed as early as 1854.

The British model of public servant protection fits best within the pragmatic Schafferian bargain, a type of bargain that was essentially derived from the British model as such. The public servant gets permanent tenure, the trust of ministers and avoidance of public blame for policy, while giving competence and loyalty to the government of the day in return. Our discussion has also made clear that the reforms proposed in the Northcote-Trevelyan report should in fact be interpreted as attempts to add some elements of a systemic Hegelian bargain, such as elitism and the idea of a separate legal position for the public servant.

Some comparative reflections and conclusions

Over the last two hundred years, the issue of describing, defining and to a certain extent codifying the rights and duties of public servants has been an important undertaking in legislation concerning administrative institutions. During the nineteenth and early twentieth centuries, in most countries the provisions surrounding the position of the public servant were a combination of old and new elements with the new elements continuously gathering strength. By old elements we mean the personalist and patronage type of features of the bargain, and by new elements we mean the rationalised and standardised features of public service arrangements. From our present-day view, we are tempted to put both kinds of features into stark oppositional relation to each other, but it is uncertain whether this was also seen that way by most contemporaries – except, perhaps, in political reformist and scholarly circles.

Conversely, we could frame the history of the protection of the public servant as providing a constant source of tension between on the one hand advocates of a conservative agenda emphasising tradition, order and stability and on the other hand proponents a newer type of society that demanded effectiveness, efficiency, professionalism and security in the sense of predictability. The latter perspective we often find embodied in political reforms and expressed in our present-day literature, while the former perspective – although supported by many at the time – nowadays generally gets considerably less attention.

Historically speaking, it is remarkable that the difference between formal-legal arrangements and informal accepted practice diverged to a considerable extent. We found evidence for two types of divergence between the juridical reality and the actual situation on the ground (*see* Raadschelders, Chapter Two in this volume). The first is that even in the absence of formal-legal protective arrangements in the pre-nineteenth century period, officials could often count on *de facto* protection, given that the behaviour of political administrators was constrained by strong social and moral norms. In our present-day view, such protection would be flawed because it was neither guaranteed nor enforceable, but this only partially diminishes its value. The second is that even after formal-legal protective arrangements were put in place, the informal practice of selection and promotion based on non-merit criteria lingered on for a considerable length of time.

The distinction between the juridical reality and the actual situation on the ground is important for two reasons. The first is that it provides us with the depth and nuance that are vital for understanding the development of norms and values concerning the public servant, which a strictly juridical approach to this topic would fail to do. The second is that it helps us understand that the gulf between juridical and sociological reality has decreased over the course of the period studied, as formal arrangements and informal practice concerning public servants' protection have grown closer towards each other during the nineteenth and twenties centuries.

The PSB perspective has proven to be helpful in understanding the negotiated and interest-driven nature of the legal position of public servants. However, its clear limitation is that it suggests a bilateral bargain between public servants and politicians only. The historical analysis shows, however, that in each of the countries studied, more parties were involved, which had a distinct impact on the institutional, legal and informal balance that was struck with respect to the position and protection of the public servant. For each country, illustrations can be given. In The Netherlands, part of the process of creating public service legislation can only be understood by looking at the increasing social-political questions surrounding the rights of employees. These made the social movement and labour unions a party of some significance. In France, the corps system presented a clear institutional framework in which interests, allegiances and functional tasks were anchored. This system – and the coalitions, resistance and power it could mobilise – has been of great importance besides the more conventional politician-public servant relations. In the German lands, as well as in The Netherlands, the pact between public officials and the monarch in the early nineteenth century complicates the picture of normal employer-employee relations. The reforms of 1848, in which the executive ministers gained more powers and the monarch lost some of his, were perceived by public servants as a deterioration of their protection rather than an improvement in it, since their trust in the political executive was lower than their trust in the king.

In Great Britain, finally, the road to public service legislation has to be viewed from the perspective of a coalition between high-minded reformers within the political-administrative class and influential outsiders wanting to modernise and professionalise the cumbersome national public service that had been left untouched by the constitutional reforms earlier in the nineteenth century.

In other words, since the early nineteenth and throughout the twentieth century, a legally protected status has become an important part of the European conception of the public servant. Despite variation across countries in timing and specific circumstances, a clear cross-national common pattern can be discerned, reflecting mechanisms of social exchange that have come over time to guarantee the protection of the public servant by the politician, in return for competence, loyalty and obedience from the public servant.

130 | The European Public Servant

References

Aberbach, J. D., Putnam, R. D. and Rockman, B. A. (1981) *Bureaucrats and Politicians in Western Democracies*, Cambridge, MA: Harvard University Press.

Aberbach, J. D. and Rockman, B. A. (1988) 'Image IV revisited: executive and political roles', *Governance*, 1: 1–25.

Bachiene, P. J. (1848) *Over de Verantwoordelijkheid en Zelfstandigheid van alle Staatsdienaars*, The Hague: Belinfante.

Barner, C. (1997) 'Remaking German politics in the 1950s: was the civil service an asset or a liability?' *German Politics*, 6(3): 16–53.

Baruch, M. O. (1997) *Servir l'État Français: L'administration en France de 1940 à 1944*, Paris: Fayard.

—— (2000) 'Vichy, les fonctionnaires et la République', in Baruch, M. O. and Duclert, V. (eds) *Serviteurs de l'État: Une histoire politique de l'administration française (1875–1945)*, Paris: La Découverte, pp. 523–38.

Bekke, A. J. G. M. and van der Meer, F. M. (eds) (2000) *Western European Civil Service Systems: Civil service systems in comparative perspective*, Cheltenham/Aldershot: Edward Elgar.

Bezes, P. and Jeannot, G. (2011) 'The development and current features of the French civil service system', in van der Meer, F. M. (ed.) *Civil Service Systems in Western Europe*, Cheltenham/Aldershot: Edward Elgar, pp. 185–217.

Bréchon, P., Laurent, A. and Perrineau, P. (2000) *Les Cultures Politiques des Français*, Paris: Presse de Sciences Po.

Cole, A., Le Galès, P. and Levy, J. (2005) *Developments in French Politics*, Houndsmill Basingstoke: Palgrave Macmillan.

Dargie, C. and Locke, R. (1999) 'The British senior civil service', in Page, E. C. and Wright, V. (eds) *Bureaucratic Elites in Western European States: A comparative analysis of top officials*, Oxford: Oxford University Press, pp.178–204.

Dijkstra, G. S. A. and van der Meer, F. M. (2011) 'The civil service system of The Netherlands', in van der Meer, F. M. (ed.) *Civil Service Systems in Western Europe*, Cheltenham/Aldershot: Edward Elgar, pp. 148–88.

Elman, B. (2002) *A Cultural History of Civil Examinations in Late Imperial China*, London: University of California Press.

Ferf, H. (1864) *Over de Regten der Ambtenaren*, Doctoral dissertation: Leiden University.

Fisch, S. (2007) 'Politische Beamten und Politisierung der Beamten in Deutschland seit 1800', in Manca, A. G. and Rugge, F. (eds), *Governo rappresentativo e dirigenze amministrative (secoli XIX e XX) Repräsentative Regierung und Führende Beambten (19.-20. Jahrhundert)*, Bologna: Il Molino/ Berlin: Duncker und Humblot.

Fry, G. (1979) *The Growth of Government: The development of ideas about the role of the state and the machinery and functions of government in Britain since 1780*, London: F. Cass.

— (2000) 'The British civil service system', in Bekke, A. J. G. M. and van der Meer, F. M. (eds) *Civil Service Systems in Western Europe: Civil service systems in comparative perspective*, Cheltenham: Edward Elgar, pp. 12–60.

Goetz, K. (2011) 'The development and current features of the German civil service system', in van der Meer, F. M. (ed.) *Civil Service Systems in Western Europe*, 2nd edn, Cheltenham/Aldershot: Edward Elgar, pp. 37–67.

Gotschmann, D. (2007) 'An der Schnittstelle zwischen Regierung und Verwaltung: Die Regierungspräsidenten im Koningreich Bayern', in Manca, A. G. and Rugge, F. (eds) *Governo rappresentativo e dirigenze amministrative (secoli XIX e XX) Reprasentative Regiering und Fuhrende Beambten in (19.-20. Jahrhundert)*, Bologna: Il Molino/Berlin: Duncker und Humblot.

Greer, S. L. and Jarman, H. (2011) 'The British civil service system', in van der Meer, F. M. (ed.) *Civil Service Systems in Western Europe*, 2nd edn, Cheltenham/Aldershot: Edward Elgar, pp. 13–37.

Grindle, M. S. (2012) *Jobs for the Boys: Patronage and the state in comparative perspective*, Cambridge, MA: Harvard University Press.

Hondeghem, A. and Van Dorpe, K. (2013) 'Performance management systems for senior civil servants: how strong is the managerial public service bargain?' *International Review of Administrative Sciences*, 79(1): 9–27.

Hood, C. (2001) 'Public service bargains and public service reform', in Peters, B. G. and Pierre, J. (eds) *Politicians, Bureaucrats and Administrative Reform*, London: Routledge, pp. 13–23.

Hood, C. and Lodge, M. (2006) *The Politics of Public Service Bargains: Reward, competency, loyalty – and blame*, Oxford: Oxford University Press.

Krabbe, H. (1883) *De Burgerlijke Staatsdienst in Nederland*, Leiden: S.C. van Doesburgh.

Krabbe, H. and Fokker, E. (1897) 'Welke is de aard der rechtsverhouding van den Staat tot zijn ambtenaren; moet zij wettelijk worden geregeld; en zoo ja, hoe in hoofdzaak?', *Handelingen der Nederlandse Juristen-Vereniging*, (28):136–255.

Meininger, M. -C. (2000) 'The development and current features of the French civil service system', in van der Meer, F. M. and Bekke, A. J. G. M. (eds), *Western European Civil Service Systems*, Cheltenham/Aldershot: Edward Elgar, pp. 188–211.

Page, E. C. (1992) *Political Authority and Bureaucratic Power*, 2nd edn, Wheatsheaf: Harvester Press.

Painter, M. and Peters, B. G. (eds) (2010) 'Administrative traditions in comparative perspective: Families, groups and hybrids', *Tradition and Public Administration*, New York: Palgrave Macmillan, pp. 19–30.

Parris, H. (1969) *Constitutional Bureaucracy: The development of British central administration since the Eighteenth Century*, London: Allen & Unwin.

Peters, B. G. (1985) 'Politicians and bureaucracies in the politics of policy making', in Lane, J. -E. (ed.) *Bureaucracy and Public Choice*, London: Sage, pp. 256–82.

Quack, H. P. S. (1913) *Herinneringen uit de levensjaren van Mr H. P. G. Quack*, Amsterdam: Van Kampen.

Raadschelders, J. and Rutgers, M. R. (1996) 'The evolution of civil service systems', in Bekke, A. J. G. M., Perry, J. L. and Toonen, T. (eds) *Civil Service Systems in Comparative Perspective*, Bloomington, Indiana University Press, pp. 67–99.

Randeraad, N. (1994) 'Ambtenaren in Nederland (1815–1915)', *Bijdragen en mededelingen betreffende de geschiedenis der Nederlanden*, CIX: 209–36.

Silberman, B. S. (1993) *Cages of Reason: The rise of the rational state in France, Japan, the United States and Great Britain*, Chicago: Chicago University Press.

Stekelenburg, M. (1999) *200 Jaar werken bij de Overheid, I, 1813–1940, II, 1940–1998*, The Hague: SDU Uitgevers.

Suleiman, E. N. (2008) *Schizophrénies Françaises*, Paris: Grasset.

Thorbecke, J. R. (1848) *Bijdrage tot de herziening der Grondwet (1848), 19–20*, Leiden: P. H. van den Heuvel.

UK Government (2007) *The Governance of Britain*. Available at http://www.official-documents.gov.uk/document/cm71/7170/7170.pdf (accessed 28 February 2014).

van den Berg, C. F. (2011) *Transforming for Europe: The reshaping of national bureaucracies in a system of multi-level governance*, Leiden: Leiden University Press.

van der Heijden, P. F. (2008) 'Ambtelijke status: Nuttig, noodzakelijk of overbodig?', *Bestuurswetenschappen*, 62(1): 32–5.

van der Meer, F. M. (2009) 'Public sector reform in Western Europe and the rise of the enabling state: an approach to analysis', in Mathur, R. (ed.) *Glimpses of Civil Service Reform*, Hyderabad: Icfai Press, pp. 171–95.

— (ed.) (2011) *Civil Service Systems in Western Europe*, 2nd edn, Cheltenham/Aldershot: Edward Elgar.

van der Meer, F. M., van den Berg, C. F. and Dijkstra, G. S. A. (2012) *De ambtenaar in het Openbaar Bestuur: De inhoudelijke en juridische herpositionering van ambtenaren vanuit internationaal-vergelijkend perspectief*, Leiden: Leiden University Press.

— (2013) 'Rethinking the "Public Service Bargain": The changing (legal) position of civil servants in Europe, *International Review of Administrative Sciences*, 79(1): 91–111.

van IJsselmuiden, P. G. (1988) *Binnenlandse Zaken: Het ontstaan van de moderne bureaucratie in Nederland, 1813–1940*, Kampen: Kok.

Weber, M. (1980) *Wirtschaft und Gesellschaft: Grundriss der verstehenden Soziologie*, Tübingen: J. C. B. Mohr.

Part Four

The Americanised Public Servant in Europe

Chapter Eight

The Role of Foreign Ideas in Identity Formation: The Hegelian Roots of Early American Public Administration

Christian Rosser

Introduction

The connection and interaction of civil society and governmental authorities is of high public and scientific interest today. An increasingly gridlocked political system in the United States and a diminishing democratic responsiveness in the European administrative apparatus are two faces of the same coin. Growing pressures to justify political and administrative practice, the neglect of the public interest, and political frustration are likely consequences of these developments (Elcock 2006). To cope with these problems, scholars of Public Administration[1] may want to look into the intellectual history of their field. The political philosophy of Georg W. F. Hegel seems to offer a starting point and abundant source of inspiration for understanding current issues concerning the public servant's public legitimacy (Stever 1990), the role of public administration as a political integrator (Seibel 2010), or the relationship between bureaucracy and freedom (Tijsterman and Overeem 2008).

This chapter may be considered a humble attempt to join the ranks of these scholars.[2] By examining Woodrow Wilson and Frank J. Goodnow's adaptation of Hegelian political philosophy, this study illustrates how the German idealistic notion of the state and public administration influenced the identity formation of early American Public Administration. It thus provides a historical example of how an idealistic notion may inspire innovative strategies to approach current problems concerning the proper role of public administration. The possibility that most readers will find Hegelian political philosophy a controversial source of inspiration for contemporary Public Administration will hopefully make this chapter all the more interesting.

Spicer (1995: 26) explains that 'public administration came of age as a discipline during the progressive era of American history'. A wealth of publications suggests that progressive intellectuals such as Wilson and Goodnow were influenced by the Hegelian line of thought (e.g. Overeem 2010; Sager and Rosser 2009; Pestritto 2007;

---

1. Upper case letters are used to refer to the scientific discipline 'Public Administration'; lower case letters are used to refer to the practice.
2. Parts of this chapter have been published in Rosser (2010, 2013 and 2014).

Rohr 2003; Miewald 1984). However, little to no primary evidence shows that Hegel's work directly influenced the two scholars.[3] The focus will therefore be on the intellectual relationship between them and Hegel, by comparing their writings with Hegel's *Philosophy of Right*.[4] Moreover, emphasising the importance of second-order reception, it is illustrated that Hegelian political philosophy was handed down to Wilson and Goodnow by scholars like Lorenz von Stein, Rudolph von Gneist, Johann K. Bluntschli, George S. Morris, Herbert B. Adams, John Burgess and Francis Lieber. Finally, by synthesising the resulting interpretations with existing literature on the subject, this chapter may substantiate and sometimes modify the state-of-the-art picture of the progressives' affinity with Hegel.

While the first section of this chapter endeavours to reconstruct Hegel's political and administrative thought, the second section traces the intellectual paths along which the Hegelian doctrine crossed the Atlantic. The reception and adaptation of Hegelian ideas by Wilson and Goodnow are examined in the third section and the reasons for this reception are discussed in the fourth section. The last section addresses the question of why contemporary administrative scholars may want to busy themselves with the Hegelian line of thought.

Hegel's *Philosophy of Right*

Hegel viewed the emergence of the rational state and modern bureaucracy as an inevitable consequence of world history. He thought that each successive historical period, corresponding with a particular form of social organisation, would correct the failures of the previous era. Freedom, both individual and collective, was finally to be realised in the absolute form of community – the rational state. As the rise of the rational state was inextricably linked with the emergence of a formalised bureaucracy, the development of an influential public administration was considered a necessary step towards the institution of freedom. The bureaucracy's task was to protect individual property and promote personal welfare while at the same time assuring that the individual pursuit of happiness did not jeopardise the general good (§ 188).

Bernard Yack (1980: 710) reads Hegel's *Philosophy of Right* as an attempt to 'reconcile the private personal freedom of individuals with the rational and free direction of public affairs'. Proceeding from the most abstract to the most concrete

---

3. While Wilson referred twice to Hegel in his writings, no explicit reference can be found in Goodnow's books, essays, speeches, lecture notes, and letters. The author gratefully acknowledges the help of Kelly Spring at Johns Hopkins University, who has searched for references to Hegel in the collection of Goodnow papers at the Milton S. Eisenhower Library.

4. For the sake of parsimony, the discussion is concentrated on *The Philosophy of Right* and supplemented with secondary literature on Hegel. *The Philosophy of Right* contains the most advanced and complete account of Hegel's political philosophy. Both the original German version (1821) and Knox's translation (1952) are used. The numbers in brackets refer to paragraph numbers. This makes it easier to compare the English translation to the original. All other German sources used in this chapter have been translated by the author.

form of freedom, Hegel started with man's abstract rights to life, liberty, and private property and ended with the state as the 'actuality of concrete freedom' (§ 260). He thought of ethical life (*Sittlichkeit*) as the 'Idea of freedom' (§ 142) and claimed that people attain freedom by pursuing 'the good knowing it to be good' (Knowles 2002: 223). He expected people to identify the state with the realised good (§ 257). Weil (1998: 45) sums it up concisely when he writes that for Hegel 'the State is the will of man insofar as he wills rationally, insofar as he wills free will'.

Hegel believed that people need collective values and norms to understand what is good. Collective values and norms are mediated through the institutions of the family, civil society (*bürgerliche Gesellschaft*), and the state (§ 157).[5] Within the family, husband and wife find freedom from personal isolation through love and concern for their 'natural unity' (§ 163). The life of family members acquires an ethical quality through the transformation of individual self-interest into care for a common purpose. However, as the unity of the family is based on feelings rather than reason, it is inadequate to cover the whole sphere of ethical life. Besides, families dissolve in the case of divorce (§ 176), the children's coming of age (§ 177), or the death of the parents (§ 177) and their members become independent personalities again. They find a 'second family' (§ 252) in civil society (Taylor 1975: 431).

Hegel's notion of civil society may best be understood as a system of needs (*Bedürfnisse*), which is characteristic of the modern economic society. What defines 'human' or 'spiritual' needs as opposed to 'animal' needs (e.g. hunger) is the recognition of others (*Anerkanntsein*) (§ 192). The satisfaction of human needs calls for social cooperation. Increased social cooperation leads to intensified social comparison. Intensified social comparison creates new needs, and so the dialectical spiral goes on. By merging individual needs with the needs of others and by cultivating people's desire for the common good, social relations acquire an ethical quality (Taylor 1975: 432–38). Accordingly, civil society forms a 'system of complete interdependence, wherein the livelihood, happiness, and legal status of one man is interwoven with the livelihood, happiness, and rights of all' (§ 183).

Hegel's normative position on civil society was ambivalent. As will be shown later, he assigned an important role to the institutions of civil society such as the estates (*Stände*) and the corporations (*Korporationen*) in safeguarding self-government and protecting the people against governmental tyranny (Church 2010). Civil society serves another function in establishing personal freedom, especially in comparison to the family. However, because of the inevitable multiplication of needs, civil society entails a tendency towards dissolution (§ 185). Therefore, its members need 'allegiance to a higher community to turn them away from infinite self-enrichment as a goal and hence the self-destruction of civil society' (Taylor 1975: 438). This higher community is to be realised in the rational state – 'the actuality of the ethical idea' (§ 257).

---

5.   This is of course a simplified way of putting it. Hegel takes a long route to arrive from the rational will of people, their individuality, abstract rights, attitudes (e.g. morality), and desires to the institutions by which they become fully developed, free people.

Hegel (§ 269) thought of the state as a self-sustaining whole, a social organism. He used the term 'organism' to illustrate the ripening process of the state to its structured form (i.e. the constitution), wherein the idea of the state realises itself (Böckenförde 1978: 584). By drawing an analogy between the state and an organism, Hegel suggested that the idea of the state determines the character of its constituent parts and that consequently, the whole state represents more than the sum of its parts. The analogy furthermore implied that it made little sense to consider the parts in isolation from each other, since they were by definition dynamically interrelated.

Such espousal of organicism aimed to refute atomistic social contract theories. For instance, Hegel insisted that the 'constitution should not be regarded as something made [...]. It must be treated rather as something simply existent in and by itself, as divine therefore' (§ 273). In this context, it may be interesting to consider Hegel's reading of Montesquieu. Even if in principle he praised Montesquieu's *trias politica*, for it contained 'the essential moment of difference', he rejected the 'false doctrine of the absolute self-subsistence [*Selbständigkeit*] of each of the powers against the others' (§ 272). In analogy to an organism consisting of different limbs serving the same purpose, Hegel accepted only an inner differentiation of organs within the unity of the state (§ 276). To use Holmes' (1995) terms, Hegel advocated 'positive constitutionalism', emphasising harmoniously cooperating powers to enable government, while he refuted 'negative constitutionalism' in the sense of checks and balances (Overeem 2010: 34). Hegel (§ 272) argued that if the legislature and the executive were arranged as independent, competing powers to ensure their mutual limitation, each branch would endeavour to obtain superiority over the other branch. This struggle for supremacy would inevitably lead to the destruction of the state's organic unity.[6]

As an alternative to Montesquieu's doctrine, Hegel postulated a differentiation between the legislature (§§ 298–320), the executive (§§ 287–97), and 'the Crown' (§§275–86). While he regarded the legislature as the 'power to determine and establish the universal' (§ 273), he depicted the executive, including the judiciary and the bureaucracy, as the branch that applied the universal rules to particular cases. Finally, he described the constitutional monarch as the 'individual, the ethical subject who unites universality and particularity in his social person' (Knowles 2002: 326). Hegel (§ 273) explicitly wrote that 'in the crown, the different powers are bound into an individual unity which is thus the apex and basis of the whole, i.e. of constitutional monarchy'. Being the 'apex of an organically developed state' (§ 286), the monarch was supposed to cut 'short the weighing of pros and cons' (§ 279) and take 'ultimate decisions' (§ 273). It thus becomes apparent that he

---

6. It should be mentioned that the rejection of Montesquieu's *trias politica* was by no means limited to nineteenth-century organic political theory. It was already common among German administrative authors of the eighteenth century such as Johann H. G. von Justi. A key difference between Hegel's rejection and that of Justi is that the latter criticised Montesquieu for challenging the virtue of the absolute monarch. As it was common among German state theorists of the eighteenth century, Justi used mechanic metaphors to reject Montesquieu (Stollberg-Rilinger 1986).

identified the crown (i.e. the sovereign) not only as an executive, but also as a legislative body (Yack 1980).

Although these quotations may suggest that Hegel was in favour of an almost omnipotent monarch, his normative stance towards the power of the crown was ambivalent. He believed that the will of the monarch ought to depend largely on the expertise of high-echelon public servants (§ 300). Besides being the advisory committee for the crown, they had to superintend 'the activities of corporations in civil society so that the latter do not degenerate into egoistic interest groups' (Shaw 1992: 382). As a mediating organ between the monarch and civil society, it was the bureaucracy's task to guarantee that good laws are executed in order to promote the welfare of the whole society. There is no doubt that Hegel saw public administration as the most important governing organisation in the rational state. Accordingly, he stated that 'civil servants and the members of the executive constitute the greater part of the middle class, the class in which the consciousness of right and the developed intelligence of the mass of the people is found' (§ 297). The bureaucratic *esprit de corps*, Hegel argued, would ensure that civil servants were in fact guardians of and servants to the common will, rather than rulers of that will (Taylor 1975: 433).

Despite his remarkable confidence in the body of public servants, Hegel saw the possibility of self-interested bureaucrats and thus the threat of an overwhelming bureaucracy. To avoid this threat, he once more stressed the 'monarch's generally accepted position as the sovereign, whose will legitimises the act of the state, places a severe limit on the ambitions of bureaucrats and politicians' (Yack 1980: 715). Hegel also relied on the 'the authority given to societies and corporations, because in itself this is a barrier against the intrusion of subjective caprice into the power entrusted to a civil servant' (§ 295). Finally, he put strong emphasis on the ethical education of public servants. He wrote that 'the fact that a dispassionate, upright, and polite demeanour becomes customary is partly a result of direct education in thought and ethical conduct' (§ 296). It was because of their thorough ethical education, Hegel believed, that public servants would internalise and act upon the idea of the state as the absolute form of community. This explains why Hegel called the body of public servants 'universal class'. His emphasis on moral education also helps explain why he believed that public servants would keep their personal and social interests apart from their professional life and fulfil their mandate independently of particular interests (§ 294). Finally, several organisational features were to serve as additional barriers against the potentially overwhelming power of the administrative apparatus (§§ 291–95). Among these features, the most important were the meritocratic recruitment of public servants as well as the formalisation, professionalisation and hierarchical organisation of the bureaucracy.

Hegel wanted the monarch to be held accountable in a similar way as he insisted on the social control of the bureaucracy. Popular control was to be carried out by the deputies of the estates. As an element in the legislative power, the estates were supposed to mediate between the sovereign and the people. In their function as a 'mediating organ', the estates prevented both 'the extreme isolation of the crown, which otherwise might seem a mere arbitrary tyranny, and also the isolation of the particular interests of persons, societies, and Corporations' (§ 302). Hegel differentiated between two estates, apparently using the term 'estate' as synonym for 'class'. On the one hand, the landed aristocracy or, as he called it, the agricultural class was by nature a support of both the monarch and civil society and was therefore 'entitled to its political vocation by birth without the hazards of election' (§ 307). On the other hand, the business class – the urban bourgeoisie – could 'enter politics only through its deputies' who were then allowed to participate at the 'summons of the crown' (§ 308). These deputies were elected not by the general public, but by the members of commercial and municipal associations. As the public servants, the deputies of the business class had to be chosen on account of their qualification. In summary, Hegel envisioned two ways by which government, consisting of the monarch and the bureaucratic executive, should be controlled. Internal control was to be achieved through the thorough education of public servants and several organisational arrangements of the bureaucracy. External control was to be exercised by elite members of the institutions of civil society.

The aim of this section has been to illustrate Hegel's reflections on the state and public administration, which have elicited both admiration and rejection from students of several political colours – fascists, conservatives, statists, liberals, communitarians and Marxists. In his controversial essay *The End of History*, Fukuyama (2006: 108) claims that 'for better or worse, Hegel's historicism has become […] inseparable from the modern understanding of man'. Although it may be doubted whether Hegel's deterministic and often metaphysical notion of progress gives way to an appropriate description of our contemporary understanding of man, it seems a fitting starting point for the discussion of the late nineteenth-century administrative discourse on both sides of the Atlantic.

The Hegelian doctrine arrives in the United States: Two waves of German influence

Gunnell (1993: 34) explains that Lieber and Bluntschli represent a 'first wave of German influence' on early American political science, including Public Administration. Both German authors, who maintained close intellectual contact, were acquainted with Hegel's political philosophy. Confident that the state was neither a 'work of contract by individuals' nor a 'machine', Lieber (1838: 183) argued that the 'state is a form and faculty of mankind to lead the species towards perfection – it is the glory of man'. He thought of the state as a sovereign organism, the purpose of which was to 'obtain the highest form of humanity' (Gunnell 1993: 29). In a similar vein, Bluntschli (1875: 18) wrote that 'the state is by no means a lifeless instrument, a dead machine, but a living and therefore organic being'. He claimed that instead of explaining the evolution of the modern state on the basis of social contract theories, one should trace the state back to its intrinsic desire for the general weal (Bluntschli 1875: 63).

In line with the Hegelian approach, Lieber and Bluntschli emphasised public administration as an essential organ of modern government. For instance, Lieber

(1835: 63) stated that the liberty of a modern nation depends at least 'as much upon the administrative branch as upon any other'. Bluntschli's (1876: 468) emphasis on an influential administration is even more obvious. He used three terminological opposites – 'constitution vs administration', 'legislation vs administration', and 'politics vs administration' – in analysing the proper role of the state's different functions. The administration represented the organ of the state being in constant contact with the people. It was not subordinate to the legislature, since it had to compensate for the gradualness of legislation and policy making. Bluntschli attributed public administration 'a separate special place within the state' (Overeem 2010: 51). He saw the public servant as a guardian and promoter of the general will, exclaiming that 'the state and the society require his service and help and are grateful for it' (Bluntschli 1876: 491).

Lieber and Bluntschli seem to perfectly suit the Hegelian approach. However, it would be inaccurate to draw too close an intellectual connection between them and Hegel (Gunnell 1993: 32–3). It was indeed not uncommon for the post-Hegelian generation of German state theorists to applaud Hegel's emphasis on the ethical significance of the state and at the same time reject his views for being too philosophical and insufficiently historical. Lieber (2000 [1859]: 5–6) and Bluntschli (1875: 76–9) accused Hegel of having interpreted the state too much as a logical abstraction and not so much as practical reality. They shared the intention of combining philosophical (i.e. abstract) and historical (i.e. practical) reasoning in order to synthesise political theory and practice (Gunnell 1993: 27–32). Bluntschli even praised Lieber as one of the first spokesmen of the peaceful alliance of the historical and philosophical methods.

Two other scholars who had considerable influence on early American Public Administration were Stein and Gneist (Miewald 1984; Fries 1973). Stein (1869: 3–12), who integrated his ideas on society with the Hegelian concept of the state, aimed at a systematic substantiation of the organic analogy when he interpreted the state as an abstract personality consisting of the self (*ich*), a will (*wille*) and deed (*tat*). While he conceived of the sovereign – a constitutional monarch with both executive and legislative functions – as the state's self-conscious self, he viewed the constitution or legislation as the state's will and the administration as its deed. The administration, determined by the state's conscience (*Gewissen*), was to protect the autonomous sphere of society while at the same time ameliorating social inequalities through socio-economic policies. He thus referred to the 'legitimation of the state not so much through its constitution as through the active, well-fare-providing administration'(Casper 1989: 325). Accordingly, Stein (1870: 3) introduced his *Handbuch der Verwaltungslehre* by stating that understanding public administration had become more important for the smooth functioning of the modern state than understanding the dynamics of constitution making.

Throughout his whole career, Gneist occupied himself with the antagonism between the state and society. The theoretical framework that he adopted to solve this antagonism was derived largely from Hegel and Stein (Hahn 1977: 1362). Gneist assumed that the mediation between state and society would be ascertained by the public service. He expressed confidence in the administrative elite, which consisted exclusively of members of the propertied classes, for they were 'elevated above the innate lure of self-interest that seeks only profit and possessions, pleasure and power' (Hahn 1977: 1364). At the heart of his theory lay the belief that popular participation in government would become unnecessary once an autonomous, formalised and rule-bound administrative apparatus had been developed (Pope 1987: 61). Gneist's writings were especially appreciated by Goodnow (2003 [1900]: 5) for whom the German legal scholar was 'almost the first student of note to call attention to the importance of administrative institutions'.

The second wave of German influence 'was a consequence of the matriculation of thousands of young American scholars in German universities' (Fries 1973: 392). The initial unavailability of a graduate education in the United States and the relative ease with which academic degrees could be attained in Germany were strong incentives to undertake a sojourn to Germany, all the more as the reputation of German academic titles promised a competitive advantage in the American academic job market (Adcock 2003: 486). It may thus not surprise that several of Wilson and Goodnow's teachers had spent some time in lecture halls at Halle, Heidelberg, or Berlin.

For instance, we know that Wilson attended George S. Morris' lectures on the philosophy of the state while he was receiving his graduate training at Johns Hopkins University (Link 1968a: 335). Morris (1885: 163) frequently referred to the *Philosophy of Right*, which he 'regarded as representing the high-water mark [...] in the treatment of the philosophical conception of the state'. Herbert B. Adams served as another essential source of inspiration for Wilson's work (Stillman 1973: 582). As Adams had completed his doctorate under Bluntschli (Fries 1973: 394), it is not surprising that his account of American history contains many organic metaphors.

Goodnow's mentor at Columbia, John W. Burgess, was also among the students who had studied in Germany – for some time under Gneist (Mahoney 2004: 134). After his return, Burgess inherited Lieber's chair as professor of political science, international law and history at Columbia (Farr 1995: 148). Burgess (1897: 403) defined history as the 'progressive realisation of the ideals of the human spirit in all of the objective forms of their manifestation' or, alternatively, as the record of 'progressive revelations of the human reason, as they mark the line and stages of advance made by the human race towards its ultimate perfection'. Considering these exemplary quotations, it becomes apparent how Hegelian Burgess' terminology actually was.

However, Burgess (1890: 84–5) expressed similar reservations to Hegel to those of Lieber and Bluntschli, regretting that the Hegelian doctrine had remained too abstract in terms of its exclusive focus on the idea of the state. He insisted that a distinction be made between the idea of the state (the realm of philosophy) and its concrete manifestation (the realm of history). According to Burgess (1897: 408), the philosophical or 'speculative element in political science' needed to be 'regulated by the historical component', i.e. the analysis of practical reality. He nevertheless arrived at the conclusion that the philosophical reasoning remains the most important aspect of political science, 'because it lights the way of progress, and directs human experience towards its ultimate purpose' (Burgess 1897: 408). He had no doubt that 'the perfection of humanity' was inextricably linked with the state (Burgess 1890: 85). On this point, he obviously agreed with Hegel.

As diverse as the theories of the above-mentioned scholars were, their ontological and epistemological foundations resonate with the Hegelian approach, emphasising the centrality of the state, public administration as the key governing organisation and the organic notion of the state. Stressing the 'historical side' of Hegel's writings, they brought the Hegelian approach to Wilson and Goodnow's attention in a compact, modified form.

Examining the Hegelian intellectual background of Wilson and Goodnow

Analysing Wilson and Goodnow's reliance on German sources helps clarify their visions of the proper relation between constitutional, political and administrative functions of government. Their remarkably similar reception of Hegelian political philosophy will be examined in the following, starting with Wilson and continuing with Goodnow.

Woodrow Wilson

In line with the Hegelian approach, Wilson declared that the state was the 'eternal and natural embodiment and expression of a form of life higher than that of the individual: that common life which gives leave and opportunity to individual life, makes it possible and makes it full and complete' (Link 1970: 13). He differentiated between the era of constitution and the era of administration as two distinct periods of the state's organic development. In an early *Essay on Administration* (1885) he noticed that:

> [the] period of constitution-making is passed now. We have reached new territory in which we need new guides, the vast territory of administration. All the enlightened world has come along with us into these new fields, and much of the enlightened world has realised the fact and is preparing itself to understand administration. (Link 1968b: 52)

Here he may have paraphrased Stein's *Handbuch der Verwaltungslehre*, which was mentioned in the previous section. At another point, Wilson underlined the historical relativity of the state's constitutional order and the historical importance of public administration by stating that the 'philosophy of any time is, as Hegel says, 'nothing but the spirit of that time expressed in abstract thought'; and political philosophy, like philosophy of every other kind, has only held up the mirror to contemporary affairs' (Link 1968b: 361).

Wilson aimed at a reinterpretation of the constitutional order of the United States, which may be exemplified with his rejection of Montesquieu's *trias politica*. He thought that his compatriots had followed Montesquieu as 'excessively practical people' rather than following him as 'philosophers' (Link 1968b: 51). These practical people had not seen that:

> Montesquieu did not hit upon exactly the right devices for practical popular government. When he said that it was essential for the preservation of liberty to differentiate the executive, legislative and judicial functions of government, he was thinking of an undemocratic state in which the executive ruled for life by hereditary right and not by virtue of popular election [...]. And he did not say that it was essential to liberty to separate, to *isolate*, these three functions of government. (Link 1968b: 51)

Wilson later resumed his criticism of Montesquieu by saying that the 'object sought is, not the effectuation of a system of mechanical, or artificial, checks and balances, but only the facilitation and promotion of organic differentiation' (Link 1969: 142). He was convinced that the American government of the late nineteenth century could not intervene according to contemporary societal needs because of strict adherence to constitutional principles. Wilson (1892: 592) therefore concluded that 'under our own system we have isolation plus irresponsibility, – isolation and therefore irresponsibility. At this point [...] our government differs from the other governments of the world. Other Executives lead, ours obeys'. These statements suggest what shall become clear in the remainder of this section: Wilson wanted above all to strengthen the national executive and administration.

Dealing with the differences between law-giving and administrative functions of the state, Wilson drew repeatedly on German sources. In *The Study of Administration* (1887: 210; *see also* Link 1968b: 371), for example, he referred to page 467 of Bluntschli's *Politik*. Wilson wrote that 'Bluntschli bids us separate administration alike from politics and from law. Politics, he says, is state activity in things great and universal, while administration, on the other hand, is activity of the state in individual and small things'. Even if this text passage may imply so, it was neither Bluntschli's nor Wilson's intention to promote an apolitical administration. On the same page from which Wilson's quote was taken, Bluntschli (1876: 467) discussed Stein's distinction between will and deed and concluded that it was inappropriate to 'parallelise administration and legislation with deed and will as if the administration had no will of its own'. Wilson seems to have agreed with Bluntschli when he claimed that Stein's 'distinction between Will and answering Deed' did not apply to the American context. The distinction had to be made instead between 'general plans and special means' (Wilson 1887: 211; *see also* Link 1968b: 372). The American public servant was supposed to have 'a will of his own in the choice of means for accomplishing his work' (Wilson 1887: 211; *see also* Link 1968b: 372). By contradicting Stein, Bluntschli and Wilson underlined the political function of public administration.

Four years after the publication of *Lehre von Modernen Staat*, Wilson had come to appreciate Stein's reflections on politics and administration. At that point, he interpreted Stein's distinction between will and deed as an analytical distinction. Wilson explained that even though the 'theory really predicates a division of organs, based upon a difference of a radical sort in the functions', there is in practice only an 'organic differentiation' (Link 1969: 383). He pictured the administration as a governmental organ that was in no sense subordinate to the legislation. According to Wilson, the administration could not wait for the legislature to enforce the state's will. While law was 'always a summing up of the past', public administration was 'always in contact with the present' (Link 1969: 138). Since both the legislature and the administration had to do with the 'active promotion of the ends of the state', they both were sources of law (Link 1969: 115). It seems plausible that the reading of Stein convinced Wilson to think of public administration as a political organ with far-reaching competences. He even quoted Stein in German to underline the political significance of public administration: '*Die Idee des Staates ist das Gewissen der Verwaltung* [the idea of the state is the administration's conscience]' (Link 1970: 28–9). Regarding concrete organisational aspects of public administration, Wilson pictured a body of public servants that was close to the concepts of Hegel and Bluntschli. In a nutshell, Wilson conceived of the administration as a science-based, formalised, hierarchical and meritocratic organisation. He assumed that the thorough training of the administrative elite would lead to a body of altruistic, dutiful public servants who would serve and promote the common will (Link 1968b: 375–6).

Frank J. Goodnow

Goodnow (2005 [1897]: 4) also distinguished between the 'constitutional era' and the 'age of administrative reform'. He lamented that Americans had usually sought their conception of liberty 'through speculation rather than observation' (Goodnow 1916: 9). Rather than 'the theory of evolutionary development' (Goodnow 1916: 18), Americans had adopted the natural rights doctrines of Rousseau and Montesquieu. These doctrines, Goodnow (1916: 18) continued, 'presupposed almost that society was static or stationary rather than dynamic or progressive in character'. Since American society was in reality dynamic in character, the ahistorical assumptions of 'old individualistic philosophy' had to be replaced with the sound epistemological basis of organic state theory. Accordingly, Goodnow's (1916: 10) understanding of democratic citizenship was informed by positive liberty, which was defined in terms of self-realisation and social expediency. He was persuaded that 'greater emphasis should be laid on social duties and less on individual rights' (Goodnow 1916: 31).

In this context we find the clearest indication of Goodnow's familiarity with Hegel's work. Goodnow (1916: 29) explicitly wrote that one should not take the 'view that the individual man lives for the state of which he is a member and that state efficiency is in some mysterious way an admirable end in and of itself'. It seems that his interpretation of the state resonates with that of the post-Hegelian generation of German scholars such as Lieber and Bluntschli. Just as they were, Goodnow was more interested in the historical or practical reality of the state than in its metaphysical purpose. But even if he contested the Hegelian approach for being too abstract or metaphysical, we still discover an elective affinity between

Goodnow and Hegel. In line with the Hegelian line of thought, Goodnow saw the state as an agent for the moral betterment of people (Pestritto 2007: 44–6).

Like Bluntschli, Goodnow (2003 [1900]: 9) observed that the organic state incorporated psychological and material forces into a consistent whole. Drawing the analogy further, he designated the two functions of expressing and executing the state's will 'respectively as Politics and Administration. Politics has to do with policies or expressions of the state will. Administration has to do with the execution of these policies' (Goodnow 2003 [1990] [1900]: 18). The organic distinction between politics and administration was meant as an alternative to Montesquieu's 'mechanic' *trias politica* (Overeem 2010: 67). Goodnow (2003 [1900]: 11) praised Montesquieu for his principle of distinguishing governmental functions. Like Wilson, Goodnow (2003 [1990]: 14) was nonetheless convinced that governmental responsibilities had been blurred because of too rigid an adherence to the separation-of-powers doctrine.

Goodnow distinguished between governmental *functions* and *authorities* (Overeem 2010: 67). He argued that the political function of the state should not be performed exclusively by the legislative branch. Depending on the level of abstraction, it was to be performed either by the people, the legislative, or the executive. Whereas the 'constitution-making authority, that is, the people', should express the will of the state 'as to the form of the governmental organisation and the fundamental rights of the individual', the legislative was to be entrusted with the expression of general rules (Goodnow 2003 [1990] [1990]: 17). The executive, on the other hand, was supposed to formulate the detailed and particular will of the state 'through the issue of ordinances' (Goodnow 2003 [1990] [1990]: 17). In a similar vein, Goodnow attributed three different administrative functions to different organs of the state. Interestingly, as did Hegel, he regarded the judiciary as part of the executive branch, explaining that the judicial authorities 'apply the law in concrete cases where controversies arise owing to the failure of private individuals or public authorities to observe the rights of others' (Goodnow 2003 [1990]: 17). Goodnow (2003 [1990]: 17) added that executive authorities should be concerned with 'the general supervision of the execution of the state will' and the actual public administration with the detailed implementation of the state will. The administrative authorities, he continued, were 'attending to the scientific, technical, and, so to speak, commercial activities of the government' (Goodnow 2003 [1990]: 17).

Finally, and like Wilson, Goodnow envisioned similar organisational arrangements for organising the administrative apparatus. For instance, Goodnow (2003 [1990]: 7) argued that 'considerable permanence of tenure' was to be given to public servants. Moreover, they were supposed to be 'selected on account of fitness for their positions'. Not only would a scientific education and a meritocratic system of personnel recruitment ensure the expertness of public servants, but also their efficiency and impartiality (Goodnow 2003 [1990]: 91). Pestritto (2007: 49) explains that the 'key to trusting administrators with the kind of discretion that Goodnow envisioned was his profound faith in the expertise and objectivity of the administrative class'. As will become clear in the remainder of this section, Goodnow attributed a decisive role to the body of public servants in solving the antagonism between government and an increasingly modernising society.

As a preliminary conclusion, one may say about Goodnow what Rohr (1986: 63) said about Wilson. Both scholars interpreted the constitution as 'the skeleton frame of a living organism' – a living organism that grows. They did not agree with the traditional American idea about the constitution as a static set of principles to ensure strictly limited government. Both authors aimed at an 'ambitious reinterpretation of the constitutional order', which included an 'expansion of federal government responsibility and action with advances on social policy and political-economic policy, and changes in the executive organisation of government and the operation of administrative systems' (Cook 2006: 328–9). It appears that both Wilson and Goodnow took sides with the post-Hegelian generation of German organicists like Bluntschli, Stein and Gneist in emphasising the developing nature of the constitutional order and the leading role that public administration had begun to play at the dawn of the twentieth century.

Hegelian political philosophy as an answer to challenges of the progressive era

One of the most important conditions for appreciating German state theory in the United States was the rapid convergence of the social landscapes of industrial capitalism on both sides of the Atlantic (Rodgers 1998: 33–51). During the late nineteenth century, the processes of industrialisation, urbanisation and democratisation led to increasing social tensions. Not only in Germany, but also in the United States, the calls for a more visible hand of the government grew ever louder. In comparison to Germany, the hand of the American government became not only more visible, but also more corrupt. Even if it remains unclear today whether corruption was bad for the growth of the American economy (Menes 2006: 67), it is important to note that around the turn of the twentieth century, progressive intellectuals believed that the corrupt relations between businessmen, politicians and public servants had harmful effects on the economy and society.

Goodnow (2003 [1990]: 192) and Wilson (Link 1968b: 363) regretted that favouritism in personnel recruitment had fostered an inefficient, incompetent and ultimately corrupt administration. As a remedy against the corruption of the spoils system, they hoped to insulate public administration from partisan politics. Using Goodnow's (2003 [1990]: 87) words to speak for both of them, legislators and high executive officers, 'to whom is entrusted the general execution of the law', should be kept accountable by voting them out of office. Well-educated, professional and tenured public servants, on the other hand, were supposed to guarantee the efficient implementation of public policy and safeguard the common good.

More generally, the Hegelian account pictured the state as the embodiment of ethical life and social responsibility and thus endorsed the possibility of positive liberty. It also endorsed the conviction that an enhanced capacity in the executive and public administration would serve as a remedy to the challenges of an industrialising society. By strengthening the executive in general and public administration in particular, progressive intellectuals sought a more interventionist government role. Furthermore, they considered it a historical necessity, i.e. a natural result of the state's organic development, that an influential administration be installed. They believed that an expansive administration would save the people from the bad influence of egoistic individualism, which was considered to be prevalent in the American *laissez-faire* economy. In his respect the Hegelian line of thought offered American progressives an alternative to the intellectual tradition of natural law and social contract theories.

Rohr's (2003: xxii) verdict about Goodnow seems to apply to Wilson as well: their work was grounded in the Hegelian philosophy of the state. Unlike Hegel, however, progressive intellectuals in the United States wanted to solve the dilemma of reconciling enhanced government capacity with *democratic* control of public action (Lynn 2001: 148). We should therefore be careful in drawing too close an intellectual connection between Hegel, Wilson and Goodnow. Obviously, Hegelian philosophy was only a part of their intellectual mix of political and administrative ideas – a part that had to be stripped of its authoritarian traces in order to be blended into a larger progressive agenda. Paradoxical as it may sound, Wilson and Goodnow attempted to separate politics from administration in order to combine efficient government intervention with democratic accountability. As a science-based, technical, meritocratic, professional and politically neutral organisation, public administration was reconcilable with democratic government, for it had nothing to do with political struggles.

Why should we bother?

Stillman (2001: 252) holds that a 'greater inclusion of historical research offers the field [of Public Administration] a better sense of what it is, why it exists, and what its fundamental human and societal purposes are'. Spicer (2008: 66) also calls 'for a more philosophical, historical, and comparative approach to public administration enquiry and education'. The findings of this chapter may contribute to furthering our understanding of the general normative orientation of early American Public Administration.

The development of Continental European Public Administration is often interpreted as fundamentally different from the development of the American field of study (Stillman 1997; Painters and Peters 2010; *see* Sager *et al.* 2012). Such narratives of European and American 'traditional flavours' (Rutgers 2001) arguably play an important role in the identity formation of a European administrative identity, since identity rests not only upon the inclusion of 'domestic' values (what belongs to us?), but also on the exclusion of 'foreign' values (what does not belong to us?). Considering the current dominance of American books and articles in administrative research, European scholars are probably forced to orient themselves explicitly or implicitly towards American scholarship in establishing a proper European administrative identity. This chapter suggests that approximately one decade ago, quite the reverse was true. It illustrates that the identity formation of American Public Administration was influenced by an idealistic notion of the state and public administration. The state was regarded as an agent for the moral betterment of American citizens and public administration was viewed as a guardian and promoter of the collective welfare.

The current interpretation of the state probably resembles a machine more closely than the organism of the German and American scholars considered in this chapter. In contrast to Hegel, we most certainly do not attribute any metaphysical purpose to the state. However, even without assuming that the individual is merely the state's functional unit subordinated to the teleological ripening process of the state, we may acknowledge progressive values when we carry on administrative research (e.g. Box 2008). There is empirical evidence suggesting that altruistic motivations are more pronounced among public servants than in the private sector. For instance, Houston and Cartwright (2007: 90) point out:

> Typical explanations of bureaucratic behaviour, such as rational choice (or principal-agent) theory, are of limited utility for understanding the commitment to public service. Based on the assumptions of the utility-maximising bureaucrat, principal-agent theory explains why bureaucrats shirk, subvert, and steal on the job but cannot account for bureaucrats who strive, support, and sacrifice on the job.

Arguably, an approach that is sensible to historical and cultural context may contribute to painting a more complex picture of Public Administration. By applying a historical or relativistic perspective to administrative ideas, we may come to the conclusion that dutifulness, honesty, and altruism are not necessarily naïve, but, depending on the context, realistic administrative values. Rothstein (2005: 10) claims that the most promising path for the near future of political science 'lies in reconnecting the normative side of the discipline – that is political philosophy – with the positive/empirical side'. According to Rutgers (2008) and Spicer (2008), this path would arguably be promising for Public Administration as well.

What about the practical benefit of a deeper knowledge of Hegelian political philosophy? Shaw (1992: 381) argues that Hegel's embrace of bureaucracy is compatible with a 'liberal theory of bureaucracy that apprehends modern political reality more adequately than the scepticism of classical liberals and contemporary libertarians about bureaucratic organisation'. It is certainly an anachronism to call Hegel a liberal philosopher. However, the 'historical' reading of Hegel is not the only way of reading Hegel. Wilson and Goodnow were aware of that and modified Hegelian political philosophy accordingly. If we follow suit with them, we may find that Hegelian administrative thought may indeed be relevant for modern liberal regimes. As Shaw (1992: 386) states.

> Governmental intervention is needed for pursuing undertakings of common good, adjusting the competing interests of producers and consumers, and supervising education crucial for training individuals to earn an independent living. Hegel's theory of the state is close to modern welfare economics, because the functions mentioned concern matters that economists designate as needing governmental intervention: either as externalities (contending interests of producers and consumers) or as public goods (undertakings of common good and education).

Against the background of the recent economic crisis, the history of ideas may illustrate that it is an option to be optimistic about public administration as a possible solution to supranational economic problems. Given the many similarities of these problems on both sides of the Atlantic, it might be an option to look back and abroad for inspiration. The transnational history of ideas will certainly not provide us with ready-made recipes that can easily be applied to our current challenges. However, it may help us to realise our high potential in problem solving.

References

Adcock, R. (2003) 'The emergence of political science as a discipline: history and the study of politics in America, 1875–1910', *History of Political Thought*, 24(3): 481–508.

Bluntschli, J. K. (1875) *Lehre vom Modernen Stat.* Vol. 1: *Allgemeine Statslehre*, Stuttgart: Cotta'schen Buchhandlung.

— (1876) *Lehre von Modernen Staat.* Vol. 3: *Politik*, Stuttgart: Cotta'schen Buchhandlung.

Böckenförde, E. W. (1978) 'Organ, Organismus, Organisation, politischer Körper', in Brunner, O., Conze, W. and Koselleck, R. (eds) *Geschichtliche Grundbegriffe*, Stuttgart: Klett-Cotta, pp. 545–622.

Box, R. C. (2008) *Making a Difference: Progressive Values in Public Administration*, Armonk: M.E. Sharpe.

Burgess, J. W. (1890) *Political Science and Comparative Constitutional Law*, Boston, MA: Ginn & Co.

— (1897) 'Political science and history', *American Historical Review*, 2(3): 401–08.

Casper, G. (1989) 'Changing concepts of constitutionalism: 18th to 20th century', *Supreme Court Review*, 311–32.

Church, J. (2010) 'The freedom of desire: Hegel's response to Rousseau on the problem of civil society', *American Journal of Political Science,* 54(1): 125–39.

Cook, B. J. (2006) 'Making democracy safe for the world: public administration in the political thought of Woodrow Wilson', in Lynch, T. D. and Cruise, P. L. (eds) *Handbook of Organization Theory and Management: The philosophical approach*, Boca Raton, FL: CRC Press, pp. 323–52.

Elcock, H. (2006) 'The public interest and public administration', *Politics*, 26(2): 101–09.

Farr, J. (1995) 'From modern republic to administrative state', in Easton, D., Gunnell, J. G. and Stein, M. B. (eds) *Regime and Discipline: Democracy and the development of political science*, Ann Arbor, MI: University of Michigan Press, pp. 131–68.

Fries, S. D. (1973) 'Staatstheorie and the new American science of politics', *Journal of History of Ideas*, 34(3): 391–404.

Fukuyama, F. (2006) 'The end of history', in Tuathail, G. Ó., Dalby, S. and Routledge, P. (eds), *The Geopolitics Reader*, New York: Routledge, pp. 107–16.

Goodnow, F. J. (1916) *The American Conception of Liberty*, Omaha, NE: Standard Printing Company.

— (2003) [1900] *Politics and Administration: A study in government*, New Brunswick, NJ: Transaction.

— (2005) [1897] *Comparative Administrative Law: An analysis of the administrative systems, national and local, of the United States, England, France, and Germany*, Vol. I, New Jersey: The Lawbook Exchange Ltd.

Gunnell, J. G. (1993) *The Descent of Political Theory: The genealogy of an American vocation*, Chicago/London: University of Chicago Press.

Hahn, E. (1977) 'Rudolf Gneist and the Prussian Rechtsstaat: 1862–78', *Journal of Modern History*, 49(4): 1361–1381.

Hegel, G. W. F. (1821) *Grundlinien der Philosophie des Rechts*, Berlin: Nicolaische Buchhandlung.

—   (1952) 'The Philosophy of Right', trans. Knox, T. M., in Hutchins, R. M. (ed.), *Great Books of the Western World, 46, Hegel*, Chicago: University of Chicago Press, pp. 1–153.

Holmes, S. (1995) *Passions and Constraint: On the theory of liberal democracy*, Chicago: University of Chicago Press.

Houston, D. J. and Cartwright, K. E. (2007) 'Spirituality and public service', *Public Administration Review*, 67(1): 88–102.

Knowles, D. (2002) *Hegel and the Philosophy of Right*, London, New York: Routledge.

Lee, D. (2008) 'The legacy of medieval constitutionalism in the Philosophy of Right: Hegel and the Prussian reform movement', *History of Political Thought*, 29(4): 601–34.

Lieber, F. (1835) *Reminiscences of an Intercourse with George Berthold Niebuhr, the Historian of Rome*, London: Richard Bentley.

—   (1838) *Manual of Political Ethics*, Part I, Boston, MA: C.C. Little and J. Brown.

—   (2000 [1869]) 'An introductory discourse to a course of lectures on the state. Delivered 10 October 1859, in the Law School of Columbia University', in Samson, S. A. (ed.), *Francis Lieber: The ancient and the modern teacher of politics: Reading and study guide*, Liberty University: Faculty Publications and Presentations, paper 154, Retrieved from: http://digitalcommons.liberty.edu/gov_fac_pubs/154

Link, A. S. (ed.) (1968a) *The Papers of Woodrow Wilson*, Vol. 4, 1885–8, Princeton, NJ: Princeton University Press.

—   (ed.) (1968b) *The Papers of Woodrow Wilson*, Vol. 5, 1885–8, Princeton, NJ: Princeton University Press.

—   (ed.) (1969) *The Papers of Woodrow Wilson*, Vol. 7, 1890–2, Princeton, NJ: Princeton University Press.

—   (ed.) (1970) *The Papers of Woodrow Wilson*, Vol. 9, 1894–6, Princeton, NJ: Princeton University Press.

Lynn, L. E., Jr (2001) 'The myth of the bureaucratic paradigm: what traditional public administration really stood for', *Public Administration Review*, 61(2): 144–60.

Mahoney, D. J. (2004) *Politics and Progress: The Emergence of American Political Science*, Lanham, MD: Lexington Books.

Menes, R. (2006) 'Limiting the reach of the grabbing hand: Graft and growth in American cities, 1880–1930', in Glaeser, E. L. and Goldin, C. (eds), *Corruption and Reform: Lessons from America's economic history*, Chicago/London: University of Chicago Press, pp. 63–93.

Miewald, R. D. (1984) 'The origins of Wilson's thought: the German tradition and the organic state', in Rabin, J. and Bowman, J. S. (eds), *Politics and Administration: Woodrow Wilson and American Public Administration*, New York: Marcel Dekker.

Morris, G. S. (1885) 'The philosophy of the state and of history', in Hall, S. G. (ed.) *Methods of Teaching History*, Vol. 1, Boston, MA: Norwood Editions.

Overeem, P. (2010) *The Politics-Administration Dichotomy: A reconstruction*, Ridderkerk: Ridderprint.

Painter, M. and Peters, B. G. (2010) *Tradition and Public Administration*, New York: Palgrave Macmillan.

Pestritto, R. J. (2007) 'The Progressive origins of the administrative state: Wilson, Goodnow, and Landis', *Social Philosophy & Policy*, 24(1): 16–54.

Pope, G. (1987) 'The political ideas of Lorenz Stein and their influence on Rudolf Gneist and Gustav Schmoller', *German History*, 4(1): 60–1.

Rodgers, D. T. (1998) *Atlantic Crossings: Social politics in a progressive age*, Cambridge: Harvard University Press.

Rohr, J. A. (1986) *To Run a Constitution: The legitimacy of the administrative state*, Lawrence, KS: University Press of Kansas.

—— (2003) 'Transaction introduction', in Goodnow, F. J. *Politics and Administration: A study in government*, New Brunswick, NJ: Transaction Publishers.

Rosser, C. (2010) 'Woodrow Wilson's administrative thought and German political theory', *Public Administration Review*, 70(4): 547–56.

—— (2013) 'Examining Frank J. Goodnow's Hegelian heritage: A contribution to understanding progressive administrative theory', *Administration & Society*, 45(9): 1063–94.

—— (2014) 'Johann Caspar Bluntschli's organic theory of the state and public administration', *Administrative Theory & Praxis*, 36(1): 32–51.

Rothstein, B. (2005) 'Is political science producing technically competent barbarians?' *European Political Science*, 4: 3–13.

Rutgers, M. R. (2001) 'Traditional flavors? The different sentiment in European and American administrative thought', *Administration & Society*, 33(2): 220–244.

—— (2008) 'The purpose of the state', *Administrative Theory & Praxis*, 30: 349–54.

Sager, F. and Rosser, C. (2009) 'Weber, Wilson, and Hegel: theories of modern bureaucracy', *Public Administration Review*, 69(6): 1136–1147.

Sager, F., Rosser, C., Mavrot, C. and Hurni, P. (2012). 'How traditional are the American, the French, and the German traditions of public administration? A research agenda', *Public Administration*, 90(1): 129–43.

Seibel, W. (2010) 'Beyond bureaucracy: Public administration as political integrator and non-Weberian thought in Germany', *Public Administration Review*, 70(5): 719–30.

Shaw, C. K. Y. (1992) 'Hegel's theory of modern bureaucracy', *The American Political Science Review*, 86(2): 381–89.

Spicer, M. W. (1995) *The Founders, the Constitution, and Public Administration: A conflict in worldviews*, Washington, DC: Georgetown University Press.

— (2008) 'The history of ideas and normative research in public administration: some personal reflections', *Administrative Theory & Praxis*, 30(1): 50–70.

Stein, L. von (1869) *Die Verwaltungslehre, Part I: Die vollziehende Gewalt*, Stuttgart: J. G. Cotta.

— (1870) *Handbuch der Verwaltungslehre und des Verwaltungsrechts*, Stuttgart: J. G. Cotta.

Stever, J. A. (1990) 'The dual image of the administrator in Progressive administrative theory', *Administration & Society*, 22(1): 39–57.

Stillman, R. J., II. (1973) 'Woodrow Wilson and the study of administration: A new look at an old essay', *American Political Science Review*, 67(2): 582–8.

— (1997) 'American vs. European public administration: does public administration make the modern state, or does the state make public administration?' *Public Administration Review*, 57(4): 332–8.

— (2001) 'Distant mirrors: Eight recent exemplary models', *Public Administration Review*, 61(2): 247–53.

Stollberg-Rilinger, B. (1986) *Der Staat als Maschine. Zur politischen Metaphorik des absoluten Fürstenstaates*, Berlin: Duncker & Humblot.

Taylor, C. (1975) *Hegel*, London: Cambridge University Press.

Tijsterman, S. P. and Overeem, P. (2008) 'Escaping the iron cage: Weber and Hegel on bureaucracy and freedom', *Administrative Theory and Praxis*, 30(1): 71–91.

Weil, E. (1998) *Hegel and the State*, Baltimore, MD: Johns Hopkins University Press.

Wilson, W. (1876) *Lehre von Modernen Staat*, Vol. 3: *Politik*, Stuttgart: Cotta'schen Buchhandlung.

— (1892) *The State: Elements of historical and practical politics: A sketch of institutional history and administration*, Boston, MA: D.C. Heath.

Yack, B. (1980) 'The rationality of Hegel's concept of monarchy', *American Political Science Review*, 74(3): 709–20.

Chapter Nine

The Dawn of French Administrative Science (1945–70): A Renewed Conception of the Public Servant

Céline Mavrot

Introduction

According to recent Public Administration[1] publications, European administrative thought typically focuses on the centrality of the state. The European 'stateness' tradition is here opposed to the American 'stateless' one. A contrast is drawn between two lines of thought: the American state's definition is claimed to be fundamentally inductive, whereas the European one would be deductive. As, in this view, the concept of the state lies at the heart of administrative science, the national state's particularities commands specific administrative theorisations. For example, the defence of individual freedoms lies at the centre of the American tradition, while the notion of *raison d'État* is the centrepiece of European thought. In this perspective, American Public Administration is impregnated with the idea of checks and balances, while European administrative thought is constituted around deductive positive law reasoning, alongside a vertical process of strong state construction (Martin 1987; Rutgers 2001; Stillman 1997). These considerations are the starting point of this chapter, which focuses on the changes in the scholarly conception of the public servant's role and place within French post-war society.

This chapter will examine important shifts in the scientific understanding of public service in France from 1945 up to the early 1970s. I will review the strong criticisms levelled at the traditional juridical mode of state regulation (Dulong 1997), which historically characterises the French model. We will see that these critiques went with important changes in the required profile of public servants and caused the rise of more technocratic senior administrators into the state apparatus. These emerging experts argued that administrative law alone could no longer resolve all the new problems. Their specific knowledge and know-how differed from those traditionally highlighted in the French administration. These partial shifts in the requisite profile of public servants are revelatory of deeper politico-administrative changes, especially the turn towards productivist and planning policies in the aftermath of the war. Organisational or economic expertise in public servants started to be increasingly valued, thus competing with the exclusively

---

1. I refer to 'Public Administration' as the academic administrative study, whereas 'public administration' designates the institutional state bodies.

juridical framing of administrative activity. In parallel, administrative law was sharply criticised for laying down rules that did not fit the new reality.

In this context, some academic and practitioners jurists reacted by attempting to renew the juridico-administrative framework. For doing so, they sought to create a new administrative science, in complement to the traditional science of state: administrative law. Administrative science was intended to help in facing the alleged problems of administrative law and to deal with what were seen as emerging challenges. The jurists recognised the fact that new public tasks, institutions, procedures and instruments were emerging, thus challenging the traditional modes of state regulation. Moreover, they argued that within these changes, the mission of public servants was different from how it had been in the past (Chevallier 1986: 36). Importantly, all administrative science's authors strongly emphasised the fact that public servants could not only be viewed as the mere executors of governmental will, but that they also had a large leeway in defining rules in the everyday administrative reality. Acknowledging the criticisms against the juridical framework, they admitted that a lot was happening in administrations beyond simply knowing and implementing the law. Recognising that fact, administrative science's authors proposed to analyse closely this leeway that public servants had, in order to see how it could be better used and framed. Basically, the purpose was to renew the juridical competencies of public servants, in accordance with the emerging challenges, in order to revalorise the role of the legal instruments in administrations.

Thus, the concern of French administrative scientists during the period of post-war reconstruction was to redefine public services and to better frame public servant activities. These attempts are indicative of the challenges faced by French scholars and practitioners at this watershed. As efforts aimed to understand the daily activity of public service in order to better orchestrate it, administrative science tells us much about the conception of French public service in this period of major changes. The present chapter particularly focuses on the work of one of the French administrative science's key precursors, Georges Langrod. Through his eyes, we will see how the public service was newly seen as a collective actor with its own will, intervening in the decision-making process and having flexibility in its tasks of organising the growth and diversification of state intervention. We will also see how, in this context, administrative scientists aimed to fill as well as to frame and control this grey area. Significantly for Langrod, administrative science was considered as a means to study the changing administrative reality, before deriving new juridical rules from it. That is to say, the emerging administrative fields and procedures had to remain in the realm of the juridical framework and expertise.

In this chapter, particular attention will be paid to some specific theoretical aspects. On the one hand, the very processes by which a 'national tradition' can perpetuate itself or not will be scrutinised (Sager *et al.* 2012). This will be done by a reconstruction of the diachronic chain of events that led to the modifications of the traditionally dominant line of administrative thought (or at least to attempts at its modification). On the other hand, in order to construct an embodied history of administrative thought, the focus will lie on the mediations (writings, actors, institutions) by which these changes were elaborated and actualised. Hence, the historical reconstruction is both discursive and configurational (Laborier and Trom 2003; Cohen *et al.* 2006; Le Strat and Pelletier 2006), in an attempt to articulate the internal and the external readings of the texts (Loiselle 2000). The chapter is structured as follows. The first section sketches the monopoly of administrative law on French administrative studies, practice and training before WW2. The second describes the post-war crisis of administrative law, as well as the emergence of new types of administrative expertise and public servant profiles; it also deals with the repercussion of these mutations on public service training. The third section exposes the project of Georges Langrod to found a French administrative science and to renew the analysis of public servants' tasks. In the fourth section, I examine how for Langrod, administrative science should serve the creation of a juridical code of administrative procedure, intended to legally frame public servants' everyday work. Finally, the last sections examine how Langrod relies on Harold Stein's case method in order to propose a renewal of public servants' training, to help them face the newly defined administrative reality.

The monopoly of administrative law

The most conspicuous characteristic of French administrative study and training is their almost total monopolisation by administrative law until WW2. This fact explains that the public service was long seen through the lens of its formally delegated tasks and duties, but this has changed with the emergence of administrative science since the middle of the 1940s. The monopoly of administrative law is rooted in the construction of the rule of law during the nineteenth century. Administrative law imposed a doctrinal edifice that had a century-long influence on the study of administration. It was mainly drawn up by one institution: the Council of State (*Conseil d'État*), one of the very highest French administrative bodies. Created in 1799 as a counsellor to the government on administrative bills, the Council of State was initially rather an instrument of the authoritarian regime of the Napoleonic Consulate. By the end of the nineteenth century, however, the Council of State was given the mission of resolving litigation between citizens and the administration. That made it the highest French administrative court. In this way, its role was progressively transformed from an absolutist tool into an organ in charge of assuring the limitation of the arbitrary state. The Council of State has nevertheless maintained – up to the present day – its function of governmental adviser on administrative bills. This makes it a peculiar jurisdictional institution, similarly responsible for co-creating administrative rules (consultative function) and exerting jurisdictional control over administrative activity (jurisdictional function) (Burdeau 1995).

Regarding the way public servants' activities are traditionally framed in France, it is important to bear in mind that the Council of State was – and still is – France's centrepiece of administrative regulation. Hence juridical rules have been the dominant way to address the issue of understanding and controlling the work of public servants. Their activities are approached from the normative perspective of what they should be, as determined by the final (litigious) administrative decision.

In this perspective, the unique rationality and motive of public servants have to be legal rules. We saw that the Council simultaneously co-creates administrative rules and judges their application by the administrative organs. This has resulted in an unprecedented construction by the Council of State of a great theoretical system based on the jurisdictional control of state activity. On one hand, the Council participates in the rule formulation process through its advice (Bertrand and Long 1960; Chevallier 1986). On the other hand, the Council adjusts these rules to the practice through its jurisdictional decisions (Latour 2004). Importantly, the Council of State's doctrinal creation has fully taken the place of what emerged simultaneously in other countries as administrative science. As a consequence, in France administrative law both regulates the state power in practice and articulates the administrative activity in theory. Thus, the behaviour of public servants is prescribed by administrative law and their effective choices and decisions are controlled through the administrative justice.

The continuous interpretative work by the Council of State has led gradually to the constitution of the prodigious corpus of administrative rules that is so specific to France. These rules were either deduced from general principles of law or from legislative and regulatory texts. As the existing legislative and executive texts on administration were sparse and fragmented, the Council of State's creative work systematised the rules guiding administrative action in its well-known jurisprudence. Thus, its case law rapidly acquired great authority, being recognised as the most accomplished and coherent body of knowledge on administration in France. The activities of the Council as a controlling authority shaped a coherent body of administrative knowledge. Since the end of the nineteenth century, the focus of administrative thought has increasingly been on the juridical framing of the state (Debbasch 1978). The main concern is the respective rights and duties of administrations and citizens. As a result, the Councillors of State successfully delimited public administration as an autonomous field of study pertaining to administrative law (Vanneuville 2003). In this process, administrative law became an autonomous and powerful scientific discipline. Thus simultaneously, administrative activity came under the influence of a strong juridification process (Ihl et al. 2003).

In the past, other administrative knowledge had in fact existed in France: the cameralist sciences. Elaborated between the seventeenth and the nineteenth centuries, these sciences were composed of non-juridical studies of various aspects of administration, such as finances or administrative techniques. However, these sciences were an accumulation of heterogeneous and descriptive knowledge (Langrod 1963a: 490). Still, the nascence of cameralist science marked a significant turning point in the socio-history of the state: the public power presented itself as no longer based on strength and secrecy, but rather as legitimised by science. In this logic, bureaucracy was seen as covering an increased number of specialised intervention fields. In parallel, public servants were henceforth the legatees of professionalised knowledge, from which they enjoyed their legitimacy, and no longer the representatives of an arbitrary power (Damamme 1988: 12; Ihl et al. 2003: 2–6). Cameralist sciences were, however, still in their infancy by the time administrative law achieved its successful emergence, and thus had no time to assert themselves (Chevallier 1986; Ihl *et al*. 2003). Whereas cameralist sciences were conducted in a scattered manner, institutional support provided by the Council of State contributed to the success of administrative law. By the end of the nineteenth century, administrative law had absorbed most of the cameralist – or administrative – sciences (Langrod 1966: 104).

Between the very end of the nineteenth century and WW2, the training of public servants was mainly shared between two institutions. Part of it was conducted at a private establishment, the *École Libre des Sciences Politiques*, founded in 1871 in order to train a new elite that would be qualified on the basis of its excellency and not of tradition any longer. The teaching gathered various types of knowledge that would be useful in the practice of future high public servants, such as political, administrative, economic, diplomatic or financial knowledge, and, of course, law. The other part of administrative training was done at the law faculties, where public law was taught in a more theoretical way via the exegetical method (Favre 1989: 25–50).[2] From this point of view, public servants principally had to know the rules and to apply them. Both institutions were in fierce competition for administrative training and for paternity on some related knowledge. The law faculties, however, managed by the end of the nineteenth century to incorporate the political and economic sciences in their own curriculum thus, once again, steering them towards a juridical orientation (Favre 1989: 92; Mazon 1988: 25). These historical developments gave to French administrative training a definitely juridical colouration, and even a litigious one to the study of administration. They are capital to understanding the later shift in the perspective on the public servant, as well as claims in favour of establishing a non-juridical science of administration and a more practical administrative training after WW2.

The crisis of administrative law

Administrative law was considered sufficient to frame and control administrative action until the first decades of the twentieth century. With its instruments, public servants were seen as sufficiently equipped to carry out their tasks of enforcing law. During the inter-war period, however, the pertinence of administrative law in accompanying the development of the state was put sharply into question (Debbasch 1973: 101). Still, the most virulent criticism emerged after WW2 (Rivero 1978). Such criticism came from various groups of actors: emerging political scientists (*see* Pelloux 1947; Rivero 1948), high public servants, technicians (Milhaud 1956), politicians (Dulong 1997) and even public law theorists themselves (Rivero 1950). In a nutshell, we can classify the criticisms of the limits of administrative law into three categories (Mavrot *et al*. 2010: 173–6). First, the politics-administration dichotomy that was found at the basis of administrative law was thoroughly contested. The dichotomy was criticised for being the gravest blind spot of

---

2.   Specific and sustainable administrative law teaching has existed since 1828 in France, at the Paris Law Faculty (Guglielmi 1996).

administrative law because it impeded the comprehension of real administrative functioning (Chevallier 1986).

Second, some voices objected to the lack of empirical evidence that characterises administrative law's abstract thought. These criticisms strongly underlined the normative and theoretical way in which administrative law was informed, leading public servants to focus on how administration should be and not on how it actually is. From now on, this top-down approach – with fixed rules defined by the high administrative jurisdiction – was seen increasingly as leading to a lack of flexibility of action. Indeed, administrative law as a unique instrument and framework for public servants was considered as too slow to adapt to the needs on the ground. The tendency of public servants to 'decide, regulate, command and obey, control and investigate, without having acquired the most basic knowledge about the numerous things which, for example, constitute the professional background of Anglo-Saxon countries' (Milhaud 1956: 208) started to be increasingly criticised.[3] In this connection, influential clubs of reformist high public servants vigorously advocated the necessity for importing non-juridical Anglo-Saxon tools into the French administration. They wanted to replace the controlling role of senior public servants by an advisory and animation role in respect of the reforms. They also demanded that all public servants acquire organisational skills in order to better use public money in times of administrative growth and diversification. These reformists were supported by newly created state bodies such as the Productivity Commission (*Commissariat général à la Productivité*, 1953–9), which promoted a productivist reform of the French public service. Since the immediate post-war period, they launched a programme of on-the-job training along that line, so as to compensate for the shortcomings of law faculties (Weexsteen 2000).[4] Hence, the productivist coalition considered public servants as needing new types of skills and knowledge, especially organisational ones.

Third, the theoretical conceptions and concepts of administrative law were denounced as being irrelevant to new modes of state interventionism as well as to the emergence of new types of institutions (Heilbronner and Drago 1959; Langrod 1956). Indeed, the restarting of industrial facilities, post-war nationalisations and productivity policies urged the state to find expertise on many new emerging technical and economic matters. Neither administrative law nor public servants exclusively trained in law were considered to be well adapted to these domains. Moreover, during the reconstruction, a great many new hybrid institutions and procedures blurring the delineation between administrative and private law emerged (Bertrand and Long 1960; Bonnaud-Delamare 1953; Pelloux 1947). The notion of public service, the centrepiece of French administrative law around which the entire doctrinal system was structured, lost its *raison d'être* (Langrod 1955: 689). The discipline thus experienced a deep theoretical crisis (Debbasch 1973). In fact, how could public servants intervene in mixed private and public institutions or procedures when the only tools at their disposal were issued by administrative

---

3. Author's translation.
4. I refer here in particular to the *Institut Technique des Administrations Publiques* (1947–74).

law, which could only apprehend purely public phenomena? For some observers, the public service was not so public any more, and hence needed new types of administrators and competencies.

Indeed, the campaigners for the obsolescence of administrative law underlined the uselessness of this rather conservative discipline for the new challenges of post-war reconstruction. The new issues were depicted as requiring prompt planning and prospective thought from public servants as well as innovative modes of controlling and ruling (Bonnaud-Delamare 1953; CFNSP 1965; Langrod 1958; Puget 1958). According to numerous commentators, public servants needed, from now on, more practical skills as well as the liberty to escape from a too constraining legal framework, and they should contribute to refining the new modes of public action. In this regard, the crisis of administrative law had many effects, such as replacing jurists by other types of experts in the state commissions for administrative reform. In the 1960s, recently defined needs such as the formalisation of the decisional process, the modernisation of the production capacity, or planning policies, opened the doors of administration to new types of high public servants, which can be generically called technocrats. Their declared will was to rationalise the state, via techniques that required the specific resources and skills that they themselves possessed. They advocated a strong executive and argued that key administrative positions should be allocated to high public servants whose legitimacy derived from the possession of technical know-how (Dubois and Dulong 1999: 13–14). Notably, at this time, new techniques for planning public action were particularly *en vogue*. Since 1966, the American Planning, Programming and Budgeting System (PPBS) had been imported into the French administration (*Rationalisation des choix budgétaires*). The Ministry of Finance was particularly interested in this government technology, as he aimed to regulate rationally the sectoral ministries and their expenses. In this context of strong governmental planning, a new profile of public servant became particularly salient: the *planificateurs*, whose economic know-how was considered crucial for running the new policies (Spenlehauer 1999). Thus, the traditional juridical mode of state regulation was challenged by the rise of the *planificateurs* at the top of the state, and new types of competencies were required for public servants (Dulong 1997). Hence, both productivism and planning emerged as new administrative reform paradigms aiming at rationalising the state, and competed with the juridical paradigm.

Indeed, the modernisers of the Plan Commission (*Commissariat général au Plan*, 1946–2006) succeeded in refining the excellence model of the public servant. The sense of hierarchy and bureaucratic formalism, associated with law, were strongly discredited, to the benefit of the vanguardist spirit and practices allowed by the economy. This redefinition of the desired properties of public servants was facilitated by the facts that the administration was being fully restructured at the time and that some of the former elites had been discredited by their attitude during the war (Gaïti 2002: 299–302). These modernisers strongly emphasised the need to allow public servants to be more innovative, in order to settle a prospective planning that was not restrained by the rigidity of the administrative law. The focus had to shift from control to action. Then from the 1970s on, the *nouvelle gestion publique* – taught in higher education institutions inside and outside the administration – became the new dominant perspective in the French public service, promoting managerial skills as the panacea (Bezes 2006; 2009: 188–98). These administrative changes are at the crossroads of two combining logics. An international one on the one hand, since the opening of the French economy to global competition with the signing of the Treaty of Rome in 1957 required the French to focus on the public decision-making process in order to provide better guidance for administrative investment policy. And a domestic one on the other hand, because the development of the welfare state since the 1960s called for a precise planning policy that profoundly reshaped the public modus operandi. These new forms of state regulation, which went together with a rationalisation of public procedures, led to a redefinition of the model of administrative competency: for public servants, the new legitimate knowledge to possess – besides being technical and economic – is operational (Bezes 2002: 310–11).

Finally, also revelatory of the decline of administrative law and of the related changes in administrative functioning were important institutional mutations in academia. The education of public servants was subjected to some change. After WW2, the criticism of law faculties – accused of being excessively abstract and literal – was very severe (Pelloux 1947). Significantly, an autonomous political science – viewed as rival to the classical juridical programme – was introduced in French schools. For example, the *Institut d'Études Politiques* (IEP) founded in 1945 in Paris was the fruit of the nationalisation of the *École Libre des Sciences Politiques* (Sadran 1999: 134). It was created together with the *École Nationale d'Administration* (National School of Administration; ENA), and prepared students for admission to the latter. Importantly, the IEP issued a fully fledged political science diploma (Favre 1981: 98), which shows the relative decline of administrative law in the field of public servant education. Very importantly, the ENA was founded in order to modernise and renew high public servant training. One of the purposes was to ensure that this education was less monopolised by a juridical approach. The composition of the ENA's teaching staff in the 1950s reflects this will to provide a more practical direction to the curriculum: 80 per cent of the professors were public servants, compared to only 20 per cent of university lecturers (Bertrand and Long 1960: 9–14). For some observers, however, the ENA still remained too academic in its approach, notably with an excessive focus on lecture-based teachings (Ayoub 1969).

To sum up, the context is one of great administrative changes and of a profound redefinition of the required skills and training of public servants. Along with these mutations, public law university professors and Councillors of State would react by reasserting the value of administrative law. Some of these administrative law experts attempted to adapt law to the administrative shifts by the means of the creation of a new discipline named administrative science. This science was intended to help study the administrative mutations in order to adapt administrative law to the changing realities and to the new requisites for public servants. We turn now to this issue, through the example of one prominent author of French administrative science, Georges Langrod.

Georges Langrod: A key promoter of French administrative science

Langrod was incontestably one of the most vocal promoters of a French administrative science as well as its most prolific author.[5] He was a law professor who specialised in comparative administrative law and participated in diverse international scientific organisations, such as the International Institute of Administrative Sciences, the International Institute of Political Sciences and UNESCO (Boulet *et al.* 1980: 463–4). On these platforms, he was notably brought into contact with American authors of Public Administration who inspired him with new approaches. We will see that one of his core purposes in attempting to establish administrative science in France was to renew the public's perception of public servants, by focusing on the importance of their role not only in applying the law, but also in co-creating it during their everyday tasks. It is difficult to assess Langrod's exact influence on the conception of administration in France in general and of public servants in particular. It can, however, be noted that he tirelessly advocated his ideas about administrative science and public servants in France between the 1940s and the 1970s throughout its teachings and its abundant bibliography.

The departure point of Langrod's will to found an administrative science is his recognition of the limitations of administrative law. His criticisms of administrative law fell within the scope of post-war denunciations of the excessive formalism of the juridical perspective and its inability to equip public servants with the right skills to face the emerging challenges. Langrod blamed the juridical reference scheme that settled for a description and an analysis of the sole structures, thus neglecting the actual administrative process. He definitely recognised the seminal contribution of administrative law in ensuring the legality of state interventions and in limiting its arbitrary power during the state's construction period. However, he proclaimed the dawn of a new era, where the traditional administrative-legal framework would no longer be sufficient to accommodate the multiple tasks of a modern state (Langrod 1957: 93; 1982). He thus criticised administrative law for its inability to understand the new phenomena and found that juridical analysis was linked to ancient forms and revolved doctrines, which resulted in an increasing 'discrepancy with life' (Langrod 1960a: 26, 55). As a consequence, he proposed the creation of an administrative science that would be able to study what had been neglected by administrative law: the informal functioning of the administration. According to him, administrative science had to analyse the activities of public servants with the help of sociological tools, in order to understand how they apply the rules in practice, and how they cope with their tasks when there is no rule.

Though Langrod claimed to break with the juridical tradition, his administrative science is primarily conceptualised as a supplement, or enlargement, of administrative law: 'its links [of administrative science] with administrative law can facilitate the progressive penetration of extra-juridical intellectual conquests into the universe of the administrative rule of law, their change into juridical norms'

---

5. No complete history of French administrative science has been written yet. About different aspects of the history of this discipline, *see* Chevallier 1986; Bezes 2002, 2006, 2009; Ihl *et al.* 2003; Payre 2006; Saunier 2003.

(Langrod 1966: 118). The aim was to bring the new administrative practices back into the realm of law. Indeed, a large part of Langrod's administrative science is dedicated to exploring parts of administrative reality that are uncovered by administrative law. Forgotten by administrative law, these aspects of reality were left to the full discretion of public servants and thus had become the subject of informal decisions. As a consequence, they suffered from the lack of juridical framing that should characterise every activity of a constitutional state (Langrod 1960a: 20–1). This resulted in the deep juridical insecurity that was firmly denounced by Langrod. In his view, a first step for administrative science was to understand when and how public servants make decisions about matters that are not (yet) fixed in the law. Then, as a second step, rules of administrative law have to be created in order to fill these blanks.

On the one hand, the lack of legal framing concerned the emerging new state activities, for which administrative law had no appropriate guiding concept, such as the administration's consultative procedures (Langrod 1972), the planning processes (Langrod 1958; 1963a: 534) and the economic activities of the state (Langrod 1966: 123). On the other hand, the increasing importance of the informal behaviour of public servants – in all domains – causes, in Langrod's view, a juridical blind spot. He sharply criticised the fact that administrative law had always ignored the day-to-day activities of public servants. In his mind, closely studying administrative behaviour was a prerequisite to later identifying rules that could be best suited to supervise such administrative behaviour (Langrod 1964: 583). In sum, Langrod's administrative science was ultimately a way to permit a juridification of what has been left out of the law.

More particularly, Langrod denounced the obstinacy of jurists in focusing on the final administrative act (the final decision made by public servants). He blamed them for their lack of concern for the sequence of acts and decisions leading to the juridical end product: the final administrative act. In fact, a focus on final administrative acts has been inherent in a tradition of administrative litigation like the French one. We saw that the nature of French administrative law was rooted in the Council of State's mission to protect the citizens against the state. Since the nineteenth century, this task has been achieved by means of administrative litigation. In this context, the final administrative acts that were attacked by citizens were elaborately examined by the Council of State. The Council decided either to validate or to revoke these final administrative acts. Consequently, the main part of the administrative law doctrine was elaborated around the question of the legality of final administrative acts from a litigious perspective, and the exact way in which these decisions were made by public servants was, according to Langrod, excessively neglected.

For Langrod, the monopoly of administrative law and its litigation perspective over the administrative study 'has created myopia in the conception of the State of law' (Langrod 1960a: 20). The focalisation on the *ex post* administrative activity by the litigation impeded understanding of the real administrative action. The administrative action that preceded the final administrative decision was disregarded: 'all that comes before [the final act], in particular, what occurs between the administration and the citizens, is relegated to the "technical" sphere, and considered as lacking in juridical interest' (Langrod 1960a: 1). As a consequence, the informal arrangements that took place during the entire administrative decision-making process had been left solely to the public servants' conscience. According to Langrod, the neglect of any analysis of the effective administrative process had many detrimental effects. Such opacity appeared in full light in the context of increased state interventionism and weakened the overall legitimacy of the state (Langrod 1960b: 407). This theme was central to Langrod's thought. By asserting the necessity to examine the process that took place before the final administrative act, he demonstrated the necessity of creating an administrative science that would be capable of achieving this task. As the traditional administrative law had no tool at its disposal to conduct this process analysis, Langrod championed the necessity of drawing upon social sciences in order to overcome the juridical impasse. In his eyes, some theoretical innovations would permit better understanding, framing and re-juridifying administrative activity.

The code of non-contentious administrative procedures

One of Langrod's primary points was his call for the creation of a Code of Non-contentious Administrative Procedures (CNCAP) (Langrod 1958, 1959, 1960a, 1963b). Briefly sketched, such a non-litigious code would assemble the entire set of rules for administrative procedures and decision-making processes to meet legal requirements. It would, thus, permit a permanent administrative auto-control during the procedure in addition to its *ex post* jurisdictional control by the Council of State. Importantly, this code of rules had to ensure the impartiality of public servants (Langrod 1960a: 31). It had to guarantee that they would not act out of their own will and that different administrators would take the same decision in similar situations. In particular, the Code would contain the norms supervising the protection of citizens during an administrative procedure that were liable to affect individual rights and interests. In Langrod's view, it was the core instrument in the democratisation of the administration (Langrod 1960b: 408) and correlatively in its legitimisation in the eyes of the citizens.

According to Langrod, administrative science should come to the rescue of administrative law by helping jurists to create a code that would be most congruent to reality. As a first step, administrative science experts had to study the motives of administrative behaviour as well as its consequences. That is, administrative science had to analyse the chain of micro-decisions that led to the final formal administrative decision. Then, as a second step, administrative law would come on stage; it would fix the rules necessary to frame this procedural administrative behaviour within the limits of what would be desirable in terms of legality. The CNCAP had to account for the necessary flexibility that required administrative action. However, its prior goal was to ensure the legality of administrative action, from which derived its legitimacy. It is amusing to notice that Langrod drew heavily on the example of the American due process administrative tradition in order to justify the necessity to establish a French Code (Langrod 1960a: 13).

He also strongly relied on Herbert Simon's psycho-sociological concepts. For Langrod, Simon had brilliantly demonstrated that public servants actually do establish political values in their day-to-day value judgements (Langrod 1954: 27). This recognition of the value-creating aspects of administrative activity was very important to Langrod, who acknowledged Simon's 'methodical introspection of the psychological mechanisms occurring within administrative activity' (Langrod 1963a: 531). Thanks to Simon, light had been thrown on the human relationships within administrative mechanisms: partnership, cooperation and cohesion, teamwork, authority and command, the division of labour, and its psycho-sociological repercussions (Langrod 1966: 116). Still citing Simon, Langrod states that all these aspects had to be treated. The purpose of administrative science was to 'find out what is the actual human behaviour in certain typical administrative situations, and consequently establishing hypothetical rules of administrative behaviour that are confirmed by the practice' (Langrod 1954: 57–8).

On this basis, Langrod defined what administrative science experts should analyse in order to create such a code: the factors on which public servants rely to make decisions, the participative procedures that administrations settle when collaborating with civil society (such as professional corporations or economic actors), the procedures used by administrations to ensure citizens' right to be heard, the way administrations justify their decisions and the administrative elaboration of prospective planning. Administrative science scholars would have to collect case studies on these themes and compare the various solutions that had been empirically elaborated by each French administration on a case-to-case basis. At the end, the aim was to find the best administrative procedures regarding the equilibrium between citizen protection and the public interest. Then, administrative law had to head the results of these studies by identifying the best rules based on these empirical observations; it would allow the organisation of administrative operations instead of hoping that decisions taken on the ground will turn out to be correct (Langrod 1960a: 27). Administration had new prerogatives of organising an increasingly complex society and this extension of its intervention in social life had to be legitimised. In particular, it had to be proven that administrative decisions were not arbitrarily made by individual public servants, but provided for by law. The conception of public service that issued from this approach was that of a neutral and egalitarian guarantor of the general interest, as an indispensable prerequisite to democracy.

As such, the Code was based on an 'understanding of the different stages of the juridical-psychological administrative acts', viewed as a process (Langrod 1960a: 26). As public servants were now considered as having their own room for manoeuvre during the administrative process, the public service was seen as a milieu on its own, having its own particular psychology and logic. Consequently, it could also be scientifically analysed (Langrod 1953), and legally framed. This juridification of the practices through administrative law was made in order to secure homogeneous administrative behaviour, thus enhancing citizens' security by predictability. Here, it is also important that public servants were considered in their relationship with citizens, as a crucial interface between the authorities and the people. In the end, the stabilisation of administrative decisions was 'a fundamental mechanism in obtaining the citizens' certitude and their confidence in the state's activity' (Langrod 1960a: 19). The Code was seen as the perfect tool for improving administrative behaviour because it would unify the rules, permit a systematisation of the doctrinal constructions, and facilitate the awareness of public servants of their own behavioural motives (Langrod 1960a: 25–6). However, in order to draw public servants' attention to their behaviour in their everyday practise, their training methods also had to be renewed. Langrod proposed to do this through an American educational tool: the case method.

The case method: Revivifying public servants' education

As part of its project to found administrative science in France, Georges Langrod proposed to renovate the education of public servants through an American-inspired teaching method. According to him, the case method was a pedagogical technique that could complete the very theoretical university teaching of law, because it focused less on the rules than on the practical skills required by public servants in their daily practical activities. In this sense, the method would help to train administrators to make good choices in the aforementioned informal part of their work. The case method is a classwork method that brings into discussion selected cases from everyday administrative life. The method is intended to train future public servants to solve concrete problems. Via this method, Langrod believed, participants could be encouraged to acquire an empirical capacity of action (Langrod 1953: 832). They simulated decision-making processes and had to analyse them (Langrod 1953: 834). According to Langrod, this pedagogic method could revolutionise the education of public servants. He criticised law professors who 'adhere to the ancient method of the dogmatic presentation of great abstract principles (Langrod 1953: 833). Just as administrative law had been overcome by reality, its teaching method had become too passive and unidirectional for contemporary training purposes. In contrast, Langrod claimed, the case method:

> introduces the readers to a given administrative climate, makes them live the administrative life as if they really were in it and had to take a decision in a concrete case: it is a sort of improved vocational training. It brings administration to class, with its proper instrumentation and the particular psychology of this milieu. (1953: 838)

We can see that the desired shift in training methods is in full accordance with Langrod's will to acknowledge the importance of the informal behaviour of public servants and their role in co-defining administrative decisions. Hence, for Langrod, the case method was a formidable laboratory of experimentation and education for future public servants, for it underlined more the nature of administrative activity than its formal structures (Langrod 1953: 838). It was a suitable tool for sensitising them to the new requirements of administrative procedures in the modern era.

We have already seen that according to Langrod, the socio-psychological process that leads to administrative decisions had to be analysed by administrative science and should then be structured by administrative law. Correspondingly, public servants had to be trained in optimal decision-making methods before taking up their offices. Langrod considered the case method as ideal for fulfilling this requirement. In this sense, the case method was the educational counterpart of the study of administrative decision-making processes. It was the necessary educational complement to administrative science and to administrative law's code of procedures. Together, the three would provide a better framework for the administrative decision-making process. Langrod relied, in particular, on Harold Stein's *Case Book* (1952). In Langrod's eyes, its virtue was that in choosing the cases for his book, Stein:

> attaches significant importance to situations where administration has to define its objectives on its own, thus becoming integrated to the political process *lato sensu*. In this conception, public servants not only interpret the objectives that are defined by the legislator, [...] but also define their proper politics. (Langrod 1953: 843)

The psychological aspects of the decision-making process in particular were considered (Langrod 1953: 834). For Langrod, it was very positive that Stein's cases were selected with special attention to situations where public servants have to take important decisions. That helps administrative science to advance in comprehending the administrative decision-making process and in analysing and supervising administrative activities.

Conclusion: The French public servant as an actor on its own

One of the most outstanding effects of the crisis of French administrative law after WW2 is the important change in perspective on public servants it caused. The key role played by public servants as full actors of the politico-administrative game was brought to light. In particular, their role in the decision-making process was acknowledged. The scope they had was highlighted, whether in interpreting the law during its application or in codetermining it in a more prospective way. These transformations especially occurred within the administrative law perspective, which formerly tended to focus on the role of public servants as purely executing the governmental will. The shift in perspective was caused by changes occurring at the institutional as well as the academic level. Basically, the post-war reconstruction, the reactivation of the economy, the growing state intervention as well as its diversification in different areas of social life necessitated a new type of public servant. These challenges were seen increasingly as requiring competencies other than the traditional juridical ones. In particular, organisational and economic know-how were seen as a requirement for running the post-war productivist or planning policies (Bezes 2009; Spenlehauer 1999). But above all, these changes in the desired conception of public servants were advocated by different groups of actors, including administrators themselves, who attempted to valorise new profiles and logics of action other than those of the traditional model (Dulong 1997). It was notably argued that the juridical mode of regulation of the state was based excessively on controlling, thus neglecting innovative and prospective thinking.

Criticisms of the juridical model were not new, but their virulence increased significantly after the war (Chevallier 1986). They emerged in different fields, such as the political, the administrative and the academic, urging the specialists of administrative law to react. They did so by attempting to regain control over the domains that were escaping the jurisdiction of law. In this sense, some of them used administrative science in order either to examine the emerging administrative procedures and domains that had not been foreseen by the law, or the infra-juridical behaviour of public servants. In this way, these phenomena could be brought back to the juridical territory by covering them under new rules. Indeed, the purpose was to legally reframe the liberty that certain categories of public servants were gaining at the time, by acknowledging and analysing it. Consequently, those developments spread the idea that public service was a milieu on its own, with a proper psychology, which had to be studied sociologically in order to be better understood. From this flew for example the two-part proposition of George Langrod to study administrative behaviour via administrative science and then to formalise it into a code of administrative procedure. Most fundamentally, these shifts in the composition of public service and of its academic conception are revelatory of the two different administrative rationalities existing in the post-war France: the emerging technocratic one and the formerly dominant juridical one (Dulong 1997). They represented two different logics: whereas the technocratic rationality valorised the possession of technical knowledge and legitimised administrative action by the achievement of practical objectives, the legal rationality highlighted the juridical knowledge and grounds administrative action in respect for procedure. Each of them underpinned a distinct figure of the public servant, and administrative science became one of the battlefields of the two approaches.

References

Ayoub, E. (1969) *La formation du personnel administratif dans la fonction publique*, Paris: Armand Colin.

Bertrand, A. and Long, M. (1960) 'L'enseignement supérieur des sciences administratives en France', *Revue Internationale des Sciences Administratives*, 26(1): 5–24.

Bezes, P. (2002) 'Aux origines des politiques de réforme administrative sous la Vème République: La construction du "souci de soi de l'État"', *Revue Française d'Administration Publique*, 2(102): 307–25.

—— (2006) 'Un jeu redistribué sous la cinquième République: Nouvelles formes et nouveaux acteurs de la réforme de l'État', *Revue Française d'Administration Publique*, 4(120): 721–42.

—— (2009) *Réinventer l'État: Les réformes de l'administration*, Paris: Presses de Sciences Po.

Bonnaud-Delamare, R. (1953) 'Progrès de la réforme administrative en France', *Revue Internationale des Sciences Administratives*, 19(3): 571–607.

Boulet, L., Dupuis, G., Menier, J., Siedentopf, H., Timsit, G. and Wiener, C. (eds) (1980) *Science et action administratives: Mélanges Georges Langrod*, Paris: Les Éditions d'Organisation.

Burdeau, F. (1995) *Histoire du droit administratif*, Paris: Presses Universitaires de France.

CFNSP/Cahiers de la Fondation Nationale des Sciences Politiques (1965) *La planification comme processus de décision*, nr. 140. Paris: Armand Colin.

Chevallier, J. (1986) *Science Administrative*, Paris: Presses Universitaires de France.

Cohen, A., Lacroix, B. and Riutort, P. (eds) (2006) *Les Formes de l'Activité Politique*, Paris: Presses Universitaires de France.

Damamme, D. (1988) 'D'une école des sciences politiques', *Politix*, 1(3): 6–12.

Debbasch, C. (1973) 'Le droit administratif face à l'évolution de l'administration française', *Revue Internationale des Sciences Administratives*, 39(2): 101–7.

—— (1978) 'La science administrative dans les pays de l'Europe occidentale continentale', *Revue Internationale des Sciences Administratives*, 44(1): 12–27.

Dubois, V. and Dulong, D. (eds) (1999) *La question technocratique*, Strasbourg: Presses Universitaires de Strasbourg.

Dulong, D. (1997) *Moderniser la politique: Aux origines de la Ve République*, Paris: L'Harmattan.

Favre, P. (1981) 'La science politique en France depuis 1945', *International Political Science Review*, 2(1): 95–120.

—— (1989) *Naissance de la science politique en France (1870–1914)*, Paris: Fayard.

Gaïti, B. (2002) 'Les modernisateurs dans l'administration d'après-guerre: L'écriture d'une histoire héroïque', *Revue Française d'Administration Publique*, 2(102): 295–306.

Guglielmi, G. J. (1996) 'Émile-Victor Foucart, ou le sacerdoce du droit public et administratif', *Revue du Droit Public et de la Science Politique*, 5: 1291–318.

Heilbronner, A. and Drago, R. (1959) 'L'administration consultative en France', *Revue Internationale des Sciences Administratives*, 25(1): 57–66.

Ihl, O., Kaluszynski, M. and Pollet, G. (eds) (2003) *Les Sciences de Gouvernement*, Paris: Economica.

Laborier, P. and Trom, D. (eds) (2003) *Historicités de l'Action Publique*, Paris: Presses Universitaires de France.

Langrod, G. (1953) 'La méthode des cas et la science administrative américaine', *Revue Française de Science Politique*, 3(4): 832–48.

— (1954) *La Science et l'Enseignement de l'Administration Publique aux États-Unis*, Cahiers de la Fondation Nationale des Sciences Politiques, nr. 59, Paris: Armand Colin.

— (1955) 'The French Council of State: its role in the formulation and implementation of administrative law', *American Political Science Review*, 49(3): 673–92.

— (1956) 'L'entreprise publique en droit administratif comparé', *Revue Internationale de Droit Comparé*, 8(2): 213–31.

— (1957) 'Science administrative ou sciences administratives?' *Annales Universitatis Saraviensis*, V(1): 92–125.

— (1958) 'Note sur les principes du code de procédure administrative de Tchécoslovaquie', *Revue Internationale des Sciences Administratives*, 24(2): 199–201.

— (1959) 'Quelques problèmes de la procédure administrative non contentieuse en droit administratif comparé', *Revue Internationale des Sciences Administratives*, 25(1): 5–20.

— (1960a) *La procédure administrative non contentieuse*, unpublished work, Cours de la faculté Internationale de droit comparé, 2nd semester, summer session, nr. A 250, Luxembourg.

— (1960b) 'Genèse et lignes directrices de la réforme de la procédure administrative non contentieuse en Pologne', *Revue Internationale des Sciences Administratives*, 26(4): 397–411.

— (1963a) 'La science de l'Administration publique (Esquisse Historique)'. Extract of vol. 1 *Studi in onore di Silvio Lessona*. Specialisation course in administrative science, University of Bologna, Bologna: Zanichelli, pp. 481–542.

— (1963b) *La preuve dans la procédure administrative non contentieuse*, Bruxelles: Éditions de la librairie encyclopédique, pp. 259–87.

— (1964) 'Ehrlich (Stanislaw) – Pressure groups and the capitalist political structure', *Revue Française de Science Politique*, 14(3): 581–3.

—   (1966) 'La science administrative et sa place parmi les sciences voisines', in Langrod, G. (ed.) *Traité de science administrative*, Paris: Mouton, pp. 92–123.

—   (ed.) (1972) *La consultation dans l'administration contemporaine*, Paris: Cujas.

—   (1982) 'France' in Heyen, E. V. (ed.) *Geschichte der Verwaltungsrechtswissenschaft in Europa*, Frankfurt am Main: V. Klostermann, pp. 67–80.

Latour, B. (2004) [2002] *La fabrique du droit: Une ethnographie du Conseil d'État*, Paris: La Découverte.

Le Strat, C. and Pelletier, W. (2006) *La canonisation libérale de Tocqueville*, Paris: Syllepse.

Loiselle, M. (2000) 'L'analyse du discours de la doctrine juridique: L'articulation des perspectives interne et externe', in CURAPP *Les méthodes au concret*, Paris: Presses Universitaires de France, pp. 187–209.

Martin, D. W. (1987) 'Déjà vu: French antecedents of American Public Administration', *Public Administration Review*, 47(4): 297–303.

Mavrot, C., Hurni, P. and Rosser, C. (2010) 'Les sciences administratives: Pérégrination des idées et lutes autour de l'appropriation d'un label', *Annuaire des Sciences Administratives Suisses*: 171–82.

Mazon, B. (1988) *Aux origines de l'École des Hautes Études en Sciences Sociales: Le rôle du mécénat américain (1920–1960)*, Paris: Éditions du Cerf.

Milhaud, J. (1956) *Chemins faisant: tranches de vie*, Paris: Hommes et techniques.

Payre, R. (2006) 'L'État vu d'en haut: la réforme de l'État au sein des espaces internationaux de la science administrative dans l'entre-deux-guerres', *Revue Française d'Administration Publique*, 4(120): 651–66.

Pelloux, R. (1947) 'L'enseignement du droit public et des sciences politiques et les projets de réforme des facultés de droit', *Revue du Droit Public et de la Science Politique*, 63: 54–67.

Puget, H. (1958) 'Le nouveau droit de l'énergie atomique', *Revue Internationale des Sciences Administratives*, 24(1): 5–16.

Rivero, J. (1948) 'Formation juridique et fonction administrative', *Revue du Droit Public et de la Science Politique*, 64: 557–64.

—   (1950) 'Les interventions de l'État dans l'économie française (1918–1948)', in UNESCO *La Science Politique Contemporaine. Contribution à la recherche, la méthode, l'enseignement*, Paris: UNESCO, pp. 494–504.

—   (1978) 'L'administration et le droit', *Revue Internationale des Sciences Administratives*, 44(1): 145–50.

Rutgers, M. R. (2001) 'Traditional flavors? The different sentiments in European and American administrative thought', *Administration & Society*, 33(2): 220–44.

Sadran, P. (1999) 'Public administration programmes in France', in Verheijen, T. and Connaughton, B. (eds) *Higher Education Programmes in Public Administration: Ready for the challenge of europeanisation?*, Limerick: Centre for European Studies, pp. 129–68.

Sager, F., Rosser, C., Hurni, P. and Mavrot, C. (2012) 'How traditional are the American, the French, and the German traditions of public administration? A research agenda', *Public Administration*, 90(1): 129–43.

Saunier, P. -Y. (2003) 'Ulysses of Chicago: American foundations and Public Administration, 1900–1960', in Gemelli, G. and Macleod, R. (eds) *American Foundations in Europe*, Brussels: European Interuniversity Press, pp. 115–28.

Spenlehauer, V. (1999) 'Intelligence gouvernementale et sciences sociales', *Politix*, 12(48): 95–128.

Stein, H. (1952) (ed.) *Public Administration and Policy Development: A case book*, New York: Harcourt Brace.

Stillman, R. J. (1997) 'American vs. European public administration: does public administration make the modern state, or does the state make public administration?', *Public Administration Review*, 57(4): 332–8.

Vanneuville, R. (2003) 'Le droit administratif comme savoir de gouvernement? René Worms et le Conseil d'État devant l'Académie des sciences morales et politiques au début du 20e siècle', *Revue Française de Science Politique*, 53(2): 219–35.

Weexsteen, A. (2000) *Le conseil aux entreprises: Le rôle de Jean Milhaud (1989–1991) dans la C.E.G.O.S. et l'I.T.A.P.*, unpublished thesis, Paris: École des Hautes Études en Sciences Sociales.

Chapter Ten

Cybernetics, German Public Administration and the Reframing of the Public Servant in the *Neo-Verwaltungswissenschaft*

Pascal Hurni

Introduction

Comparative Public Administration tends to treat the development of national public administration (the practice) and Public Administration (PA; the study) as distinct traditions (Sager *et al.* 2012; Raadschelders 2008; Rugge 2003; Bevir *et al.* 2003; Rohr 2002; Rutgers 2001; Smith 2001; Stillman 2001; Painter and Peters 2010; Kickert and Stillman II 1999). The notion of intellectual tradition is used as an ideal type, path-dependency or cultural variation on a macro level. It is uncontested that traditions can function as useful conceptual maps to explain many similarities and dissimilarities on conceptions of the state, the role of public servants and the relationship between state and administration (*see* Stillman 2001, 1997; Kickert and Stillman II 1996; Overeem and Rutgers 2003; Rutgers 2000, 2001; Rosser 2010; Sager and Rosser 2009; Rohr 2002). However, it is debatable to what degree such schematic models are empirically valid (Sager *et al.* 2012).

Arguably, the dilemma of being concise and correct at the same time lies in the very nature of model building in social science. As models are abstractions of an overly complex reality, simplifications are conducted to separate relevant and irrelevant factors and, thus, to arrive at observations which beforehand had been clouded by too much data (Diekmann 2005: 122–8; Goertz 2005). However, as the vivid discussion following Hobsbawm and Ranger's (2009) influential essay *The Invention of Tradition* shows, one must be aware that traditions are often constructed to build identity. Hitherto, there have been hardly any primary source-based empirical studies that tried to validate the theoretical reasoning on traditions of PA (e.g. Rosser 2010; Sager and Rosser 2009). The analysis of the transfer of ideas examines in how far traditions have been formed under foreign influence to establish the validity of national PA traditions as self-referential path dependencies, and thus aims to separate the fact and the fiction of PA tradition (Sager *et al.* 2012: 1).

This chapter examines the origin of the *Neo-Verwaltungswissenschaft* by inspecting the import of ideas from the USA. As will be shown, this coincides with a reframing of the role of the public servant. It has been argued that external inspiration tends to have a relatively strong influence in the forming stages of a scientific field of research (Bevir 2002; Flyvbjerg 2006; Kuhn 1996). A qualitative content analysis promises to provide a deepened knowledge at the level of originality and independence. By analysing citations and references in primary sources and how these ideas have been introduced to the new context, insight can be gained into the validity of PA traditions. It will be shown that the introduction of the cybernetic approach by Karl W. Deutsch's *The Nerves of Government: Models of Political Communication and Control* (1963) was a fruitful stimulation of German political sciences and PA, as it provided the epistemological foundation of public administration being part of the political–administrative system (PAS) (e.g. Luhmann 1966b). Cybernetics contributed to the new understanding by emphasising a more system-oriented approach, a positivistic methodology and the ability to deal with automation and with intelligent organisations (e.g. Simon 1947).

Thus, public servants were no longer conceived as merely tools of political power. As individuals and constituting members of an intelligent organisation, they received discretionary power to decide how best to achieve outcome goals. Their contribution to society was thus reframed, and the evaluation of their work consisted no longer of checking compliance with standard bureaucratic procedure. This legitimised gain in power contrasted with the threatened loss of job security, and also provided Public Administration with the solution to this tension: whereas budgetary restraints and technological progress placed humans and machines in competition, humans were capable of reframing their actions according to set goals following unexpected turns and in complex societal settings.

The chapter is structured as follows: First, the origin and the concept of cybernetics will be introduced. Next, its influence on German PA is elaborated. Thereby, three aspects will be discussed in greater detail: *why* the new paradigm was added to the theoretical framework, *how* methodological standards of empirical analysis have been changed, and *what* new questions have entered the scholarly discussion. Thereafter the conclusion shall provide exemplary insights and discuss the implications of the notion of tradition in PA.

Wiener, Shannon, Deutsch: A general introduction

Cybernetics is derived from the Greek κυβερνήτης (kybernetes; steersman). The notion has a rich tradition in political theory, as the Greek state philosophers Plato and Aristotle had used the steersman as a metaphor applied to the governor of the *polis* (Lang, 1966, 1970: 17–50; Vogl 2004; Klaus 1964). Additionally, the physicist André-Marie Ampère (1843: 140–1) had used the notion *cybernétique* as a classification of the art of governing. Norbert Wiener (1950: 11) was not aware thereof, but adopted the notion from Clerk Maxwell's essay 'On governors' (1868), the first article applying the concept of a feedback mechanism in the context of political systems and public servants. Although the notion of cybernetics remained rather undefined (Pias 2004b) this would not infringe with its popularity, and cybernetics became a buzzword in the USA and in Germany from the 1950s to the mid-1970s. As a working definition, cybernetics can be defined as the control, design and analysis of complex systems and the organisational self-adaptation to meet predefined goals.

In the early 1940s, the mathematician Wiener and the physician Arturo Rosenblueth developed a model to grasp the transfer of information in complex systems such as in body cells and machines (Wussing 2009: 529). They soon realised that machines and organs can be described as isofunctions by applying a purpose-oriented behaviourist and a rationalistic functionalist perspective (Rosenblueth *et al.* 1943). Their research first stirred interest among computer engineers as it became clear to Wiener and John von Neumann that their subject of interest was largely the same (Wiener 1963: 44). Soon the group of interested scholars stemmed from a variety of fields of research such as psychology, sociology, anthropology, philosophy, economics, ecology, engineering, neurophysiology and opinion research – among others Paul Lazarsfeld, Margaret Mead, Lawrence K. Frank and the mathematician and engineer Claude E. Shannon. After their initial success, the reunions were institutionalised and became known as Macy Conference (Pias 2003, 2004a).

Wiener had first encountered Shannon's writings while contributing to the development of automatic target systems during WW2 (*see* Conway and Siegelman 2005: 127). After the first Macy Conference, Shannon broadened his scope so that information theory was applicable to all forms of communication including neuronal transmission (*see* Werner 2002: 2). His seminal essay 'A mathematical theory of communication' (1948) laid the foundation of information theory. While social scientists referred only vaguely to Shannon, they widely applied his vocabulary and definitions to their respective fields of research when dealing with information transfer, i.e. communication. As Wiener (1950: 16) stated, communication is of uttermost importance, as:

society can only be understood through a study of the messages and the communication facilities which belong to it; and [...] in the future development of these messages and communication facilities, messages between man and machine, between machines and man, and between machine and machine, are destined to play an ever-increasing part.

Although Wiener omitted communication between man and man, clearly this was in his mind as well:

The existence of Social Science is based on the ability to treat a social group as an organization and not as an agglomeration. Communication is the cement that makes *organizations*. Communication alone enables a group to think together, to see together, and to act together. All sociology requires the understanding of communication. [...] Certain aspects of the theory of communication have been considered by the engineer. While human and social communication are extremely complicated in comparison to the existing patterns of machine communication, they are subject to the same grammar; and this grammar has received its highest technical development when applied to the simpler content of the machine. (Wiener cited in Deutsch 1963: 77, emphasis in the original)

As Robert Theobald (1966: 59) argued, 'to run the complex society of the second half of the twentieth century' one would have to 'use the computer'.

Apart from the theoretical framework, this latter aspect was very relevant for social scientists as they dwelled upon questions on the possibilities of how the potential of objectifying intellectual processes would affect society and how society would be affected by automation. Although the notion of automation had already been coined in the 1930s (Pietsch 1957), it was John Diebold (1952) in *Automation: The Advent of the Automatic Factory* who presented an applicable framework by including the objectification of intellectual processing from Shannon's information theory (Frank 1969: 12–40; Bull 1964: 49). Most prominently treated by social scientists was the threat of mass unemployment (e.g. Carleton 1965; Friedman 1953; Schelsky 1957; Pollock 1956).

The application of cybernetics to the political system was initiated by Deutsch in *Nerves of Government: Models of Political Communication and Control* (1963). The cybernetic approach was intended to go beyond the old state concepts and not to use them merely as a metaphor (Luhmann 1966b: 41). As Deutsch (1963: 26–34) argued, cybernetics represented a more appropriate starting point for reasoning on the state than either the mechanical or the organic model. The cybernetic model combined the clear-cut analytical categories of the mechanical model while being as dynamic as the organic model, but without either being a simple synchronic conception or lacking theoretical definition and thus being unsuitable for rigorous analysis.

The reception by PA in Germany

After the schism of the rational-explanatory and the rational-normative approaches of social science in general and Public Administration in particular in the mid-nineteenth century, jurisprudence and the concept of the *Rechtsstaat* dominated the German scientific debate on public administration, the conception of the public servant and the terms of the nascent German nation state (Luhmann 1966b: 33). It was not until the early 1970s that the social science-based German Public Administration could establish itself as an academic branch (Seibel 1996; Jann 2003, 2009; Bogumil 2005; Bogumil and Jann 2009; Fisch n.d.). This was largely due to the reception of *The Nerves of Government: Models of Political Communication and Control* (Deutsch 1963) respectively its translation *Politische Kybernetik: Modelle und Perspektiven* (1966). Based thereupon, the function of public administration and the role of the public servant were no longer seen as being restricted to the role of an instrument of the executive branch, but were conceived as part of the PAS. Cybernetics thus contributed to an understanding of the various tasks of the public servant by promoting the more holistic approach of systems theory, the inclusion of automation, and rigorous positivistic, quantitative research methods.

Systems theory

In the beginning, cybernetics was about the study of communication and control of organic and mechanical systems. But when Stafford Beer's (1962, 1959) focus on the effectiveness of organisations was combined with Herbert Simon's (1947, 1955: 5) notion of decision-making, this provided the starting point for applying the concept of cybernetics to social systems such as the state. As Deutsch (1963: 42) stated:

> Unfortunately, Simon has not applied his powerful and suggestive models to large-scale political and social processes, although he has applied his style of thinking with excellent effect to problems of private and public administration, the business firm, and the study of organizations.

Thus, when German political scientists combined the concepts of Beer, Simon and Deutsch, they broadened their initial research scope of the analysis of parties, the parliament and democracy. Although public administration had not been a quintessential element in democracy theory, it has become a research subject in its own right. The conception of a political system has allowed political scientists to examine how, by whom, and to what extent public servants partake qualitatively and quantitatively in decision-making (Hartfiel *et al.* 1964: 80–1). This reassessment challenged the traditional doctrine of public administration being an instrument of the executive branch, and the clear-cut distinction of administration's role in the political process. Consequently, public servants were no longer expected to follow orders, but to contribute to the outcome that had been decided upon politically. Nonetheless, Niklas Luhmann (1972, 1966b) was unwilling to renounce the politics–administration dichotomy in his theory. Rather, he chose to redefine politics and administration so that *Politik*[1] was concerned solely with the meta-legitimisation of decision-making and institutions, whereas *Verwaltung* was concerned with applying the rules of legitimate decision-making (Hesse 1982: 18; Luhmann 1972, 1969). In other words, *Politik* was largely restricted to constitution making and polity. But as this collided with the very foundations of political science, Luhmann's proposition was not favourably received or applied – except by Luhmann himself (Dammann 1973, 1971).

Luhmann's (1966b) theory of Public Administration had at least one lasting influence. It helped to establish a holistic view of the PAS by making Talcott Parsons' (1956, 1958) structural-functional systems theory better known. Additionally, Luhmann (1966b: 31–2) introduced Robert K. Merton (1940, 1945) who had examined the functioning of bureaucracy and exerted a strong influence on the sociology of organisations (*see* Selznick 1943, 1949, 1948; Blau 1955, 1956: Blau and Scott 1962; Gouldner 1954; Clark 1956, 1960). Most importantly, by adding internal and informal structures within complex organisations to the functionalist approach, Luhmann explained how unintended side-effects as well as organisational dysfunctions occurred when goals on the individual level or

---

1. It should be noted that the differentiation of politics, policy and polity had not yet been established in Germany.

specific goals on the organisational level (*Zielvorgaben*; such as efficiency) clash with the system's purpose (*Systemzweck*; such as good governance). Approving of organisation sociology's findings that humans tend to behave tactically and rationally in their respective environment, Luhmann (1966b: 33) concluded that organisational dysfunction would best be explained by structural tension and the inherent contradictions of organisations rather than by the alleged conservatism of public servants, their non-openness to change or their individual failings.

Whereas such arguments were quite new in Germany, these findings had long been published in US organisational sociology (e.g. Wilensky 1956; Dalton 1959; Moore 1959; Burns 1955, 1961, 1962; Strauss 1962; Presthus 1962; Wildavsky 1964; Morstein-Marx 1959a: 75–82; Crozier 1963; Sjoberg 1960; Merton 1940, 1945, 1957). Organisational sociology displayed difficulties in incorporating individual rationality into a system's rationality, and consequently failed to explain and correct the empirical observations (Luhmann 1966b: fn 42: 33). Disregarding the misdemeanour of individuals, cybernetics dealt with these organisational pathologies by the notions of flawed feedback (Deutsch 1969: 193). Thus information processing played an eminently important role not only in the systems-environment interaction but also in organisational learning.

Figure 10.1: Model of the state as a control chain

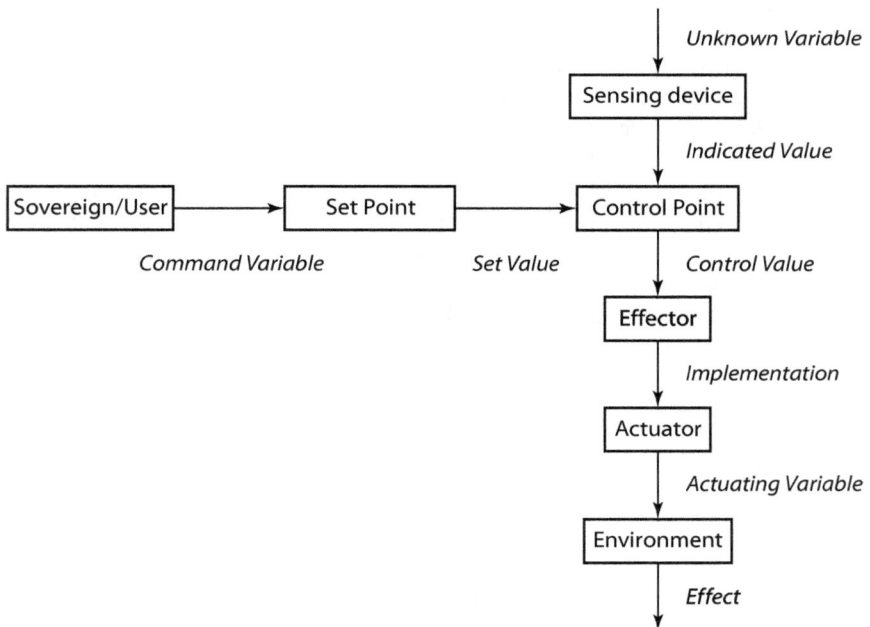

Note: Aderhold's (1973: 77) model depicts the concept of the control chain as it was applied to the organisations.

Luhmann distinguished three different kinds of systems-environment reaction: a fully determined causal reaction, a more complex stimulus-response reaction and a systems-environment interaction, where organisations render their environment and themselves. The first two models corresponded largely to public administration as an instrument. Dieter Aderhold's (1973: 75) diagram may provide some help for better understanding (*see* Figure 10.1). Here, the system receives an input and processes the information. But due to the linear information processing and lacking the means of intelligent reaction to environmental effects, these two models were deemed too simplistic, unrealistic and not fit for application in social science (Luhmann 1966b: 41). Nonetheless, they provided the theoretical grounds for numerous publications (e.g. Angermann 1959; Adam 1959; Haberstroh 1960; Nürck 1960b; 1960a; Langen 1964). Tying in with the criticism that the mechanical model was too rigid (*see* Deutsch 1963: 26–30), organisations of these two types would be unable to sense any change in the environment, let alone react to it. As Eberhard Lang (1966: 21, 80) put it, initiative to change was limited to the sovereign/user (*Regler*). Thus control was not only time-intense but – as there was no systematic way of gathering and processing information – nobody in a position to decide further action could base their decisions or actions on assured facts.

Figure 10.2: Model of the state as an intelligent organisation

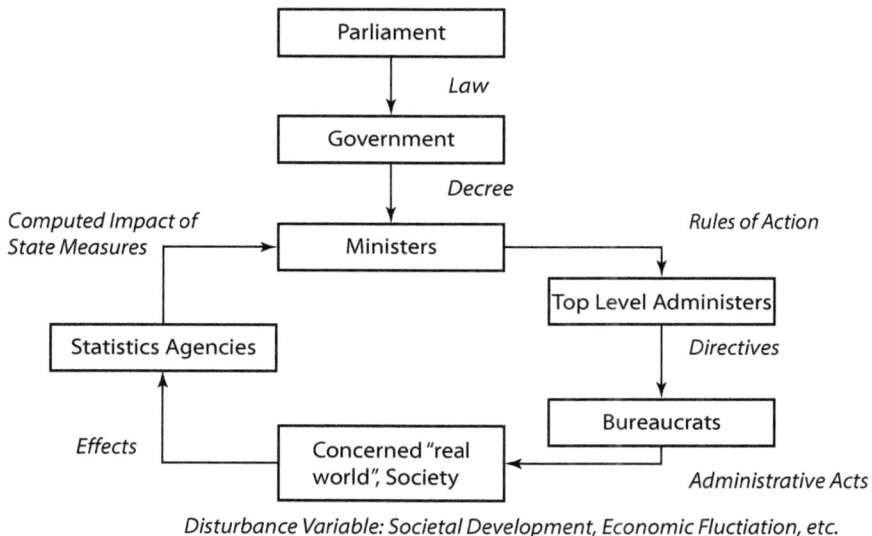

Disturbance Variable: Societal Development, Economic Fluctiation, etc.

Note: Aderhold's (1973: 77) model depicts not only the internal structure of the system, which corresponds with the ways of communication, but also the institutions of knowledge gathering, memory and retrieval. Additionally it shows how new normative goals are inducted into the system by the political authorities.

Alternatively, in systems-environment interaction, systems were conceived to be a sensitive and sensible institution. Thus, intelligent systems were capable of distinguishing what *ought to be* from what actually *is*. Once the normative *ought* is given by the sovereign, the organisation specifies them into means. An analysis of the outcome then provides the data to adjust the means accordingly. This should result in an intelligent proceeding wherein the organisation automatically, or in other words intelligently, adapts its behaviour to pursue the goals (*see* Figure 10.2). This form of interaction can arguably be understood as communication or control (Senghaas 1966:256; Flechtner 1966; Naschold 1969), being reminiscent of Wiener's *Cybernetics: Or the Control and Communication in the Animal and the Machine* (1948). The intelligent behaviour of organisations was tied to an elaborate feedback system, whereby public servants supplied the organisation with knowledge about the environment, knowledge of the past and also knowledge about itself (Deutsch 1966: 193–4; 1969: 300–3; Senghaas 1967: 386–99; 1966: 256–9). If one or more of these conditions were lacking, dysfunctions or pathologic behaviour resulted. Also, dysfunctions might result if organisations could not assert themselves, missed the means to absorb information and act accordingly, or lost the potential for reorganisation (Naschold 1969: 144–6; 161–3; Narr 1969: 104–10; Lang 1970). Thereby an inherent problem of all recursive feedback systems emerged: the resulting lag in perception-action cycles (Aderhold 1973: 78).

Scholars applied the notion of feedback as a means of automatic control. Whereas the term itself and the formulation as an abstract concept were relatively new, the concept of self-regulating systems had been known in technology and economics since well before Adam Smith (Mayr 1971: 2). Otto Mayr established three criteria for intelligent organisations' behaviour in complex systems: First, the system must carry out commands and maintain the controlled variable equal to the command signal in spite of external disturbances; second, the system operates as a closed loop with negative feedback to correct perceived errors; third, the system includes a sensing element and a comparator, at least one of which can be distinguished as a physically separate element. The expected behaviour fits the empirical data. In particular, this provided an explanation of how organisations were evolving on the individual, organisational and at times even the purpose level, while at the same time remaining remarkably stable. This dynamic stasis was called hyperstability.

One of the main reasons why the cybernetic approach proved so fruitful was the inherent openness of the isofunctional approach, which even led to claims of cybernetics being the universal science, or at least that it could combine the various approaches in political science (e.g. Guntram 1985: 296; Kannegiesser and Kelm 1965: 32; Naschold 1969: 23; Steinbuch 1965: 324, 359; Narr 1969: 88–9, 124; Aderhold 1973: 73–4; Senghaas 1967: 186). However, Renate Mayntz (1964: 385) warned this might lead to blindness of the specifics of social systems. Nonetheless she concluded that cybernetics might best be applied to goal-oriented and planned organisations.

The relocation of the PAS and the claim that public administration's functions should be analysed by political science rather than jurisprudence, marks the starting point of the *Neo-Verwaltungswissenschaft*. As a social science it emphasised empirical studies over normative prescriptions, and thus the public servant's role in the PAS became an important research topic. *Neo-Verwaltungswissenschaft*'s proponents abandoned the politics-administration dichotomy as being unrealistic and, in the end, irrelevant concerning all functionalistic criteria of the state in the PAS (*see* Hirsch 1969: 276). This was most clearly expressed in Scharpf's (1971) seminal paper 'Verwaltungswissenschaft als Teil der Politikwissenschaft' [Public Administration as Political Science], which today is accepted as one of the founding publications of modern German PA.

Quantitative methods

According to Senghaas (1966: 254), German political science had stagnated as it predominantly discussed definitions. In cases where theses were empirically tested, this happened with a 'disproportion of methodological expense and substantial results'. As Senghaas continued, Deutsch's cybernetic model could be a remedy as it had been devised to be operationalised.

Naschold (1969: 22–3) provided an example of how this could be done concerning the PAS:

> Given is a system with several variables. The dependent variable (the system's output) is a function of several input variables. The output is set with a value defined by the system or the system's environment. The control deviation, i.e. the offset between the respective current output value [*Ist-Wert*] (in control systems, the technical term is a controlled process variable) and the set point [*Soll-Wert*], shall approach zero. However, the output value depends on various independent variables, the environmental disturbance variables, which can fluctuate widely. To allow the possibility that output and process value become identical, at least one of the disturbance variables, the so-called actuating variable, has to be accessible and adjustable. Therefore, the system has to have at the very least one degree of freedom, if the set point is to be realisable. (Author translation)

This quote corresponds well with Aderhold's model of the intelligent state (*see* Figure 10.2). In the 1960s, scholars still lacked sufficient knowledge of how to select variables and assess their interrelation, especially when evaluating disturbance values and their correlation with other systems' behaviour (*see* Guetzkow 1962, 1963; Verba 1964). This led Naschold (1969: 18) to the conclusion that rigorous research based on cybernetics and information theory may perhaps never be feasible.

A possible long-term solution was presented by the rise of simulations, where complex political decision-making situations could be simplified (Lang 1966: 36). According to Dieter Senghaas (1966: 267), the idea of simulations had been introduced by engineers to arrive at simplified conditions. Relying on the logics of simulation by Raymond Boudon (1965: 11), it was claimed that all processes could be simulated if a coherent framework of quasi-laws could be described and if all variables were known and well determined. Adapted to the PAS, computers would simulate behaviour in social systems (Hauff 1965).

To his German peers, Senghaas (1966: 267) recommended several US authors (e.g. Helmer 1965; Crane 1962; Hovland 1963) and the section on gaming in the *Journal of Conflict Resolutions* as introductory reading on simulations in political science.

By reducing the number of variables, simulation did not represent a solution by itself. However, the 'mathematically rather complex procedure' (Mayntz 1964: 380) of factor analysis might be able to contribute to reducing the encountered problems. One of the first introductions to factor analysis in German had been written by Peter Hochstätter (1962) and was explicitly directed at scholars in social science. However, as Deutsch (1969: 85–8) explicitly stated, it would not be advisable for social scientists to require additional education in higher mathematics. Better could be expected if research was conducted in teams of social scientists with enough analytical understanding to formulate their research question in an operationalised manner, with mathematicians who knew enough about social science to understand the fundamental problems and provide the adequate mathematical instruments. The use of computers seemed a promising approach to overcome these difficulties. In German social science, among the first to rely on computers as an analytical instrument was survey research. According to Mayntz (1964: 380), the IBM 101 Statistical Sorting Machine aided in handling the data gained from several thousand interviewees. Thus, factor analysis and simulations led to a broad integration of computers in social sciences and to new ways of gathering knowledge (*see* Fruchter and Jennings 1962).

Whereas the time required for a correlation of variables, scaling schemes, and factor analysis was shortened significantly, the complexity of the analysis and the limited understanding and access to computers made it increasingly difficult for peers to evaluate the results. Thus, on the downside, it became more difficult to discern if constants and coefficients had been added arbitrarily to provide better results that in reality were lacking in meaning (Deutsch 1969: 86–7). In systems theory no system exists completely isolated from others. Consequently, interdependencies of the parameters need to be taken into consideration. This led to highly complex results that were either difficult to interpret or that were not based stringently on operationalisation and had rather heuristic value (Jänicke 1973: 213; Habermas 1973: 15; Aderhold 1973: 79).

Automation

Aside from the theoretical framework and the rise of methodological concepts, it was the implementation of cybernetics that captured the interest of German PA. At the beginning of the twentieth century, automation had been limited to power, endurance and – to a certain extent – precision. With the development of computers it was the intellectual capability that could be automatised. Algorithms contain well-defined specifications and a set of rules as to the order, and under which circumstances, a procedure has to be carried out (Frank 1969: 34). Arguably, operationalisation in scientific research is an analogy thereof.

As a topic for social scientists in Germany, automation had been introduced by Friedrich Pollock (1955) in 'Automation in USA: Betrachtungen zur "Zweiten Industriellen Revolution"' ['Automation in the USA: reflections on the "second Industrial Revolution"']. Choosing the USA as a study topic seemed most reasonable: on the one hand, the development could be observed best, as it was most advanced. On the other hand, US literature provided the best insight into the subject (e.g. King 1952; Tustin 1952; Ridenour 1952; Nagel 1952). Additionally, Pollock referred to the German translations of Wiener's *The Human Use of Human Beings: Cybernetics and Society* (1950) and Diebold's *Automation: The Advent of the Automatic Factory* (1952).

Pollock (1955: 80) observed that automation led to the exclusion of humans from the production chain. When humans were compared to machines, they were usually considered less reliable and more expensive (Pollock 1955: 146). Thus, the role of humans became limited to being a servo-component: on the one hand for the maintenance and service of the machines and on the other hand for adjusting the algorithms to the specific tasks required (Greene 1954: 58). As the goal of automation was to free technology from human limitations (Pollock 1955: 147), many contributions to the discussion on automation revolved around questions of mass unemployment and its effects on laid-off individuals and the society as a whole if humans were subsequently replaced by machines (e.g. Carleton 1965; Friedman 1953; Schelsky 1957; Pollock 1956).

Thus, relevant to political science were questions concerning social welfare, but also the introduction of machines to the political sphere. Dominique Dubarle (1948) had envisioned a *machine à gouverner*, which would choose the best measures to reach any given political goal in any given situation with the greatest probability based on pure logics (Pollock 1955: 154). As Hans Peter Bull (1964: 40) maintained, this vision was disturbing, as these *Befehlsmaschinen* would argue flawlessly and opposition to their decisions would be at least illogical, if not unreasonable (*see* Zeidler 1959: 31; Schelsky 1957: 11–12, 19; Ridenour 1957: 167–71). Albeit futuristic, cybernetics and automation allegedly had the potential of providing a perfect state and putting humanity under tutelage.

More relevant to PA was the danger for white-collar workers of being outperformed. Traditionally, it had been the unqualified workforce who had to cede their jobs to machines in industrial production. But now qualified workers such as public servants were concerned. Public administration was torn between its goals of efficiency and effectiveness and the guaranteed job security for the *Beamte*, which had been reinstated in 1957. According to Bull (1964: 37) the benefits of public administration's automation were self-evident: For example, when Fiscal Authorities North automatically processed tax reimbursement claims, they finished two months faster (*see* Michael 1962: 10; Maass 1961; Pollock 1956: 31–2, 174–5). However, the legal status was unclear when state services such as tax assessments, statistics, or traffic regulations, relied on machines (Bull 1964: 37–40; Maass 1961: 141–2; Haupt 1961: 12; Pollock 1955: 80). How could administrative measures such tax evaluations or speed ticketing be appealed in court when they had been computed and sent by machines? Further discussions evolved around e-government *avant la lettre*.

For example, Fritz Morstein-Marx (1959b: 212–13) discussed the launch of so-called *Antragshäuser* where citizens could deposit requests that thus would be transferred automatically to the competent authority. Bull (1964: 40) further developed this vision: he hoped that in the foreseeable future requests could be answered (and billed) automatically and immediately if the request were deposited in the correct form.

Scholars of administrative law were rather hesitant to consider the implementation of cybernetics and drew analogies of the tasks of public servants' implementation of orders and judges' sentencing (*see* Seibel 1982: 187). A trial may seem to be a fitting opportunity insofar its function is to apply the correct sentence according to the crime committed. According to Friedrich List (1955: 10), automation of case law would lead to undue simplification, which fails to consider the relevant singular particularities of the individual case. Interestingly, Bull (1964: 108: fn 559) largely agreed with List's assessment. However he drew contrary conclusions: as automation of the law would lead to less arbitrariness of jurisdiction, this would result in more justice. Luhmann (1966a: 134) demanded that legislation and proponents of automation should form an alliance to reduce the (illegitimate) power of the judges. However, this position represented only a minority (Seibel 1982: 187–9).

The fundamental limits of automation in jurisprudence were best stated by Spiros Simitis. In accordance with Deutsch (1969: 95), Simitis (1964: 354–6) maintained that a structural-functional analysis could not provide answers to normative questions as cybernetic systems are value-indifferent (*Wertindifferent*). Their output depends on predefined axiomatic operating rules and societal development could not be predefined. 'The tendency of extensive axiomatisation will thus be restricted to totalitarian political orders, or to those who believe that the historicity of human beings is foreseeable and thus declaring their own solutions to be general and eternally valid' (Simitis 1964: 356).

Conclusion

Regarding the reception of the cybernetic approach by German Public Administration, its use in reframing of the public servant and the role of transferred ideas in establishing the *Neo-Verwaltungswissenschaft*, it has been shown that cybernetics has exerted considerable influence. This observation strengthens Mark Bevir's (2002: 198) statement that when reflecting on existing beliefs does not lead to satisfactory answers to the encountered question, new understandings can enter scientific discourse.

Considering the notorious vagueness of the notion of cybernetics (Güldenberg 2003: 31; Pias 2004b), in this context, cybernetics may be best understood as a label used to claim membership of group identity or to classify contributions to the respective discourse. Common ground was found on three levels: first, cybernetics constituted a new form of institutionalism. Second, cybernetics promoted more 'mathematical', i.e. quantitative and/or operationalised scientific approaches. Third, cybernetics was interested in the objectification of intellectual processing and its effects on society, which was often discussed referring to notions of automation. Thus, sharing epistemological grounds with their US peers, the considerable influence observed can hardly be surprising.

Aderhold (1973: 10) praised cybernetics as an 'original, thought-provoking impulse', which was not euphorically or naïvely received, but rather applied to the specific socio-political context of Germany. For German scholars, political cybernetics provided the background of the PAS and thus acted as the distinguishing feature *vis-à-vis* the approach of jurisprudence to public administration. Although cybernetics dealt with systems and organisations, it can be argued that the emphasis of the important political role of public administration and the public servant legitimised the *Neo-Verwaltungswissenschaft* as a field of study. Henceforth, the traditional doctrine of public administration as an instrument of the executive branch, as conceived by jurisprudence, was challenged by political science. Although this criticism was not new at all (e.g. Jastrow 1902), the political role of the public servant was broadly recognised only after the new theoretical framework was established. Thus the criteria of qualifications for good public servants were extended beyond being law-abiding and efficient.

The focus of PA scholars broadened also: it became clear that the knowledge gap in the various aspects of planning were of greatest importance (*see* Naschold 1972: 166). Further development would follow the models of the policy cycle, which led to implementation studies, the policy approach, and so on, which all were acknowledged to be inspired by US-American examples (Pollock 1956: 18–19, 26; Mayntz 1980, 1996). Although cybernetics, the rise of the systems theory, and the conceptual shift of public administration from an instrument to an integral subsystem of the PAS seem to be linked (Aderhold 1973: 10; Naschold 1969: 22–3), this might be purely coincidental.

Scholars refer to the US not only when discussing the effects of automation on society, but also when discussing the use of computers in public administration (*see* Michael 1962: 10; Maass 1961; Pollock 1956: 31–2, 174–5). Although the vocabulary of cybernetics is used in reassessing public administration's function and functioning in the PAS, German scholars' clear distinction of *Regelung* and *Steuerung* when discussing control shows significant difference with that of the USA (*see* Lang 1966: 21). Arguably reasons for this were rooted in the broader context of German political discussion and resulted from the emancipation of public administration from its role as an instrument of the executive branch. Acceptance of public administration as an important part of the politics-administration system in its own right, and not only as an instrument for the executive's branch, may be due partly to the reception of cybernetics. This shift of role implicated a reframing of public servants' role. As the discussion of the politics-administration dichotomy and problematisation of the small recruiting base of public servants has a long history, postulating this change as caused by the transfer of ideas seems farfetched. Nonetheless, Deutsch's *Nerves of Government* (1963) did have a significant influence on German PA scholars and the autopoiesis of academic institutions and the *Neo-Verwaltungswissenschaft*. Although this may be a temporal coincidence, the transfer of ideas should not be neglected. Foreign influence has played an important role and should not be systematically underestimated when referring to PA traditions.

However, the dissemination of ideas does not represent the key to identity and tradition on its own, as other factors might be far more important. Apparently being a member of the cybernetic discourse and the underlying web of belief has played a decisive role in the autopoiesis of the *Neo-Verwaltungswissenschaft*. A closer look at the most often-mentioned scholars in this chapter should be interesting as not only the internationally known Luhmann and Mayntz, but also Aderhold, Bull, Hirsch, Narr, Naschold, Pollock, Schelsky, Senghaas and Simitis pursued successful academic careers. Apparently, membership in the cybernetics circle served as a network and to a certain extent contributed to the formation of the modern German PA. To evaluate its importance, the history of ideas needs to be complemented by further studies.

References

Adam, A. (1959) *Messen und Regeln in der Betriebswirtschaft*, Würzburg: Physica-Verlag.

Aderhold, D. (1973) *Kybernetische Regierungstechnik in der Demokratie: Planung und Erfolgskontrolle*, Munich: Olzog-Aktuell.

Ampère, A. -M. (1843) *Essai sur la Philosophie des Sciences: Ouqq Exposition analytique d'une Classification Naturelle de Toutes les Connnaissances Humaines*, Paris: Bachelier.

Angermann, A. (1959) 'Kybernetik und betriebliche Führungslehre', *Betriebswirtschaftliche Forschung und Praxis*, 11(5): 257–67.

Beer, S. (1959) *Cybernetics and Management*, London: English Universities Press.

— (1962) *Kybernetik und Management*, Frankfurt am Main: S. Fischer Verlag.

Bevir, M. (2002) 'The role of contexts in understanding and explanation', in Bödeker, H. E. (ed.) *Begriffsgeschichte, Diskursgeschichte, Merapherngeschichte*, Göttingen: Wallstein Verlag, pp. 159–208.

Bevir, M., Rhodes, R. A. W. and Weller, P. (2003) 'Traditions of governance: interpreting the changing role of the public sector', *Public Administration*, 81(1): 1–17.

Blau, P. M. (1955) *The Dynamics of Bureaucracy*, Chicago: Chicago University Press.

— (1956) *Bureaucracy in Modern Society*, New York: Random House.

Blau, P. M. and Scott, W. R. (1962) *Formal Organizations: A comparative approach*, San Francisco, CA: Standford University Press.

Bogumil, J. (2005) 'On the relationship between political science and administrative science in Germany', *Public Administration*, 83(3): 669–84.

Bogumil, J. and Jann, W. (2009) *Verwaltung und Verwaltungswissenschaft in Deutschland: Einführung in die Verwaltungswissenschaft*, Wiesbaden: Verlag für Sozialwissenschaft.

Boudon, R. (1965) 'Réflexions sur la logique des modèles simulés', *Archives Européennes de Sociologie*, 6(1): 3–20.

Bull, H. P. (1964) *Verwaltung durch Maschinen: Rechtsprobleme der Technisierung der Verwaltung*, Köln: Kommunale Gemeinschaftsstelle für Verwaltungsvereinfachung.

Burns, T. (1955) 'The reference of conduct in small groups: cliques and cabals in occupational milieux', *Human Relations*, 8(4): 467–86.

— (1961) 'Micropolitics: mechanisms of institutional change', *Administrative Science Quarterly*, 6(3): 257–81.

— (1962) 'Des fins et des moyens dans la direction des entreprises', *Sociologie du Travail*, 4(3): 209–29.

Carleton, W. G. (1965) 'The century of technocracy', *Antioch Review*, 25(4): 487–506.

Clark, B. R. (1956) 'Adult education in transition: a study of institutional insecurity', Berkeley, CA: University of California Publications in Sociology and Social Institutions, 1(2): 43–202.

—   (1960) *The Open Door College: A case study*, New York/Toronto/ London: McGraw-Hill.

Conway, F. and Siegelman, J. (2005) *Dark Hero of the Information Age: In search for Norbert Wiener, the father of cybernetics*, New York: Basic Books.

Crane, D. (1962) 'Computer simulation: new laboratory for the social sciences', in Philipson, M. (ed.) *Automation: Implications for the future*, New York: Random House, pp. 339–54.

Crozier, M. (1963) *Le phénomène bureaucratique*, Paris: Le Seuil.

Dalton, M. (1959) *Men Who Manage*, New York: John Wiley.

Dammann, K. (1971) 'Vom "Arbeitenden Staat" zur "Politischen Verwaltung"', *Neue Politische Literatur*, 16(1–2): 188–204, 457–81.

—   (1973) 'Verwaltungswissenschaft und Rechtswissenschaft', in Grimm, D. (ed.) *Rechtswissenschaft und Nachbarwissenschaften*, Frankfurt: Athenäum-Fischer, pp. 107–39.

Deutsch, K. W. (1963) *The Nerves of Government: Models of political communication and control*, New York: Free Press.

—   (1966) *Politische Kybernetik: Modelle und perspektiven*, Freiburg im Breisgau: Rombach.

—   (1969) *Politische Kybernetik: Modelle und perspektiven*, Freiburg im Breisgau: Rombach.

Diebold, J. (1952) *Automation: The Advent of the Automatic Factory*, New York: Van Nostrand.

Diekmann, A. (2005) *Empirische Sozialforschung: Grundlagen, Methoden, Anwendungen*, Reinbek bei Hamburg: Rowohl Taschenbuch Verlag.

Dubarle, D. (1948) 'Une nouvelle science: la cybernéthique – vers la machine à gouverner?', *Le Monde*, 28 December, p. 3.

Fisch, S. (n.d.) *60 Jahre Deutsche Hochschule für Verwaltungswissenschaften Speyer*. Available at: http://www.hfv-speyer.de/sfisch/Stefan_Fisch_60_ Jahre_DHV.pdf (accessed 27 February 2014).

Flechtner, H. -J. (1966) *Grundbegriffe der Kybernetik*, Stuttgart: Wissenschaftliche Verlagsgesellschaft.

Flyvbjerg, B. (2006) 'Five misunderstandings about case-study research', *Qualitative Inquiry*, 12(2): 219–45.

Frank, H. (1969) *Kybernetische Grundlagen der Pädagogik: Eine Einführung in die Pädagogistik für Analytiker, Planer und Techniker des didaktischen Informationsumsatzes in der Industriegesellschaft*, Baden-Baden: Agis-Verlag.

Friedman, M. (1953) 'The methodology of positive economics', in Friedman, M. (ed.) *Essays in Positive Economics*, Chicago: University of Chicago Press.

Fruchter, B. and Jennings, E. E. (1962) 'Factor analysis', in Borko, H. (ed.) *Computer Applications in the Behavioral Sciences,* Englewood Cliffs: Prentice Hall, pp. 238–65.

Goertz, G. (2005) *Social Science Concepts: A user's guide*, Princeton, NJ: Princeton University Press.

Gouldner, A. (1954) *Patterns of Industrial Bureaucracy*, Glencoe, IL: Free Press.

Greene, J. (1954) 'Man as a servo component', *Control Engineering*, 1(2): 54–5.

Guetzkow, H. (1962) *Simulation in Social Science*, Englewood Cliffs: Prentice Hall.

— (1963) *Simulation in International Relations*, Englewood Cliffs: Prentice Hall.

Güldenberg, S. (2003) *Wissensmanagement und Wissenscontrolling in lernenden Organisationen: Ein systemtheoretischer Ansatz*, Wiesbaden: Deutscher Universitäts-Verlag.

Guntram, U. (1985) 'Die Allgemeine Systemtheorie: Ein überblick', *Zeitschrift für Betriebswirtschaft*, 55(3): 296–323.

Habermas, J. (1973) *Legitimationsprobleme im Spätkapitalismus*, Frankfurt am Main: Suhrkamp.

Haberstroh, C. J. (1960) 'Control as an organisational process', *Management Science*, 6(2): 165–71.

Hartfiel, G., Sedatis, L. and Claessens, D. (1964) *Beamte und Angestellte in der Verwaltungspyramide: Organisationssoziologische und verwaltungsrechtliche Untersuchungen über das Entscheidungshandeln in der Kommunalverwaltung*, Berlin: Duncker & Humblot.

Hauff, V. (1965) 'Simulation sozialer Systeme und politischer Alternativen', *Atomzeitalter*, 7(3): 80–4.

Haupt, W. (1961) 'Der mechanisierte Lohnsteuer-Jahresausgleich 1959', *Der Steuerbeamte (Beilage zur Steuer-Warte)*, p. 12.

Helmer, O. (1965) *Social Technology*, Santa Monica: Rand Corporation.

Hesse, J. J. (1982) 'Einführung', in Hesse, J. J. (ed.) *Politische Vierteljahresschrift*, special issue 13: *Politikwissenschaft und Verwaltungswissenschaft*, Opladen: Westdeutscher Verlag, pp. 9–33.

Hirsch, J. (1969) 'Ansätze einer Regierungslehre', in Kress, G. and Senghaas, D. (eds) *Politikwissenschaft: Eine Einführung in ihre Probleme*, Frankfurt am Main: Europäische Verlagsanstalt, pp. 269–85.

Hobsbawm, E. J. and Ranger, T. (2009) *The Invention of Tradition*, 7th edn, Cambridge: Cambridge University Press.

Hochstätter, P. R. (1962) 'Faktorenanalyse', in König, R. (ed.) *Handbuch der empirischen Sozialforschung*, Stuttgart: Enke Verlag, pp. 385–414.

Hovland, C. I. (1963) 'Computer simulation in the behavioral sciences', in Berelson, B. (ed.), *The Behavioral Sciences Today*, New York: Harper Torchbooks, pp. 77–88.

Jänicke, M. (1973) *Herrschaft und Krise*, Opladen: Verlag für Sozialwissenschaften.

Jann, W. (2003) 'State, administration and governance in Germany: competing traditions and dominant narratives', *Public Administration*, 81(1): 95–118.

— (2009) 'Praktische Fragen und theoretische Antworten: 50 Jahre Policy-Analyse und Verwaltungsforschung', *Politische Vierteljahresschrift*, 50(3): 476–505.

Jastrow, I. (1902) *Sozialpolitik und Verwaltungswissenschaft*, Berlin: Georg Reimer.

Kannegiesser, K. and Kelm, G. (1965) 'Das Vertragssystem unter dem Systemaspekt der Kybernetik', *Staat und Recht* 14(1): 32.

Kickert, W. J. M. and Stillman, R. J., II (1996) 'Changing European states: changing public administration', *Public Administration Review*, 56(1): 65–7.

—— (1999) *The Modern State and its Study: New administrative sciences in a changing Europe and United States*, Cheltenham: Edward Elgar.

King, G. W. (1952) 'Information', *Scientific American*, 187(3): 132–48.

Klaus, G. (1964) *Kybernetik in philosophischer Sicht*, Berlin: Dietz Verlag.

Kuhn, T. S. (1996) *The Structure of Scientific Revolutions*, Chicago: University of Chicago Press.

Lang, E. (1966) *Staat und Kybernetik: Prolegomena zu einer Lehre vom Staat als Regelkreis*, Salzburg/Munich: Anton Pustet.

—— (1970) *Zu einer kybernetischen Staatslehre: Eine Analyse des Staates auf der Grundlage des Regelkreismodells*, Salzburg: Pustet.

Langen, H. (1964) *Der Betrieb als Regelkreis*, Berlin: Ducker & Humblot.

List, F. (1955) *Verwaltungsrecht technischer Betriebe*, Baden-Baden: Verlag für angewandte Wissenschaften.

Luhmann, N. (1966a) *Recht und Automation in der öffentlichen Verwaltung*, Berlin: Duncker & Humblot.

—— (1966b) *Theorie der Verwaltungswissenschaft. Bestandsaufnahme und Entwurf,* Köln/Berlin: Grote.

—— (1969) *Legitimation durch Verfahren*, Neuwied, Berlin: Luchterhand.

—— (1972) 'Politikbegriffe und die "Politisierung" der Verwaltung', *Demokratie und Verwaltung, 25 Jahre Hochschule für Verwaltungswissenschaften Speyer*, Berlin: Duncker & Humblot, 211–28.

Maass, W. (1961) 'Die Mechanisierung von Aufgaben der Steuerverwaltung in den Vereinigten Staaten und in Deutschland', *Verwaltungsarchiv*, 52(52): 113–59.

Maxwell, J. C. (1868) 'On governors', *Proceedings of the Royal Society*, 16(100): 270–83.

Mayntz, R. (1964) 'Anwendung der Kybernetik in der Soziologie', in Frank, H. (ed.) *Kybernetische Maschinen*, Frankfurt am Main: Fischer.

—— (ed.) (1980) *Implementation politischer Programme: Empirische Forschungsberichte*, Königstein: Verlagsgruppe Athenäum, Hain, Scriptor Hanstein.

—— (1996) 'Politische Steuerung: Aufstieg, Niedergang und Transformation einer Theorie', in von Beyme, K. and Offe, C. (eds) *Politische Theorien in der ära der Transformation*, Opladen: Westdeutscher Verlag, pp. 148–68.

Mayr, O. (1971) 'Adam Smith and the concept of the feedback system: economic thought and technology in 18th-century Britain', *Technologie and Culture*, 12(1): 1–22.

Merton, R. K. (1940) 'Bureaucratic structure and personality', *Social Forces*, 18(4): 560–8.
— (1945) 'The role of the intellectual in public bureaucracy', *Social Forces*, 23(4): 405–15.
— (1957) *Social Theory and Social Structure*, Glencoe, IL: Free Press.
Michael, D. M. (1962) *Cybernation: The silent conquest,* Santa Barbara, CA: Center for the Study of Democratic Institutions.
Moore, D. G. (1959) 'Managerial Strategies', in Warner, W. L. and Martin, N. H. (eds) *Industrial Man: Businessmen and business organizations*, New York: Harper, pp. 219–26.
Morstein-Marx, F. (1959a) *Das Dilemma des Verwaltungsmannes*, Berlin: Duncker & Humblot.
— (1959b) *Einführung in die Bürokratie: Eine Vergleichende Untersuchung über das Beamtentum,* Neuwied: Hermann Luchterhand Verlag.
Nagel, E. (1952) 'Automatic control', *Scientific American*, 187(3): 44–7.
Narr, W. -D. (1969) *Theoriebegriff und Systemtheorie,* Stuttgart: Verlag W. Kohlhammer.
Naschold, F. (1969) *Systemsteuerung,* Stuttgart: Verlag W. Kohlhammer.
— (1972) 'Zur Politik und ökonomie von Plaungssystemen', *Politische Vierteljahresschrift*, special issue, 4: 13–53.
Nürck, R. (1960a) 'Funktions- und strukturbedingte Regelungsmassnahmen der Unternehmung', *Zeitschrift für Betriebswirtschaft*, 30(12): 744–56.
— (1960b) 'Unternehmensführung – ein Regelungsproblem', *Betriebswirtschaftliche Forschung und Praxis*, 12(4): 230–8.
Overeem, P. and Rutgers, M. R. (2003) 'Three roads to politics and administration: ideational foundations of the politics/administration dichotomy', in Rutgers, M. R. (ed.) *Retracing Public Administration*, Boston, MA: Elsevier: 161–84.
Painter, M. and Peters, B. G. (2010) *Tradition and Public Administration*, New York: Palgrave Macmillan.
Parsons, T. (1956) 'A sociological approach to the theory of organisations', *Administrative Science Quarterly*, 1(1/2): 63–85, 225–39.
— (1958) 'Some ingredients of a general theory of formal organization', in Halpin, A. W. (ed.) *Administrative Theory in Education*, New York/ Chicago: Macmillan, pp. 40–72.
Pias, C. (2003) *Cybernetics/Kybernetik: The Macy-Conferences 1946–1953*, Vol. 1: *Transactions/Protokolle*. Zürich/Berlin: Diaphanes.
— (2004a) *Cybernetics/Kybernetik: The Macy-Conferences 1946–1953*, Vol. 2: *Essays and Documents/Essays und Dokumente,* Zürich/Berlin: Diaphanes.
— (2004b) 'Zeit der Kybernetik – eine Einstimmung', in Pias, C. (ed.) *Cybernetics – Kybernetik: The Macy-Conferences 1946–1953*, Vol. 2: *Essays & Documents/Essays und Dokumente*, Zürich, Berlin: Diaphanes, pp. 9–41.

Pietsch, M. (1957) 'Automation', in *Staatslexikon*, 6th edn, Freiburg im Breisgau: Verlag Herder/Spalte, p. 794.

Pollock, F. (1955) 'Automation in USA: Betrachtungen zur "Zweiten Industriellen Revolution"', in Adorno, T. W. and Dirks, W. (eds) *Sociologica*, Frankfurt am Main: Europäische Verlagsanstalt, pp. 77–156.

—— (1956) *Automation: Materialien zur Beurteilung der ökonomischen und sozialen Folgen*, Frankfurt am Main: Europ- Verlagsanstalt.

Presthus, R. V. (1962) *The Organizational Society*, New York: Alfred A. Knopf.

Raadschelders, J. C. N. (2008) 'Understanding government: four intellectual traditions in the study of public administration', *Public Administration*, 86(4): 925–40.

Ridenour, L. N. (1952) 'The role of the computer', *Scientific American*, 187(3): 116–30.

—— (1957) 'Die Befehlsmaschine', *Das Elektronengehirn: Theorie und Praxis der Automation: Zwölf Beiträge führender amerikanischer Wissenschaftler*, Wiesbaden: Rhein, Verlags-Anstalt.

Rohr, J. A. (2002) 'Musings on the state: a reply to Mark Rutger's "Traditional flavors"', *Administration & Society*, 33(6): 664–70.

Rosenblueth, A., Wiener, N. and Bigelow, J. (1943) 'Behavior, purpose and teleology', *Philosophy of Science*, 10(1): 18–24.

Rosser, C. (2010) 'Woodrow Wilson's administrative thought and German political theory', *Public Administration Review*, 70(4): 547–56.

Rugge, F. (2003) 'Administrative traditions in Western Europe', in Peters, B. G. and Pierre, J. (eds) *Handbook of Public Administration*, London/ Thousand Oaks/New Dehli: Sage, pp. 177–91.

Rutgers, M. R. (2000) 'Public administration and the separation of powers in a cross-Atlantic perspective', *Administrative Theory and Practice*, 22(2): 287–308.

—— (2001) 'Traditional flavors? The different sentiments in European and American administrative thought', *Administration & Society* 33(2): 220–44.

Sager, F. and Rosser, C. (2009) 'Weber, Wilson, and Hegel: theories of modern bureaucracy', *Public Administration Review*, 69(6): 1136–47.

Sager, F., Rosser, C., Hurni, P. and Mavrot, C. (2012) 'How traditional are the American, French and German traditions of public administration? A research agenda', *Public Administration*, 90(1): 129–43.

Scharpf, F. W. (1971) 'Verwaltungswissenschaft als Teil der Politikwissenschaft', *Annuaire Suisse de Science Politique*, 11(1): 7–24.

Schelsky, H. (1957) *Die sozialen Folgen der Automatisierung*, Frankfurt/Cologne: Diederichs.

Seibel, W. (1982) '"Regierbarkeits"-Krise und Verwaltungswissenschaft: Eine ideengeschichtliche Systematik der Stabilisierung krisengefährdeter sozialer Ordnungen und ihrer Berücksichtigung in den Wissenschaften vom programmierten Staatshandeln', doctoral dissertation, Kassel: Gesamthochschule.

—   (1996) 'Administrative science as reform: German public administration', *Public Administration Review*, 56(1): 74–81.

Selznick, P. (1943) 'An approach to a theory of bureaucracy', *American Sociological Review*, 8(1): 47–54.

—   (1948) 'Foundations of the theory of organization', *American Sociological Review*, 13(1): 23–35.

—   (1949) *TVA and the Grass Roots: A study in the sociology of formal organization*, Berkeley/Los Angeles: University of California Press.

Senghaas, D. (1966) 'Kybernetik und Politikwissenschaft', *Politische Vierteljahresschrift*, 7(2): 252–79.

—   (1967) 'Sozialkybernetik und Herrschaft', *Atomzeitalter* 9(3): 186–99.

Shannon, C. E. (1948) 'A mathematical theory of communication', *Bell System Technical Journal*, 27(3–4): 379–423, 623–56.

Simitis, S. (1964) 'Rechtliche Anwendungsmöglichkeiten kybernetischer Systeme', in Frank, H. (ed.) *Kybernetische Maschinen*, Frankfurt am Main: S. Fischer Verlag.

Simon, H. A. (1947) *Administrative Behavior: A study of decision-making processes in administrative organization*, New York: Macmillan.

—   (1955) *Das Verwaltungshandeln: Eine Untersuchung der Entscheidungsvorgänge in Behörden und privaten Unternehmen*, Stuttgart: W. Kohlhammer.

Sjoberg, G. (1960) 'Contradictory functional requirements and social systems', *Journal of Conflict Resolution*, 4(2): 198–208.

Smith, A. (2001) 'Studying administrative reform in Britain and France: academic questions, traditions and debates', *Public Policy and Administration*, 16(4): 9–19.

Steinbuch, K. (1965) *Automat und Mensch*, Berlin/Heidelberg/New York: Springer Verlag.

Stillman, R. J., II (1997) 'American vs. European public administration: does public administration make the modern state, or does the state make public administration', *Public Administration Review*, 57(4): 332–8.

—   (2001) 'Toward a new agenda for administrative state research? A response to Mark Rutger's "Traditional flavors?" essay', *Administration & Society*, 33(4): 480–8.

Strauss, G. (1962) 'Tactics of lateral relationship: the purchasing agent', *Administrative Science Quarterly*, 7(2): 161–82.

Theobald, R. (1966) 'Cybernetics and the problems of social reorganization', in Dechert, C. R. (ed.) *The Social Impact of Cybernetics*, Notre Dame: University of Notre Dame Press.

Tustin, A. (1952) 'Feedback', *Scientific American*, 187(3): 48–55.

Verba, S. (1964) 'Simulation, reality, and theory in international relations', *World Politics*, 16(3): 490–519.

Vogl, J. (2004) 'Regierung und Regelkreis: Historisches Vorspiel', in Pias, C. (ed.) *Cybernetics/Kybernetik: The Macy-Conferences 1946–1953*, Vol. 2: *Essays & Documents/Essays & Dokumente*, Zürich: Diaphanes, pp. 67–79.

Werner, M. (2002) *Information und Codierung: Grundlagen und Anwendungen,* Braunschweig/Wiesbaden: Vieweg und Teubner.

Wiener, N. (1948) *Cybernetics: Or the control and communication in the animal and the machine,* Paris/Cambridge/New York: Hermann et Cie, Technology Press, John Wiley & Sons.

— (1950) *The Human Use of Human Beings: Cybernetics and society,* Boston, MA: Houghton Mifflin.

— (1963) *Kybernetik: Regelung und Nachrichtenübertragung im Lebewesen und in der Maschine,* Reinbek bei Hamburg: Rowohlt.

Wildavsky, A. (1964) *The Politics of the Budgetary Process,* Boston/Toronto: Little Brown.

Wilensky, H. (1956) *Intellectuals in Labor Unions: Organizational pressures on professional roles,* Glencoe, IL: Free Press.

Wussing, H. (2009) *6000 Jahre Mathematik: Eine kulturgeschichtliche Zeitreise,* Vol. 2: *Von Euler bis zur Gegenwart,* Berlin/Heidelberg: Springer Verlag.

Zeidler, K. (1959) *Über die Technisierung der Verwaltung: Eine Einführung in die juristische Beurteilung der modernen Verwaltung,* Karlsruhe: C. F. Müller.

Part Five

The Europeanised Public Servant in the EU

Chapter Eleven

Developing a Hybrid Identity? The Europeanisation of Public Servants at the Continent's Far West

Bernadette Connaughton

Introduction

The pervasiveness of Europeanisation is more apparent in the politics and policies of the member states than in their institutional architecture and administrative systems. Public administrations remain conditioned by features of national administrative traditions (Knill 2001; Harmsen 1999) reflecting the history, identity and traditions of a specific state and its society. This is reflected in European public administration, which is composed of European Commission services and a variety of arrangements in the twenty-eight member state administrations. It contrasts with a well-defined European concept of public administration in the form of a 'European administrative space' (EAS), which denotes that public administration is guided and managed on the basis of common European principles through rules, standards and practices (OECD 1998; *see* Chapter One). The public servants operating within this European administrative space constitute a crucial 'living institution', the identities, preferences, training and role perceptions of which are influenced by their interactions with the EU policy bureaucracy and participation in policy networks. Simultaneously, the identity of officials is moderated by national political–administrative cultures, the ways in which the concept of the public servant has developed over time, through changes in organisational and societal context (*see* Raadschelders, Chapter Two in this volume). Understanding European official identity as a part of the development of the EAS requires an exploration of the circumstances through which a sense of administrative loyalty and role is developed, lost and defined (Olsen 2002).

This chapter explores how Irish public servants have developed an official identity in central government departments, how they go about their EU policy work as 'street-level diplomats', and whether participation in the EU policy-making process shapes their role perceptions. In the first section of the chapter, interpretations of Europeanisation are considered as a means of understanding how official engagement with the EU has the potential to shape national official identity. The second unpacks the characteristics of public service that have influenced the identity of the Irish public servant from independence in 1922 to EU membership in 1973. Several 'mediating' characteristics are identified as influential for our understanding of what appears to be a limited 'Europeanisation' of Irish official identity. This is further considered in the third section, which presents an overview of how Irish officials approach their EU policy work. The discussion offers insights into their attitudes, practices, career trajectories and identities through a review of the literature and several interviews undertaken with central government officials.

Europeanisation and bureaucrats: Identity and roles

Europeanisation is regarded by scholars as critical to our understanding of the transformations of national systems and the salience of the EU for its member states. The concept describes 'a set of interrelated processes that go well beyond the traditional focus of scholars interested in how state bargaining and elite identification affect the evolution of the EU' (Checkel and Katzenstein 2009: 9). A prominent definition by Radaelli (2003: 30) considers Europeanisation as:

> processes of (a) construction, (b) diffusion, and (c) institutionalisation of formal and informal rules, procedures, policy paradigms, styles, 'ways of doing things' and shared beliefs and norms which are first defined and consolidated in the making of EU decisions and then incorporated in the logic of domestic discourse, identities, political structures and public policies.

Of interest to this discussion is how EU norms and 'ways of doing things' are mediated by domestic variables to affect officials' roles and identities. Bulmer (2007: 55) contends that changes in the work of individual national public servants are not usually labelled as Europeanisation but acknowledges that the subject matter falls within most of its definitions. It is also asserted in the literature that the impact of Europeanisation on collective identities and shifting loyalties is not only controversial but also poorly understood (Risse 2001: 198). This reference to Europeanisation and the evolution of a nation state identity is, arguably, directly relevant to national officials since they engage as conduits, decision makers, and policy or rule bearers between the EU and the national level, not least through their participation in a variety of EU fora.

Assuming that an emerging European polity impacts on the domestic one and produces challenges to 'social' identity, we would also expect there to be a degree of impact on 'official' identity. EU policy making is both a political and a bureaucratic process and is characterised by increasing bureaucratisation, since national officials dominate domestic EU-related policy making. The emergence of greater centralisation for coordinating EU business has led to the emergence of powerful EU core executives. Does this result in officials acquiring a more European identity, a hybrid identity, or do they maintain a distinctly national identity? Laffan (2007a) asserts that in practice we know relatively little about official attitudes, practices, career trajectories or identities. But knowing about this is essential if we are to develop a deeper understanding of EU-domestic dynamics. Her view is generally reinforced by the commentary in studies that focus on the *roles* and *socialisation* of domestic bureaucrats in the EU policy-making process. *Role* is defined as referring to 'a more or less systematic pattern of relations between actors and specific position' (Beyers 2005), whereas *socialisation* refers to individuals acquiring preferences by 'internalising norms, values, and principles' embodied by the groups or institutions that are 'important to their personal dispositions' (Hooghe 2001: 14), and is motivated by a 'logic of appropriateness'. European socialisation entails:

> that the involvement in European venues causes a redefinition of norms and practices, and these European norms and values gradually become 'internalised' as part of the self. More generally, European socialisation refers to the adaptive learning processes of national organisational structures, and the individuals representing these, to a changing, or changed, and increasingly Europeanised political environment. A better understanding of socialisation processes may thus contribute substantially to the study of Europeanisation and European integration. (Beyers 2010: 909–10)

The literature shows that across the continent of Europe public servants draw on a number of roles and identities in dealing with EU business, and it explores the dominance of either an intergovernmental or supranational role conception. This includes officials of functional national agencies (Egeberg 1999), bureaucratic elites developing shared governance beliefs (Radaelli and O'Connor 2009), and experts whose professional knowledge is shared across a multi-level EU administration (Egeberg 2006). Central to these identities is the national administration, which remains the key point of reference for national officials; supranational loyalties remain secondary. In the EU policy-making process, however, officials are not acting just as national representatives but are encouraged to engage as technical experts, which may induce a deeper attachment to European ideals, knowledge or ways of doing things. Other work that increases our understanding of a potential European or hybrid official identity are studies that observe how individual public servants are 'doing policy work' and experience their craft as participants in a multi-levelled process ('t Hart *et al.* 2007) or narratives of their personal 'lived' experiences as negotiators (Clark and Jones 2011).

The various studies on the socialisation of officials participating in working groups within the Council, however, assign a limited socialisation potential to EU institutions and highlight the continuing importance of domestic factors such as state structure and involvement in domestic coordination networks. The national administration is core to officials engaging in European policy making and their identity is significantly conditioned by their 'domestic institutional embeddedness' (Beyers and Trondal 2004).[1] Hence, despite an

---

1. Beyers and Trondal (2004) substantiated this argument in their comparison of Belgian and Swedish officials attending working groups within the Council of Ministers. Belgian officials are more supranationally oriented than their Swedish colleagues.

inclination to regard national perspectives as coinciding and intersecting with European developments, officials continue to classify themselves as national agents, although they perform both national and European roles. Administrative tradition and culture should not be excluded when considering official identity since administrative cultures (and sub-cultures) embody more specific patterns of behaviour and orientations of officials (*ibid.*). In the remainder of this chapter, an analysis of the adaptation of Irish officials to the EU and considerations of the way in which this affects identity is complemented by an exploration of the factors that moderate their beliefs and practices and account for national identity. The following section considers the development of an official identity in the emerging independent Irish state.

Official identity: Irish nationalism and British norms

The desire for Irish independence in the late nineteenth and early twentieth centuries was founded on both political and cultural nationalism. Despite a political mood in 1922 reflecting distance from Great Britain, however, it was never in doubt that the Irish Free State (IFS) would adopt a form of representative parliamentary government, since the experience of Westminster politics and administration had deep roots in Ireland (MacCarthaigh 2005: 63). Institutions of the British state – parliament, judiciary, policy and military – were replaced with native institutions and Irish public administration closely emulated the English model. It is recorded that 98 per cent of central government officials transferred from the service of Great Britain to the Irish Provisional Government (Fanning 2007). The stability of Irish democracy in the aftermath of a revolution and civil war is generally explained by the new government's retention of the state structures and especially the bureaucratically embedded public service. The assimilation of British structure and officials that served in the previous regime is worth considering further to understand the identity formation of officials in what was to become the native public service.

Characteristics of civic and ethnic nationalism that shaped a particular Irish identity also influenced the beliefs of Irish officials, even if the majority of public servants resisted an active role in the fight for independence. Public servants' sympathy for and adaptation to separatism was initially cultural, then political and finally revolutionary (Fanning 2007; Maguire 2008). Social conservatism was compounded by the absence of a strong labour movement in Ireland and the dominance of the national question laid a peculiar foundation for the nature of Irish politics rather than a more usual split along class lines. Maguire (2008: 29) argues that the Irish public servants developed a 'pious dislike' of England arising from the opinion that 'England had treated Ireland badly'. In December 1921, the Anglo-Irish Treaty was signed, and this led to the partition of Ireland and the formation of the IFS (twenty-six counties). This split was contentious in Republican ranks and led to civil war. Despite their Republican sympathies, many public servants remained at their desks after 1921 and 'the new leaders able to rely on their bureaucrats did not have to turn Ireland into a military dictatorship to stay in power' (Velychenko 2005: 18). Stability was also upheld in the religious composition of the top officials who transferred to the IFS since they were about evenly divided into Catholic and Protestant Irish with a slight majority of Catholics (McBride 1991: 310; Lee 1989: 90). These officials served their new IFS masters loyally, much as they had done their unionist masters under the British.

The identity of the Irish public servant in an independent Irish state was also characterised by a recognition of the rights and entitlements that had been introduced through reforms ranging from the implementation of the Northcote-Trevelyan recommendations published in 1854 (*see* Chapter Seven in this volume), to the Royal Commission of the Civil Service chaired by Anthony Patrick MacDonnell (1912–14), to the Warren Fisher reforms in Dublin Castle (1920). The latter resulted in a hardcore unionist element being ousted from Dublin Castle and the rejuvenation of an outmoded, demoralised administration into an efficient and modernised public service just in time for treaty settlement. These advances were not lost on the senior administrators who transferred, and their high consciousness of those reforms provided a durable administrative legacy. The distraction of the civil war also provided senior public servants with the opportunity to set up the administration of an independent Ireland 'without the meddlesome interference of politicians' (Fanning 2007: 9). The identity of Irish officials became moulded by the formal institutional arrangements and the service modelled itself strongly on what it deemed to be the virtues of the British system. Moody and Martin (2011: 291) comment that 'after 1922 Merrion Street became Whitehall writ small'. Three features laid the foundation of this system. First, a Ministers and Secretaries Act, which became the legal basis for the public administration in 1924, exacerbated the characteristics of centralisation and control. Second, centralisation was further accentuated by the copper fastening of what Fanning (2007: 10) describes as the 'fundamental principles' of the role of the British Treasury and their emulation by the Irish Department of Finance. In the first administration the Minister of Finance was also head of government, which afforded immense advantages to the senior officials seeking to embed the British legacy, since the general public service organisation and regulation was vested in the Department. Third, features of merit and political impartiality endured through indigenous recalibrations of British institutional features that included the Civil Service Commission in 1924 and the Local Appointments Commission in 1926. Lee (1989: 93) comments that the adherence to the British model dominated mentalities as well as institutional structures. At one level it contributed significantly to establishing standards of personal integrity and at another level it enshrined the 'cult of the amateur' in administration. In particular, the idea of administrative impartiality endured and remained central to the self-image of Irish public servants (Collins *et al*. 2007: 15).

Official identity: Institutional embeddedness, culture and opportunity

As Raadschelders comments (Chapter Two in this volume), public servants are always rooted in a specific political–administrative tradition. The social profile of the Irish public servant in the early decades of independence also provides insight into their developing identity. The comparison with British administrative legacies demonstrates that the administrative system was not unique, but also that the nature of the wider society at the time of independence was exceptional. The new state enjoyed the resources of a highly developed civil society that had been put together by the British state and the Irish churches in the nineteenth century. Garvin (2004: 27) comments that 'legitimacy was lent to the new Free State regime by a popular Catholic church determined that a Catholic electorate should enjoy that apparent contradiction in terms, a Catholic liberal democracy'. To a large degree this was reflected in official identity, which was shaped by deeply conservative views. For example, official attitudes towards women showed the political conservatism of the new state. Women had played a significant role in Irish revolutionary politics, but 'the return to normalcy' in the post-civil war period extinguished opportunities for women to contribute to aspects of Irish life outside the roles of wife and mother (Keogh 2005: 39). Officials preferred to keep women out of posts, beginning at the junior executive grade, though this was not legally possible (*ibid.*). This contrasted with the growing employment of women in the public service between 1914 and 1918 when they were substituted for enlisted men in the First World War. After 1922 the introduction of a 'marriage bar' assured that women remained a significant minority within the bureaucracy. Until 1973 women had to retire from most public service positions after marriage. This archaic measure denied the state the benefit of a reservoir of talent.

The social profile of male public servants was very different from that of their British counterparts. Over time the service became composed of principally young men from similar backgrounds in rural Ireland, typically educated by the Christian Brothers[2] and from families that were unable to afford third-level education. They were described as intellectually able and hardworking, but rather narrowly practical in their approach, and deeply conservative (*see* Chubb 1992). Barrington (1974) argued that the Irish public service was anti-intellectual and too representative of a small homogeneous society, since Irish administrators tended to be the children of small farmers, small shopkeepers and the petit bourgeois, not drawn from some hereditary or economic elite (cited in Fanning 2008: 204). The image of the Irish public servant has been unflatteringly described as 'of a lowly clerk, a cheap-suited, Fáinne-wearing bumbler, or a cold-eyed spinster with a rosary, a sharp tongue and a well-worn pair of knitting needles' (O'Halpin, cited in McCarthy 2005).

The political elite seemed to lack the ideas and ability to change things, a tendency reinforced by both structural features and the distinctive culture. Despite the advantages of inheriting a functioning administration and its consolidation through centralisation, the structural features of the electoral system did not foster a

---

2.   The Christian Brothers were founded in 1808 to provide education for poor boys but came to provide education for all classes, especially at the second level.

professional cadre of political policy makers and cultivated a personal and informal dimension to Irish politics. Bureaucratic continuity was enforced by the electoral system since senior public servants served essentially inexperienced governments and ministers who were reliant on their expertise. Hence, another maxim of British public service, that of 'clear sight over short distances', also became a hallmark of the Irish administration (Barrington 1980: 31). The background and training of public servants had closed their minds to most ideas outside the British liberal and *laissez-faire* tradition (Fanning 2008: 293). Public servants saw their role as administering the system as it existed. In the words of a senior official, 'we are concerned, not with ends, which is politics, but with means, which is administration. We are concerned not with why a service is provided but with how it is provided' (Barrington, cited in Fanning 2008: 193). Commentators also became scathing of the fictional division between politics and administration in the policy-making process promoted by public servants, criticising this idea as naïve, misleading and promoting bureaucratic inflexibility (Fanning 2008: 201). It enshrined a false dichotomy that misrepresented the workings of the policy-making processes and the activities of the 'permanent government'. The conservative intellectual climate in the administration was unlikely to promote a spirit of innovation, especially after the onset of the depression in the early 1930s. As a consequence, policy steering was shaped by the conventions of the political culture and informal approaches rather than clear strategic planning and rational structures.

By 1957, the boundaries and philosophy of the central administration seemed reasonably settled and were very similar to the institutions set up on the foundation of the state (Gaffey 1982: 115). From the 1930s to the 1950s, economic, foreign and social policies promoted isolationism and self-sufficiency. This reinforced a nationalism that advocated cultural monochromism, social homogeneity and political solidarity. The 1937 constitution gave normative effect to these core values of Irish national identity, which fashioned official identity. The delay in abandoning protectionism was a significant policy mistake (Garvin 2004). Such delays were also evident later on in the failure to invest in education earlier and implement policy recommendations to address the problems of indigenous industry. Clearly necessary reform was not only a matter of structures but also of culture, ideas and intellectual influences shaping the public service. Despite the inspiration of talented individuals like T. K. Whitaker, a Secretary of the Department of Finance, there was no drive or encouragement from public servants to rethink the system. The initiatives taken by Whitaker and his colleagues, however, marked a critical juncture in the way the administration affirmed its role as a nexus between political leadership and the socio-economic development. These officials acknowledged that cultural change and new skills were needed in the public sector (Fanning 2008) and bureaucratic inflexibilities needed to be overcome. Prior to this point, the bureaucratic elites in the Department of Finance had perceived their mission as one to promote the self-sufficiency of the state. An Institute of Public Administration (IPA) was established in 1957 to assist with training and critical thinking. But by the early 1970s, it was acknowledged that the public service had lost its influence to attract the top ranks of school leavers and had little ability to attract the small pool of university graduates (Fanning 2008: 202). All in all, this trajectory did not inspire confidence that 'elitist claims of modern administrators [were sufficiently able] [...] to represent the public interest when it came to understanding complex issues' (*ibid.*).

So, we can conclude that in the first two-thirds of the twentieth century, the identity of the Irish public servant was conservative (even for the times), pragmatic, but with a weak internal logic for dealing with robust state development, influenced by the political culture emerging in the new state, and demonstrating adherence to apolitical, impartial, meritocratic principles and the idea of 'public service', which manifested distinct modes of handling problems and solutions. The incorporation of British norms and traditions through assimilating a model of durable democratic institutions and administrative system endured, as did the hard-won rights and entitlements introduced through reforms in Dublin Castle prior to independence. These are factors that sculpted the identity of Irish officials serving in the early decades of independence and that until today moderate the impact of Europeanisation, as we will see now when we consider the more recent decades.

Joining the EU

On the eve of EU membership in 1973, Irish public servants maintained a conservative identity, had not engaged with reform, and had very little experience of internationalisation. A former senior official recalls his early days in the service:

> For example, I joined a Civil Service in the 1970s, which paid men and women different rates, which required women to resign on marriage, which was still preparing for entry into the 'Common Market', which was concerned about how to react to the eruption of 'the Troubles' in Northern Ireland, which was serving a population in which the first generation to benefit from free post-primary education was still at school, which operated in a tightly defined and largely homogenous cultural context and in which the most sensational media stories tended to reflect only the more risqué elements of the Late Late Show. It was widely perceived, as a career, to be worthy but dull, earning its keep on the basis that most people, including Ministers, believed that, in the words of a former Department Secretary, 'the best way to get results was to allow an old and well-tried machine to function efficiently. (Dermot McCarthy (2005) (Secretary General, Department of Taoiseach and Secretary General to the Government 2001–11))

In the years after the war, the public service had begun to reach out tentatively towards involvement in international organisations such as the Organisation for European Economic Co-operation (OEEC), the UN (membership in 1955), and the IMF and World Bank (membership in 1957). The idea of becoming engaged in alliances that might involve a mutual defence commitment was not attractive, however, and public servants shared a common vision for the country with their political masters. A formal end to protectionism was signalled in 1961 with the application for full membership of the European Economic Community (EEC). This impetus for change arose from that citadel of conservatism, the Department of Finance, and highlighted a 'significant domestic victory which the Taoiseach and a small group of officials enjoyed over the traditionalists in the ruling Fianna Fáil party' (Keogh and Keogh 2007: 8). Despite this, the road to membership proved rather tortuous as it was not until 1969 that accession negotiations commenced. Irish policy makers were naïve in their understanding of how European politics functioned and inexperienced in the art of international diplomacy. A small group of politicians and senior public servants from the Department of Finance was responsible for drafting and managing the application and for the subsequent negotiations, which finally led to a positive decision. The implications of membership were outlined in White Papers produced in 1970 and 1972, but they made no reference to the public service (Barrington and Cooney 1984: 172), nor did they consider the political dimensions of membership in any detail. The officials whose professional lives were to change considerably did not address the reality of this substantial new dimension to their work. Paradoxically, accession may well have posed a greater challenge to public servants than the emergence of the independent state.

Laffan (2007b) argues that adapting public administration to EEC membership challenged the capacity of the system to cope with the demands of the European policy process and modernisation in general. In respect to the three-fold categorisation of coordination systems by Bartlett and Ghoshal (1989) – centralisation, formalisation and socialisation – the Irish case introduced all three (Laffan 2007b: 191). However, 'the dominant mode of coordination on a day-to-day and week-to-week basis is undoubtedly socialisation' (*ibid.*) and the system channels political and administrative resources towards the big issues of significance to Ireland. In general, the Irish officials who have written about their work experience as 'bureaucrat diplomats' do so in a positive light and have augured that the system served Ireland relatively well:

> The obvious fact that EU policy measures play a central role in shaping domestic policy across a range of fields means that EU policy work is critical to the operation of the Irish State. Moreover, the debate also allows us an opportunity to help shape EU policy in a larger sense, which has obvious opportunities for Ireland (in terms of shaping external positions and the orientation of markets and measures within the EU) and an opportunity to contribute to policy making on a larger scale than would ever arise on a solely national basis. (Personal interview, July 2012)

The views of ministers about the Irish capability to cope with European policy have also been largely constructive, with some undertones of scepticism reserved for particular issues.[3] In order to provide an overview of the processes of socialisation and learning triggered by EU membership and moderated by the characteristics inculcated in Irish officials since independence, the following issues are taken together and explored: organisational dimensions (e.g. training, instruction and guidance; career development) and role orientations (what do national public servants see as their chief tasks, to what extent do they see themselves as involved, how big a part of daily working life do they devote to European matters?).

Living with Brussels

Although there were individual exceptions it appears that in the advent of EU membership government departments and their officials were slow to move away from the comfort of old orthodoxies. Overall, little attention had been paid to 'living with the system', in contrast with the effort attributed to preparation by the UK and Denmark (Laffan 2007b). The pressure was felt as officials attempted to graft new duties onto the scaffold of an old system.

A critical requirement for partaking in EU business is the development of a cadre of suitably qualified officials who can combine technical expertise with knowledge of the EU policy-making process. From the very beginning the officials from the Department of Foreign Affairs were able to conform to this identity of EU bureaucrat-diplomats since it was their *métier* to live much of their professional lives abroad and be in regular contact with foreign officials. Cromien (2000: 148) notes that this was not the case for other public servants, who 'initially had something of an inferiority complex, or at least a sense of unease, operating in an international milieu'. Irish officials were not comfortable working in a multilingual environment and while early Irish governments had made much of translating official documents into Irish to mark a distinct Irish identity, the promotion of the language in the national education system did not ultimately deliver an Irish language revival debate. In addition, few officials were trained in foreign languages and at that time most officials had little, if any, contact with other administrations or experience of travel abroad. Likewise no specific training emerged within the system. It remained ad hoc and the administration did not develop a fast stream for Brussels high-flyers. This has not changed; there still is an absence of career planning in a European context. Irish officials remain largely

---

3. For example, Minister Roche in 2007 commented that policy makers regard Ireland as a small state and this has implications for how Ireland positions itself in the Union. 'Far from suffering our identity and sovereignty have both been enhanced by the impact of membership' (Roche 2007). In 2000, two government ministers interpreted identity from a different perspective. Minister Síle de Valera attempted to excuse Ireland's poor compliance with the habitats directive: 'But it is not the cornerstone of what our nation is or should be. We have found that directives and regulations agreed in Brussels can often seriously impinge on our identity, culture and traditions'. Minister and Tánaiste Mary Harney referred to Ireland as 'geographically closer to Berlin than Boston [...] spiritually we are probably a lot closer to Boston than Berlin' (O'Mahony 2004). These comments were in marked contrast to a positive speech delivered by Taoiseach Bertie Ahern that year at the Institute of European Affairs (Ahern 2000).

a group of policy process generalists who learn on the job and have very little training in formal policy analysis techniques. Nor are departments likely to have a cadre of trained lawyers, which has proven problematic for implementation in complex areas such as environmental policy. A dearth of specialist staff can also be an inhibition in technical negotiations. Despite this, the learning obtained from participating in Council working groups also presents opportunities:

> The range of subject areas we are exposed to is interesting in and of itself, but the exposure we get to the position and practice of other member states is particularly interesting in that it gives ready comparison with our own situation and allows for very useful discussion around best practice, both in terms of process and in terms of measures taken. This (informal) process has proven to be hugely influential in informing the policy-making process here. (Personal interview, July 2012)

In all, Irish officials are rarely rewarded in their careers for becoming EU experts and this tends to militate against the development of a European identity. It can also be difficult to recruit officials for secondment to the Permanent Representation from line departments since career progression is more secure for those who do not break their service in their own department. Officials who have served in the Permanent Representation appear to be the officials with the most robust socialisation experience, though they are regarded as a close-knit Irish mini-civil service. The Permanent Representation is not composed wholly of diplomats from Foreign Affairs but also staffed from line departments and is Ireland's largest external mission. These officials are supported by what Laffan and O'Mahony (2007) refer to as 'Brussels insiders' and boundary spanners, namely the few key experts in sectoral departments and those within the 'holy trinity' of Foreign Affairs, Finance and the Taoiseach (Prime Minister's Office). They understand Brussels and have an innate sense of the constraints of Ireland's position, resources and size. These insiders are European experts who are called upon for high-level negotiations and the same names tend to be mentioned over and over, which is also typical of the realities in a relatively small administration. Generally, these officials are most likely to have served in the Permanent Representation, the EU institutions or agencies, or they have worked on EU affairs in Dublin. Their insights from abroad facilitate the transfer and absorption of ideas and practices, or provide an argument for introducing change. For example, the continental idea of the Commissioner's personal cabinet was loosely experimented with by the Labour Party in the early 1990s through the introduction of a programme manager system and the subsequent growth in the number of special advisers (Connaughton 2010). However, the initiative came from the political elites and was strongly resisted by the 'permanent government', who consider any ideas of a cabinet system as unacceptable, since it threatens their role and non-political tradition (Connaughton 2006: 274).

What is discernible is that the socialisation of Irish public servants in the management of EU business became reliant on informal contacts given the intimacy of a small administration with small numbers of officials working on EU affairs in the departments. This appears to clash with the feature of hierarchy and operating in silos entrenched by the Ministers and Secretaries Act (1924). It is apparent, however, that departmental cultures do matter and officials within line departments retain well-embedded norms that respect the primacy of a 'lead department'. In other words, officials from departments such as Finance, Agriculture, Justice or Environment are loyal to the departmental line and the fragmented nature of the Council negotiations themselves in separate councils exacerbates the segmentation at national level (Laffan 2007b). As Egeberg (2001) has noted, the role perceptions of these public servants are likely to be moulded by those institutions that are primary and immediate to them and organise their routines in daily practice. Between the Permanent Representation and line departments there are several European 'official identities', the development of which was noted by one official as follows:

> To a certain degree, such an identity (or rather a series of them) has long since evolved. The 'Brussels Community' of those attachés and those permanently stationed there (meaning three to four year rotations) forms one such community, with its own implicit norms and modes of behaviour. Those attending meetings from national capitals have a slightly different set of cultural norms associated with them, varying substantially by Council Formation. Fisheries or Agriculture is a very different sector within which to operate than more esoteric sectors like the cultural or diplomatic 'communities'. (Personal interview, July 2012)

Within departments the EU coordination units do not play a major role in directing departments to address European issues substantively or to 'think European' (Egeberg 2001). The emphasis is rather on adapting to the changes in EU policy work over time and the legislative process as 'the tactical approach taken to debating issues, contributing to discussions, or raising concerns will (predictably) change as dossiers develop and morph; the role played by member state officials shift to reflect this' (personal interview, August 2012). This is lamented by Foreign Affairs officials who are more likely to concentrate on the broader canvass of EU developments than the immediate interests of line departments who sometimes regard Foreign Affairs as too quick to compromise. Despite this, Laffan (2004) comments that in key negotiations all Irish officials 'sing from the same hymn sheet', showing collegiality and high levels of trust.

During the mid-1990s public servants began to grapple with the ramifications of the modernisation of the public administration via mild new public management (NPM) reforms, shifts towards governance and networks and a rapid growth in the economy. As Raadschelders (Chapter Two in this volume) comments, it is evident that the context to which public servants work has changed. The challenges of combining the traditional role and culture of officials with a public service modernisation programme prompted the establishment of a new type of mixed economy and a shift in the role of the public service from providing services to regulating or enabling them. Bureaucratic tasks became more complex and fragmented with corresponding impacts on the capacity for policy making and implementation – domestic and EU. The identity of public servants as a collective was also affected by the decision of the Irish government on Budget Day 2003 to commence a decentralisation of public servants from departments in the capital to various towns throughout the country. This scheme, which was rescinded by 2011, impacted on the effective running of government departments. It caused a hollowing-out of the centre, which made engagement with the EU more challenging at a time when the 2004 and 2007 enlargements were taking place and the Irish system for EU business remained under-institutionalised by continental standards. Formalising the coordination system was not championed by public servants as a collective, despite their induction to the EU fora. They largely interpreted formal structures as an impediment to efficiency. To a certain extent an attitude prevailed that 'if it ain't broke don't fix it', with a preference for informal contacts. The system of engagement for public servants began to be more institutionalised after the Nice Treaty, which was initially rejected by voters. A second Nice Treaty referendum was held and greater effort was made to address accountability concerns. This was illustrated in the introduction of a new system to manage executive-legislature relations for the scrutiny of proposals originating from the EU legislative process. After 2005, a number of officials began to voice concern about the lack of formalisation and the difficulties of coping in the new phase of EU development. Ministerial attendance in Council meetings was also low in comparison to other similar-sized member states, which placed further burdens on the public servants representing Ireland. What is evident about the Irish case is that significant resources go into having 'a good presidency' but in the aftermath of Irish EU Presidencies a strong level of commitment is not sustained.

It has been argued that after 1999 Ireland lost its coherence on European policy and the political and administrative elite did not develop a strategy for the different circumstances arising from the period of Ireland's economic success or its implications for EU membership (Laffan 2010; NESC 2010). Nor did the elite pay sufficient attention to the growing importance of the European Parliament (EP). In other words, the strategy of concentrating on a number of key priorities after the Celtic Tiger years (1995–2001) may have served well in the past but was no longer sufficient. This criticism did not receive much attention. Neither was it new, since as far back as the late 1980s the ability and skill of the Irish public servant in choosing the ground on which to negotiate longer-term issues had been questioned (Lee 1989). While Irish officials became quite adept at working in the Brussels system they employed a tactical rather than strategic game, in line with the developed characteristics of the service – pragmatic rather than ideological, reactive not proactive.

This can be illustrated in sectoral policy where it is evident that Ireland is a 'taker', not a 'shaper', of EU policy. Individual officials working in specific sectoral areas have considerable autonomy in the development of national positions, as they partake in follow-on meetings and can be subject to fewer procedural constraints than their counterparts in other member states. From the point of view of resources, an Irish delegation at working-party level may be composed of only one (junior) official, which places considerable personal responsibility on that individual.

They may have some room for manoeuvre in their negotiating brief, but the scenario may fuel cautiousness, which is ingrained in how the official hierarchy has operated since the Ministers and Secretaries Act (1924).[4] Officials in the Permanent Representation also have to rely on personal judgement rather than instruction from at home. Laffan (2001: 96) provides an account from interviews with Irish public servants who participated in Council working groups:

> Inevitably the strategy is defensive and is compared to 'shooting ducks in an arcade game'. Put simply you shoot down the problems one by one [...] Individual officials tend to work on the basis of trying to shape or reshape the five or six problem areas in any proposal for Ireland. This is achieved by using an informal checklist of the kinds of issues that need watching.

This contrasts with the shared governance beliefs and socialisation referred to in the literature, which emphasises the potential of technical experts to deepen their engagement with European policy making. Laffan (2001: 96–7) surmises that 'this problem solving approach to negotiations means that the Irish delegates tend only to intervene on specific issues but have little to say on the broad thrust of policy'. Kirby and Murphy (2010: 154) reinforce this commentary in their analysis that the collapse of the Celtic Tiger raises questions about the extent to which EU membership has served to transform Irish economic decision making and social policy: 'Evidence shows that the Irish policy community remains relatively insular, strategically using European and international discourse to selectively amplify domestic policy agendas.'

A European official identity?

There is no doubt that the Irish bureaucracy did undergo modernisation and during the ten-year boom delegations from other countries (in particular Central and Eastern Europe) typically came to visit government departments to learn more about the Irish areas of success. The roles undertaken by Irish officials in the Brussels arena have been viewed in both a positive and a negative light. On the one hand, Irish officials undertake roles whereby their quest to 'fight for Ireland Inc.' is pursued through a strategy which is as communitarian as possible. In the words of the former Permanent Representative, Ambassador Bobby McDonagh:

> Many ingredients have contributed to our success but none have been more important than goodwill. The goodwill of partners and EU institutions has been built up painstakingly through constructive engagement, several successful Irish Presidencies, and respecting the concerns and aspirations of others. (Houses of the Oireachtas 2008)

---

4.   The 1924 Act and its amendments remain central to the functioning of the public service despite modernising legislation in the form of the Public Service Management Act (1997), which has attempted to clarify the roles of the political and administrative elite in particular.

In negotiations on Common Agricultural Policy (CAP) reform and structural funds, Irish officials are regarded as skilful in negotiation and as exhibiting good judgement in situations to make the most of the national view. On the other hand, official strategies have also been regarded as reinforcing the 'sponger' in the Irish value system through demands to be treated as a special case without making concessions. And while symptomatic of the realities of being a small state, Ireland rarely takes a lead in proposing new schemes for the EU or strengthening it. From 2000 it has been perceived that Ireland shifted from a communitarian approach to a more focused domestic agenda. Laffan and O'Mahony (2008) assert that Irish politicians and officials presented a 'begging bowl mentality' in their approach to EU outcomes. After forty years of membership, limitations of Irish officials in the command of foreign languages remain, as does a lack of exposure of officials to the European experience. The lack of a European background may be a factor contributing to the failure of Irish political and administrative elites to communicate Europe effectively to Irish citizens. Following the initial rejections of the Nice Treaty in 2001 and the Lisbon Treaty in 2008 Ireland's influence has waned. The country has been regarded as a problem partner (O'Mahony 2012), and this prompted the Fine Gael-Labour coalition government who took office in 2011 to promote engagement with Europe as a priority.

On reflection, the Lisbon Treaty was a critical juncture, which exposed the fact that the Irish political and administrative elite had to adapt to the way Brussels currently does its business. The interaction and intersection of the financial crisis and new rules of the game in Brussels have altered the dynamic of Ireland's engagement with Europe (Laffan 2010; NESC 2010). The more regular meetings of heads of state, in particular since the start of the financial crisis, are also an indication of this change. The increase in multilateral diplomacy has led to a greater European and international dimension in the traditionally very conservative Department of the Taoiseach. This is a coordination issue, since the Taoiseach mediates domestic issues in cabinet. The move does not appear to have any impact on role perceptions of officials. When in autumn 2011 a group of officials moved to Government Buildings from the Department of Foreign Affairs to embed the EU division there, they retained their grading and identities as career diplomats. There is a markedly different relationship with Europe since 2011. Officials are now active in attempts to build rapport and the role of embassies has increased. In the words of one official:

we have salvaged our reputation in Europe, our missions work hard, and the message out there is how important our programme and attitude is in meeting commitments signed up to [...] [we are] prepared to work hard, explain when we have issues. (Personal interview, August 2012)

In conclusion, national-level public servants are key actors operating in the broader European administrative space (EAS), and for many of them their work requires participation in policy networks and constant interaction with the EU bureaucracy. In the words of one official, 'a European official identity is essential in relation to discussion at UN level. However, it is important that member states retain their own identities' (personal interview, August 2012). The organisational and societal context within which the Irish public servant works would perhaps have evolved over time in any case, but was influenced by EU membership while still moderated by tradition.

The discussion indicates that in comparison to our knowledge of structural issues there is little comprehensive information about cultural aspects such as the adaptation and socialisation of individual officials to Europe, or how they affect change. In the Irish case, few senior officials become embedded into Europe and their identity remains influenced by the ethos, norms and routines of the national public service. What is evident from the Irish experience is that the commitment of a relatively small cadre of senior officials undertaking both advisory and management roles is highly influential in developing an effective strategy towards Europe. These are the officials that are more likely to assume a hybrid rather than a national identity, but their beliefs and experience do not permeate throughout the service. However, the very work of the EU as a policy bureaucracy requires significant input from middle-ranking staff or 'senior operational officials'. Further insights into the work of these types of 'bureaucrat–diplomats' and 'street-level entrepreneurs' ('t Hart *et al.* 2007) would enhance our understanding of the Europeanisation of the public servant.

References

Ahern, B. (2000) 'Shaping a new Union: an Irish contribution', address by the Taoiseach, Bertie Ahern TD, to The European Movement Ireland, Dublin Castle, 6 November.

Barrington, T. J. (1980) *The Irish Administrative System*, Dublin: Institute of Public Administration.

Barrington, R. and Cooney, J. (1984) *Inside the EEC: An Irish guide*, Dublin: O'Brien Press.

Bartlett, C. A. and Ghoshal, S. (1989) *Managing Across Borders: The transnational solution*, Boston, MA: Harvard Business School Press.

Beyers, J. (2005) 'Multiple embeddedness and socialisation in Europe: the case of Council officials', *International Organization*, 59(4): 899–936.

—— (2010) 'Conceptual and methodological challenges in the study of European socialisation', *Journal of European Public Policy*, 17(6): 909–20.

Beyers, J. and Trondal, J. (2004) 'How nation states "hit" Europe: ambiguity and representation in the European Union', *West European Politics*, 27(5): 919–42.

Bulmer, S. (2007) 'Theorising Europeanization', in Graziano, P. and Vink, M. P. (eds) *Europeanisation: New research agendas*, Basingstoke: Palgrave, pp. 46–58.

Checkel, J. T. and Katzenstein, P. J. (2009) 'The politicisation of European identities', in Checkel, J. T. and Katzenstein, P. J. (eds) *European Identity*, Cambridge: Cambridge University Press, pp. 2–28.

Chubb, B. (1992) *The Government and Politics of Ireland*, 3rd edn, London: Longman.

Clark, J. and Jones, A. (2010) '"Telling stories about politics": Europeanization and the EU's Council working groups', *Journal of Common Market Studies* 49(2): 341–66.

Collins, N., Butler, P. and Cradden, T. (2007) *Modernising Irish Government*, Dublin: Gill & Macmillan.

Connaughton, B. (2006) 'Reform of politico-administrative relations in the Irish system: clarifying or complicating the doctrine of ministerial responsibility?', *Irish Political Studies*, 21(3): 257–76.

—— (2010) '"Glorified gofers, policy experts or good generalists": a classification of the roles of the Irish ministerial adviser', *Irish Political Studies*, 25(3): 347–70.

Cromien, S. (2000) 'Serving in new spheres', in O'Donnell, R. (ed.) *Europe: The Irish experience*, Dublin: Institute for Public Administration, pp. 148–60.

Egeberg, M. (1999) 'The impact of bureaucratic structure on policy making', *Public Administration,* 77(1): 155–70.

—— (2001) 'How federal? The organisational dimension of integration in the EU (and elsewhere)', *Journal of European Public Policy*, 8(5): 728–46.

—— (2006) *Multilevel Union Administration: The transformation of executive politics in Europe*, Basingstoke: Palgrave Macmillan.

Fanning, R. (2007) 'Picturing the public service in 1922', in Callanan, M. (ed.) *Ireland 2022 Towards One Hundred Years of Self-Government*, Dublin: Institute of Public Administration, pp. 6–15.

— (2008) *The Quest for Modern Ireland: The battle of ideas 1912–1986*, Dublin: Irish Academic Press.

Gaffey, P. (1982) 'The central administration', in Litton, F. (ed.) *Unequal Achievement: The Irish experience 1957-1982*, Dublin: Institute of Public Administration, pp. 115–32.

Garvin, T. (2004) *Preventing the Future: Why was Ireland poor for so long?*, Dublin: Gill and Macmillan.

Harmsen, R. (1999) 'The Europeanisation of national administrations: a comparative study of France and The Netherlands', *Governance*, 12(1): 81–113.

't Hart, P., Geuijen, K., Princen, S., Yesilkagit, K. and Mastenbroek, E. (2007) *The Europeanisation of Civil Service Craft*, report presented to the Dutch Ministry of the Interior (BZK), University of Utrecht.

Hooghe, L. (2001) *The European Commission and the Integration of Europe*, Cambridge: Cambridge University Press.

Houses of the Oireachtas (2008) *Ireland's Future in the European Union–Report*, 27 November.

Keogh, D. (2005) *Twentieth Century Ireland*, Dublin: Gill & Macmillan.

Keogh, D. and Keogh, A. (2007) 'Ireland and European integration: from the Treaty of Rome to membership', in Callanan, M. (ed.) *Foundations of an Ever Closer Union: An Irish perspective on the fifty years since the Treaty of Rome*, Dublin: Institute of Public Administration, pp. 6–50.

Kirby, P. and Murphy, M. P. (2010) *Towards a Second Republic: Irish politics after the Celtic Tiger*, London, Pluto.

Knill, C. (2001) *The Europeanisation of National Administrations: Administrative patterns of institutional change and persistence*, Cambridge: Cambridge University Press.

Laffan, B. (2001) 'Organising for a changing Europe: Irish central government and the European Union', Dublin: Policy Institute, Trinity College Dublin.

— (2004) 'Irish government and European governance', in Garvin, T., Manning, M. and Sinnott, R. (eds) *Dissecting Irish Politics: Essays in honour of Brian Farrell*, Dublin, University College Dublin Press, pp. 116–33.

— (2007a) 'Core executives', in Graziano, P. and Vink, M. P. (eds) *Europeanisation: New research agendas*, Basingstoke: Palgrave Macmillan, pp. 128–40.

— (2007b) 'Managing European dossiers in the Irish civil service: living with the EU system?' in Callanan, M. (ed.) *Foundations of an Ever Closer Union: An Irish perspective on the fifty years since the Treaty of Rome*, Dublin: Institute of Public Administration, pp. 175–94.

— (2010) *Ireland and Europe 2010: An unwelcome critical juncture*, Dublin: Institute of International and European Affairs.

Laffan, B. and O'Mahony, J. (2007) 'Managing Europe from an Irish perspective: critical junctures and the increasing formalisation of the core executive in Ireland', *Public Administration,* 85(1): 167–88.

—   (2008) *Ireland and the European Union*, Basingstoke: Palgrave.
Lee, J. (1989) *Ireland 1912-1985: Politics and Society*, Cambridge: Cambridge University Press.
McBride, L. W. (1991) *The Greening of Dublin Castle*, Washington: Catholic University of America Press.
MacCarthaigh, M. (2005) *Accountability in Irish Parliamentary Politics*, Dublin: Institute of Public Administration.
McCarthy, D. (2005) 'Public service reform in Ireland', paper to Annual Kenmare Economics Workshop, 15 October.
Maguire, M. (2008) *The Civil Service and the Revolution in Ireland, 1912-38: Shaking the blood stained hand of Mr Collins*, Manchester: Manchester University Press.
Moody, T. W. and Martin, F. (2011) *The Course of Irish History*, Cork: Mercier Press.
National Economic & Social Council (NESC) (2010) *Refinding Success in Europe: The challenge for Irish institutions and policy*, Dublin: National Economic and Social Council.
OECD (1998) *Preparing Public Administrations for the European Administrative Space*, Sigma Papers No. 23, Paris: Organisation for Economic Cooperation and Development.
Olsen, J. P. (2002) *Towards a European Administrative Space?* ARENA working papers WP 02/06, Oslo: ARENA Centre for European Studies.
O'Mahony, J. (2004) 'Ireland and the European Union', in Collins, N. and Cradden, T. (eds) *Political Issues in Ireland Today*, Manchester: Manchester University Press, pp. 21–32.
—   (2012) 'When Europe hits home: government and the European Union', in O'Malley, E. and MacCarthaigh, M. (eds) *Governing Ireland from Cabinet Government to Delegated Government*, Dublin: Institute for Public Administration, pp. 190–214.
Radaelli, C. M. (2003) 'The Europeanization of public policy', in Featherstone, K. and Radaelli, C. M. (eds) *The Politics of Europeanization*, Oxford: Oxford University Press, pp. 27–56.
Radaelli, C. M. and O'Connor, K. (2009) 'How bureaucratic elites imagine Europe: towards convergence of governance beliefs?' *Journal of European Public Policy*, 16(7): 971–89.
Risse, T. (2001) 'A European identity? Europeanization and the evolution of nation-state identities', in Cowles, M. G., Caporaso, J. and Risse, T. (eds) *Transforming Europe: Europeanization and domestic change*, Ithaca, NY: Cornell University Press, pp. 198–216.
Roche, D. (2007) 'Ireland's vision of European integration', remarks by the Minister for European Affairs, Dick Roche TD at NUI Galway, September.
Velychenko, S. (2005) 'Bureaucrats and revolutionary state-building in Ireland and Russia: was Weber right?' *Canadian Journal of Political Science*, 38(1): 1–22.

Chapter Twelve

European Values and Practices in Post-Communist Public Administration: The Baltic States

Karin Hilmer Pedersen and Lars Johannsen

Introduction

The 'return to Europe' after independence implied a fundamental reconstruction of the political, economic and administrative systems of the Baltic States. Public servants had to conform to principles of democracy, to private and competitive markets and to serving the people instead of the rulers. The accession to and subsequent membership of the European Union only exacerbated the need to reshuffle and radically change the administration and administrative values. In this volume, Raadschelders (Chapter Two) contends that the development during the last century is a convergence towards a bureaucratically embedded public servant who operates within clear legal boundaries, is professional and meritorious, observes equality under the law but also enjoys full-time employment, a decent salary, pensions and legal protection under the Civil Service Acts. Controversies over different administrative principles and national traditions aside, the bottom line of extensive administrative reforms after communism is to enhance public servants' integrity over ideological and political loyalty and their responsiveness to interest organisations and citizens. This chapter asks whether and how public servants in post-communist countries, in this case the Baltic States, merge with a common European administrative identity.

Comprehensive public administration reforms are not simply a matter of passing relevant legislation. The litmus test lies in the values, attitudes and beliefs of the individual public servant. This chapter focuses on values that qualify the structures and processes of public administration with respect to public servants' integrity by examining (1) perceptions of integrity (formal rule-abiding norms, commitment to the arm's-length principle in concrete cases and intentions to blow the whistle if administrative misconduct is discovered), and (2) the significance of responsiveness (a positive value of citizen participation in public administration). While the first part reflects a bottom-line consensus about public administration values, the second part concerns the understanding of modern administration to be inclusive and more serving than steering *vis-à-vis* the citizens (OECD 2001; EU Commission 2001; Johannsen and Pedersen 2008).

The countries formed after the collapse of the Soviet Union did not constitute a coherent sample for studying social transformation (Bunce 1995; Johannsen and Pedersen 2009a). Among the post-communist countries, the three Baltic States constitute an ideal laboratory for studying social transformation that highlights similarities in the background variables, such as late statehood, the degree of inclusion in the Soviet economic, political and administrative practices, and the post-transitional choices of political institutions as well as proximity to the EU (Johannsen and Pedersen 2011a). The similar system design implies that background variables are held constant. This means that we cannot make inferences about the Soviet legacy effect on the values of present-day public servants. But as a common denominator, the Soviet legacy serves as a shared understanding of public administration, which may even work as an antithesis of good practice.

Country differences may be explained by national sentiments, but with an institutional approach, administrative structures and processes can be seen as an underlying explanation (Charron and Lapuente 2010; Charron et al. 2012; Przeworski 2004). In a broader theory of human behaviour, administrative structures and processes are seen to shape informal values and norms (March and Olsen 1989, Ostrom 2010: 160–1). The fact that the speed and scope of administrative reform were not uniform across countries, departments and administrative levels implies specifically that we seek to explain differences by looking into particular aspects of the public administration. We follow the management maxim: 'Where you stand depends on where you sit', known as Miles' Law (Miles 1978), but add, 'and how you sit'. Thereby we stress the impact of administrative structures and processes on public servants' individual judgements.

The chapter builds on a survey among Baltic public servants conducted in spring 2011.[1] Their values are held up against the administrative structures and processes they experience in their organisation: hierarchical chain of demand, meritocratic recruitment, coordination with other public authorities and cooperation with private actors as well as administrative-level (state sub-national[2]) and management obligations (with/without staff responsibility). Although the design holds background country variables constant, we do examine whether there is an Estonian exceptionalism as argued by Panagiotou (2001) or whether different choices in the process towards EU membership matter (Johannsen and Pedersen 2009b).

After a discussion of the historical background and public administration ideas that melt together in the process of public administration reforms after communism, the formal changes in public administration (PA) are described. The presentation of methodological issues of case selection and the survey is followed by a discussion of public servants' values. Next follows a discussion, based on regression analysis, of the relation between administrative structures and processes and values of integrity and responsiveness. Finally, we conclude and sum up.

---

1.   The survey was carried out by the authors with assistance from TNC-Gallup International Denmark and national offices and funded by Danish Research Council grant no. 10-080446. We thank our research assistant Charlotte Brandsborg for assistance with the statistics.

2.   We use the term 'sub-national' instead of 'local' or 'regional' due to country-specific territorial-administrative set-ups.

Mapping the dependent variable: Legacy, independence and transfer of 'European administrative values'

When the Soviet Union collapsed in 1989–90, research on societal changes split into two approaches (Crawford and Lijphart 1995). The legacy approach emphasises the impact of institutionally established practices and norms of appropriateness during the Soviet period, predicting inertia and gradual reform processes. As far as administrative reform and changes in public servants' norms and values were concerned, the legacy approach predicts that surviving institutional norms of appropriate conduct will be traced back to either pre-Soviet history or the fifty years of Soviet occupation. In contrast, the *tabula rasa* approach contends that the so-called 'Washington consensus', the ethos of democracy and liberal market economy, would erase the Soviet legacy and pave the way for a rapid and focused reform process. The pre-accession process of EU membership builds by and large on this perception. It seems, however, that neither prediction fully matches reality but depends on the specific country and the policy area under scrutiny. Before turning to administrative reforms and related public servant values, we discuss the pre-Soviet and Soviet legacies and the content of external recommendations.

Pre-Soviet and Soviet legacies

If historical legacies matter it is either through direct personal experience or ideas about what people believe is proper behaviour. In the Baltic States, pre-Soviet public administration history reflects late statehood and periods of either German or Russian dominance with respect to public service practices. In the short inter-war period, the only time the countries were independent states in modern time, Estonian and Latvian national administrations resembled a German-inspired Weberian practice, whereas Lithuanians were more inspired by American traditions (Domarkas and Gineitine 2000; Randma 2000; Vanags 2000). Although countries differ in their pre-Soviet administrative history pre-Soviet practices are unlikely to transcend to present-day values through 'person-to-person' relations. In Estonia, Soviet occupation effectively destroyed inter-war public service cadres (Sootla and Roots 1999: 238). In Latvia, the German occupation (1941–5) led to a reorganisation of most of the public administration according to the German military structure. An attempt to reinvent national public administration traditions in the 1950s was oppressed and countered by increased appointment of Russian officials to top administrative positions (Jansone and Reinholde 2001: 208). Thus if pre-Soviet history matters it is the effect of ideas about proper, democratic and just administration and not about concrete organizational structures that prevails (Kitschelt 2003: 62).

Besides different ideas about public administration, public servants and state administrators are met with different public sentiments. Georg Sootla contends that the history of inter-war Estonia reflects duality between the state as foreign and coercive *vis-à-vis* a caretaking community of ethnic Estonians (2001: 124–6). During the period of independence, Lithuanian government was preoccupied with security issues and ignored 'the public service functions of public administration'

(Lazareviciute *et al.* 2001: 248–9). In consequence serving in the public service in Estonia and Lithuania was not prestigious, unlike in Latvia where public servants enjoyed general respect and status (Jansone and Reinholde 2001: 208). Whether these sentiments can be depicted in public servants' values today is, however, a question that our survey cannot answer.

The Soviet legacy is rooted in the fifty years of Soviet occupation during which an administrative structure was imposed on all Soviet republics. The implications for public servants' values of administrative integrity and responsiveness are not documented, but rely on theoretical inference. First with respect to integrity, the legacy of Soviet administration was an over-politicised system. Personnel policy was organised in a *nomenclature* system in which the Communist Party monopolised recruitment and promotion decisions (Goetz and Wollmann 2001: 865). In this system, merit became synonymous with party loyalty and a formal legislative practice where strict rule abidance became a source of power indicating 'allowed' and 'forbidden', not 'right' or 'wrong' (Ahdieh 1997: 98). On many accounts the internal organisation of Soviet bureaucracy appeared to resemble the Weberian centralised hierarchy of control, rational management and technical competencies (Brzezinski 1970: 152–4). However, this interpretation overlooks the legal-rational thinking in Weber's bureaucracy model with its emphasis on equality and impartiality, which was alien to Soviet reality (Pakulski 1986: 5–6).

Second, responsiveness to the public was part of the official doctrine of 'democratic centralism'. The doctrine combined the centralised leadership of the Communist Party with the formal institutionalisation of inclusion (Soviet Constitution 1977: Articles 3, 8 and 6 respectively). In praxis, however, civic engagement outside the realm of the Communist Party was effectively destroyed and civic apathy was the rule rather than the exception. The detailed administrative instructions characteristic for Soviet administrations hindered the development of professional standards necessary 'to strike the balance between uniformity [...] flexibility and adaptability', creating a culture that was aversive to responsibility (Johannsen 2003: 25–6).

The legacy approach predicts continuity, which may run through either institutional or cognitive patterns. After 1990, the public service personnel changed extensively due to available and more lucrative jobs in private companies and the active utilisation of positions to engage the privatisation process, but also staff reductions due to budgetary shortages (Lazareviciute *et al.* 2001: 239; Jansone and Reinholde 2001: 211). In contrast with other post-communist countries, the Baltic States did not execute comprehensive lustration processes (Letki 2002). However, the Estonian 1990 constitution and subsequent language laws *de facto* cleaned the public service of Russophone staff, and 37 per cent of public servants were hired in 1994 after the regime change (Sootla 2001: 128–9). The change of administrative personnel makes it unlikely that Soviet legacy has travelled through personal experience. Given the widespread upheavals against Soviet rule followed by a comprehensive and consistent pro-Western strategy during the 1990s, it is more likely that values held by present-day public servants are antithetical to a Soviet past (Nakrošis 2001: 172).

Independence and the European administrative space

The discontinuity assumption underlining the liberal imperative approach is connected to the process towards EU membership. Public administration reforms were formally not a requirement, but in practice the accession process implied a spillover into public service reform along the lines of the 'principles of a European Administrative Space', which reflect 'Weberian' criteria by stressing (1) reliability and predictability (legal certainty); (2) openness and transparency; (3) accountability and (4) efficiency and effectiveness (OECD 1999: 8). The notion of a shared 'administrative space' builds on a baseline approach, which is relatively silent about the precise institutional set-up. The guiding aim of administrative reforms was to implement changes that qualified as a 'modern, competitive public administration on a global basis' so that national decisions remain 'open to ideas and practices being utilized in non-European countries' (Nunberg 2000: 3–4).

Emphasis on the legal-rational aspects of traditional Weberian bureaucracy was justified because the effective implementation of EU law in all member states forms the basis of both the EU governance system and the functioning of the internal market. The Weberian basis was accordingly set up against a Soviet legacy of flexible and politicised rule application. The argument was that PA had to follow reforms reflecting a Weberian model before experimenting with the managerial approaches advocated in new public management (NPM) (Verheijen and Coombes 1998; Drechsler 2005: 96; Meyer-Sahling 2011: 240).

Besides concrete public administration reforms along the lines described, the European Union emphasises dialogue with and responsiveness to interest organisations and the public (EU Commission 2001, 2004; OECD 2001). Responsiveness is a property of an administration in which accountability not only travels through the normal procedures of representative democracy, but also through cooperation with citizens through various institutional arrangements such as public hearings, parent councils in schools or interest groups in the formulation and implementation of policies (Johannsen 2002; Johannsen and Pedersen 2008). In choosing the term 'responsiveness', we draw extensively on the democratic discourses of public society as the 'infrastructure and organisational bedrock of democratic societies' (Zimmer 2005: 11), while at the same time emphasising the independence of public administration from political influence (Evans 1995).

Direct citizen participation in public administration is not an uncontested issue. On the positive side, it is believed to make citizens more responsible and engaged (Barber 1983; Putnam with Leonardi and Nanetti 1993; Habermas 1996), to work as a 'checks and balances mechanism' and watchdog (Ostrom and Ostrom 2011: 115), and to improve implementation (Kathi and Cooper 2005: 559). In this perspective, the inclusion of different interests moves the public service away from reliance on the technical and expertise models of administration and is expected to create more enlightened decisions and increased legitimacy, thus avoiding complaints and obstructions once decisions have been made (Irvin and Stansbury 2004: 56–7). On the negative side, citizen participation challenges representative democracy when it opens for decentralised decision making at lower levels of government

(Peters and Pierre 2000: 14; Kathi and Cooper 2005: 560). A more serious consequence is that including citizens directly in public administration increases the risk of 'capturing', which may open a Pandora's box of particularism and inequality.

Irrespective of the pros and cons, Irvin and Stansbury (2004: 59) contend that ill-considered inclusion of citizens in the decision-making process may backfire in terms of efficiency, because projects may become more expensive when citizens are heard on sometimes highly technical matters. Thus the positive effect is only likely if public servants are sincere and include citizens in order to achieve better and more efficient decisions and not merely as lip service to a principle or manipulation (King *et al.* 1998: 321). These concerns shed light on the importance of public servants' attitudes towards the inclusion of citizens. Citizens' participation reframes the relationship and the interaction of citizens and public servants by highlighting the importance of public servants with a positive view on inclusion. At the same time it is important that the values of inclusion go together with the values of administrative integrity to avoid particularism and unequal treatment of citizens, if not direct corruption.

Formal changes in public administrations

The changes towards democracy and the market have not been smooth. With frequent political changes and high turnover rates among public servants it is no small feat that formal legislation governing the public service was in place less than a decade after independence (*see* Table 12.1). In time, all three countries fulfilled the public administration baseline requirement for EU membership stressing political neutrality, professionalism and transparency, competitiveness, and accountability as functional equivalents of competencies and public service neutrality (Palidauskaite 2011). The emphasis was on formal changes such as public service legislation (Randma-Liiv and Järvalt 2011: 39), meritocratic recruitment and promotion and the introduction of codes of ethics and official oaths known from some EU members, for example The Netherlands (*see* Rutgers, Chapter Four in this volume).

Table 12.1 illustrates core elements in the formal basis for Baltic public servants. It is difficult to disagree with Palidauskaite *et al.*'s conclusion that 'the civil service systems in all three Baltic countries are more or less similar' (2010: 49). This said, the implementation of the legal framework has been found to be incomplete (Unpan 2004a, 2004b, 2004c; Dimitrova 2005: 84), which opens up for country differences when it comes to practices.

Meritocratic recruitment to the public service is in place in all three states. It follows the departmental or specialist system where recruiters in each public body search for the candidate with the relevant or specialised expertise to fill the vacancies and have adopted the same principles at the core with respect to recruitment and promotion. A slight difference is that Lithuania has established a centralised system of admission and assessment to oversee recruitment, whereas Latvia and Estonia give more discretion to each department. In June 2013, the Lithuanian admission and assessment system was strengthened, which suggests that the difference may in practice not have been significant.

Table 12.1: Core elements in public service legislation concerning recruitment and ethics

	Estonia	Latvia	Lithuania
Legal basis	1996: 'The Public Service Act' 1999: 'The Anti-Corruption Act'	1994: 'Law on the State Civil Service' 1995: 'Law on Preventing Corruption' (amendments 1999, 2012) 2001: 'The Civil Service Law' 2002: 'The Law on the Anti-Corruption Bureau'	1995: 'Law on Officials' 1997/1999: 'The Public Service Law' (amendments 2010) 2002: 'The Law on Corruption Prevention'
Meritocratic recruitment and promotion	Yes: Discretion in each department	Yes: Discretion in each department	Yes 2002: Centralised system of admission and assessment 2013: Legal strengthening of admission and assessment system
Ethics	1999: 'The Public Service Code of Ethics'	2001: 'The Civil Service Code of Ethics'	Ethical principles established in 'The Law on Public Service'

Sources: Authors' compilation based on Unpan (2004a, b, c), Dimitrova (2005), Palidauskaite (2011), Estonian, Latvian and Lithuanian Constitutions and relevant legal acts.

In addition, codes of conduct and judicial principles for maintaining integrity have been emphasised through legislation. Examples of the judicialisation of the ethical principles are the Lithuanian Law on Public Service, establishing the arm's-length principle that a public servant:

> [must not] enter into contracts on behalf of the state or municipal institution or agency, at which he holds office, with individual (personal) enterprises, partnerships whose owner, general or limited partner are him or his spouse, close relative or a person related to this public servant by marriage[.] (Art. 17)

Similarly, responsiveness is codified in the Estonian Public Service Code of Ethics, where the first line simply states: 'An official is a citizen in the service of people', indicating that the public servant is not an instrument of the state for steering behaviour, but rather a mediator between the state and the citizens. In contrast to Estonia, both Latvia and Lithuania grant citizens constitutional rights to direct participation in the work of state/local government in addition to voting rights (arts 101 and 33 respectfully). However, as noted, citizens' inclusion in public administration can be a double-edged sword, and differences in the formal-legal provision may transform into how positive public servants believe participation to be.

The EU has had a strong influence, mediated by internal interests and conditions, on the intense reorganisation of PA (Nakrošis 2001: 176; Sarapuu

2012: 818; Nakrošis and Budraitis 2012; Sarapuu 2011). However, as noted by Palidauskaite (2011: 205–6), we should be aware that 'changes in the observable written legislation may have served as lip service to a critical (EU) environment which had placed public service system reform in a weakly defined public administration 'acquis'. Since EU membership, the focus has thus switched to the behavioural aspects of reforms and whether formal changes have rubbed off on practices and values (Dimitrova 2010; Sedelmeier 2008). In contrast to studies of the formal changes after 1990, our survey studies the link between the context within which public servants work, i.e. the extent of meritocracy, hierarchy, coordination and cooperation, and the public servants' intrinsic values of neutrality and responsiveness to the public. In other words, it examines the validity of Miles' Law that your views depend on where and how you sit, but it also reflects the Thomas theorem presented by Raadschelders (Chapter Two in this volume) that 'when people perceive situations as real, then they are real in their consequences'.

Towards explanations: An explorative analytical framework

Administrative structures are understood here to determine whether the respondents work at state or sub-national level and whether they have staff responsibility or not. Because of the more frequent contact with other European colleagues we expect norms of integrity as well as responsiveness in the form of citizens' participation to be higher in the state administration and among public servants with staff responsibility. Administrative processes are not measured by formal regulations but according to how the respondents perceive the characteristics of their own organisation. We look into four organisational variables: hierarchy, meritocracy, coordination among agencies and cooperation with private actors. Highly hierarchical structures subsume a chain of command running from higher to lower levels, which we expect to enhance integrity but reduce positive views on participation. Meritocratic procedures may enhance integrity, but may also encourage participation because of the higher professionalism implied by it. With respect to coordination among public agencies, we expect it to go hand in hand with increased integrity because it inserts an element of control but citizens' participation may not be welcomed in an already complex organisational environment. In contrast, we expect that if cooperation with private actors is common, public servants will be more cautious and value integrity more, while the impact of citizens' participation on values could go either way depending on whether experiences are positive or negative.

Adding to administrative structures and processes, we look at two individual characteristics. Studies on corruption have shown that women have greater integrity than men (Goetz 2007). We therefore include gender as a control variable to see if this applies to other dimensions of integrity. With respect to responsiveness, however, we do not expect gender to be important. The second control variable, age, serves as an indirect measure of the Soviet legacy approach and therefore adds to the country comparison analysis. Although we do not expect many of the public servants to have served during the Soviet period, we do expect the older generation to be more sensitive to questions of integrity and responsiveness. Cultural theory contends that rapid social changes are not common because it takes time for people's mind-set to adapt to changes. However, a prime example of discontinuity is Germany after WW2 (Eckstein 1988). The Soviet legacy may matter exactly for this reason and thus serve as a negative standard. This is more so, as older public servants may have been active during the uprising in the 1990s and therefore hold integrity and responsiveness dearer than the younger generations. The following analysis digs into the link between these variables on the one hand and public servants' integrity and their positive view of citizens' participation on the other. Before turning to the analysis a few words concerning the survey and research design are in order.

Research design: Method of analysis and survey

The choice of the Baltic countries highlights the logic of a most similar systems design as the three countries share a comprehensive set of common features, i.e. late statehood, degree of inclusion in Soviet economic, political and administrative practices, and post-transitional choices of political institutions and inclusion in the European Union (Johannsen and Pedersen 2011a).

Even though background variables are held constant, country variation cannot be excluded. In particular, we expect Estonia to stand out for several reasons. Culturally, Estonia is tied to Finland, its closest neighbour, and the countries share linguistic similarities. It is even argued that Estonian uniqueness in relation to the two other Baltic States can be traced back to different experiences during the Soviet period and especially less cultural integration or assimilation with Russians (Panagiotou 2001: 269). Economically, Estonia fared substantially better than Latvia and Lithuania throughout the 1990s, partly because it was not plagued by a legacy of large-scale heavy industry (Panagiotou 2001: 264; Johannsen and Pedersen 2009b). Politically, Estonia took the lead with a stronger change team abolishing trade barriers, cutting taxes, promoting foreign investment and so on. Finally, Estonia stands out as more successful in terms of curbing corruption (Transparency International 2011; Pedersen and Johannsen 2004, 2006). According to perception studies, the relatively lower degree of corruption may be especially important in understanding public servants' values on the integrity of public administration.

The analysis is based on a survey conducted in April 2011 as part of a project questioning administrative capacity and corruption. Given this focus, respondents were selected randomly among public servants who, according to national codes, possess decision authority, per instruction or discretion, typically carrying the title 'head of section' or higher to distinguish them from public servants like librarians, nurses or teachers. In order to fully capture administrative capacity, given that a growing number of public servants are employed at sub-national level, it was important that the respondents were representative of public servants at both national and sub-national levels.

Table 12.2: Sample size: distribution in countries and among levels of administration (numbers and percentages)

	Estonia		Latvia		Lithuania		Total	
	N	%	N	%	N	%	N	%
State	155	22.0	123	24.6	152	30.4	430	25.2
Sub-national	551	78.0	377	75.4	348	69.6	1276	74.8
Total	706	100.0	500	100.0	500	100.0	1706	100.0

To be representative of Baltic public servants a minimum of 500 respondents (with completed or almost completed interviews) was stipulated. In addition, a quarter should be employed at the national level. The total number of respondents, their distribution among countries and their level of administration are reported in Table 12.2.

Differences in national views on how best to approach public servants resulted in different sampling strategies: web surveys were used in Estonia, telephone interviews in Latvia and Lithuania. Moreover, the Latvian bureau used a more elaborate introduction to the project. The response rates were 37, 76 and 25 per cent for Estonia, Latvia and Lithuania respectively. The sampling strategies may have introduced a bias in whom the researchers reach and how they respond. A web survey may affect answers, as it is less intrusive and suffers less from a social desirability effect. Because public servant integrity and administrative neutrality are core values not only in a European baseline approach but also especially in the formal legislation and codes of all three countries, a desirability effect – i.e. that respondents overestimate their own neutrality – can be expected. Accordingly, the survey method would predict relatively less reported integrity in the Estonian sample than in Latvia and Lithuania. Moreover, the different introduction notes might introduce some bias between Latvia and Lithuania causing Latvians to be more politically correct than Lithuanians. Besides this caution and the implications for the discussion below, the high number of respondents and the overall representativeness should compensate. The survey is a closed questionnaire. The appendix lists the precise wording of the questions and discusses how each variable is handled. The next sections give an overview of the dependent variables using descriptive statistics, and develop the causal analysis using standard OLS and logistic regression with Estonia as the reference case.

Where do they stand: Descriptive analysis

If Baltic public servants were once inclined towards Soviet administrative practices and values, it is safe to say that something has changed.

Table 12.3 shows that Baltic public servants value integrity and responsiveness, but to a varying degree. Of the respondents, 92.2 per cent adhere to the arm's-length principle. The fairly small differences between countries on this item indicate consensus among Baltic public servants that they should not become involved in cases in which friends or relatives have private interests. The table also

Table 12.3: Overview of public servants' values on neutrality and responsiveness (numbers and percentages)

		Bending rules (1=no)	Arm's length principle (1=yes)	Whistle blowing (1=always)	Citizens' participation (1=yes)
Total (%)		46.9	92.2	60.8	47.8
Country	Estonia (%)	33.0	90.0	65.4	43.2
	Latvia (%)	53.5	94.1	54.3	57.2
	Lithuania (%)	59.0	91.9	62.5	45.0
N		1.647	1.494	1.517	1.706

Note: The value 1 is an expression of integrity/responsiveness in the following variables: bending rules, arm's length, whistle blowing and participation.

reports that less than 50 per cent will bend the rules to achieve policy objectives, but there are notable differences between Estonia on the one hand and Latvia and Lithuania on the other. The country differences may partly be a result of the variance in the surveys, i.e. that the Estonian web survey may reflect the truer – and less politically correct – state of affairs. Because of this consideration and to maximise variation we maintain the Likert scale in the causal analysis.

In any case, the public servants are caught in the dilemma of getting the job done and upholding the rules. With a Soviet legacy of over-regulation and formalisation, rule bending might be the only way to get things done in conjunction with the European Union's emphasis on strict rules and hierarchical structures. Some public servants probably feel that this undermines their professional assessment and consideration of local circumstances (Pivoras 2010: 111–12).

Public servants' inclination to blow the whistle and to view citizens' participation positively varies between the countries and is not indicated by overwhelming majorities. Whistle blowing may remind some of KGB informers, and citizens' participation may also resemble Soviet times when participation was cherished but in practice ignored if not directly unwanted. If so, it is hardly surprising that less than half of the respondents find that including citizens would make a positive difference to their organisation. However, the legacy approach would predict that country differences are negligible, which is not so.

The institutional stand behind values of integrity and responsiveness: Causal analysis

The general overview when the three expressions of integrity and the item of responsiveness are regressed against administrative structures and processes is shown in Table 12.4. On all four items there is a significant relation with being Latvian, administrative level, and perception of own organisation as meritocratic. The degree to which coordination with other public authorities is common relates significantly with the three items of integrity, but not with responsiveness. Note that in this context the degree of hierarchy is negatively related to responsiveness

Table 12.4: Values of integrity and responsiveness

	Linear regression			Logistical regression			
	Bending rules (1–7, 7=never)	Arm's length (0–1, 1=yes)		Whistle-blowing (0–1, 1=always)		Responsive (0–1, 1=yes)	
	B	B	Exp (β)	B	Exp (β)	B	Exp (β)
Constant	5.254	-1.279		-0.680		-2,299	
Estonia	(Ref.)	(Ref.)		(Ref.)		(Ref.)	
Latvia	0.235 (0.111) *	-0.084 (0.325)	0.920	-0.697 (0.164) ***	0.498	0.553 (0.155)	1.739 ***
Lithuania	0.078 (0.138)	-0.415 (0.376)	0.660	-0.397 (0.200) *	0.672	0.128 (0.193)	1.137
Gender (0=female, 1=male)	-0.285 (0.093) **	-0.440 (0.262)	0.644	0.217 (0.133)	1.242	0.027 (0.129)	1.027
Age	0.000 (0.004)	0.030 (0.013) *	1.031	0.001 (0.006)	1.001	0.002 (0.006)	1.002
Level (0=state, 1=sub-national)	-0.499 (0.105) ***	-1.260 (0.402) **	0.284	-0.571 (0.155) ***	0.565	1.214 (0.152)	3.366 ***
Staff responsibility (0=no, 1=yes)	0.002 (0.117)	0.549 (0.303)	1.731	0.162 (0.172)	1.176	0.073 (0.161)	1.076
Hierarchy	-0.048 (0.024)	-0.010 (0.069)	0.990	0.030 (0.035)	1.030	-0.109 (0.034)	0.896 ***
Merit	0.119 (0.036) ***	0.349 (0.085) ***	1.418	0.137 (0.052) **	1.147	0.164 (0.052)	1.179 ***
Coordination	0.132 (0.042) **	0.327 (0.111) **	1.387	0.133 (0.061) *	1.143	0.004 (0.059)	1.004
Cooperation	-0.069 (0.026) **	0.003 (0.078)	1.003	0.015 (0.038)	1.015	0.133 (0.037)	1.142 ***
N	1.153	1.055		1.082		1.178	

Note: Level of significance: ***; **; *: 0.001; 0.01; 0.05 (two-sided test). Bending rules: Linear regression. Model constructed with OLS. Unstandardised coefficients and standard errors in parentheses. Adjusted R^2 = 0.071. Arm's length: Logistical regression. Model constructed with binary logistics. Logit-coefficients, odds-ratios and standard errors in parentheses. Nagelkerke R^2 = 0.153; Cox and Snell R^2 = 0.062; Hosmer and Lemeshow: $\chi^2(8)$ = 7.313, p = 0.503. Whistle-blowing: Logistical regression. Model constructed with binary logistics. Logit-coefficients, odds-ratios and standard errors in parentheses. R^2 = 0.064; Cox and Snell R^2 = 0.048; Hosmer and Lemeshow: $\chi^2(8)$ = 9.864, p = 0.275. Responsive: Model constructed with binary logistics. Logit-coefficients, odds-ratios and standard errors in parentheses. Nagelkerke R^2 = 0.144; Cox and Snell R^2 = 0.108; Hosmer and Lemeshow: $\chi^2(8)$ = 6.244, p = 0.620.

but not to the integrity items. The degree of cooperation with private actors is related with a negative view on increasing flexibility and discretion, but relates positively with values of responsiveness. The age variable is only significant with respect to accepting the arm's-length principle, and men are more likely than women to bend rules. This confirms the traditional stereotype of men cherishing efficiency and women being more caring and thus more inclined to protect the values of equality. Before turning to institutional explanations some words on country differences are in order.

Country differences are not consistent across all four items. Estonia is expected to differ from the two other countries as explained above and is therefore the reference case in the analysis. Although there is reason to believe that Latvia and Lithuania differ from Estonia, they differ only on some issues. Against expectations, due to higher levels of corruption, Lithuanians and Latvians are less willing to blow the whistle on administrative irregularities. This is notable because Latvia and Lithuania have established independent anti-corruption agencies and maintain a high profile in combating corruption (Johannsen and Pedersen 2011b). Reluctance to blow the whistle may be caused by acceptance, i.e. corrupt practices are internalised, or by outright fear of reprisals (Johnson 2003).

Latvians also stand out with respect to rule bending. Rerunning the analysis with Lithuania as reference case (not shown) confirms that Latvians are less prone to bend rules and much more sympathetic to the effect of citizens' participation. The conservative stand on rule bending is surprising, as Latvians are believed to have been more favourable to NPM and its emphasis on administrative results (Jansone and Reinholde 2001: 209). However, as responsiveness implies the risk of capture and favouritism it appears logical that the positive stand on citizens' participation is balanced by strict rule compliance.

Although Estonia did stand out in choosing a more radical economic reform strategy than Latvia and Lithuania, our survey questions Estonian uniqueness when it comes to public servants' values. Instead, it seems that 'where and how you sit' in the administrative system matters more than nation.

There are consistent and significant differences between the national and sub-national levels. Public servants at the sub-national level are more inclined to bend the rules, to disrespect the arm's-length principle and to keep the whistle in their pocket, but also to be more responsive to the public. In other words, state public servants have a higher degree of integrity but a lower degree of responsiveness. This may reflect the insight that collaborative decision-making is especially efficient and thus valued in smaller settings more than in larger ones (Ostrom 1990). However, including citizens may also be a way to get the job done and a strategy to build alliances on increased funding. Peters and Pierre (2000) note the downside of participation is that it increases demands for public spending. Due to the distribution of tasks between state and sub-national administration this may be more outspoken at sub-national level. Furthermore, the sub-national administrative levels in all three countries, but in particular Latvia and Estonia, consists of small units that are in general starved of financial resources and have difficulties in keeping qualified personnel (Ruus 2011; King *et al.* 2004; Vanags and Vilka 2006). This implies that value differences between administrative levels may be explained by a more professional central administration and/or socialisation into European values brought about by close contacts to European bureaucrats (Hofmann 2008). But it is not only a question of distance from Brussels. Finding practical solutions to day-to-day problems is another. Sub-national administrations are closer to citizens who demand that the job gets done making public servants value flexibility. This may indicate that the inclination to be more flexible is not about integrity but simply a matter of different tasks.

With respect to administrative processes, meritocratic recruitment and promotions together with coordination practices in public administration are key factors in shaping public servants' values. The virtue of meritocracy lies in the legal-rational selection mechanism of hiring and promoting public servants, which means that it is in their self-interest to perform in the interest of the public. Across the board, meritocracy is significantly and positively related to integrity and responsiveness. As a consequence of professionalisation, where formal qualifications are more important than personal loyalties and political affiliations (O'Dwyer 2006: 30–1), it is not surprising that the more meritocratic the organisation is, the more public servants cherish integrity. This confirms previous findings that meritocracy decreases the temptation to abuse office, i.e. to become corrupt (Rubin and Whitford 2008), and, according to Dahlström *et al.* (2011: 3), generates an 'esprit de corps' fostering impartiality and non-corrupt behaviour. This may also be why meritocracy fosters the values of participation as public servants' professional ethos protects against temptations of preferential treatment when they come in close contact with citizens. Uncertainty remains, however, if it is the mechanism of meritocracy or security in employment that makes it more costly for public servants to part with integrity principles (Rubin and Whitford 2008: 405; de Graaf 2007: 52–3). In any case, it is fairly certain that if you sit in an organisation that complies with the norms of meritocracy, you are more likely to hold values of integrity. This is particularly interesting, because meritocratic recruitment is one of the administrative benchmarks recommended by the EU.

The degree of coordination among public agencies also holds a positive and strong relation across the three integrity items, but not with responsiveness. This effect is not surprising because coordination implies that other agencies can supervise and control practices in the organisation. Coordination may thus increase the professional ethos through social control and increased citizens' participation may add another level of complexity to policy programmes where multiple agencies are already involved. Cooperation with private actors carries a risk of particularity. It is therefore somewhat disturbing that the more one cooperates with private actors the more willing one is to bend the rules. One explanation is pressure from private actors, who focus on efficiency, effectiveness and profitability and are perhaps less concerned with due process. This finding corresponds to concerns that the focus on efficiency and effectiveness in NPM may neglect the values of equality and accountability (Maravic and Reichard 2003; Raadschelders, Chapter Two in this volume). This may be the exact reason why, according to the EU, formal meritocratic structure recommendations should be enforced before engaging in NPM experiments.

Another lesson learned is that experience with involving private actors in implementation makes public servants perceive citizens' participation as positive for the administration. Repeating the regression model for each country individually (not shown) reveals that much of the effect is driven by Lithuania, where few have experience with inclusion, and by Estonian public servants who frequently involve private actors in the implementation of public policy. This structure indicates that there may be a floor and a ceiling to the lesson: citizens' can be involved too little, but also too much.

Concluding: A European neutral yet responsive public servant

There is a change underway in the Baltic administrations. It is perhaps too optimistic to claim that the values of public servants in the Baltic States have become the negated image of Soviet administrative practice. But it is a fair conclusion that the public servants in the three states do indeed embrace modern European administrative values as there is a high degree of support for the neutrality of the public service and many, though not all, see responsiveness to citizens' participation as positive in administrative development.

In terms of differences in national administrative cultures Latvia stands out. Latvian public servants uphold higher standards for rule compliance but are less willing to blow the whistle on misconduct; and they are more positive towards citizens' participation than their colleagues in the two other states. A possible explanation is that the Latvian public service is more formal and rigid than our controls can capture through the measure of hierarchy. Thus, citizens' participation can, indeed, make a positive change. A more comprehensive explanation of why Latvians stand out is beyond this study.

The primary difference is not found between the countries, however, but between different levels of administration. The state administrations have embraced the values of integrity to a larger extent than sub-national administrations, which, in turn, are much more responsive to citizens' participation. It appears that public servants are developing in two different directions or, alternatively, in two tempi. The former explanation is rooted in the task differences and contact with citizens, whereas the latter indicates differences in European exposure. As for instilling integrity, there is quite a job ahead in terms of training and raising awareness among public servants at the sub-national level, but there is equally a call to open the central administrations to inclusion and responsiveness to citizens.

Concerning the influence of administrative processes upon the formation of value systems, hierarchy is found to be detrimental to responsiveness. Flatter and more flexible administration may promote efficient citizens' participation. Although it appears that citizens' participation is good only up to a certain point, support for citizens' participation is high among public servants who in practice involve outside actors in implementation. Finally, meritocracy is highlighted because it almost appears to be a panacea for developing modern European administrative values. Practising meritocracy is closely related to the development of both integrity and responsiveness. In sum, there is a clear tendency that Baltic public servants do hold European values of public administration, but also that country-specific issues still matter.

References

Ahdieh, R. B. (1997) *Russia's Constitutional Revolution: Legal consciousness and the transition to democracy 1985–1996*, Pennsylvania, PA: Pennsylvania State University Press.

Barber, B. R. (1983) *Strong Democracy: Participatory politics for a new age*, Berkeley, CA: California University Press.

Brzezinski, Z. (1970) *Between Two Ages*, New York: Penguin.

Bunce, V. (1995) 'Should transitologists be grounded?', *Slavic Review*, 54(1): 111–27.

Charron, N. and Lapuente, V. (2010) 'Does democracy produce quality of government?' *European Journal of Political Research*, 49(4): 443–70.

Charron, N., Dahlström, C. and Lapuente, V. (2012) 'No law without a state', *Journal of Comparative Economics*, 40(2): 176–93.

Crawford, B. and Lijphart, A. (1995) 'Explaining political and economic change in post-communist Eastern Europe: old legacies, new institutions, hegemonic norms, and international pressure', *Comparative Political Studies*, 28(2): 171–99.

Dahlström, C., Lapuente, V. and Teorell, J. (2011) 'The merit of meritocratization: politics, bureaucracy, and the institutional deterrents of corruption', *Political Research Quarterly*, XX: 1–13.

de Graaf, G. (2010) 'A report on reporting: why peers report integrity and law violations in public organizations', *Public Administration Review*, 70(5): 767–79.

Dimitrova, A. (2005) 'Europeanization and civil service reform', in Schimmelfennig, F. and Sedelmeier, U. (eds) *The Europeanization of Central and Eastern Europe*, Ithaka, NY: Cornell University Press, pp. 71–90.

— (2010) 'The new member states of the EU in the aftermath of enlargement: do new European rules remain empty shells?', *Journal of European Public Policy*, 17(1): 137–48.

Domarkas, V. and Gineitine, D. (2000) 'Lithuania Historical framework: development of public administration as an academic field of study', in Lithuania, retrieved from http://www.nispa.org/reports/Lithuania/Part1.htm (accessed 2 February 2014).

Drechsler, W. (2005) 'The re-emergence of "Weberian" public administration after the fall of new public management: the Central and Eastern European perspective', *Halduskultuur*, 6: 94–108.

Eckstein, H. (1988) 'A culturalist theory of political change', *American Political Science Review*, 82(3): 789–804.

EU Commission (2001) *White Paper on Governance*, retrieved from http://eur-lex.europa.eu/LexUriServ/site/en/com/2001/com2001_0428en01.pdf (accessed October 2013).

— (2004) 'A new partnership for cohesion: convergence, competitiveness, cooperation', *Third Report on Economic and Social Cohesion*, http://ec.europa.eu/regional_policy/sources/docoffic/official/reports/pdf/cohesion3/cohesion3_part4_en.pdf (accessed September 2013).

Evans, P. (1995) *Embedded Autonomy: States and industrial transformation*, Princeton, NJ: Princeton University Press.

Goetz, A. M. (2007) 'Political cleaners: women as the new anti-corruption force?', *Development and Change*, 38(1): 87–105.

Goetz, K. and Wollmann, H. (2001) 'Governmentalizing central executives in post-communist Europe: a four-country comparison', *Journal of European Public Policy*, 8: 864–87.

Habermas, J. (1996) *Between Facts and Norms: Contribution to a discourse theory of law and democracy*, Cambridge: Polity.

Hofmann, H. C. H. (2008) 'Mapping the European administrative space', *West European Politics*, 31(4): 662–76.

Irvin, R. A. and Stansbury, J. (2004) 'Citizen participation in decision making: is it worth the effort?', *Public Administration Review*, 64(1): 55–65.

Jansone, D. and Reinholde, I. (2001) 'Politico-administrative relations: the case of Latvia', in Verheijen, T. (ed.), *Politico-Administrative Relations, Who Rules?* Bratislava: NISPAcee, pp. 203–25.

Johannsen, L. (2002) 'The responsive state', *Baltic Defence Review*, 2(8): 9–20.

—— (2003) 'The effective state', *Baltic Defence Review*, 2(9): 23–33.

Johannsen, L. and Pedersen, K. H. (2008) 'The responsive state: openness and inclusion in the policy process', in Dani, A. A. and de Haan, A. (eds) *Inclusive States: Social policy and structural inequalities*, Washington, DC: International Bank for Reconstruction and Development, World Bank, pp. 73–95.

—— (2009a) 'Keys leading to transition and paths leading beyond', in Johannsen, L. and Pedersen, K. H. (eds) *Pathways: A study of six post-communist countries*, Aarhus: Aarhus University Press, pp. 155–67.

—— (2009b) 'When nation building is at odds with economic reform and EU membership', *Politics in Central Europe*, 5(2): 55–77.

—— (2011a) 'Path making: democracy in the Baltic States twenty years after', *Politics in Central Europe*, 7(1): 57–73.

—— (2011b) 'The institutional roots of anti-corruption policies: comparing the three Baltic States', *Journal of Baltic Studies*, 42(3): 329–46.

Johnson, R. A. (2003) *Whistleblowing: When it works - and why*, Boulder, CO: Lynne Reiner Publishers.

Kathi, P. C. and Cooper, T. L. (2005) 'Democratizing the administrative state: connecting neighborhood councils and city agencies', *Public Administration Review*, 65(5): 559–67.

King, C. S., Feltey, K. M. and O'Niel Susel, B. (1998) 'The question of participation: toward authentic public participation in public administration', *Public Administration Review*, 58(4): 317–26.

King, G. J., Vanags, E., Vilka, I. and McNabb, D. E. (2004) 'Local government reforms in Latvia, 1990–2003', *Transition to a Democratic Society Public Administration*, 82(4): 931–50.

Kitschelt, H. (2003) 'Accounting for postcommunist regime diversity: what counts as a good cause?' in Ekiert, G. and Hanson, S. E. (eds) *Capitalism and Democracy in Central and Eastern Europe: Assessing the legacy of communist rule*, Cambridge: Cambridge University Press, pp. 49–86.

Lazareviciute, I., Tirviene, J. and Poniskaitis, J. (2001) 'Politico-administrative relations in Lithuania', in Verheijen, T. (ed.) *Politico-administrative Relations: Who Rules?*, Bratislava: NISPAcee, pp. 226–67.

Letki, N. (2002) 'Lustration and democratisation in East-Central Europe', *Europe-Asia Studies*, 54(4): 529–52.

Maravic, P. von and Reichard, C. (2003) 'New public management and corruption: IPMN dialogue and analysis', *International Public Management Review*, 4: 84–130.

March, J. G. and Olsen, J. P. (1989) *Rediscovering Institutions: The organizational basis of politics*, New York: Free Press.

Meyer-Sahling, J.-H. (2011) 'The durability of EU civil service policy', *Governance*, 24(2): 231–60.

Miles, R. E., Jr (1978) 'The origin and meaning of Miles' Law', *Public Administration Review*, 38(5): 399–403.

Nakrošis, V. (2001) 'Lithuanian public administration: a usable state bureaucracy?' *Journal of Baltic Studies*, 32(2): 170–81.

Nakrošis, V. and Budraitis, M. (2012) 'Longitudinal change in Lithuanian agencies: 1990–2010', *International Journal of Public Administration*, 35(12): 820–31.

Nunberg, B. (1999) The State after Communism: administrative transitions in Central and Eastern Europe, Washington DC: World Bank.

—— (2000) 'Ready for Europe: public administration reform and European Union accession in Central and Eastern Europe', World Bank Technical Paper no. 466, Washington DC: World Bank.

O'Dwyer, C. (2006) *Runaway State-Building: Patronage, politics and democratic development*, Baltimore, MD: Johns Hopkins University Press.

OECD (1999) *European Principles for Public Administration*, SIGMA papers no. 27, retrieved from http://www.oecd.org/site/sigma/publicationsdocuments/36972467.pdf (accessed November 2012).

—— (2001) *Citizens as Partners: OECD Handbook on Information, Consultation and Public Participation in Policy-Making*, Paris: OECD.

Ostrom, E. (1990) *Governing the Commons*, New York: Cambridge University Press.

—— (2000) 'Crowding out citizenship', *Scandinavian Political Studies*, 23(1): 3–16.

—— (2010) 'Analyzing collective action', *International Association of Agricultural Economists*, 41: 155–66.

Ostrom, E. and Ostrom, V. (2011) 'The institutional perspective on values and virtues', in de Vries, M. S. and Kim, P. S. (eds) *Value and Virtue in Public Administration: A comparative perspective*, London: Palgrave Macmillan, pp. 115–34.

Pakulski, J. (1986) 'Bureaucracy and the Soviet system', *Studies in Comparative Communism*, XIX(1): 3–24.

Palidauskaite, J. (2011) 'The value profile of civil servants in new European democracies through the lens of embedded ethics', in de Vries, M. S. and Kim, P. S. (eds) *Value and Virtue in Public Administration: A comparative perspective*, London: Palgrave Macmillan.

Palidauskaite, J., Pevkur, A. and Reinholde, I. (2010) 'A comparative approach to civil service ethics in Estonia, Latvia and Lithuania', *Journal of Baltic Studies*, 41(1): 45–71.

Panagiotou, R. A. (2001) 'Estonia's success: prescription or legacy', *Communist and Post-Communist Studies*, 34: 261–77.

Pedersen, K. H. and Johannsen, L. (2004) 'The real challenge for change: public administration in new EU member states', *Welt Trends*, 12: 93–105.

— (2006) 'Corruption: commonality, causes and consequences in fifteen post-communist countries', in Rosenbaum, A. and Nemec, J. (eds) *Democratic Governance in Central and Eastern European Countries*, Bratislava: NISPAcee, pp. 311–36.

Peters, B. G. and Pierre, J. (2000) 'Citizens versus the new public manager: the problem of mutual empowerment', *Administration & Society*, 32(1): 9–28.

Pivoras, S. (2010) 'Model of civil service in Lithuania's public policy', *Baltic Journal of Law & Politics*, 3(1): 99–124.

Przeworski, A. (2004) 'Institutions matter?', *Government and Opposition*, 39(4): 527–40.

Putnam, R. D. with Leonardi, R. and Nanetti, R. Y. (1993) *Making Democracy Work: Civic traditions in modern Italy*, Princeton, NJ: Princeton University Press.

Randma, T. (2000) 'Estonia: historical framework', retrieved from www.nispa. org/reports/Estonia/Part1.htm (accessed 2 February 2014).

Randma-Liiv, T. and Järvalt, J. (2011) 'Public personnel policies and problems in the new democracies of Central and Eastern Europe', *Journal of Comparative Policy Analysis: Research and Practice*, 13(1): 35–49.

Rubin, E. V. and Whitford, A. (2008) 'Effects of the institutional design of the civil service: evidence from corruption', *International Public Management Journal*, 11(4): 404–25.

Ruus, J. (2011) 'Democratic participation at the local level in post-communist states: Estonia, Latvia, Lithuania', in Schiller, T. (ed.) *Local Direct Democracy in Europe*, Wiesbaden: VS Verlag für Sozialwissenschaften, pp. 268–89.

Sarapuu, K. (2011) 'Post-Communist development of administrative structure in Estonia: from fragmentation to segmentation', *Transylvanian Review of Administrative Sciences*, special issue, pp. 54–73.

— (2012) 'Administrative structures in times of changes: the development of Estonian ministries and government agencies 1990–2010', *International Journal of Public Administration*, 35(12): 808–19.

Sedelmeier, U. (2008) 'After conditionality: post-accession compliance with EU law in East Central Europe', *Journal of European Public Policy*, 15(6): 806–25.

Sootla, G. (2001) 'Evolution of roles of politicians and civil servants during the post-communist transition in Estonia', in Verheijen, T. (ed.) *Politico-Administrative Relations: Who Rules?*, Bratislava: NISPAcee, pp. 107–46.

Sootla, G. and Roots, H. (1999) 'The civil service in the Republic of Estonia', in Verheijen, T. (ed.) *Civil Service Systems in Central and Eastern Europe*, London: Edward Elgar, pp. 235–66.

Soviet Constitution (1977), retrieved from http://www.constitution.org/cons/ussr77.txt (accessed August 2013).

Transparency International (2011) *Transparency International*, retrieved from http://cpi.transparency.org/cpi2011/ (accessed August 2013).

Unpan (2004a) 'Republic of Latvia: public administration country profile', UN: Division for Public Administration and Development Management (DPADM), Department of Economic and Social Affairs (DESA), retrieved from http://unpan1.un.org/intradoc/groups/public/documents/un/unpan023216.pdf (accessed August 2013).

— (2004b) 'Republic of Estonia: public administration country profile', UN: Division for Public Administration and Development Management (DPADM), Department of Economic and Social Affairs (DESA), retrieved from http://unpan1.un.org/intradoc/groups/public/documents/un/unpan023213.pdf (accessed August 2013).

— (2004c) 'Republic of Lithuania: public administration country profile', UN: Division for Public Administration and Development Management (DPADM), Department of Economic and Social Affairs (DESA), retrieved from http://unpan1.un.org/intradoc/groups/public/documents/un/unpan023217.pdf (accessed August 2013).

Vanags, E. (2000) 'Latvia: historical framework', retrieved from www.nispa.org/reports/Latvia/Part1.htm (accessed 2 February 2014).

Vanags, E. and Vilka, I. (2006) 'Local government in the Baltic States: similar but different', *Local Government Studies*, 32(5): 623–37.

Verheijen, T. and Coombes, D. (1998) *Innovations in Public Management: Experiences from East and West Europe*, Aldershot: Edward Elgar Publishers.

Zimmer, A. (2005) 'Civil society organization in Central and Eastern European countries: introduction and terminology', in Zimmer, A. and Priller, E. (eds) *Future of Civil Society: Making Central and Eastern European nonprofit organizations work*, e-book, Berlin and Münster: Leske+Budrich, pp. 11–27.

Appendix: Survey Questions

Dependent variables

Bending rules:

20A: On a scale of 1 to 7, where '7' means 'in all cases' in favour and '1' means 'in no cases', given the risk of not treating all citizens equally, are you in favour of bending the rules in order to achieve policy objectives?
20B: On a scale of 1 to 7, where '7' means 'in all cases' and '1' means 'in no cases', do you accept bending the rules in order to achieve policy objectives?

> The variable *bending rules* used in the analysis is a pooled variable consisting of QA20A and QA20B and ranging from 1 to 7. The two questions do not give any convincing difference in the respondents' answers. The only difference made by the stimulus is that the Latvians are more discouraging if there is a risk of unequal treatment (from 67 to 51 per cent), which is the opposite of what we would expect.

Arm's length:

25A: I will now give you a complicated, but important question, so please take some seconds before answering it. Let us imagine that a public servant has to deal with a case in which his friends/relatives have personal interests; however, favouring his friends/relatives would not accord strictly with current regulations. What do you think a public servant in your organisation would typically do?
25B: I will now give you a complicated, but important question, so please take some seconds before answering it. Let us imagine that a public servant has to deal with a case in which his friends/relatives have personal interests; however, favouring them would not accord strictly with current regulations. On the other hand, making a decision in favour of his friends or relatives would contribute to the common good. What do you think a public servant in your organisation would typically do?
Respondents were asked to choose between:
1. Hand over the case to a colleague.
2. Make a decision in favour of his friends/relatives.
3. Make a decision not in favour of his friends/relatives.

The variable *arm's length* consists of the variables QA25A and QA25B, where QA25B has a stimulus with respect to promoting the common good. There are statistically no differences between the responses of the two groups and answers to the two questions are therefore merged. On a side note, however, with respect to gender there is a small difference associated with gender between the answers to the two questions. While 93.5 per cent of both women and men will maintain neutrality as a starting point, women are consistent and maintain an arm's length, even if their decision does not contribute to the common good of society (93.5–92.5 per cent). In contrast men are less likely to keep the arm's length (93.5–88.1 per cent), if they know that their decision contributes to the common good.

Whistle-blowing:

42–6: I will read out some statements in the following. On a scale of 1 to 7, where '7' means 'always' and '1' means 'never', If you found out that one of your colleagues had accepted a bribe, how would you act?

In the regression we use answers to Q46 where the respondent says, 'Do nothing'.

Responsiveness:

22: In your view, how many of the following items would make a decisive and positive change for your organisation? 'Increase in citizen participation' – Yes, No, Do not know.

Independent variables

Merit:

I will read out some statements in the following. On a scale of 1 to 7, where '7' means 'always' and '1' means 'never', how often do you think that the following applies to your organisation? Recruitment of employees is based on the skills and merits of the applicant.

Hierarchy:

On a scale of 1 to 7 where '7' means 'totally agree' and '1' means 'totally disagree', please tell me to what extent you agree or disagree with the following statement: Your organisation is hierarchically structured.

Employment at administrative level:

At what level of public administration do you work? (State, regional, local.)

Regional and local levels have been merged and in the text we use the term sub-national level for this variable.

Staff responsibility:

What is your position in your organisation? Possibilities given were 'head of section' and 'head of office', in both cases distinguished with or without staff responsibility.

Coordination:

On a scale of 1 to 7, where '7' means 'always' and 1' means 'never', when thinking about the relation between your organisation and other actors how often do you think that tasks relating to your organisation and other actors are highly coordinated?

Cooperation:

On a scale of 1 to 7, where '7' means 'always' and 1' means 'never', when thinking about the relation between your organisation and other actors how often do you think that private parties (individuals, firms, NGOs) are involved in implementing the organisation's policy objectives?

Part Six

Conclusion: A Shared Administrative Identity?

Chapter Thirteen

Shared Values for a European Administrative Identity? A Cross-National Analysis of Government Employees' *Basic Human Values*

Julia-Carolin Brachem and Markus Tepe[1]

Introduction

In the various EU institutions in Brussels, Strasbourg and elsewhere, government employees from different European countries with distinct administrative approaches work together and shape EU policies. Although there are shared principles of EU administration, as for example codified in the community *acquis*, the normative ingredients and motivational foundations for a common European administrative identity remain an open question (e.g. Cardona 2009; OECD 1999). While institutional changes in the European administrative space (EAS) have already received much scholarly interest (e.g. Balint *et al.* 2008; Hofmann 2008; Olsen 2003), research on the motivational foundations and the features of a potential European administrative identity is still in its infancy. This chapter considers the acknowledgement and mutual recognition of shared motivational values to be prerequisites for the development of a European administrative identity, and therefore puts government employees' motivational values at the centre of investigation. Focusing on government employees' self-perception, it explores the possibility of identifying a shared motivational conception among European public servants (compared to the US) that may serve as a building block for a common European administrative identity.

Linking the discussion about *Public Service Motivation* (e.g. Coursey and Pandey 2007; Hammerschmid *et al.* 2009; Perry 1996)[2] with psychological research on *Basic Human Values* (e.g. Davidov *et al.* 2008; Lyons *et al.* 2006; Schmidt *et al.* 2007; Schwartz 2005) and the so-called *Person-Environment Fit* (e.g. Kristof-Brown *et al.* 2005; Leisink and Steijn 2008), we compare *Basic Human Values* among government employees from EU countries and the US. In doing so, we pay particular attention to the conditioning role of a nation's administrative tradition,

---

1.   This study is part of an ongoing research project exploring 'The Transformation of the State as Employer' at the Collaborative Research Center Transformation of the State (CRC) 597, http://www.sfb597.uni-bremen.de. We gratefully acknowledge financial support from the German Research Foundation. The dataset and Stata command files are available for replication purposes.

2.   Also *see* Anderfuhren-Biget (2012), Rayner *et al.* (2010), Vandenabeele (2008), Van der Wal and Huberts (2008) and Wright and Pandey (2008).

as the historical, institutional and sociological backgrounds that are condensed in these traditions are presumed to shape government employment policies and thereby affect the attractiveness of government employment for different motivational types.

The comparative public administration literature offers various possibilities for describing and classifying the institutional features of national administrative systems (e.g. Lodge 2009, Painter and Peters 2010a; 2010b; Pollitt and Bouckaert 2011; Rugge 2009; Sager *et al.* 2012). We make use of these contributions and investigate the value orientations of government employees in five countries, namely the United States, Great Britain, France, Germany and Sweden. We have chosen these five countries since they have repeatedly been depicted as representative cases for the Anglo-American, Napoleonic, Germanic and Scandinavian administrative traditions (e.g. Painter and Peters 2010b), and thereby serve as empirical reference points for a classification of *Western Administrative Traditions* (also *see* Raadschelders, Chapter Two in this volume). If country-specific differences in government employees' *Basic Human Values* do exist, this sample of countries with most different administrative traditions should be able to reveal them.[3]

The empirical analysis utilises data from the World Values Survey 2005/6, in which subjects' value orientations are measured with the *Basic Human Values* inventory as developed by Schwartz (Schwartz *et al.* 2001; Schwartz 2006). It proceeds in two steps: first, in order to see whether European (or continental European) idea(l)s of the public servant can be discerned or not, we adopt a between-country perspective and investigate whether government employees from countries with a Napoleonic, Germanic or Scandinavian administrative tradition have more values in common than their colleagues from countries with an Anglo-American tradition. Second, from a within-country perspective, we seek to explore whether government employees have a distinct profile of motivational values as compared to their private sector counterparts (e.g. Hammerschmid *et al.* 2009; Ritz 2011).

The chapter proceeds as follows. The next section provides a brief review of the concept of *Basic Human Values*. This is followed by a discussion of contemporary typologies of *Administrative Traditions*, the *Public Service Motivation* literature and the *Person-Environment Fit* approach. The fourth section presents the dataset, the definition of variables and the statistical models. Empirical findings are presented in section five. The final section summarises the chapter and discusses its potential implications for further research.

Basic Human Values

In general, values are 'what people consider important' (Roccas *et al.* 2002: 790). They 'serve as guiding principles in life [...] [and] are acquired [...] through socialization [...] and [...] the [...] learning experiences of individuals'

---

3.   The United States and Great Britain are certainly not considered as 'most different' administrative traditions. Yet, while some authors underline that the two countries share a common Anglo-American administrative tradition (Painter and Peters 2010b), others have pointed out consistent differences in their administrative practices (Pollitt and Bouckaert 2011). In order to inform this discussion on empirical grounds, we have chosen to explore both countries.

(Schwartz 1994: 21). Following this definition, values 'motivate action' (Schwartz 1994: 21) and help to understand the direction and speed of organisational changes (Schwartz 2006: 929; Davidov *et al.* 2008: 3). Shared motivational values are expected to constitute the normative basis for developing a consistent group identity. Consequently, government employees' motivational values should be essential for the development of a common European administrative identity.

In methodological terms, motivational values have been measured via the *Basic Human Values* inventory (e.g. Schwartz and Bilsky 1990; Schwartz 1992, 1994, 2001, 2005; Schwartz and Sagiv 1995).[4] This inventory has been designed to cover a broad range of value orientations, independent from national context and culture. Building on Rokeach's (1973) conceptualisation of human values, Schwartz's ambitious research agenda aimed to identify 'a limited set of value types that are recognized in various human groups [and] a structure in [...] [their] relationships' (Schwartz 1994: 20), in order to create 'a systematic theory of the content and organization of value systems' (Schwartz *et al.* 2001: 519).

Using samples from forty-four countries with about 26,000 respondents (Schwartz 1994: 27), Schwartz discovers 'ten motivationally distinct types of values' (Schwartz 1994: 21), which are considered to capture the major value orientations across cultures. These *Basic Human Values* are (Schwartz 1994: 22): *Power* ('Social status and prestige, control or dominance over people and resources'), *Achievement* ('Personal success through demonstrating competence according to social standards'), *Hedonism* ('Pleasure and sensuous gratification for oneself'), *Stimulation* ('Excitement, novelty, and finding a challenge in life'), *Self-Direction* ('Independent thought and action – choosing, creating, exploring'), *Universalism* ('Understanding, appreciation, tolerance, and desiring protection for the welfare of all people and for nature'), *Benevolence* ('Preservation and enhancement of the welfare of people with whom one is in frequent personal contact'), *Tradition* ('Respect, commitment, and acceptance of the customs and ideas that traditional culture or religion provide'), *Conformity* ('Restraint of actions, inclinations, and impulses likely to upset or harm others and violate social expectations and norms') and *Security* ('Safety, harmony, and stability of society, of relationships, and of self').

These ten *Basic Human Values* can be arranged in a circle (Schwartz 1994: 24), with conceptually closer values lying closer together. The order is as follows: *Power, Achievement, Hedonism, Stimulation, Self-Direction, Universalism, Benevolence, Tradition, Conformity* and *Security*. The circular structure of value relations implies that values that are closer to each other are based on a similar underlying motivation. In order to condense the ten values into analytically more feasible dimensions, the opposition between competing value types can be arranged in two bipolar dimensions (Schwartz 1994: 25). One dimension opposes *Self-Enhancement* (*Power, Achievement*) and *Self-Transcendence* (*Universalism, Benevolence*) values. The two poles on this dimension contrast the importance of one's own success and dominance with the importance of accepting others as equal and caring for them. The second dimension opposes *Openness to Change*

---

4. Also *see* Davidov *et al.* (2008), Lyons *et al.* (2006) and Schmidt *et al.* (2007).

(*Stimulation, Self-Direction*) and *Conservation* (*Tradition, Conformity, Security*) values. The two poles on this second dimension contrast the importance of one's own independent thought and action with the importance of traditional practices and stability. *Hedonism* is the only value that belongs to both *Self-Enhancement* and *Openness to Change* (Schwartz 1994: 25).

Theoretical framework

Why would we expect government employees' *Basic Human Values* to vary across administrative traditions?[5] In order to answer this question, the theoretical framework builds on three so-far separated strands of literature; namely the typology of *Administrative Traditions*, the flourishing *Public Service Motivation* literature and the *Person-Environment Fit* approach.

Administrative Traditions

Whether a common European administrative identity is based on common motivational values among government employees can be approached from different theoretical and methodological angles (*see* Raadschelders, Chapter Two in this volume for an overview). From a cross-national perspective it is easy to see that the role and position of government employment differs between the US and European countries. In order to know whether there are any typical European idea(l)s of the public servant, understanding the role of administrative traditions is essential. A country's administrative tradition is presumed to influence not only the institutional arrangement of public administration systems (context), but also government employees' attitudes towards organisational change via self-selection into government employment (Peters and Painter 2010: 234).[6] Although public administration systems have undergone several reforms and changes, there are persistent patterns of administrative thought and practice (Painter and Peters 2010a: 3). Along these patterns, countries have been classified into distinct groups of administrative tradition (e.g. Painter and Peters 2010b; Pollitt and Bouckaert 2011). We expect that if there are any typical European idea(l)s of the public servant – at least present in government employees' motivational self-perception – the *Basic Human Values* of government employees should vary across administrative traditions.

The comparative public administration literature provides various typologies of administrative traditions. Painter and Peters (2010b: 19) identify, among others, the Napoleonic, Germanic, Scandinavian and Anglo-American administrative traditions. The Napoleonic administrative tradition – in our study represented by France – stands for a strong legal foundation of the state. Public law regulates the state-society relation and assures accountability. The organisation of the state is hierarchical and centralised, and the government exercises the important task

---

5. *See* Tepe (2012) for an exploration of public *vs.* private sector employees' political attitudes.
6. *See* Tepe *et al.* (2014) on the temporal stability of the administrative regime and the specific stability of the public/private sector wage gap.

of nation building. In this system, in which government employees are recruited through elite training, the public service in general has a rather high status. The elitist recruitment of top bureaucrats is coupled with an integrated and politicised relationship between the political and the administrative space (e.g. Ongaro 2010).

In the Germanic administrative tradition, here typified by Germany, the state also has a strong legal foundation in public law and regulates both the state-society relation and legal mechanisms. The organisation of the state, however, is federalist and cooperative. Moreover, it assures public action with and through non-state corporations. In these cooperative contexts, public service employment has rather high formal entry barriers. In contrast to the Napoleonic administrative tradition, the relations between politics and public administration are separated and fairly politicised (Painter and Peters 2010b: 22–3).

In the Scandinavian administrative tradition, in this study represented by Sweden, the state has a strong legal foundation and the state-society relation is grounded in a broad welfare regime. The organisation of the state is decentralised, in both administrative and political terms. As in the Germanic administrative tradition, politics and administration are separate (e.g. Painter and Peters 2010b: 23; Pierre 2010), but status differences between public and private sector employment are far less pronounced.

The Anglo-American administrative tradition, in this study typified by Great Britain and the United States, can be considered as being 'stateless' (Stillman 1990; Painter and Peters 2010b: 20). The state has limited legal foundations and the accountability mechanisms are of a political rather than a legal nature. The state-society relation is essentially pluralist and gives more responsibility to the market and to a lively civil society, which represents the public interest. Government employees' training puts emphasis on public management skills. The overall relations between politics and administration are distant (Painter and Peters 2010b: 20–1).

However, a closer look at Great Britain and the United States reveals consistent differences in their administrative practices. Regarding the state structure and the organisation of government, Great Britain is a unitary and centralised state. In contrast, the United States are federal, rather fragmented and rely strongly on self-organised forms of governance (Painter and Peters 2010b: 20–1; Pollitt and Bouckaert 2011: 50). Concerning accountability, administrative oversight by the courts plays an important role in the United States, whereas in Great Britain parliamentary sovereignty is more important (Painter and Peters 2010b: 21). With regard to the public service, American government employees, especially those in the upper ranks, hold only temporary positions and are highly politicised, whereas British government employees hold permanent positions and operate in a neutral way (Painter and Peters 2010b: 20; Peters 2010: 120; Pollitt and Bouckaert 2011: 50).

This refinement indicates that the United States may serve as the ideal reference category for the Napoleonic, Germanic and Scandinavian administrative traditions, all of which share a common understanding of the state-society relationship. Rutgers (2001) shows how different attitudes towards the concept of state have influenced the study of public administration in the US and European contexts. These concern in particular the legal tradition of the state, the legal accountability mechanisms and the special role of the public service. A common state-society conceptualisation in the Napoleonic, Germanic and Scandinavian administrative traditions becomes even more obvious if we consult Pollitt and Bouckaert's (2011) dichotomy of *Rechtsstaat* and *public interest* administrative cultures. According to their typology of administrative systems, the Napoleonic, Germanic and Scandinavian traditions are considered to be sub-categories of the legalistic oriented *Rechtsstaat* culture, whereas the Anglo-American tradition is based on a *public interest* culture.

The institutional and inherited structural differences in administrative traditions are expected to find their expression in government employment regulations and in particular in the recruitment policies, pay and career options that are offered to government employees. Following this line of reasoning, government employment in different countries should attract different motivational types. While we remain agnostic about which administrative tradition attracts which motivational type of government employee, the substantially different arrangement of the state-society relationship between the Napoleonic, Germanic and Scandinavian traditions on the one hand and the Anglo-American tradition on the other hand leads us to the following proposition:

> *P1 Administrative Tradition*: Government employees from countries with a Napoleonic, Germanic or Scandinavian administrative tradition share more values with each other than with government employees from countries that belong to the Anglo-American administrative tradition.

Public Service Motivation and the Person-Environment Fit assumption

The role of motivational values is most prominently discussed in the *Public Service Motivation* literature (e.g. Anderfuhren-Biget 2012; Behnke 2011; Brewer 2003; Coursey and Pandey 2007; Crewson 1997; Hammerschmid *et al.* 2009; Norris 2003),[7] which assumes that government employees have a work orientation that differs from private employees and is based mainly on values that are related to the public interest and compassion. The idea of a distinct *Public Service Motivation* (Perry and Wise 1990: 367) has been developed against the background of rational choice-oriented analyses of bureaucratic behaviour (e.g. Downs 1967; Niskanen 1971). From the early 1990s onwards, Perry and Wise have been promoting research on *Public Service Motivation*, building on Knoke and Wright-Isak's (1982) typology of rational, norm-based and affective public service motives. While rational motives are 'grounded in individual utility maximization' (Perry and Wise 1990: 368), norm-based motives include the aim to conform to social norms, and affective motives refer to 'emotional responses to various social contexts' (Perry and Wise 1990: 368).

---

7.   Also *see* Perry and Wise (1990), Perry (1996), Rayner *et al.* (2010), Vandenabeele (2008), Van der Wal *et al.* (2006), Van der Wal and Huberts (2008), Wright (2001) and Wright and Pandey (2008).

Perry has created a twenty-four item scale that differentiates between four *Public Service Motivation* dimensions (Perry 1996: 16–17): first, *Attraction to public policy-making* as a rational dimension, relating to the fascinating task of policy making and increasing government employees' feelings of self-importance; second, *Commitment to the public interest/civic duty* as a norm-based dimension, describing government employees' altruistic aim to serve the public interest (Perry 1996: 6); third, *Compassion*, which is another norm-based dimension that refers to government employees' sympathy for regime values and other persons; fourth, *Self-sacrifice* as an affective dimension covering government employees' 'willingness to substitute service to others for tangible personal rewards' (Perry 1996: 7).

The empirical benefits of the *Basic Human Values* concept presented above have been utilised in various studies.[8] But although the *Public Service Motivation* literature provides strong theoretical grounds for expecting motivational differences between government employees and their private sector counterparts, so far the *Basic Human Values* concept has not been used to explore government employees' motivational value orientation. Nevertheless, one can draw various conceptual linkages between the dimensions of *Public Service Motivation* and *Basic Human Values* (e.g. Hammerschmid *et al.* 2009; Ritz 2011). The values *Power* and *Achievement*, for example, could be associated with an *Attraction to public policy-making. Universalism* could embrace social norm-based motives such as *Commitment to the public interest/ civic duty. Benevolence* can be linked to *Compassion* and to a lesser extent to the affective motive *Self-sacrifice*. Even though we will not be able to test the direct relationship between items that measure *Public Service Motivation* and those items that measure *Basic Human Values*, there is substantial theoretical and empirical overlap.[9]

Following the implicit assumptions from the *Public Service Motivation* literature, the public sector is expected to constitute a specific work environment that attracts employees with unique public service motives. This assumption is taken up and made explicit in the *Person-Environment Fit* approach (e.g. Leisink and Steijn 2009). Kristof-Brown *et al.* (2005) summarise the existing *Person-Environment Fit* literature and differentiate between four distinct types of fit. On the formal level, they identify the *Person-Organisation Fit*, which describes the compatibility between persons and the organisation they work for (Kristof-Brown *et al.* 2005: 285) as well as the *Person-Job Fit*, which

---

8. Kulin and Svallfors (2011), for example, explore the nexus between motivational values and attitudes towards redistribution. They find that the impact of *Basic Human Values* on policy attitudes is stronger in more privileged classes, depending on a country's level of equality and poverty (Kulin and Svallfors 2011). Also *see* the study of Reeskens and Wright (2011), who show that civic nationalism, which reflects *Self-Transcendence* values, is positively associated with subjective well-being, whereas ethnic nationalism, which reflects *Self-Enhancement* values, is associated with lower subjective well-being.

9. The *Basic Human Values* inventory is understood as a complementary and easily accessible inventory rather than an alternative to the established *Public Service Motivation* items.

reflects 'the relationship between a person's characteristics and those of the job or tasks [...] performed at work' (Kristof-Brown *et al.* 2005: 284). On the interpersonal level, Kristof-Brown *et al.* identify the *Person-Group Fit*, which concentrates on the relationship between persons and their work groups as well as the *Person-Supervisor Fit*, which indicates goal congruence or even personal similarity between supervisors and subordinates (Kristof-Brown *et al.* 2005: 286–7). In general, the *Person-Organisation Fit* and the *Person-Job Fit* have become two of the most important criteria in the field of human recruitment and selection research.

A neighbouring approach to the *Person-Environment Fit* is Schneider's *Attraction-Selection-Attrition* model, which explains how the range and internal heterogeneity of persons working for one organisation is restricted. According to Schneider (1987: 442–5), the same types of persons are attracted to an organisation with a certain philosophy and goal manifestation. The organisation itself restricts the range of persons by selecting only those that have the kind of competencies needed in the organisation. Finally, people whose characteristics and expectations fit the organisational environment (*Person-Organisation Fit*) stay, whereas those whose characteristics do not fit leave after a while. The *Attraction-Selection-Attrition* cycle implicates that organisations consist of more or less homogeneous personnel.

Basic Human Values *and sector choice across Administrative Traditions*

The main question raised by the *Public Service Motivation* and *Person-Environment Fit* literature is which *Basic Human Values* are associated with government employment. Or to put it more simply, does the public sector in different administration tradition contexts attract employees with different values?

As to this question, there exist at least two alternative views. Following the *Public Service Motivation* approach, the primary aim of government employees is to serve the public interest. This is reflected by the affective motives in Perry's and Wise's (1990: 368–9) *Public Service Motivation* approach, and is corroborated by empirical findings which show that government employees place a high value on the intrinsic reward of work and are motivated to support the common welfare (Behnke 2011; Buurman *et al.* 2012; Houston 2000; Leisink and Steijn 2008). With regard to the four main dimensions of the *Basic Human Values* concept, we can therefore expect the following relationship:

> *P2a Self-Transcendence*: Government employees are more likely to have stronger *Self-Transcendence* (*Universalism, Benevolence*) values than their private sector counterparts.

Government employees are frequently blamed for strictly rule-bound behaviour and their limited openness towards change (e.g. DeHart-Davis 2007; Merton 1940; Thompson 1961). This perspective is to a certain extent reflected by Perry and Wise's (1990: 368–9) rational and norm-based motives and is empirically supported by different studies indicating that government employees are risk-averse (Bellante and Link 1981; Buurman *et al.* 2012; Pfeifer 2010). Moreover, traditional democratic values such as legitimation, control and accountability still seem to play an important role in the public sector (Behnke 2011). Referring to Schwartz's bipolar value dimensions (1992: 43; 1994: 25; Schwartz and Sagiv 1995: 94–6), this perspective on government employees' value orientation is summarised in an alternative proposition:

> *P2b   Conservation*: Government employees are more likely to have stronger *Conservation* (*Tradition, Conformity, Security*) values than their private sector counterparts.

Following the stylised relationship between *Administrative Traditions, Basic Human Values* and *Person-Environment Fit*, illustrated in Figure 13.1, P2a/b should be contingent upon government employees' affiliation to a certain administrative tradition.[10]

Figure 13.1: Stylised relationship between Basic Human Values, Person-Environment Fit *and* Administrative Tradition

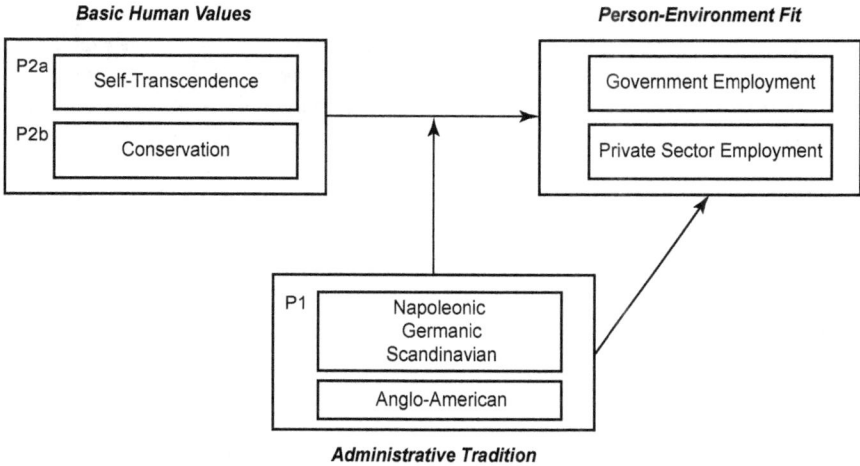

Basic Human Values   **Person-Environment Fit**

P2a — Self-Transcendence

P2b — Conservation

Government Employment

Private Sector Employment

P1 — Napoleonic / Germanic / Scandinavian

Anglo-American

Administrative Tradition

---

10. Alternatively, one might assume that certain work socialisation experiences in the private and public sectors will result in sector-specific *Basic Human Values*. To explore this reversed link – which is equally plausible – would require panel data, which is not available with respect to the research question in this chapter. Addressing the effect of work socialisation on government employees' *Basic Human Values* must therefore be left to future research.

11. Although we sought to avoid any bias in our sample, it must be stated that the nature of government employment differs from country to country. Therefore, government employees remain to some extent a heterogeneous group in the different countries.

Data and method

Dataset and variables

The three propositions are tested with data from the World Values Survey 2005/6 for France, Germany, Sweden, Great Britain and the United States. The country selection is motivated by the countries' ability to serve as representative cases of a distinct administrative tradition. Against the background of a most different regime scenario, the study concentrates on France, standing for the Napoleonic administrative tradition, Germany, typifying the Germanic administrative tradition, Sweden, representing the Scandinavian administrative tradition, and Great Britain and the United States, representing the Anglo-American tradition. The United States serves as the reference country. We exclude persons younger than eighteen, persons who never had a job, students, pensioners, the self-employed, and persons working in private non-profit organisations. Finally, the dataset consists of 2,660 observations; 798 of the respondents (30 per cent) are government employees.[11]

Government employees' value orientation is operationalised with the ten items from Schwartz's (2006: 939–41) *Portrait Values Questionnaire* as utilised in the World Values Survey. The *Portrait Values Questionnaire* originally consists of forty short verbal portraits, each describing 'a person's goals, aspirations, or wishes that point implicitly to the importance of a value' (Schwartz *et al.* 2001: 523). The abbreviated ten item *Portrait Values Questionnaire* measures value orientation indirectly (Schwartz *et al.* 2001: 523). The respondents have to answer the question *How much is this person like you?* on a 6-point scale (1 *Very much like me*, 2 *Like me*, 3 *Somewhat like me*, 4 *A little like me*, 5 *Not like me*, 6 *Not like me at all*) (Schwartz *et al.* 2001: 523). In the World Values Survey 2005/6 each *Basic Human Value* (*Power, Achievement, Hedonism, Stimulation, Self-Direction, Universalism, Benevolence, Tradition, Conformity, Security*) is covered by one portrait.

The respondents' employment sector is operationalised with the question *Are you working for the government or public institution, for private business or industry, or for a private non-profit organisation?*, while only respondents working in the public or private sector remain in the sample.

In order to reveal alternative explanations for government employees' value orientations, we include a full set of socio-demographic control variables, reflecting standard predictors such as gender, age, family status, educational level, employment status and income. Furthermore, we control for the respondents' occupation, which is measured by the question *In which profession/occupation do you do most of your work?* For the analysis we create five occupational categories: Employer/manager, professional, office worker, manual worker and unskilled worker. For further information, the definitions and descriptive statistics of all variables used in the statistical analyses are given in Tables 13.1 and 13.2.[12]

---

12. Since these items are available only in the World Values Survey 2005/6, we cannot take into account how recent public sector reforms might have affected government employees' value orientation.

Table 13.1: Definition and coding of variables

Variable type	Variable name	Source
Countries	France	WVS 2005/6 (v2)
	Germany	WVS 2005/6 (v2)
	Sweden	WVS 2005/6 (v2)
	Great Britain	WVS 2005/6 (v2)
	United States	WVS 2005/6 (v2)
Basic Human Values	Power	WVS 2005/6 (v81)
	Achievement	WVS 2005/6 (v85)
	Hedonism	WVS 2005/6 (v83)
	Stimulation	WVS 2005/6 (v86)
	Self-direction	WVS 2005/6 (v80)
	Universalism	WVS 2005/6 (v88)
	Benevolence	WVS 2005/6 (v84)
	Tradition	WVS 2005/6 (v89)
	Conformity	WVS 2005/6 (v87)
	Security	WVS 2005/6 (v82)
	Self-Enhancement (Power + Achievement)	
	Openness to Change (Stimulation + Self-direction)	
	Self-Transcendence (Universalism + Benevolence)	
	Conservation (Tradition + Conformity + Security)	
Employment	Employment sector (1 = Public sector | 2 = Private sector)	WVS 2005/6 (v243)
	Occupation (1 = Employer/manager | 2 = Professional | 3 = Office worker | 4 = Manual worker | 5 = Unskilled worker)	WVS 2005/6 (v242)
Socio-demographics	Gender (1 = Male | 2 = Female)	WVS 2005/6 (v235)
	Age	WVS 2005/6 (v237)
	Family status (1 = Married | 2 = Separated/Divorced/ Widowed | 3 = Single)	WVS 2005/6 (v55)
	Educational level (1 = No formal education/Primary school | 2 = Secondary school | 3 = University)	WVS 2005/6 (v238)
	Employment status (1 = Employed | 2 = Unemployed/ Housewife/Other)	WVS 2005/6 (v241)
	Income	WVS 2005/6 (v253)

Table 13.2: Descriptive statistics

Variable	Mean	Std. Dev.	Min.	Max.
France	0.19	0.39	0	1
Germany	0.25	0.44	0	1
Sweden	0.23	0.42	0	1
Great Britain	0.17	0.38	0	1
United States	0.15	0.36	0	1
Power	0.30	0.24	0	1
Achievement	0.50	0.28	0	1
Hedonism	0.58	0.27	0	1
Stimulation	0.39	0.28	0	1
Self-direction	0.66	0.24	0	1
Universalism	0.65	0.24	0	1
Benevolence	0.73	0.22	0	1
Tradition	0.52	0.30	0	1
Conformity	0.59	0.28	0	1
Security	0.63	0.27	0	1
Self-Enhancement (Power + Achievement)	0.40	0.21	0	1
Openness to Change (Stimulation + Self-direction)	0.53	0.21	0	1
Self-Transcendence (Universalism + Benevolence)	0.69	0.18	0	1
Conservation (Tradition + Conformity + Security)	0.58	0.20	0	1
Public sector	0.30	0.46	0	1
Employer/manager	0.09	0.28	0	1
Professional	0.12	0.33	0	1
Office worker	0.42	0.49	0	1
Manual worker	0.32	0.47	0	1
Unskilled worker	0.05	0.22	0	1
Female	0.51	0.50	0	1
Age	41.60	11.80	18	80
Family status	1.52	0.79	1	3
Married	0.67	0.47	0	1
Separated/Divorced/Widowed	0.14	0.35	0	1
Single	0.19	0.39	0	1
No formal education/Primary school	0.12	0.32	0	1
Secondary school	0.58	0.49	0	1
University	0.30	0.46	0	1
Employed	0.82	0.38	0	1
Unemployed/Housewife/Other	0.18	0.38	0	1
Income	5.43	2.49	1	10
Income (centred)	−6.65	2.19	−5.80	6.22

Statistical models

The empirical analysis is based on a series of binary and multinomial regression models, estimating the effect of *Basic Human Values* on the likelihood of working as a government employee. The primary goal is to find out whether government employees in countries with a Napoleonic, Germanic or Scandinavian tradition (France, Germany, Sweden) have more motivational values in common than with government employees from an Anglo-American administrative tradition (Great Britain, United States) (P1). The empirical analysis proceeds in three steps: after presenting descriptive evidence, we restrict the sample to include only those respondents that considered themselves as government employees and estimate the effect of *Basic Human Values* on the likelihood of being a government employee in France, Germany, Sweden, Great Britain or the United States using a multinomial logit model. Thereafter, we estimate the association between government employment and *Basic Human Values* on country-specific samples and compare these associations between countries to identify whether government employees from different administrative traditions hold different motivational values. This enables us to explore P1 and P2, which assume that government employees are likely to have stronger *Self-Transcendence* (P1a) or *Conservation* (P1b) values than private sector employees, in a joint set-up without ignoring general cross-national differences in *Basic Human Values*.

In order to evaluate the overall fit of the statistical models, the Pseudo-$R2$, Akaike Information Criterion (AIC) and Bayesian Information Criterion (BIC) are displayed at the bottom of the regression tables. The likelihood-ratio test, which provides a comparison of the fit of two alternative model specifications, is used to evaluate the extent to which the inclusion of the *Basic Human Value* items improves the ability to predict government employment.[13]

Empirical analysis

Descriptive analysis

The descriptive analysis, illustrated in Table 13.3, displays the average response for Schwartz's *Basic Human Values* dimensions among government and private sector employees in the United States, Great Britain, France, Germany and Sweden. In general, one can state that *Self-Transcendence* values seem to be more important for government employees (Government: 72 per cent, private: 68 per cent), whereas *Self-Enhancement* values seem to be more important for private sector employees (Gov.: 38 per cent, Priv.: 43 per cent). Regarding the average level of importance, *Self-Transcendence* values (*Universalism, Benevolence*) achieve the highest levels,

---

13. 'Predict' is used as a technical term in the context of statistical inference. With respect to the cross-sectional dataset at hand, the multivariate analysis is used to identify statistical associations between an individual's *Basic Human Values* and the likelihood that this individual is a government employee.

Table 13.3: Basic Human Values *by institution of occupation and country*

Country	Self-Enhancement		Openness to Change		Self-Transcendence		Conservation	
	Private (%)	Gov. (%)	Private (%)	Gov. (%)	Private (%)	Gov. (%)	Private (%)	Gov. (%)
USA	42	42	55	52	66	65	62	60
Great Britain	40	35	54	56	72	74	67	66
France	36	36	52	49	70	73	60	61
Germany	51	45	50	47	61	68	54	54
Sweden	39	34	57	55	72	76	54	54
Total	43	38	53	52	68	72	59	58

Note: Values standardised to range from 0 to 100 percentage points, weighted by v259.

followed by *Conservation* (*Tradition, Conformity, Security*), *Openness to Change* (*Stimulation, Self-Direction*), and *Self-Enhancement* (*Power, Achievement*) values.

A closer look at country-specific differences reveals that in the case of *Self-Transcendence* and *Self-Enhancement*, the value orientation in European countries (France, Germany, Sweden and Great Britain) is quite similar. This stands in contrast to the United States as a non-European country. Moreover, *Self-Transcendence* values seem to be more important for government than for private employees in all four European countries – in Great Britain, however, to a lesser extent. The *Self-Enhancement* values seem to be more important for private sector employees in Great Britain, Germany and Sweden. With regard to *Openness to Change* values, all five countries show limited sector differences. The biggest deviations between government and private employees' average *Basic Human Values* can be found in Germany with *Self-Transcendence* values, which are apparently much more important for government employees (government: 68 per cent, private: 61 per cent), and *Self-Enhancement* values, which are apparently much more important for private employees (government: 45 per cent, private: 51 per cent). This last striking deviation in the field of *Self-Enhancement* values can be observed in the same manner in Great Britain (government: 35 per cent, private: 40 per cent) and Sweden (government: 34 per cent, private: 39 per cent).

Multivariate analysis

In order to find out whether government employees in countries with a Napoleonic, Germanic or Scandinavian administrative tradition (represented by France, Germany, Sweden) share more motivational values than they share with government employees from an Anglo-American administrative tradition (represented by Great Britain, United States), Table 13.4 presents a multinomial logistic model. This model estimates the effect of the four *Basic Human Values* dimensions on the likelihood of working as a government employee in Great Britain, France, Germany and Sweden, using government employees in the United States

Table 13.4: Determinants of government employees' nationality

	Great Britain	France	Germany	Sweden
	(Reference = government employees from the United States)			
Self-Enhancement	−3.634***	−1.923*	1.990*	−1.704*
	[0.00]	[0.08]	[0.06]	[0.08]
Openness to Change	2.154**	−0.371	−2.031*	0.841
	[0.02]	[0.72]	[0.05]	[0.37]
Self-Transcendence	2.429***	3.294***	2.123**	4.445***
	[0.01]	[0.00]	[0.02]	[0.00]
Conservation	2.658**	0.288	−2.275**	−1.558
	[0.01]	[0.78]	[0.03]	[0.12]
Female	0.387	−0.394	0.363	0.0859
	[0.27]	[0.26]	[0.30]	[0.80]
Age	−0.0184	−0.0207	−0.00247	0.0346**
	[0.30]	[0.27]	[0.89]	[0.04]
Married	−0.106	0.214	0.562	0.648
	[0.84]	[0.68]	[0.28]	[0.18]
Separated/Divorced/Widowed	0.175	0.292	0.189	0.341
	[0.79]	[0.67]	[0.78]	[0.58]
Secondary school	−0.913	−3.530***	−2.884**	−1.808
	[0.53]	[0.01]	[0.03]	[0.14]
University	0.824	−1.260	−0.922	1.830
	[0.59]	[0.35]	[0.50]	[0.17]
Unemployed/Housewife/Other	16.90***	16.27***	17.00***	15.24***
	[0.00]	[0.00]	[0.00]	[0.00]
Income	0.335***	0.172*	0.121	−0.0692
	[0.00]	[0.07]	[0.22]	[0.46]
Employer/Manager	−1.584	−2.277	−1.312	−20.34***
	[0.20]	[0.21]	[0.45]	[0.00]
Professional	−2.423**	15.09***	0.750	−4.353***
	[0.04]	[0.00]	[0.57]	[0.00]
Office worker	−1.211	18.05***	4.267***	−0.245
	[0.30]	[0.00]	[0.00]	[0.83]
Manual worker	−0.977	17.00***	3.182**	0.587
	[0.38]	[0.00]	[0.01]	[0.59]
Observations	798			
Pseudo R2	0.272			
AIC	2,028.2			
BIC	2,327.9			
Likelihood-ratio test (*p*-value)	0.00			

Note: Multinomial logistic regression with robust standard errors, p-values in brackets, weighted by v259.

as the reference category. Since this model takes into account only government employees, the number of observations decreases to 798 respondents.

We start with a likelihood-ratio test to explore whether the inclusion of the four *Basic Human Values* dimensions helps to predict government employment in different countries. With a *p*-value of 0.00 the likelihood-ratio test clearly supports the inclusion of the *Basic Human Values*. A closer look at the four single dimensions indicates that value preferences of *Self-Enhancement*, *Self-Transcendence*, and to a lesser extent of *Openness to Change* and *Conservation* show statistically significant associations with government employment in the European countries (Great Britain, France, Germany, Sweden) in contrast to the United States. Apart from *Self-Transcendence*, however, the direction of these associations does not offer a clear pattern. Table 13.5 reveals that higher *Self-Transcendence* values are characteristic among European government employees, when compared to government employees from the United States.[14]

With respect to our first proposition P1, which expects government employees from a country with a Napoleonic, Germanic or Scandinavian tradition to share more motivational values with each other than with government employees from an Anglo-American administrative tradition, the conclusion is twofold. First, only one out of four *Basic Human Values* dimensions shows a consistent pattern, and therefore becomes a candidate for a shared motivational value. Second, compared to government employees from the United States, not only do government employees from the Napoleonic, Germanic and Scandinavian cases show higher levels of *Self-Transcendence*, but so do government employees from Great Britain.

In order to find out whether government employees across different European countries have distinct motivational values even after taking into account country-specific differences in overall *Basic Human Values*, Table 13.5 presents a series of binary logistic regressions, estimating the effect of *Basic Human Values* on the likelihood of working as a government employee. In all of these models private sector employees serve as the reference category.

The pooled Models 1–3 take into account 2,660 observations from all five countries (United States, Great Britain, France, Germany, Sweden). Models 1–3 serve to calibrate Models 4–8, which are estimated on country samples. While Model 1 only includes the socio-demographic and occupational control variables as potential determinants for government employment, Model 2 adds the four *Basic Human Values* dimensions (*Self-Enhancement, Openness to Change, Self-Transcendence, Conservation*).[15] In Model 3 these four dimensions are disentangled into the ten single *Basic Human Values*, thus offering a more detailed look at the influence of single motivational values. Each of

---

14. We have replicated the multinomial model presented in Table 13.5 on the sample that includes only private sector employees. This specification also shows that higher values of *Self-Transcendence* are a distinct feature of Europeans. Only in the German case the *Self-Transcendence* orientation is not significantly higher than the *Self-Transcendence* orientation of private sector employees from the United States.

15. The correlations of the ten single *Basic Human Values* as well as a factor analysis support Schwartz's theoretical four dimensions.

Table 13.5: Determinants of government employment

	Model 1	Model 2	Model 3	Model 4 (US)	Model 5 (GB)	Model 6 (FR)	Model 7 (DT)	Model 8 (SE)
			Government employment = 1, Private sector employment = 0					
Female	0.944***	0.877***	0.859***	0.846***	1.327***	-0.168	1.014***	1.089***
	[0.00]	[0.00]	[0.00]	[0.01]	[0.00]	[0.51]	[0.00]	[0.00]
Age	0.0257***	0.0224***	0.0227***	0.0138	0.0219*	0.0509***	0.00678	0.0410***
	[0.00]	[0.00]	[0.00]	[0.32]	[0.09]	[0.00]	[0.56]	[0.00]
Married	0.00862	-0.0383	-0.0597	-0.0190	0.0686	0.216	-0.201	0.434
	[0.95]	[0.80]	[0.69]	[0.96]	[0.87]	[0.52]	[0.57]	[0.20]
Separated/Divorced/Widowed	-0.0166	-0.0341	-0.0543	-0.195	0.248	-0.199	0.0801	0.147
	[0.93]	[0.86]	[0.77]	[0.69]	[0.61]	[0.68]	[0.87]	[0.69]
Secondary school	0.448**	0.440**	0.443**	-0.0819	-0.531	0.152	0.415	0.910**
	[0.02]	[0.02]	[0.02]	[0.93]	[0.51]	[0.69]	[0.22]	[0.05]
University	1.109***	1.115***	1.094***	0.690	-0.207	1.182***	1.638***	1.440***
	[0.00]	[0.00]	[0.00]	[0.52]	[0.81]	[0.01]	[0.00]	[0.00]
Unemployed/Housewife/Other	-0.349**	-0.358**	-0.362**	p.p.	-0.0953	-0.920***	-0.182	-0.244
	[0.02]	[0.02]	[0.02]		[0.79]	[0.00]	[0.52]	[0.54]
Income_c	-0.0401	-0.0320	-0.0251	0.0454	0.122*	-0.0115	-0.0168	-0.182***
	[0.14]	[0.24]	[0.37]	[0.61]	[0.07]	[0.87]	[0.81]	[0.00]
Employer/manager	-0.373	-0.308	-0.355	-0.472	0.738	p.p.	-0.572	p.p.
	[0.30]	[0.39]	[0.33]	[0.61]	[0.17]		[0.71]	
Professional	1.561***	1.578***	1.542***	1.024	1.911***	13.90***	3.24***	0.189
	[0.00]	[0.00]	[0.00]	[0.24]	[0.00]	[0.00]	[0.01]	[0.77]
Office worker	0.894***	0.915***	0.886***	-0.217	0.721	13.85***	2.663**	0.0750
	[0.00]	[0.00]	[0.00]	[0.81]	[0.12]	[0.00]	[0.01]	[0.89]
Manual worker	0.575**	0.579*	0.556*	-0.377	0.709	12.70***	1.497	0.456

Table 13.5 (continued)

	Model 1	Model 2	Model 3	Model 4 (US)	Model 5 (GB)	Model 6 (FR)	Model 7 (DT)	Model 8 (SE)
	Government employment = 1, Private sector employment = 0							
	[0.04]	[0.05]	[0.05]	[0.66]	[0.14]	[0.00]	[0.17]	[0.40]
France	0.0653 [0.74]	-0.0278 [0.89]	-0.0476 [0.83]					
Great Britain	0.159 [0.43]	0.0675 [0.74]	0.0911 [0.66]					
Sweden	0.650*** [0.00]	0.551*** [0.01]	0.565*** [0.00]					
Germany	0.186 [0.32]	0.231 [0.24]	0.236 [0.25]					
Self-Enhancement		-0.509* [0.08]		0.486 [0.62]	-1.246* [0.07]	0.404 [0.52]	-0.895 [0.20]	0.0302 [0.96]
Openness to Change		-0.281 [0.31]		-1.114 [0.26]	0.829 [0.23]	-1.283** [0.01]	-0.303 [0.66]	0.101 [0.86]
Self-Transcendence		1.089*** [0.00]		-0.275 [0.78]	-0.0893 [0.91]	1.491** [0.02]	1.635** [0.02]	1.388** [0.04]
Conservation		-0.0643 [0.81]		-0.973 [0.27]	0.572 [0.40]	-0.114 [0.85]	-0.000708 [1.00]	-0.381 [0.49]
Power			-0.658** [0.01]					
Achievement			0.0632 [0.77]					
Hedonism			-0.0498 [0.83]					

Table 13.5 (continued)

	Model 1	Model 2	Model 3	Model 4 (US)	Model 5 (GB)	Model 6 (FR)	Model 7 (DT)	Model 8 (SE)
			Government employment = 1, Private sector employment = 0					
Stimulation			−0.263 [0.22]					
Self-Direction			0.0319 [0.89]					
Universalism			0.349 [0.14]					
Benevolence			0.637** [0.03]					
Tradition			−0.0548 [0.76]					
Conformity			−0.0341 [0.87]					
Security			0.0357 [0.87]					
Observations	2,660	2,660	2,660	398	471	507	672	544
Country sample	All	All	All	US	Great Britain	France	Germany	Sweden
Pseudo R^2	0.127	0.134	0.136	0.137	0.170	0.151	0.215	0.123
AIC	2,994.0	2,980.4	2,985.2	419.1	503.0	554.3	719.1	702.4
BIC	3,094.1	3,104.0	3,144.2	482.8	573.6	622.0	795.8	771.5
Correctly classified (%)	73.98	73.76	74.14	76.13	78.13	79.65	68.23	78.13
Likelihood-ratio test (p-value)	0.00	0.00	0.03	0.73	0.40	0.05	0.04	0.58

Note: Binary logistic regression with robust standard errors, p-values in brackets, p.p. = predicts failure perfectly, weighted by v259.
Note: see Table 13.4.

the three pooled models includes a set of country dummies for the European countries (Great Britain, France, Germany, Sweden; using the United States as the reference country). Models 4–8 replicate the specification used in Model 2, but estimate this specification on separate country samples for the United States (Model 4), Great Britain (Model 5), France (Model 6), Germany (Model 7) and Sweden (Model 8).

Before we go on to discuss the statistical associations between the *Basic Human Values* and government employment, let us take a look at the socio-demographic and occupational control variables. First, being female is positively associated with government employment, which indicates that compared to private sector employees a larger share of government employees are women. This observation, however, cannot be replicated on the French sample. Age is positively associated with government employment in the pooled models. Second, concerning the educational profile, Models 1–3 show that government employees tend to have higher formal degrees (secondary school and university) than their private sector counterparts. This observation is particularly strong in the French and German sample, the two countries in which government employment has high formal entry barriers. Overall, these findings are consistent with prior findings (e.g. Tepe 2012; Tepe *et al.* 2014) on the socio-demographic characteristics of government employees, which also indicates that government employment attracts female employees and sets high formal entry barriers (e.g. a university degree). Third, concerning the occupational composition of government employment, Models 1–3 suggest that compared to private sector employment a larger share of government employees are working in professional occupations. This finding, however, varies across country samples (*see* Models 4–8), thus indicating country-specific differences in the occupational composition of the public workforce. Fourth, country-specific differences in the size of the public workforce are captured with the set of country dummies (Models 1–3). Compared to the United States (reference country), Sweden has a significantly larger share of government employees, which is hardly surprising if we compare the role of the state in public service production in the two countries.

Let us now take into account the association between the *Basic Human Values* and government employment as represented in the pooled models. In Model 2 *Self-Enhancement* is negatively associated with government employment, while the opposite is the case with *Self-Transcendence*. In substantive terms, the likelihood of government employment decreases by 9.82 percentage points when *Self-Enhancement* increases from its minimum to its maximum. If *Self-Transcendence* increases from its minimum to its maximum, the likelihood of government employment increases by 19.4 percentage points. Compared to the impact of socio-demographic factors (e.g. being female increases the likelihood of government employment by 17.1 percentage points), these are relevant effect sizes. The likelihood-ratio test for the four *Basic Human Values* dimensions is statistically significant at the highest margin and thereby also supports the conclusion that including the *Basic Human Values* in our statistical model improves our ability to predict government employment.

Splitting up the *Basic Human Values* into ten values (*see* Model 3) and including these ten values into the statistical model provides a robustness check on the use of the aggregated four dimensions and also allows us to find out which values are behind the pattern observed in Model 2. First, even though only two out of ten values reach conventional levels of statistical significance, the likelihood-ratio test confirms that including these ten variables improves the ability to predict government employment. Second, the negative association between *Self-Enhancement* and government employment is driven by the value *Power* rather than *Achievement* (these two values constitute *Self-Enhancement*). As a refinement to the previous conclusions, government employees do not value *Achievement* less than their private sector counterparts; it is the value *Power* that government employees value less than their private sector counterparts. Third, a similar refinement can be made with respect to the positive association between government employment and *Self-Transcendence. Self-Transcendence* consists of the two values *Universalism* and *Benevolence*, and only the latter shows a statistically significant association with government employment. As a reminder: higher levels of *Benevolence* mean that the respondents care about the enhancement of other people's welfare. This pro-social value orientation seems to be a distinct feature of government employees compared to their private sector counterparts.

The next step in the empirical exploration is to test whether the pattern that has been observed in Model 2 and refined in Model 3 applies to the respective administrative tradition contexts of all five countries under investigation. Replicating the specification used in Model 2 on separate country samples (*see* Models 4–8) reveals that only in the three continental European countries – France, Germany and Sweden – *Self-Transcendence* is positively associated with government employment. The negative association between *Self-Enhancement* and government employment, which we have observed in the pooled model, can be replicated only in the British sample. Another statistical artefact (spurious finding) might be the negative association between *Openness to Change* and government employment in the French sample. Despite the limitations that are caused by the use of country sample-specific regressions, we find that in the three continental European countries higher levels of *Self-Transcendence* are a distinct feature of government employees rather than of their private sector counterparts.

This observation provides some empirical evidence to proposition 2a, which has been derived from the *Public Service Motivation* framework. Proposition 2b, which argues that government employees are more likely to hold stronger *Conservation* values, receives no empirical support, not even in the country-specific analysis (Models 4–8). The country-specific analysis, however, indicates that higher levels of *Self-Transcendence* as a distinctive feature of government employees' value orientation are a robust pattern in the three continental European countries (France, Germany and Sweden).

Discussion and conclusions

This chapter explored the question of whether it is possible to identify a shared motivational conception among public servants that can serve as a building block for a common European administrative identity. Linking the discussion about *Public Service Motivation* with psychological research on *Basic Human Values* and the so-called *Person-Environment Fit*, we investigated the value orientation of government employees in five countries (United States, Great Britain, France, Germany and Sweden), each of them representing a distinct administrative tradition.

From a between-country perspective, administrative traditions remain an important contextual factor that shapes government employees' value orientation (P1).[16] The review of administrative traditions has shown that the Napoleonic, Germanic and Scandinavian traditions share a rather similar conceptualisation of the state-society relationship. This conceptualisation is rather different from the state-society relationship that is dominant in countries with an Anglo-American administrative tradition. The comparison between countries of government employees' value orientation reveals that values of *Self-Transcendence* are a common and distinct feature of continental European government employees compared to government employees from the United States. Hence, there seems to exist some congruence in the field of *Self-Transcendence* values among the European government employees, which is in line with previous research on *Basic Human Values* in Western Europe (Arzheimer 2012). The simultaneity of homogeneous and heterogeneous motivational values might help to keep the EAS flexible and sensible towards national particularities. But above all, it provides a promising basis for further research on the development of a European administrative identity.

In accordance with previous research on government employees' work motivation (e.g. Perry 1996; Wright and Pandey 2008) and social attitudes (e.g. Brewer 2003), the empirical evidence presented in this chapter indicates that there are systematic differences between government and private employees' *Basic Human Values* (Schwartz 1994). From a within-country perspective, government employees have higher values of *Self-Transcendence* than private sector employees, especially with regard to the value *Benevolence*. In addition, *Self-Enhancement* values, especially the value *Power*, are significantly less important for government employees than for their private sector counterparts. These differences in the motivational values of government and private sector employees are particularly dominant in the three continental European countries France, Germany and Sweden. These statistical associations are consistent with the notion that government employees have a distinct pro-social orientation, which can be traced back to the *Public Service Motivation* framework (P2a). The expectation that government employees might also have stronger *Conservation* values than their private sector counterparts (P2b), however, receives no empirical support.

To conclude, the empirical analysis presented in this chapter indicates that European government employees in fact have a distinct and sector-specific value profile. A deeper understanding of these motivational values is not only important to refine the concept of the European public servant and its

---

16. *See* Tepe *et al.* (2010) on the association between administrative traditions and the configuration of the state-market relationship.

development over time (*see* Raadschelders, Chapter Two in this volume), but might also help to choose the appropriate recruitment and pay policies in the public sector. Other scholars have stressed the risk of crowding out government employees' intrinsic motivation by implementing human resource management tools that have been adopted from the private sector (e.g. Weibel *et al.* 2009). The motivational value patterns that have been revealed in this chapter provide some empirical evidence for such fears. If policy makers ignore government employees' value orientations, they could in the long run risk crowding out intrinsic *Self-Transcendence* motives from their workforce.

References

Anderfuhren-Biget, S. (2012) 'Profiles of public service-motivated civil servants: evidence from a multicultural country', *International Journal of Public Administration*, 35(1): 5–18.

Arzheimer, K. (2012) 'Europa als Wertegemeinschaft? Ost und West im Spiegel des "Schwartz Value Inventory"', in Keil, S. I. and van Deth, J. W. (eds) *Deutschlands Metamorphosen: Ergebnisse des European Social Survey 2002 bis 2008*, Baden-Baden: Nomos, 73–98.

Balint, T., Bauer, M. W. and Knill, C. (2008) 'Bureaucratic change in the European administrative space: the case of the European Commission', *West European Politics*, 31(4): 677–700.

Behnke, N. (2011) 'Alte und neue Werte im öffentlichen Dienst', in Blanke, B. *et al.* (eds) *Handbuch zur Verwaltungsreform*, 4th edn, Wiesbaden: VS, 340–9.

Bellante, D. and Link, A. N. (1981) 'Are public sector workers more risk averse than private sector workers?', *Industrial and Labor Relations Review*, 34(3): 408–12.

Brewer, G. A. (2003) 'Building social capital: civic attitudes and behavior of public servants', *Journal of Public Administration Research and Theory*, 13(1): 5–26.

Buurman, M., Delfgaauw, J., Dur, R., Van den Bossche, S. (2012) 'Public sector employees: risk averse and altruistic?', *Journal of Economic Behavior & Organization*, 83(3): 279–91.

Cardona, F. (2009) 'Integrating the national administrations into the European administrative space', paper presented at Sigma Conference on Public Administration Reform and European Integration, March 2009.

Coursey, D. H. and Pandey, S. K. (2007) 'Public service motivation measurement: testing an abridged version of Perry's proposed scale', *Administration & Society*, 39(5): 546–68.

Crewson, P. E. (1997) 'Public service motivation: building empirical evidence of incidence and effect', *Journal of Public Administration Research and Theory*, 7(4): 499–518.

Davidov, E., Schmidt, P. and Schwartz, S. H. (2008) 'Bringing values back in: the adequacy of the European Social Survey to measure values in 20 countries', *Public Opinion Quarterly*, 72(3): 420–45.

DeHart-Davis, L. (2007) 'The unbureaucratic personality', *Public Administration Review*, 67(5): 892–903.

Downs, A. (1967) *Inside Bureaucracy*, New York: Little, Brown Company.

Hammerschmid, G., Meyer, R. E. and Egger-Peitler, I. (2009) 'Das Konzept der Public Service Motivation: Status Quo der internationalen Diskussion und erste empirische Evidenzen für den deutschsprachigen Raum', *Der Moderne Staat*, (1), 73–92.

Hofmann, H. C. H. (2008) 'Mapping the European Administrative Space', *West European Politics*, 31(4): 662–76.

Houston, D. (2000) 'Public service motivation: a multivariate test', *Journal of Public Administration Research and Theory*, 10(4): 713–27.

Knoke, D. and Wright-Isak, C. (1982) 'Individual motives and organizational incentive systems', *Research in the Sociology of Organizations*, (1): 209–54.

Kristof-Brown, A. L., Zimmerman, R. D. and Johnson, E. C. (2005) 'Consequences of individuals' fit at work: a meta-analysis of person–job, person–organisation, person–group, and person-supervisor fit', *Personnel Psychology*, 58(2): 281–342.

Kulin, J. and Svallfors, S. (2011) 'Class, values, and attitudes towards redistribution: a European comparison', *European Sociological Review*, 29(2): 155–67.

Leisink, P. and Steijn, B. (2008) 'Recruitment, attraction, and selection', in Perry, J. L. and Hondeghem, A. (eds) *Motivation in Public Management: The call of public service*, Oxford University Press, 118–35.

—   (2009) 'Public service motivation and job performance of public sector employees in The Netherlands', *International Review of Administrative Sciences*, 75(1): 35–52.

Lodge, M. (2009) 'Administrative patterns and national politics', in Peters, B. G. and Pierre, J. (eds) *Handbook of Public Administration*, 2nd edn, London: Sage, 285–97.

Lyons, S. T., Duxbury, L. E. and Higgins, C. A. (2006) 'A comparison of the values and commitment of private sector, public sector, and parapublic sector employees', *Public Administration Review*, 66(4): 605–18.

Merton, R. (1940) 'Bureaucratic structure and personality', *Social Forces*, 18, 560–668.

Niskanen, W. (1971) *Bureaucracy and Representative Government*, Chicago: Aldine Atherton.

Norris, P. (2003) 'Is there still a public service ethos? Work values, experience, and job satisfaction among government workers', in Donahue, J. D. and Nye, J. S. (eds) *For the People: Can we fix public service?* Washington DC: Brookings Institution Press, pp. 72–89.

OECD (1999) 'European principles for public administration', SIGMA Papers No. 27. Available at http:// www.oecd.org/site/sigma/publicationsdocuments/ 36972467.pdf.

Olsen, J. P. (2003) 'Towards a European administrative space?', *Journal of European Public Policy*, 10(4): 506–31.

Ongaro, E. (2010) 'The Napoleonic administrative tradition and public management reform in France, Greece, Italy, Portugal and Spain', in Painter, M. and Peters, B. G. (eds) *Tradition and Public Administration*, Hampshire: Palgrave Macmillan, pp. 174–90.

Peters, B. G. (2010) 'Public administration in the United States: Anglo-American, just American, or which American?' in Painter, M. and Peters, B. G. (eds) *Tradition and Public Administration*, Hampshire: Palgrave Macmillan, pp. 114–28.

Painter, M. and Peters, B. G. (2010a) 'The analysis of administrative traditions', in Painter, M. and Peters, B. G. (eds) *Tradition and Public Administration*, Hampshire: Palgrave Macmillan, pp. 3–16.

— (2010b) 'Administrative traditions in comparative perspective: families, groups and hybrids', in Painter, M. and Peters, B. G. (eds) *Tradition and Public Administration*, Hampshire: Palgrave Macmillan, pp. 19–30.

Perry, J. L. (1996) 'Measuring public service motivation: an assessment of construct reliability and validity', *Journal of Public Administration Research and Theory*, 6(1): 5–22.

Perry, J. L. and Wise, L. R. (1990) 'The motivational bases of public service', *Public Administration Review*, 50(3): 367–73.

Peters, B. G. and Painter, M. (2010) 'Conclusion: administrative traditions in an era of administrative change', in Painter, M. and Peters, B. G. (eds) *Tradition and Public Administration*, Hampshire: Palgrave Macmillan, pp. 234–7.

Pfeifer, C. (2010) 'Risk aversion and sorting into public sector employment', *German Economic Review*, 12(1): 85–99.

Pierre, J. (2010) 'Administrative reform in Sweden: the resilience of administrative tradition?' in Painter, M. and Peters, B. G. (eds) *Tradition and Public Administration*, Hampshire: Palgrave Macmillan, pp. 191–202.

Pollitt, C. and Bouckaert, G. (2011) *Public Management Reform: A comparative analysis: New Public Management, governance, and the neo-Weberian state*, 3rd edn, Oxford: Oxford University Press.

Rayner, J., Williams, H. M., Lawton, A. and Allinson, C. W. (2010) 'Public service ethos: developing a generic measure', *Journal of Public Administration Research and Theory*, 21(1): 27–51.

Reeskens, T. and Wright, M. (2011) 'Subjective well-being and national satisfaction: taking seriously the "proud of what?" question', *Psychological Science*, 22(11): 1459–62.

Ritz, A. (2011) 'Attraction to public policy making: a qualitative inquiry into improvements in PSM measurement', *Public Administration* 89(3): 1128–47.

Roccas, S., Sagiv, L., Schwartz, S. H. and Knafo, A. (2002) 'The Big Five personality factors and personal values', *Personality and Social Psychology Bulletin*, 28(6): 789–801.

Rokeach, M. (1973) *The Nature of Human Values*, New York: Free Press.

Rugge, F. (2009) 'Administrative traditions in Western Europe', in Peters, B. G. and Pierre, J. (eds) *Handbook of Public Administration*, 2nd edn, London: Sage, pp. 113–27.

Rutgers, M. R. (2001) 'Traditional flavors? The different sentiments in European and American administrative thought', *Administration and Society*, 33(2): 220–44.

Sager, F., Rosser, C., Hurni, P. Y. and Mavrot, C. (2012) 'How traditional are the American, French and German traditions of public administration? A research agenda', *Public Administration*, 90(1): 129–43.

Schmidt, P., Bamberg, S., Davidov, E., Herrmann, J. and Schwartz, S. H. (2007) 'Die Messung von Werten mit dem Portaits Value Questionnaire', *Zeitschrift für Sozialpsychologie*, 38(4): 261–75.

Schneider, B. (1987) 'The people make the place', *Personnel Psychology*, 40(3): 437–53.

Schwartz, S. H. (1992) 'Universals in the content and structure of values: theoretical advances and empirical tests in 20 countries', in Zanna, M. (ed.) *Advances in Experimental Social Psychology*, Vol. 25, New York: Academic Press, pp. 1–65.

— (1994) 'Are there universal aspects in the structure and contents of human values?', *Journal of Social Issues*, 50(4): 19–45.

— (2005) *Basic Human Values: An overview*, Jerusalem: Hebrew University.

— (2006) 'Les valeurs de base de la personne: théorie, mesures et applications', *Revue française de sociologie*, 47(4): 929–68.

Schwartz, S. H. and Bilsky, W. (1990) 'Toward a theory of the universal content and structure of values: extensions and cross-cultural replications', *Journal of Personality and Social Psychology*, 58, 878–91.

Schwartz, S. H. and Sagiv, L. (1995) 'Identifying culture-specifics in the content and structure of values', *Journal of Cross-Cultural Psychology*, 26(1): 92–116.

Schwartz, S. H., Melech, G., Lehmann, A., Burgess, S., Harris, M. and Owens, V. (2001) 'Extending the cross-cultural validity of the theory of Basic Human Values with a different method of measurement', *Journal of Cross-Cultural Psychology*, 32, 519–42.

Stillman, Richard J., II. (1990) 'The peculiar "stateless" origins of American public administration and consequences for government today', *Public Administration Review,* 50(2): 156–67.

Tepe, M. (2012) 'The public/private sector cleavage revisited: the impact of government employment on political attitudes and behavior in eleven West European countries', *Public Administration*, 90(1): 230–61.

Tepe, M., Gottschall, K. and Kittel, B. (2010) 'A structural fit between states and markets? Public administration regimes and market economy models in the OECD', *Socio-Economic Review*, 8(4): 653–84.

— (2014) 'The competing state: Transformation of the public/private sector earnings gap in four countries', in Schneider, S. and Rothgang, H. (eds) *State Transformations in the Post-National Constellation*, Houndsmills: Palgrave Macmillan.

Thompson, V. (1961) *Modern Organisation*, New York: Knopf.

Vandenabeele, W. (2008) 'Government calling: public service motivation as an element in selecting government as an employer of choice', *Public Administration*, 86(4): 1089–105.

Van der Wal, Z. and Huberts, L. (2008) 'Value solidity in government and business: results of an empirical study on public and private sector organizational values', *American Review of Public Administration*, 38(3): 264–85.

Van der Wal, Z., Huberts, L., van den Heuvel, H. and Kolthoff, E. (2006) 'Central values of government and business: differences, similarities and conflicts', *Public Administration Quarterly*, 30(3): 314–64.

Weibel, A., Rost, K. and Osterloh, M. (2009) 'Pay for performance in the public sector – benefits and hidden costs', *Journal of Public Administration Research and Theory*, 20(2): 387–412.

Wright, B. E. (2001) 'Public-sector work motivation: a review of the current literature and a revised conceptual model', *Journal of Public Administration Research and Theory*, 11(4): 559–86.

Wright, B. E. and Pandey, S. K. (2008) 'Public service motivation and the assumption of person–organisation fit: testing the mediating effect of value congruence', *Administration & Society*, 40(5): 502–21.

Chapter Fourteen

Models of Public Servants' Training and the Crisis of Democracy: From 'Politics as Vocation' to the 'Effective Bureaucrat'?

Gayil Talshir

Introduction

> Bureaucracy inevitably accompanies mass democracy [...] This results from a characteristic principle of bureaucracy: the abstract regularity of the execution of authority, which is a result of the demand of 'equality before the law' in the personal and functional sense – hence, the horrors of 'privilege' and the principled rejection of doing business 'from case to case'. (Weber 1958: 224)

This chapter situates the image of the public servant in the context of the crisis of democratic legitimacy. Working within the framework set by Raadschelders in this volume (Chapter Two), it argues that while the bureaucrat was the quintessential figure of the modern political order in the wake of the modern state, it is precisely the role of bureaucracy that is at the heart of the contemporary crisis of democratic legitimation of advanced welfare national democracies. Bureaucrats were endowed with the claim to the generality of the state for thinkers as Hegel and Weber. They represented the era of the rational-legal order, but also the crisis of political disenchantment. With the advent of history, crystallised after WW2, the state employee was the prime manifestation of the welfare state and the figure that facilitated the economic miracle and the affluent society (Galbraith 1963). However, the bureaucrat, representing the 'big state', became an enemy of the dominant ideology of the 1980s onwards. The bureaucracy was interestingly attacked from both the new right and the new left, by both neoliberals and communitarians. The status of the public servant, like his changing role in view of privatisation, new public management (NPM) and globalisation, inevitably had to change too. The Europeanisation of the image of public service was part of this ongoing process. But has a new model emerged, one rethinking the role of the state, and hence refashioning the function of the public service in advanced democracies? While this book has fleshed out different dimensions of this question, this chapter takes the angle of the training of public servants as a mirror of the image, status and role in understanding the interacted relationships between the state and public service in advanced democracies.

On the grand-theory level, I want to offer a different reading of Weber's idea of disenchantment. The main argument I forward is that 'enchantment' is an immanent part of human society, of societal political being. It does not disappear; it merely transposes itself to other realms of the polity. Thus, while the first crisis of legitimacy, with the emergence of modernism, shifted the 'charm' or the order of symbolism from religion and kingdom to nation and state, whereby the public servant embodies the rationale of the new world order of the modern state apparatus, the second crisis of legitimacy is double-edged. It has challenged both 'nation' and 'state': the nation, as the 'soul' of the state, is undermined simultaneously by the spirit of local communities and by the European or global village. The crisis of the state is omnipresent in terms of the weaknesses of institutional democracies in delivering the promise of engaged citizenship and sovereign people, as well as in the people's distrust of the state apparatus. However, the theoretical reactions to the crisis – multiculturalism and deliberative democracy – have not necessarily strengthened representative democracy; furthermore, in both, the public servant has presented part of the problem of distance rather than the solution. So the public servant, the paradigmatic role model of the modern state, is being cast out as embodying the problematic 'big state' image of a previous generation. A thin, technocratic image is now holding sway. Is it the case that the time of public service has passed, or can the crisis of legitimation be mended from within, and with it a new vision of the role of the state, and a new function and status for public service be enhanced?

The chapter analyses the transformation of the role of the public servant in the context of these two crises of legitimation: the first crisis, described by Weber and maturing after WW2; and the contemporary crisis of legitimation, analysed by Habermas and others as a crisis of late modernity. The image of the bureaucrat is analysed as a function of the qualifications and training he received within the nation state: it thus examines the role of the public servant in close connection to the particular political cultures within three European democracies, presenting alternative models of public service: the English, French and German systems (Sager *et al.* 2012). The first section of the chapter presents the image of the bureaucrat following Hegel and Weber and the complexity of his role in view of political disenchantment. The second section examines comparatively the images of public service as enshrined in the training schools of public servants in the UK, France and Germany, portraying the bureaucrat's role and status in accordance with national traditions. The third section analyses the contemporary crisis of democratic legitimation and the negative role assigned to the bureaucracy within it, looking at economic, social and political dimensions. The fourth section analyses the changing, converging training programmes in the UK, France and Germany in the era of NPM. The final discussion analyses these changes critically and puts forward an alternative approach to the training and role of public service in democratic polity.

The first legitimation crisis: The bureaucrat, the rational-legal order, and political disenchantment

Hegel famously argued that '(t)he modern state has enormous strength and depth, in that it allows the principle of subjectivity to complete itself to an independent extreme of personal particularity, and yet at the same time brings it back into the substantive unity, and thus preserves particularity in the principle of the state' (Hegel §260, 2001: 198). Crucially, in Hegel's view the person who embodies this unity of the particular and the general, the one that elevates his role to embody freedom in the state, is the public servant:

> The state cannot rely upon service which is capricious and voluntary, such, for example, as the administration of justice by knights-errant [...] The public service requires the sacrifice of independent self-satisfaction at one's pleasure, and grants the right of finding satisfaction in the performance of duty, but nowhere else. Here is found the conjunction of universal and particular interests, a union which constitutes the conception and the internal stability of the state. (Hegel §294, 2001: 237)

Thus, the modern state is represented in Hegel's account by the role and materialisation of the public servant. The bureaucracy is at once the highest manifestation of the universal and the general embodied in the role of the individual bureaucrat who acts in the public interest as his own mission. Despite Marx's critique of those who present themselves as embodying the general will while in fact acting from their own interest, Weber offered a perspective more akin to that of Hegel concerning the particular question of the importance of the role of the bureaucracy; while the bureaucrat, as part of the bourgeoisie and the intelligentsia, is a unique embodiment of the modern rational-legal order, he also bears the brunt of popular disenchantment with politics.

In his *Politik als Beruf*, Weber distinguishes between two notions of politics as vocation:

> Either one lives 'for' politics or one leaves 'off' politics. By no means is this contrast an exclusive one [...] He who strives to make politics a permanent source of income lives 'off' politics as a vocation, whereas he who does not do this lives 'for' politics. (Weber 1958: 84)

Several points are in order: first, note that both politicians and bureaucrats are thus part of the ruling political elite of the modern state; the public servant is a political actor. Second, it is not only the politician, but also crucially the public servant that experiences 'politics as vocation' and has a calling for public service as his motivation. And third, it is the state that pays the salary of those who live 'off' politics and thus facilitates this role: the modern state and the bureaucrat are closely entangled. Thus, the public service is part and parcel of the political strata of modern society; the distinction is not between the political and administrative elites but within the political elites, and even there the distinction is archetypal, in a Weberian way, not in praxis, where one man may be both living 'for' and 'off' politics or be in transit between the two manifestations of politics as vocation.

Crucially, while in this lecture Weber is interested in highlighting political leaders, and therefore it is the figure of the politician that is usually associated with a political calling, the fact of the matter is that the figure linked most strongly with Weber's analysis of the modern era is nevertheless the bureaucrat. For the simple reason that while the leader possesses either the authority of traditional domination or that of charisma, both these types have been active throughout history. It is the third type of authority, that is, domination emanating from the rational-legal order, that characterises the rise of the bureaucrat:

> Finally, there is domination by virtue of 'legality', by virtue of the belief in the validity of legal statute and functional 'competence' based on rationally created *rules*. In this case, obedience is expected in discharging statutory obligations. This is domination as exercised by the modern 'servant of the state' and by all those bearers of power who in this respect resemble him. (Weber 1958: 79)

Thus, the social role that manifests the modern state *par excellence* is that of the public servant. It is he who embodies the rationale of the legal order that underpins the legitimacy of the rule of law, and that manifests this public position as part of a democratic order of equality before the law, as part of a system and not of this or that individual or case; 'the modern state is a compulsory association which organizes domination' (Weber 1958: 82). The prime actor, the executer of this order, is the public servant.

However, whereas for Hegel the bureaucrat embodies the highest form of ethical life, for Weber it is rather a tragic role, for in the modern era, the public servant manifests at once the most sophisticated form of public service and the disinterested, disenchanted dimension of politics. For Weber analyses the price of modernity precisely in political disenchantment. He famously argued in *Science as Vocation* that:

> the fate of our times is characterized by the rationalization and intellectualization and, above all, by the 'disenchantment of the world'. Precisely the ultimate and most sublime values have retreated from public life either into the transcendental realm of mystic life or into the brotherliness of direct and personal human relations. (Weber 1958: 155)

This was not merely a displacement of religion from the centre stage of public life to the privacy of the human soul or one's community. Rather, the processes of rationalisation and intellectualisation, identified with the bureaucracy, are the trademarks of modernity and can be analysed in science, law, politics and society. The crisis of modernity has therefore entailed the break away from the symbolic order of the old regime. Instead, modernity was characterised by the emergence of empirical sciences, and an alternative legal order and bureaucratic apparatus, which facilitated the legitimacy of state and society based on processes of scientification and institutionalisation of the public sphere. It is the close association of the public servant with the mechanistic system and the functionalism of the state that will be key to his demise as the role model of modernity as the analysis of the contemporary crisis of legitimacy would later demonstrate.

An alternative analytical framework: Re-enchantment and the politics of identity

I want to challenge Weber's thesis by rethinking the role of disenchantment in the current crisis of legitimacy. While still holding to the trade-off between the disillusionment with the old regime's power – divinity and kingdom, in all their magical glory and transcendence – and the rationalisation of modernity, the main question is whether the 'magic' had indeed disappeared or merely migrated to other realms of social life. I want to argue that 'enchantment' – symbolism, belief, emotionality, solidarity and shared identity – is an immanent feature of human society. Indeed, it symbolises the sense of belonging to a unified entity, a collective identity. Thus, the crisis of legitimacy is a crisis of identity, namely, of identification and belonging. In juxtaposition to Weber's argument, disenchantment did not mean the end of 'magic' in public life, and transcendence beyond the rational order or individualism, but its relocation. From religion and knighthood the symbolism of collective identity was transferred to other arena, most notably to nation and state.

Thus, the twentieth century was called 'the age of ideologies' (Bracher 1984) and grand ideas, embedded in different holistic ideologies, provided the alternative glue to human social fabric. The new 'spell' was especially strong since the world became a world of modern states, and the ideology of the state, whether nationalism, democracy, communism or other, remarried form with content, administration with values. The nation state has become the centrepiece of the new world order.

The argument therefore is that enchantment is an immanent part of human society and the crisis of modernity did in fact culminate in the disenchantment of the public sphere in its traditional loci, which was ultimately transferred to a different arena – the nation state. This also explains why Weber himself was a nationalist – or even more so, an *étatist*. Indeed, since he believed in *Wertrationalität* – using his rationality rather than sentiment to form his nationalism – it could indeed be seen as the predecessor of Habermas' constitutional patriotism – based on rationality rather than emotionity. This is why Weber did not consider his nationalism to be of sociological significance. Thus, the first crisis of legitimation, despite the new rational-legal order, is a crisis of collective identity. 'Sentiment of solidarity', in Weber's terms, far from being a concept that disappeared from sociological analysis, is precisely the hidden agenda of modernism, and nationalism is one important manifestation of it. The sense of belonging and the idea of symbolic politics was transferred from the traditional agents of authority and relocated to the nation within the state as an alternative locus of identification, in a new moral and metaphysical realm. But the nation state really had three facets: the nation, the state and democracy. At the crossroads of all three accounts lay the bureaucracy. For Weber the features that exemplify the bureaucracy are those of hierarchy, the official public domain, expertism, social esteem, tenure and legal authority (Weber 1958: 197–202). It was both the infrastructure of the modern state, and it acted in the national interest, embodying the new politician of democracy – the one that saw politics as its vocation. Rather than disenchantment, the public servant encompassed the new ideal of involved, state-centred political actor. However, for both Weber and Hegel, what distinguishes the public servant is his training and education. For Hegel:

> The members of the executive and the state officials constitute the main part of the middle class, in which are found the educated intelligence and the consciousness of right of the mass of a people. The institutions of sovereignty operating from above and the rights of corporations from below prevent this class from occupying the position of an exclusive aristocracy and using their education and skill wilfully and despotically. (Hegel §297; 2001: 239)

For Hegel, the substance of their training, which symbolises the ethical life in the state, is that of 'integrity of conduct, gentleness, and freedom from passion' (Hegel 2001: 238). For Weber it would rather be the specialised knowledge of the expert (Weber 1958: 235). It is to the question of the special training and education of the public servant, as a means of distinguishing different political cultures in Europe, that we now turn.

Models of public servants in national democracies

The origin of the public service is closely related to nation state development in general. Public servants were very much personal servants to the king; one could speak even of a 'household servant'. There was still no strict distinction between the public and the private realm. There was, however, a shift in political ideology; the monarchy came to be regarded increasingly as an instrument for providing for the public welfare. The separation of the public and private was important for the creation of the public service (Raadschelders and Rutgers 1996: 89).

The relation between the public service and the rise of the nation state is at the heart of this section. It is the strong bond between the emergence of the modern state, the concept of the national interest, and the crystallising political culture and the role of the public service, that is to be disentangled. One level of analysis is the relation between politicians and bureaucrats, which is already an issue in Weber's writing and would serve one distinguishing factor among the different national traditions in Europe. However, the key dimension that is to be compared is the training and education of the public service: as Hegel and Weber strongly stressed, it was the background of public servants in the educated middle classes that qualified them for their role and crowned their status and position in the ruling elites. The argument here is that despite the convergence of processes in the European context, and mutual learning from sister countries, distinct traditions have evolved in the formative years of the rise of the nation state that were institutionalised after WW2.

The Whitehall model: The public servant as the enlightened Englishman

When discussing public service in the context of the rise of the nation state, 'the United Kingdom is in fact "an aberrant case" among the nations of Europe' (Parris 1987: 42). For the concept of 'state', it is argued, was never a preoccupation of the British discourse as was the case in the continental counterparts. Rather than a legal existence, the UK was united under one crown and the public servants were, to begin with, the servants of the king. Still, in terms of democratic roots the UK has perhaps the longest roots, going back to the Magna Carta through the Glorious Revolution to the political thinkers Hobbes, Locke, Smith and Mill. Furthermore, England has landmark commissions on the issue of the public service, notably the Nortcote-Trevelyan report of 1853 and the Fulton Committee's recommendations of 1968, which resulted in the Wilson government's decision to create Civil Service College. Curiously, as of 2012, the Said School of Business at Oxford University would be the hub for public service in the UK. It is therefore fascinating to view the training of the public service in relation to the emergence of the political institutions side by side with the monarchy.

The thread that runs throughout the reports – from the mid-nineteenth century to the late twentieth century – has to do with the training of the public servants and their qualifications and recruitment. The Northcote-Trevelyan report is concerned particularly with the lack of ambition and competition among public servants, compared with the private business sector, whereas the Fulton Committee is concerned with the 'generalist' education with which most public servants enter their public role (*see* Chapter Seven in this volume). With historic irony, both their recommendations – a unified examination in the former case, a specialist university degree in the latter – have actually crystallised the root phenomenon of the British public service: the economic and political elites as the key social strata from which the public service is recruited. But what was the vision enshrined in the idea of the generalist education, and what model of public service does it entail?

The transformation experienced by the UK system in the second half of the nineteenth century was one from patronage – both of personal aristocrats and later on of parties – to a neutral and nonpartisan service. In fact, the Civil Service Commission established in 1855 following the Northcote-Trevelyan report, sought to centralise the examinations and create free and equal competition. While competition – with the growing rise of the numbers of public servants – was open in most departments in the 1870s, the unified competition was such that 'the subjects and rules of the examinations were defined in such a way as to give advantages to those who had been through the public schools and the old universities of Oxford and Cambridge' (Parris 1987: 51). As late as 1914 almost half of the recruits studied in public (i.e. private) schools, and 90 per cent of the graduate degrees came from Oxbridge, two-thirds of which were in classical languages, ancient history and philosophy. This phenomenon was dubbed by politicians and scholars alike as 'generalism':

> Generalism, which the Fulton commission called 'the philosophy of the amateur' (or 'generalist' or 'all-rounded') means that public servants in the UK are trained and socialized to apply general skills of policy and politics rather than in the details of their policy sector or indeed of any one academic discipline (most clearly seen in the long tradition of officials studying 'Greats', i.e. classics, at university). (Greer and Jarman 2011: 17)

Note the scorn and the tone with which the term 'generalists' is referred to. Interestingly, this critique comes from the historical actors (i.e. Gladstone) and contemporary politicians, both from the left – such as Wilson's critique of the conservative dominance of the public service – and the right – such as the Thatcherite attempt to weaken the big government and privatise the public service, from politicians and scholars alike. What interests us, however, is the ideal that stood at the root of the 'generalist'.

Who is the citizen that studies the classics? That is versed in ancient languages and history? That reads the Greek plays and modern poetry? That is trained in ethics and philosophy? He is the Englishman. He is the enlightened, educated, moral gentleman, with broad horizons and an ability to learn from history. He is at once humble before the 'Greats' and perceives himself in their tradition. He is acting on behalf of the national interest because he can see beyond his own interest and recognises the counters of the big historical picture. He is at once aware of the different points of view and capable of making his decision and lead. The 'classic' or 'generalist' was not just a trick of the aristocracy to let only those of its own into the public service, it encompassed an ideal of the English citizen. It was the same dilemma that Mill introduced in *On Liberty*: once recognise the citizen as free, equal and seeking self-fulfilment as part of a political community, capable of forming an opinion while tolerating others' ideas and being able to argue with them, striving to the truth but accepting that no one party possesses it all and hence one needs a majority decision – this ideal can hardly be met by the commoners, by the workers, by the mass society.

The English public servant was supposed to be acting on behalf of the public, supposed to be neutral and non-partisan, with wide horizons that trained him to move between positions, strive forward and see big pictures, but he can hardly be 'any' citizen. It is this paradox that modern mass democracy brought about, reflected in its most severity in the critique of the public servant. The training as a 'generalist' in the top universities portrayed the ideal with which ordinary citizens met when they came to the bureaucrat, the governmental ministries or to the public sector. It was an ideal that they could understand but rarely accomplish themselves. Mill notoriously suggested that the intelligentsia would have a double vote, and later stressed public education and socialisation as the main state mechanisms that would allow this ideal to be democratised. This was precisely what the different reports tried to do. But the introduction of the centralised exams demanded by the Northcote-Trevelyan report strengthened even further the ability of those whose upbringing was in the private schools and elitist universities to qualify; even the call of the Fulton Committee to professionalise the public service was more likely to send the elites to study a more specialised discipline than to open the gates for the middle classes to enter the public sector. The fact that the Said Business School at Oxford University was chosen for the task of 'professionalising' the British public service carries a historic irony, but this will be discussed later.

The French ENA model: The serviteur public as the democratic Frenchman?

The French case is a classic example of co-evolution of public service and the modern state (Bezes and Jeannot 2011: 187; *see* Chapter Nine in this volume). Crucially, it was imbued with the values of the French revolution and the spirit of democracy, despite the fact that the actual regimes included the Napoleonic reign, the Vichy regime under German occupation and the Gaullist regime among others. What is notable in the French case is of course the centralisation effort, which at once aimed at unified socialisation and democratisation, but in fact made manifest the close relation between a strong centralist state and the ideal of the national interest or general will embodied by the public service. In the French case, the very institutionalisation of education and public service go hand in hand to create the realm of this analysis. Thus, the *Grand Corps d'État* (main state bodies) were set up by the creation of the *grandes écoles* (higher education schools) designed to impart the said knowledge (Bartoli 2008: 16). In it, the values of loyalty, discipline and devotion to the public interest were crystallised in the powerful tradition of the French public service to date. The students of these institutions were segregated from society and were trained as 'the future bearers of sacerdotal state dignity considered themselves to be instrument of a transcendental rationalism *vis-à-vis* adverse social conflicts and their various manifestations' (Birnbaum 1987: 74). They lived behind closed doors deprived of personal belongings and under constant guardianship of their superiors: they were sacrificed to the ideals of general interest and loyal spokespersons of the state. Nevertheless, the first attempt to create a national school of administration by Carnot actually failed (Herper 1987: 75). Indeed, as in the British case, the examinations, which relied heavily on the classics, favoured an elite. In 1840, 68 per cent of public servants were sons of public servants (Herper 1987: 77). In fact, this charge that a discrepancy exists between the content of the examinations and the requirement of the jobs is still made today (Bartoli 2008: 21).

But of course the main development in the French model of public servant occurred with the establishment of the national school of administration, ENA. It had two aims initially: to democratise and open the lines for recruits from different walks of life; and to provide training that fed directly to the job of the public servant. However, as usual, the institutionalisation of the school meant, first, that the exams needed specific training that was biased towards the middle classes and facilitated by courses given in Paris (Owen 1990: 76), and second that the training itself was provided by teachers of whom 80 per cent were senior public servants themselves, thus promoting socialisation into the traditional public service with less room for innovative thinking. In terms of the programme, after a few weeks the students of ENA were sent to hands-on training – a placement for one year – and worked under senior public servants. Back in Paris the idea of a non-technical administrator was developed: this included decision making, problem solving and research techniques (Owen 1990: 77). The actual studies were in administration and economics (Bartoli 2008: 31).

What can we learn from these conditions about the model of the public servant in France? Here there is less room for guessing: the French design is oriented towards crystallising the public sector with a strong ethos of guarding the national interest. The centralised training ensures a single dominant interpretation of what this national interest is. The general will is endowed less by the content of the training than by the socialisation process, which is entangled with the unified examinations that are open to all, with apprentice-style hands-on training, and the fact that 80 per cent of the teachers are themselves senior public servants. The actual content is that of public policy. It thus exposes a different approach to the separation of the politician as a decision maker from the bureaucrat as a mere implementer: whereas in the British case the neutrality was crucial (though it never quite materialised) in order to separate the policy maker from the official, in France the education of the bureaucrat gave him authority as a professional administrator and a saviour of the public good and national interest, and hence capable of judging a case on its merits and in the public interest and not through a political or partisan perspective.

The German model: The Rechtsstaat *and the* Juristenmonopol *prevail?*

While the British and French models have each entertained a different prospect of democracy – the neutral serving elite in the former and the principally open professional guardian of public interest in the latter, the role of the German public service *vis-à-vis* the state and democracy is somewhat more complicated (*see* Chapters Five and Ten in this volume). If the convergence of the emerging nation state, democracy, nationalism and welfare provision gradually reinforced one another in twentieth-century UK and France, in Germany it can be argued that Bismarck's welfare state was instated to rebuff the aristocracy on the one hand and mass democracy on the other; if the rule of law was, in the UK and France, enshrined in equality before the law and human rights, it is only in the post-WW2 era – and in fact coerced by the Allies – that such a strong linkage was attempted in the Federal Republic of Germany (FRG) (Goetz 2011: 45). In many ways the structures of the state, held by the public service, preceded and sometimes made redundant the impulse to democratise. This reached its peak in the Nazi regime where the public service became the backbone of the total state (Derlien 1987: 99). Thus, it can be argued that in belated nationalism the co-evolution of federal union, welfare structures, a national army and the public service established a top-down approach that was problematic for the emergence of a participatory political culture (A. R. Peters 1990: 184). Or, to use Goetz's terms, the German *Nationalstaat*, *Rechtsstaat*, *Bundersstaat*, and *Sozialstaat* facilitated the role of the public service as a modernising agent. It is only in the post-WW2 era in Germany that the two other building blocks – a fully-fledged party democracy and a Europeanised state – flourished (Goetz 2011: 43–4).

Crucially, the *Rechtsstaat* is instrumental to understanding the German public service not only because of its complex relations with democracy, but also because of the central role that law studies instituted in the public service. In fact, the key element in German public service training, since the inception of the federal state in the late nineteenth century, has been the overrepresentation of law graduates in the public service. This in part allowed for a quick recovery after 1918 and 1945, but it also meant that while in the UK and France the public service had a collective consciousness as agents of democracy, acting in the name of the people for the public good, the role of the jurists in the German system was much more to interpret the laws and act within their structures than to embody a democratic spirit. In fact, Habermas' constitutional patriotism can be viewed as one way to try to force the German system at once to accept civil rights as the basis of democracy and the *Rechtsstaat*, to rebuke nationalism and to refashion democracy as the spirit in which the public service and political culture operate. Thus, what came to be called *Juristenmonopol* stresses that training in the public service in Germany has always been heavily influenced by law studies, and this is true today, when 65 per cent of senior positions are held by lawyers (Dose 1999; Reichard 2007: 52). It is therefore of secondary importance that the Speyer school, established in 1947 in the French influence zone in the FRG, has closely followed the model of ENA. The basic training, the teachers and the internship in the public service were under a supervision and ethos that were entangled with the law faculty.

Comparative discussion: The public servant as the prototype of the modern citizen

The heyday of the public servant as the role model of the nation state came with the post-WW2 era, when the infrastructures of Europe had to be built and the state, which sent its citizens as military servants to die, was now the sole actor capable of producing a public service that would rebuild the social and economic infrastructures. The economic miracle was such that the role of bureaucracy – in education, social security, work, pensions, health, childcare and old age – was instrumental to the make-up of the nation states. The teacher, the postman, the policeman, local representatives – were all employed by the state and all provided for social welfare. It was also the peak of the democratic moment: with the moral victory over the totalitarian (fascist, racist and soon communist) regimes, democracy (that is, the liberal democratic welfare state) became the only game in the advanced town (Bell 1960). Democracy, as the ruling institutional design, facilitated the emergence of the affluent society and linked economic success with political liberalism. The bureaucracy held the trio – welfare state, nation state, and democracy – together.

The three models of public servants, this section argued, have portrayed the specific national traditions that emerged with the rise of the nation state, democracy and the welfare state. Each model entails a different ethos or vision of politician–bureaucrat relations and ideal of the democratic citizen. Thus, the UK model put forward the serving elite ideal: neutral, non-partisan and with a classical education that makes the public servant part of the chain of the 'Greats' and interprets his role as crucial for the working of the state, with the downside of being open to only a small aristocratic elite with public school and Oxbridge education. The French model embodied the universalist ethos that every citizen can become a public servant with total devotion to the state and the public good, in the tradition of Rousseau's general will and Hegel's general class, with the distinct curriculum that centres on policy studies, thus perceiving the public servant not merely as an implementer but as a professional policy shaper working for the common good. The German model perceived the public servant as acting within the legal structures of the rule of law, and thus that people trained in the law are best equipped in this vision to be part of the intuitional design of a functioning state. In a way, Germany operated the classic Weberian model encompassing at once the rational-legal order, in which the public servant, trained in law, functions within the legal order but also lacks the enchantment of politics for he is part of the structure of the state rather than an engaged, committed politician. The lack of immediate understanding of a democratic spirit was compensated only after WW2, when the rule of law was crystallised as the key to German party democracy, with both its underpinning of individual rights and its post-national ethos rejecting nationalism in favour of democratic étatism. It is to the crisis of democratic legitimation that we now turn.

The second legitimation crisis: The crisis of rationality, political re-enchantment and the national bureaucrat

The contemporary legitimation crisis has long been described as a crisis of democracy. The mainstream way to understand this crisis takes Weber's analysis of the rational-legal order and argues that the contemporary crisis is one of a crisis of rationality. One central analyst of the current crisis is Habermas. We first present briefly his analysis and then bring the role of the public service into play. Habermas' preoccupation with the contemporary legitimation crisis stems from the inherent legitimation deficit of modern society and therefore constitutes a fundamental problem for the survival of these polities (Plant 1982: 341). His analysis rests to a great extent on Weber's characterisation of the first legitimation crisis of authority and political power of the old regime – the aristocracy and the church. While the first crisis was solved by the development of the rational-legal order, disenchanted as it was, the current crisis focuses on the lack of a common value-base on which to found the legitimation of late capitalistic democratic society. Both the diagnosis and the solutions that Habermas offers pertain to the centrality of rationality in terms of consolidating the common ethos of modern society and the need to preserve this rationality in order to enable the preservation of these societies.

There are three roots to this legitimation crisis. One has to do with the capitalistic society and its belief in the neutral invisible hand of the market as the sole legitimate mechanism for determining economic decisions. Instrumental rationality distinctively characterises this sphere, yet the zealous separation of the economy and politics in the capitalist *Zeitgeist* proves too thin to provide a political moral tissue on which overall legitimacy can develop. In order to legitimise the intervention of politics in the economy, society needs a moral foundation. It is a political and cultural crisis of legitimation, based precisely on the need to go beyond the separation of market and polity:

> Recoupling the economic and the political [...] creates an increased need for legitimation. The state apparatus no longer, as in liberal capitalism, merely secures the general conditions of production [...] but is now actively engaged in it. It must therefore – like pre-capitalist state – be legitimated. (Habermas 1976: 36)

The second root has to do with the scientific civilisation – empirical sciences and technology. The conflict between dogmatism and positivism constitutes rationality as the underlying premise of empirical science theories. There is an implicit concept of rationality, of reason, which is defined in terms of efficiency and economy. But in order for technological rationality to prevail, the same dilemma as that of the capitalist ethos emerges:

> It desires rationality as a value, because it has the advantage over all the other values of being implicit in the rational modes of procedures themselves. Because this value can be legitimized by pointing to the process of scientific investigation and its technical application, and does not have to be justified in terms of pure commitment alone, it has a preferential status as against all other values. (Habermas 1973: 269–70)

The very emblem of neutrality, or value-free science, necessitates rationality as a precondition. Here, religion is a clear counterpart of science. Rationality and legality are juxtaposed both to the traditional archetype of authority and to the mystical, utterworldliness of religion. Weber's characterisation of modernisation is enhanced.

The third root has to do with democracy. Analysing democracy as part of the rational-scientific order, following Weber, would entail viewing democracy as a political mechanism, a web of institutions, procedures and processes, that provides the political setting in which the rational order occurs. This would actually become a dominant thesis of political scientists, from Schumpeter's 'other theory of democracy' to Lipset and Rokkan's characterisation of social cleavages, party systems and voters' alignment, to Schattschneider's party democracy (Schumpeter 1942; Lipset and Rokkan 1967; Schattschneider 1968). It translates, in Habermasian terms, into constitutional patriotism (Habermas 1998). As Calhoun explains, constitutional patriotism:

> [entails] a commitment to the justification of collective decisions and the exercise of power in terms of fairness. It is thus compatible with a wide range of specific constitutional arrangements, and with a variable balance between direct reference to universal rights and procedural norms on the one hand and a more specific political culture on the other. (Calhoun 2002: 147).

Thus, in understanding modernisation and placing democracy within the counters of this project, Habermas follows Weber in maintaining democracy as a neutral arena, a superstructure in which constitutional, legal and procedural arrangements provide a framework in which the population acts. The contemporary crisis is thus characterised as a crisis of legitimation, for which expanding social discourse within the public sphere and enhancing constitutional patriotism serve as a remedy (*see* Figure 14.1).

However, there is a hidden dimension lacking from Habermas' analysis. If we apply our different framework of analysis to the contemporary crisis, and bring in political re-enchantment, we may indeed perceive it in terms of a crisis of collective identity and provide a more complex understanding of modern evolution. The locus of the nation state provided an alternative locus for the nineteenth-century identity crisis of the capitalist society on both grounds: nationalism re-enhanced the collective spirit of the people, while the democratic state offered belief in the democratic creed – civil rights and the rule of law, political and social rights

Figure 14.1: Legitimation crises: Hegemonic theory

1st Legitimation crisis: Modernisation (Weber)

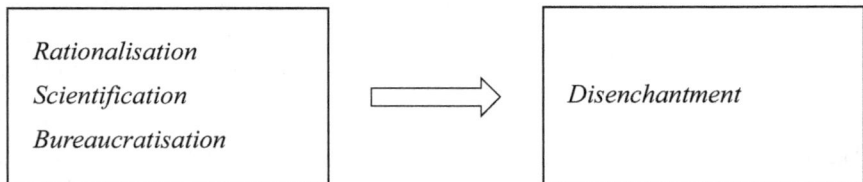

2nd Legitimation crisis: Late modernity (Habermas)

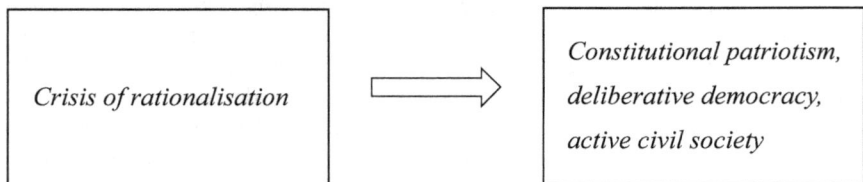

(Marshall 1950) – as a complementary layer of social trust and solidarity. Today's crisis is severe as both these loci of collective identity and identification are suffering a crisis of legitimation. Nationalism is acutely challenged by globalisation as an economic force and multiculturalism as an ideological rival. Democracy suffers a crisis of legitimation as observed in phenomena such as decreasing trust in central democratic institutions, depleting turnouts in most of the democratic world, the decline of political parties as the main vehicle of democracy, the volatility of voting patterns, the personalisation of politics, the emergence of the cartel party model, and a host of other political indicators of the processes of dealignment. Crucially, this crisis is a crisis not merely of the procedures of democracy, but a one of trust, of identity, of legitimacy. Disenchantment haunts once again; this time the nation state is being challenged by both global (i.e. European and cosmopolitan) and local (i.e. ethnic, national, sexual, cultural) identities, and civil society is being identified as a prime arena for the rising new identities: a total eclipse of the state? Representative democracy is challenged by alternative, participatory forms of democracy: this is a challenge to the cartel party system, but not less to the 'expertocracy' of the bureaucracy (see Figure 14.2).

It is now time to bring back in the public service. For the first crisis of legitimation was encapsulated in designing the model of the public servant to coincide with the democratic public servant's national role. Contrary to Weber's analysis, political re-enchantment saw the rise of the nation state as the new collective identity and public service provided the backbone for the new institutional design. As we saw, on the socio-economic level, the crucial role of the bureaucrat was pervasive with the rise of the welfare state in the aftermath of WW2. The state became the only legitimated agent for reconstructing national infrastructure, the job market, welfare

Figure 14.2: An alternative theoretical framework

1st Legitimation crisis: Modernity

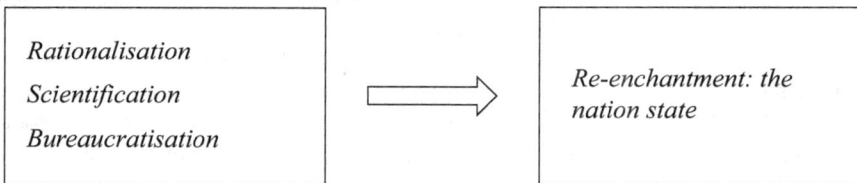

Rationalisation *Scientification* *Bureaucratisation*	⟹	*Re-enchantment: the nation state*

2nd Legitimation crisis: Late modernity

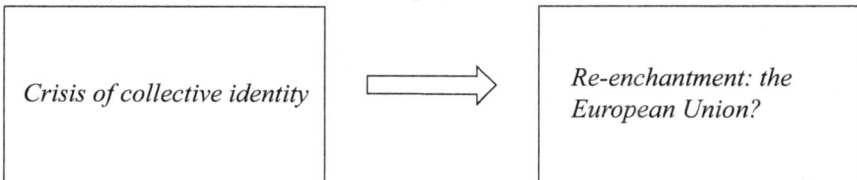

Crisis of collective identity	⟹	*Re-enchantment: the European Union?*

provision and social security. So much so, that Daniel Bell called the phenomenon that the welfare state model was accepted by both left- and right-wing governments 'the end of ideology' (Bell 1960). Crucially, this consensus was not to live long, as politics caught up with economic theories in the 1980s and neoliberalism became the new dominant ideology. The bureaucracy was now at the centre of the attack, blamed for all the economic ills, stagnation and mediocrity. The bureaucrat was to blame for the inefficiency of the economy, the mediocrity of education, the appalling service that citizens received and the monumental public sector threatening to drag society down with its irresponsible collective bargaining and outrageous pensions scheme. Against this image emerged the discourse of consumerism, with the entrepreneur and start-up initiator as the new role model: creative, daring, innovative, dynamic, market-breaking, adapting: everything the bureaucrat was not. Neoliberalism, moving from an economic theory to a political ideology, swept advanced democracies and enchanted most of the mainstream political parties.

Indeed, the attack on the 'big state' has not come only from the new right: the new left has been as eager to challenge the anonymous state as the prime location of collective interest and identity: the vast theoretical and empirical analysis of communitarianism, multiculturalism and collective rights made manifest the move away from the universal rights of all citizens within the democratic polity to a society divided into identity groups with competing narratives and the demand for collective rights, recognition of values and right to education. Not only the welfare consensus but also the national ethos, both components central to the role of the public servant in European nation states, has been severely challenged. The bureaucracy, once the general class acting in the national interest, has now become the antagonist: the faceless, neutral, rational, professional bureaucrat is everything the new social movements want to get away from: they seek a person rooted in her community, other-regarding, seeking self-expression, passionate, involved, spontaneous and experiencing democracy as a participatory way of life. If once the public servant was the protagonist of the educated middle classes, the late twentieth century saw the rise of the new middle classes, with university education as their prime feature, and their post-material values as their distinguishing character (Inglehart 1977, 1990).

The third facet of the crisis is that of democratic legitimation. Habermas and others have interpreted this as a crisis of rationality. Therefore much theoretical writing about democracy is devoted to discursive, reflexive, participatory, grassroots and deliberative democracy, hoping to restore trust in the system (Dryzek 2010). Crucially, these alternative models of democracy – that centre on the active participation of citizens in civil society, involved individuals and groups, citizens' juries, deliberative polls and so on – entail great animosity not only from party democracy, but from public service expertise. The one ethos that all three states shared was that of the professional public servant, who had the ability to see the national interest and the common good. All alternative models of democracy actually reject expert democracy and vow for a more participatory model with the premise that the layperson, if just given the chance and the time, would produce policies as good as those of the expert. The crisis of democracy is portrayed well in the changing training of the public service and its ethos.

Training the new manager: Governance and the effective bureaucrat model

The reform of public service and the rise and perhaps downfall of NPM are well documented in public administration (Dunleavy *et al.* 2006; De Vries 2010). In order to complete the picture, it is crucial to understand the close connection between the changing training of the public servants all over Europe, the new model of the public servant and the crisis of democracy. In a nutshell, does the new managerial approach to public service, with its conversion on a European model, single a way out of the crisis of legitimation and a new horizon for the revival of democracy? Or is it, on the contrary, further eroding the democratic ethos that is viable mainly in a national context?

The grave critique of the ENA model, coming both from the left, accusing the conservatism of the system and the undemocratic praxis of maintaining the public domain in the hands of those who do well in the examinations that originally set to serve them, and from the right, that vows to dismantle the big state manifested in the public sector led in the last generation to vast changes in the model of training both inside ENA and outside it. Notably, the core curriculum is now composed of three areas of study: Europe; local government and public sector administration; and management (ENA 2013). Interestingly, there is now an ENA-Potsdam shared MA programme: Masters in European Governance and Administration. It has a clear focus on management skills, the tools of governance and has a European emphasis. The British case is even more telling: as of October 2012, top public servants seeking responsibility for national projects would have to take a course not in a school of public policy or public administration, but in the Said School of Public Business, at Oxford University. If in the aftermath of WW2 the states took upon themselves to train the public service for its crucial role in building the welfare state and becoming the backbone of advanced democracies, the proliferation of public administration programmes in universities and colleges, with their ultimate model being the business schools and the MBA masters degree, reflects the privatisation and changing face of the concepts of public service training. Attacks came not only from the established political system, but also from citizens angry with the lack of service, and from the neoliberal ideology – concerned with efficiency, intervention in the free market and a cutting-red-tape obsession. The *Zeitgeist* has completely changed. The changes in training only manifest these changes.

If indeed our grand-theory is at work, then surely process of re-enchantment has occurred once again, and a move away from the nation state to the European Union and the global market is reflected in the move away from the public servant as the protagonist. What, then, is the new role model? What are the core values behind the new curricula in public management? What is the model of the public servant in the twenty-first century? In the knowledge society, in the age of globalisation, the ideal type becomes the private sector entrepreneur. The post-industrial society shifted the outlook from the state to the market and from the policy maker to the start-up companies. Instead of state apparatus we find the individual competitive initiator, creative, inventive and innovative, and acting within the private market. There is deep disdain from the state: we envision a move away from the government to governance, away from policy makers to policy networks, a move from state organs to a diverse and complex web of institutions, such as private companies, international institutions, civil society organisations and transnational financial corporations (Bevir 2010). Within this framework, the distinct role of the government, and with it of the public service, is on the wane. The web of institutional actors in a globalised world weighs less on the government and much more on individuals and international players. The tools for contemporary public servants in Europe, judging from the programmes on offer, are those of management courses, leadership, budgeting and European outlook. Even the internships are not exclusively in public service but in public and private sectors, in both Europe and in other countries. Thus, the generalist education of the Englishman, the policy orientation of the Frenchman, even the *Rechtsstaat* dimension of the legally trained German public servant, give way to the business-like, managerial, effective model of the European bureaucrat. The MBA model has won; instead of politics and policy there are globalism and governance, and hardly any mention of democracy.

The European model: Enhancing or further eroding democracy?

It is perfectly consistent with the analysis of the contemporary crisis of democracy to argue that the recurring crisis of political disenchantment has found its honourable outlet in the European Union; that the new model of the public servant, as reflected in the innovative and creative entrepreneur manager, with leadership skills and diversified experience in public and private sector governance, portrays a dynamic, vibrant model of democracy at the local, national and European levels. However, as has been argued throughout this volume, while some common features emerge there are still essential differences so there might be room for rethinking this model: in what ways is it democratic? Perceives shared interests? Provides tools for policy analysis, decision making and acting on behalf of the public good? What are the values it entails, or is it all about efficiency and budgeting, thin government and living as much as possible in the free market and globalisation? Is there no more role for the public servant and the democratic state?

The contemporary literature on the limited success of NPM in transforming the public service (Raadschelders *et al.* 2007, 2014) as well as the recent crises in the global economy have led to new thoughts about a third model of public service and state relationships. Against the Weberian model of politician/bureaucrat separation, and the NPM model of minimising the role of the state using privatisation and outsourcing to reduce state interference and adopting the economic manager as the model of consumer-oriented public service, there are new venues for rethinking the relationship in the public sphere between the government, the private sector and civil society. Whether the public values management or democratic governance (Stoker 2006), the limits of the manager ideal type come to the fore. Rather than distrust of the state, and alternative models to representative democracy, the beginning of a new model emerges. The policy maker and the public servant have changed their roles as the sole conductors of the policy process in the welfare state model, and the minimal regulative role in the NPM model, to one in which the state is a hub of policy network, with a distinct role of summoning the different key players – international, national and local – using the image of innovative policy making. In forming new ways of structuring the function of the public service, focused on integrative thinking, systems approaches and working in the national interest towards the public good using strategic thinking and long-term planning, as well as regulation, standard shaping and coordination skills to forge, lead and supervise the complex policy processes in advanced democracies. Such processes also involve public participation, deliberation and empowerment of civil society, in order to enhance representative democracy and public trust. What shape such a model might entail, and what the training might be for a public service that supports democratic governance, are yet to be established.

References

Aberbach, J. D., Putnam, R. D. and Rockman, B. A. (eds) (1981) *Bureaucrats and Politicians in Western Democracies*, Cambridge, MA: Harvard University Press.

Bartoli, A. (2008) 'The study of public management in France', in Kickert, W. M. J. (ed.) *The Study of Public Management in Europe and the US*, London: Routledge, pp. 14–41.

Bell, D. (1960) *The End of Ideology: On the exhaustion of political ideas in the Fifties*, Glencoe, IL: The Free Press.

Bevir, M. (2012) *Governance: A very short introduction*, Oxford: Oxford University Press.

Bezes, P. and Jeannot, G. (2011) 'The development of the French civil service system', in van der Meer, F. M. (ed.) *Civil Service Systems in Western Europe*, Cheltenham: Edward Elgar, pp.185–216.

Birnbaum, P. (1987) 'France: polity with a strong state', in Heper, M. (ed.) *The State and Public Bureaucracies: A comparative perspective*, New York: Greenwood Press.

Bracher, K. (1984) *The Age of Ideologies*, London: Methuen.

Calhoun, C. (2002) 'Imagining solidarity: cosmopolitanism, constitutional patriotism and the public sphere', *Public Culture*, 14(1): 147–71.

Derlien, H.-U. (1987) 'State and bureaucracy in Prussia and Germany', in Heper, M. (ed.) *The State and Public Bureaucracies: A comparative perspective*, New York: Greenwood Press, pp. 89–108.

De Vries, J. (2010) 'Is New Public Management really dead?', *OECD Journal on Budgeting*, 1: 1–5.

Dose, N. (1999) 'Teaching Public Administration in Germany', *Public Administration*, 77(3): 652–6.

Dryzek, J. (2010) *Foundations and Frontiers of Deliberative Governance*, Oxford, Oxford University Press.

Dunleavy, P., Margetts, H., Bastow, S. and Tinkler, J. (2006) 'New Public Management is dead – Long live digital-era governance', *Journal of Public Administration Research and Theory*, 16: 467–94.

ENA (2013) 'The 24-month program' Available at http://www.ena.fr/index.php?/en/formation/initiale/24-month-program (accessed 1 December 2013).

Galbraith, J. K. (1963) *The Affluent Society*, Harmondsworth: Penguin.

Goetz, K. H. (2011) 'The development of the German civil service system', in van der Meer, F. M. (ed.) *Civil Service Systems in Western Europe*, Cheltenham: Edward Elgar, pp. 37–66.

Greer, S. L. and Jarman, H. (2011) 'The British civil service system', in van der Meer, F. M. (2011) *Civil Service Systems in Western Europe*, Cheltenham: Edward Elgar, pp. 13–36.

Habermas, J. (1973) *Theory and Practice*, Boston, MA: Beacon Press.

—— (1976) *Legitimation Crisis* (translation and introduction by McCarthy.), London: Heinemann.

— (1998) *The Inclusion of the Other: Studies in political theory*, in Cronin, C. P. and de Greiff, P. (eds) Cambridge, MA: MIT Press.

Hegel, G. W. F. (2001) *Philosophy of Right* (translation by Dyde, S. W.), Kitchener: Batoche.

Herper M. (ed.) (1987) *The State and Public Bureaucracies* NY: Greenwood Press, pp. 89–108.

Ingelhart, R. (1977) *The Silent Revolution: Changing values and political styles among Western publics*, Princeton, NJ: Princeton University Press.

— (1990) *Culture Shift in Advanced Industrial Society*, Princeton, NJ: Princeton University Press.

Lipset, S. M. and Rokkan, S. (1967) *Party Systems and Voters Alignments: Cross-national perspectives*, New York, Free Press, pp. 1–64.

Marshall, T. H. (1950) *Citizenship and Social Class and Other Essays*, Cambridge, Cambridge University Press.

Owen, B. G. (1990) 'France', in Kingdom, J. E. (ed.) *The Civil Service in Liberal Democracies: An introductory survey*, London: Routledge, pp. 64–89.

Parris, H. (1987) 'Developments of the unpretentious bureaucracy: the case of England', in Heper, M. (ed.) *The State and Public Bureaucracies: A comparative perspective*, New York: Greenwood Press, pp.41–58.

Peters, A. R. (1990) 'West Germany', in Kingdom, J. E. (ed.) *The Civil Service in Liberal Democracies: An introductory survey*, London: Routledge, pp. 182–207.

Plant, R. (1982) 'Jurgen Habermas and the idea of legitimation crisis', *European Journal of Political Research*, 10(4): 341–52.

Raadschelders, J. C. and Rutgers, M. R. (1996) 'The history of civil service systems', in Bekke, A. J. G. M., Perry, J. L. and Toonen, T. A. J. (eds) *Civil Service Systems in Comparative Perspective*, Bloomington, IN: Indiana University Press, pp. 67–100.

Raadschelders, J. C. N., Toonen, T. A. J. and van der Meer, F. M. (eds) (2007) *The Civil Service in the 21st Century*, London: Palgrave.

Reichard C. (2007) 'The study of public management in Germany: poorly institutionalized and fragmented' in Kickert W. (ed.) *The Study of Public Management in Europe and the US*, London: Routledge, pp. 42–69.

Sager, F., Rosser, C., Hurni, P. and Mavrot, C. (2012) 'How traditional are the American, the French, and the German traditions of Public Administration? A research agenda', *Public Administration*, 90(1): 129–43.

Schattschneider, E. E. (1968) *Party Government*, New York: Holt, Rinehart & Winston.

Schumpeter, J. A. (1942) *Capitalism, Socialism and Democracy*, New York: Harper & Row.

Stoker, G. (2006) 'Public value management: a new narrative for networked governance?' *American Review of Public Administration*, 36(1): 41–57.

Weber, M. (1958) *Essays in Sociology*, Gerth, H. H. and Mills, C. W. (eds) New York: Oxford University Press.

Chapter Fifteen

Conclusions: Common Ground for a Common Future?

Patrick Overeem and Fritz Sager

Introduction

In 1841, Honoré de Balzac painted a humoristic and largely ironic portrait of the public servant in his *Physiologie de l'Employé* (*see* Rutgers 2009). His booklet reveals much about the contemporary prejudices against 'bureaucrats' in France – prejudices that still exist today, of course, and can be encountered in many other countries, too. What is fascinating about ironic accounts like Balzac's, however, is their tendency to present a positive ideal or model of their object of ridicule in negative terms, so to speak. Unfortunately, however, both ironic and serious accounts of the 'public servant' are rare. Our understanding of that concept therefore remains dim and fragmented, albeit a little bit less so, we hope, at the end of this study.

The project of this volume could be compared to a jungle expedition in search of a particular species: is there such an animal as the *European* public servant and if so, what are its traits? Or perhaps our endeavour rather resembles a biologist's analysis of different species from various ages and countries to assess whether they belong to the same genus. More prosaically put, this volume has sought to explore whether in European thought and practice (across different times and places) a shared concept of the public servant can be found that might serve as a building block of a common administrative identity in our integrating continent. To our knowledge, this is the first study addressing this question and therefore it still bears an exploratory character.[1] At the same time, it brings together strong strands of ongoing research from different sub-disciplines in political science and public administration, such as the history of political concepts, comparative administrative science and Europeanisation studies. This kind of broad-ranging collaboration is, in our opinion, too rare in today's highly specialised social science and we hope to have shown that it can be very fruitful.

Several questions, multiple answers

In Chapter One, we announced that this volume would attempt to answer a cumulative set of four sub-questions. Now, at the end of our journey, we can look back and try to formulate answers to each of them. As our volume could treat its

---

1. The study by Giancarlo Vilella (2010) has to be mentioned here, although it concentrates on the role of the Eurocrat rather than on historical understandings of the public servant across Europe.

vast and under-researched subject only in a selective and exploratory manner, the answers we give will unavoidably also be partial and tentative. They can be taken as hypothetical, in the sense that they are testable by future research. Indeed, we would be pleased to see (parts of) our project carried on and, if necessary, corrected by the research of others. Nevertheless, we do think the work presented in this volume can already help us to develop better answers than we have had so far.

Conceptual history

Our first and most basic sub-question was thus formulated: *How has the public servant been conceived (in different periods of time and at different places) throughout the history of European thought?* This question was addressed specifically in Parts Two and Three, but also on many places elsewhere in the volume. We have met the public servant in a range of different capacities and roles, for instance as a loyal yet frank adviser at court (*see* Joanne Paul in Chapter Three), as a political actor in the newly emerging *Verwaltungsstaat* (Niels Hegewisch in Chapter Five), as a modern bureaucrat with legally protected status (Caspar van den Berg, Gerrit Dijkstra and Frits van der Meer in Chapter Seven), as an 'administrative diplomat' involved in European policy making in Brussels and EU member state capitals (*see* Chapter Eleven by Bernadette Connaughton and Chapter Twelve by Karin Hilmer Pedersen and Lars Johannsen), and so on. We have seen an evolutionary process in which the public servant developed from a personal footman to a state servant and eventually a public manager (*see* Gayil Talshir in Chapter Fourteen). This variety could perhaps be described by means of Weber's distinctions between various rationalities, vocations, or even 'life orders' (*Lebensführungen*) (Hennis 1988; *see* Du Gay 2000: 9–11). Serving a monarch is clearly a different task, bringing different responsibilities and moral concerns, than serving an abstract entity like a state, or even a supranational organisation. If this is the case, the continuity of our storyline may be questioned: are the public councillor to the English monarch and the present-day networking Eurocrat indeed of the same species or not? We think they are, but the evolution that has taken place is undeniable.

Determining whether any characteristics are common to *all* conceptions of the public servant in Europe is far from easy. Public servants do nowadays have to administer an oath of office in most countries, but not everywhere; they have a special, protected status in most cases, but again not, or not similarly, in all. It seems advisable, therefore, not to look for just one common denominator that characterises 'the' European public servant, but rather to apply Wittgenstein's idea of 'family resemblances'.

As is fairly well known, Wittgenstein argued in his *Philosophical Investigations* (1967: §§66–7; *see* Wennerberg 1967) that the multitude of games humans play do not have one single characteristic in common. Some are played with balls, others with cards, some by adults only (drinking games), others by children too, some in teams (soccer), others in couples (chess) or even alone (Solitaire), in many games points are scored, but not in all, and so on. Indeed, the rules, the stakes, and the purposes of games vary widely. It is not even true that all games are played for fun (think of Russian roulette). So there is not one single trait, Wittgenstein argued, that is common to all games. The only reason why we can call them all by one name is that they are part of an interlocking network of overlapping subsets. Games share 'family resemblances', just as in a family, where every member shares physical characteristics (the deep eyes, the hooked nose, the curly hair) with some others but not with all. Important characteristics are shared in related but never-exhaustive combinations.

This notion of family resemblances seems applicable to European conceptions of the public servant, too. Public servants in Europe (or rather the ways we think about them) are a big family through which ancient ideals of republican virtue, Christian ideas of service, and modern notions of professionalism, among others, run liberally. Some characteristics are widely present (e.g. having a legally protected status), whereas others are more rare (e.g. having a symbolic connection to the monarchy, as in 'Her Majesty's Civil Service').

Of special interest to European thinking about the public servant are the ideas developed by Hegel and Weber. They have been highly influential, not only in American administrative thought (Hegel in the second half of the nineteenth century and Weber in the second half of the twentieth), but from the very moment of their writing onwards also in Europe (*see* Chapters Five, Eight (Christian Rosser) and Fourteen). They are important, however, not only because of their direct influence on later conceptions, but also because of their paradigmatic, even ideal-typical status. Indeed, their conceptions represent two extremes on a scale that still seems to underlie much of European thinking on public administration as such. One pole is the Hegelian concept of the public servant as a member of the 'universal class', the true representative of the state and guardian of the public interest; the other is the Weberian concept of the competent, professionally trained bureaucrat, who is strictly subordinate and loyal to his political superiors. These two archetypes are undoubtedly better at home in theory than in praxis, have figured on our stage as well (particularly in Chapters Eight and Seven, respectively) and they can still be encountered. Writing about the administrative apparatus of the EU, Anne Stevens notes:

> What is essentially in conflict within the EU administration are two modes of legitimacy. The first is a legitimacy which is derived from constitutionally embedded and legally based structures designed to embed the administration within society and allow it to fulfil certain key social functions. This results in a relatively autonomous administration. The second is a procedural legitimacy, based upon outcomes, responsiveness, effectiveness and accountability. This administrative model is an essentially instrumental one [.] (Stevens 2002: 5)

In this contrast, we can still recognise the Hegelian and the Weberian understandings of the role of the public service and hence of the public servant. The duality and even tension between these idea(l)s of the good administrator seem particularly characteristic of European administrative thought – more so, for sure, than for American thought, although traces of it can be found there too.

Transatlantic comparisons and influences

In his discussion of family resemblances, Wittgenstein has further noted that it tends to be very difficult to draw borders around a group sharing these (1967: §68). Where does one family with overlapping traits stop and another begin? Distinguishing between families will unavoidably be somewhat arbitrary. This problem certainly emerges when we turn to our second sub-question: *How do the European conceptions of the public servant compare with and/or reflect the influences of other conceptions, in particular American ones?* Although addressed most directly in Part Four, our treatment of non-European conceptions has admittedly been limited. In Chapter Three (by Joanne Paul), we came across ancient Greek and Roman ideas (such as the fascinating notion of *parrhesia* – which basically meant 'speaking truth to power') that were a central part of the humanist view on the king's councillor and thenceforth of the modern concept of the public servant. And in Chapter Seven, Van den Berg, Dijkstra and Van der Meer noted that British policy makers drew on Chinese examples for introducing exam-based selection of new officials. But, for reasons set out in the first chapter, most attention in the volume has been paid to American ideas and influences. Since the mid-nineteenth century, fruitful intellectual exchanges across the Atlantic have taken place, first mainly westbound and then to an even stronger degree *vice versa*. After a general analysis of the transatlantic interplay of administrative ideas on the public servant in the late nineteenth and early twentieth centuries (Chapter Eight by Christian Rosser), we examined how the European public servant became considerably 'Americanised' after WW2. Concentrating on two significant countries in particular, namely France (Chapter Nine) and Germany (Chapter Ten), Céline Mavrot and Pascal Hurni have shown how administrative ideas on decision making and cybernetics, respectively, were imported from the United States and adapted to fit the administrative traditions of both countries. The processes they describe imply that currently, in the early twenty-first century, much American blood runs through the veins of the European public servant.

European convergence?

In Part Five in particular, but also in its surrounding chapters (Nine, Ten, and Thirteen), we aimed to find answers to our third sub-question: *To what extent do different conceptions of the public servant converge in times of European integration?* If, indeed, the metaphor of family resemblances suits our subject, one might think that intra-family intercourse spreads the genes and will gradually lead to greater homogeneity among European public servants ('isomorphism').

On the basis of this volume, we can safely conclude that this does indeed seem to happen. Especially within the EU, but probably also in European countries outside it (Norway, Switzerland), one can observe the 'Europeanisation' of the public servant. Two processes are at work here. One is the formal process in which requirements from the EU's *acquis communautaire* and various forms of 'soft law' (more or less formalised in the so-called 'open method of coordination') are implemented, especially in new member states in Central and Eastern Europe. These may, for instance, require a considerable degree of administrative independence from and neutrality towards partisan politics. The other is a more informal process in which public servants are socialised in European administrative culture and identity by international contacts and cooperation. This volume does not empirically assess the absolute and relative strength of these two well-documented processes, but it definitely does show instances of both (in Chapters Twelve and Eleven, respectively).

A more general comparison is offered in Chapter Thirteen by Julia-Carolin Brachem and Markus Tepe, who in a detailed empirical study manage to reveal that public servants in various European states tend to espouse a closely similar and unique set of public service values. In clear contrast to their colleagues from the US, government employees from France, Germany, Sweden and even Great Britain show higher values of *Self-Transcendence*, that is to say: *Universalism* (meant as an understanding, appreciation, tolerance and desire to protect the welfare of all people and for nature) and *Benevolence* (meant as the preservation and enhancement of the welfare of those people with whom one is in frequent personal contact). This typical motivational pattern among European employees comes as close to a positive answer as we can give to the question whether in Europe anything like 'a shared administrative identity' exists.

Building block for European integration?

This brings us to our last sub-question: *Is it possible to identify a shared conception of the public servant that can serve as a building block for a common European administrative identity?* Currently, European integration seems to be in a more critical phase of its history than it has been for a long time. The financial crisis (often dubbed the Euro-crisis) and the strongly Eurosceptic mood among many European voters and politicians make the prospect for further integration far from bright. In these circumstances, it is not to be expected that the discovery and development of a shared European idea(l) of the public servant can contribute very much to the creation of 'an ever closer Union'. Indeed, it is far from obvious that we, as social scientists and historians, should aspire to promote actively such a controversial political goal. We can, however, contribute to a fair assessment of the chances of success for actors such as the European Commission, who are working to develop an EAS as an important component of a further integrated Union (and conversely of other actors who might want to prevent such a development). In other words, *if* you strive to develop (or prevent) the EAS, what support does the search for shared European conceptions of the public servant lend to your endeavour? Is there enough unity (or enough diversity) to build on?

These questions are, of course, difficult to answer equivocally. This volume contains chapters that could give hope to either side in the integration debate. On the one hand, the empirical analysis in Chapter Thirteen clearly shows that, indeed, there is a set of values endorsed by many European public servants from different member states – and significantly more so by them than by their colleagues from elsewhere. So there seems to be a shared administrative identity, or at least a shared moral outlook among European administrators that is unique to them and different from that of others (namely Americans). On the other hand, several chapters (Seven, Nine, Eleven and Fourteen) also show the remaining strength and impact of national and transnational administrative traditions. The Oxbridge-educated amateur generalist, the ENA-trained professional, and the lawyer-bureaucrat in the *Rechtsstaat* tradition may increasingly be stereotypical characters of the past, but frequently their offspring is still easily recognisable (*see* Chapter Fourteen by Gayil Talshir). We must also not neglect the power of context. National administrative systems are parts of national political systems, and just as political systems influence their administrative elements, subsequently administrative systems impact the public servants who work in them. Europeanisation literature shows how national political systems prevail, and the same is true for their bureaucrats. Finally, the impact of present-day attempts to develop a shared idea(l) of 'good governance' on a global scale may in the long run have more impact on the administrative identity of public servants working on European soil than historical national traditions and the contemporary efforts of Europeanisation. During the sovereign debt crisis in Greece, to mention a recent example, the impact of IMF policies on public servants seemed at least as strong as that of local and national traditions or even those of the European Union.

All in all, we would conclude that there is probably not one single conception of the public servant that could serve as a building block for European administrative integration, but rather a complex network of concepts and associations to concepts (a semantic field) that shows very easy connections as well as highly difficult disconnections. Working on further European integration by employing the former and avoiding the latter requires an amount of analytical subtlety that will probably be hard to achieve in a muddled political process.

Research gaps and future research

Although our volume spans a long time period (from the sixteenth to the twenty-first century) and a vast area (from Ireland to the Baltic States), there is of course still very much it does not cover. One conspicuous limitation is given by its strong focus on the greater countries in north-western Europe (Germany, France and Great Britain) and thereby its limited attention to southern, central and eastern Europe as well as Scandinavia. Historically, the picture is clearly also far from complete. For instance, the development of the bureaucratic manager, depicted and criticised by Alasdair MacIntyre as one of the few typical *characters* of modern Western society (1984: Chapters Three and Four), should be described in much more detail. High on the agenda should therefore be research attempting to fill the evident gaps herein not covered. Likewise, one could further strengthen the active use of multiple disciplinary perspectives, including contributions from not only historians and political scientists, but also economists, sociologists, philosophers and others. Indeed, cross-disciplinary cooperation could be employed still more effectively.

A second desiderate is a more comparative research agenda than we were able to deliver in this volume. While some chapters provide transatlantic comparisons with the US, comparative public administration should have a more global scope. Even if there is a European public servant, how does she/he differ from counterparts like the African or the Asian public servant? Such broad comparison may clarify a set of salient questions such as: are the similarities of the American and the European public servant greater than their differences? What is the role of colonial legacies, i.e. how similar is the South American public servant to his/her southern European colleagues? And when and where does the concept reach its limits? In which cases can we no longer meaningfully speak of 'public servants'? Given the growing interest in comparative public administration, much will be learned by taking advantage of the existing variance in administrative identities across the globe.

Even more important, finally, seems to us the challenge of gradually developing a useful body of theory that helps us make better sense of the wealth of historical and contemporary material about this topic. In the development of modern, continent-wide conceptions of the public servant, what is important and why? Although in this volume Chapter Two (by Jos Raadschelders) has provided some helpful analytical tools that could be employed in all other chapters, in our choice of chapter topics we had by and large to proceed inductively. In future projects one could try to have a better-developed analytical framework in advance (to see what is most needed) as well as afterwards (to give findings their rightful place). As we understand it, this book has both set the stage for such a framework and underscored the need for its further development.

References

Du Gay, P. (2000) *In Praise of Bureaucracy: Weber, organization, ethics*, London: Sage.

Hennis, W. (1988) *Max Weber: Essays in reconstruction*, London: Allen & Unwin.

MacIntyre, A. C. (1984) *After Virtue: A study in moral theory*, 2nd edn, Notre Dame, IN: University of Notre Dame Press.

Rutgers, M. R. (2009) 'Reflections on Balzac's *Physiology of the Bureaucrat* (1841): tracing popular opinion and the problems of irony', *Public Voices*, X(2): 58–67.

Stevens, A. (2002) 'Europeanisation and the administration of the EU: a comparative perspective', Queen's Papers on Europeanisation, no. 4/2002, Belfast: Queen's University), retrieved from http://www.qub. ac.uk/schools/SchoolofPoliticsInternationalStudiesandPhilosophy/ FileStore/EuropeanisationFiles/Filetoupload,38421,en.pdf (accessed on August 2014).

Vilella, G. (2010) *The European Civil Servant: An introductory essay*, Brussels: Euroeditions.

Wennerberg, H. (1967) 'The concept of family resemblances in Wittgenstein's later philosophy', *Theoria*, 33(2): 107–32.

Wittgenstein, L. (1967) *Philosophical Investigations*, Oxford: Blackwell.

Index

Page numbers in italics refer to Figures and Tables